The Complete Beginner's Guide to
Genealogy, the Internet, and Your Genealogy Computer Program

by Karen Clifford

Copyright © 2001
Genealogy Research Associates, Inc.
Monterey, California
All Rights Reserved. No part of this publication
may be reproduced, in any form or by any means,
including electronic reproduction or reproduction
via the Internet, except by permission of the publisher.
Published by Genealogical Publishing Co., Inc.
1001 N. Calvert St., Baltimore, MD 21202
Library of Congress Catalogue Card Number 00-130060
International Standard Book Number 0-8063-1636-5
Made in the United States of America

Table of Contents

Chapter 5 Printing Your Records

Chapter 6 Your Family History Notebook

Chapter 7 Developing a Sense of Our Ancestors' Environment

Chapter 8 Resolving Conflict

Chapter 9 State Vital Record Offices, Public Libraries, Courthouses and Local Repositories

Chapter 10 Resources of the Family History Library

Chapter 11 Major Databases of the Family History Library

Chapter 12 Using Local Family History Centers

Chapter 13 National Archives and Regional Records Services Facilities

Chapter 14 Census Records Between 1850-1920

Chapter 15 Analysis and Goal Setting

Chapter 16 Sharing Your Family History Research

Appendix A

The Internet and Genealogy

Appendix B

Genealogical Forms

Index

ACKNOWLEDGMENTS

Gratitude is extended to Maureen Girard for reading every word and offering wonderful counsel and support in the writing of this book. Thanks also to Pat Miljarak for supporting the production of the project and doing the things in the office that needed to be done so I could write, write, write! David McPhail and Michael Clifford did a professional job on the graphics and pulled together many supportive documents for this book.

Introduction

The purpose of this book is to demystify genealogy and its supportive tools—genealogy computer programs and the Internet. It is a guide for the beginning family historian. It contains the information you need to get started in your family history research. It shows you how to organize your family papers and how to enter information into a genealogy computer program so that you can easily manage, store, and retrieve your data. It also shows you how to put together a Family History Notebook to help you organize and archive your records and supporting documents.

HOW THIS BOOK IS ARRANGED

Each chapter in this book has several components—each of which serves a complementary purpose.

- The main body of the text provides instruction supported by illustrations, charts, and examples.
- "Your Turn" activities serve as application modules asking the reader to apply the instruction to his or her own research needs.
- Assignments serve as a review and comprehension check.
- Computer checklists give the reader hands-on experience with his or her personal genealogy computer program.
- Web site addresses are also listed at the end of each chapter to guide the reader to valuable Internet resources related to the topics.
- Entries in the chapter bibliographies serve as resources for further study of the topics covered.

Taking advantage of these resources before beginning each new chapter will provide the knowledge-base and experience needed to do well in subsequent chapters.

THE ROLE OF THE TEACHER

The value of this book multiplies when a good instructor provides experiences, case studies, and first-hand knowledge. If that instructor can "hold your hand" for that first visit into the deep recesses of a "strange and awesome library" haunted by family historians, you will be doubly blessed.

SUPPORTING MATERIALS

Whether you are working with an instructor or on your own, be sure to take advantage of the supporting materials to this textbook.

- The CD *The Great Ancestral Hunt* provides access to additional resources, including Internet sites and forms that help with the chapter assignments. You may order the CD from GRA, Inc., 2600 Garden Road, Suite #224, Monterey, CA 93940 or online at *http://www.GRAonline.com.*
- Web page supplements, also located at *http://www.GRAonline.com,* contain additional information. For instance, information about various genealogy computer programs can be found in the supplemental Web materials. Individual features of each program are taught and applied in practical applications, allowing you to compare and decide which program(s) best meets your needs.

This book continues with guidelines for using public libraries, courthouses, and archives to their greatest advantage. The value of Family History Centers and Regional Records Services Facilities of the National Archives, as well as other repositories, is explained, and a step-by-step guide for using the records in each facility is provided, including general background information on how to obtain vital, probate, military, and census records. This book will help you master the foundation skills of this most fascinating pursuit as you confidently probe further into your family's history. And now let us begin this great adventure.

Karen Clifford

CHAPTER 1

Principles of Success for the Family Historian

Some have been denied families of example, but somewhere on every family tree there is a hero. There are also explanations for feelings, for traditions, for understanding ourselves. There are examples of histories we don't want to see repeated, lessons learned, and visions of what we may become.

—Karen Clifford

So much has been located, organized, inventoried, cataloged, shared on computer programs or online systems, microfilmed, photocopied, and alphabetized, that genealogy "research" is much more reliable, fulfilling, and easier to do today than ever before.

There was a time when the pursuit of family genealogy was left to the lone aunt or widower uncle who had plenty of time and nothing else to do. Times have changed!

Today this fascinating pursuit is being accomplished by rising executives, young mothers with growing children, teachers, construction workers, retired couples, high school and college students and many others. In fact anyone who enjoys putting together a puzzle, reading mystery stories or historical novels, or solving problems will find genealogy utterly absorbing.

Even with our many other family, educational, civic, and professional pursuits, there are formulas, techniques, flow charts, computer programs, and the Internet to help the would-be "family historian" be successful in limited time. Even the amateur can produce a praiseworthy family history on a limited budget in a short period of time.

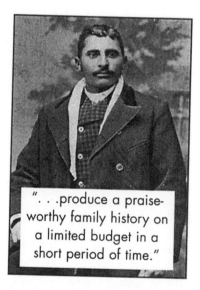

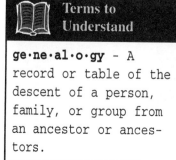

". . .produce a praise-worthy family history on a limited budget in a short period of time."

FAMILY HISTORY

Genealogy is a branch of history--Family History. At its best, it also involves scientific study to determine family relationships. "Only when systematic knowledge is derived from observation, study, and experimentation to arrive at a hypotheses, does genealogy become a true science. When sloppy methods are used, it is lowered to the level of a mere pastime built upon false premises. It really is unworthy of all your fine efforts." (See Chapter 1, "Understanding Genealogical Research," in *The Researcher's Guide to American Genealogy* by Val Greenwood.)

> 📖 **Terms to Understand**
>
> **ge·ne·al·o·gy** - A record or table of the descent of a person, family, or group from an ancestor or ancestors.

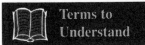

Terms to Understand

vi·tal rec·ord - An account made in an enduring form, especially in writing, that preserves the knowledge or memory of data pertinent to the birth, marriage or death of an individual.

In the past, genealogy was limited in scope to one or more ancestral lines. It concentrated on **vital records**. Its concern was primarily kinship and matters of descent. It did not engage in reasoned argument as to why certain events occurred.

Family History, on the other hand, is an extension of genealogy but with more depth. Meat is put on the bones of genealogy by including historical information in a narrative form. As someone once stated, "What is the use of digging up the skeletons in your closet, if you're not going to put flesh upon their bones." Genealogy in its expanded view, termed Family History, is what we will study. It includes an examination of individuals against the background, location and circumstances of their lives, because people and places are really inseparable.

This book will attempt to set forth the principles of success for the family historian using a variety of methods, sources, and repositories.

Bring your skeletons to life!

Sometimes, in the past, less effective techniques were followed, and these need to be corrected as they are discovered. For example, looking up everyone in the entire country with the last name you are seeking has been replaced with looking up your surname in the time period, locality, and among associates, starting from where your ancestor was last positively known to have been. In other words, always go from the *known to the unknown.*

Some research principles have never before been recorded. Some have yet to be discovered. Our success, however, depends upon our effectiveness as discoverers and followers of all those principles that will influence our success. Principles have great value. They outline what we must actually do to be successful. They are the ideas that we are willing to put into practice to accomplish our goals.

This book will cover the Sixteen Steps shown in Illustration 1-1. It will demonstrate how to organize, document, print, analyze, and locate the best places and types of records for answering your family history questions. This first chapter will cover the principles of genealogy research and formulas for the successful investigation of your family.

SIXTEEN STEPS TO ORGANIZED RESEARCH

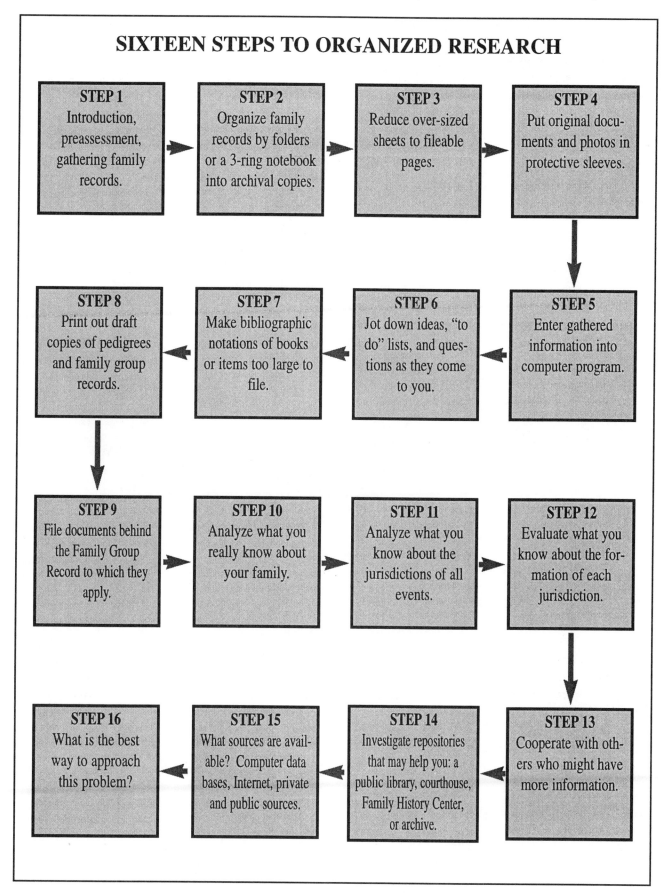

STEP 1
Introduction, preassessment, gathering family records.

STEP 2
Organize family records by folders or a 3-ring notebook into archival copies.

STEP 3
Reduce over-sized sheets to fileable pages.

STEP 4
Put original documents and photos in protective sleeves.

STEP 8
Print out draft copies of pedigrees and family group records.

STEP 7
Make bibliographic notations of books or items too large to file.

STEP 6
Jot down ideas, "to do" lists, and questions as they come to you.

STEP 5
Enter gathered information into computer program.

STEP 9
File documents behind the Family Group Record to which they apply.

STEP 10
Analyze what you really know about your family.

STEP 11
Analyze what you know about the jurisdictions of all events.

STEP 12
Evaluate what you know about the formation of each jurisdiction.

STEP 16
What is the best way to approach this problem?

STEP 15
What sources are available? Computer data bases, Internet, private and public sources.

STEP 14
Investigate repositories that may help you: a public library, courthouse, Family History Center, or archive.

STEP 13
Cooperate with others who might have more information.

Illustration 1-1 Research Flow Chart

Terms to Understand

ju·ris·dic·tion - The territorial range of authority or control.

Terms to Understand

e·val·u·a·tion - To determine the value, worth, or quality of what you have found in light of the customs, events, time period, locality, and goal upon which you are working.

Terms to Understand

fact - Something that is real or actual determined by evidence; an event.

Terms to Understand

tra·di·tion - The passing down of unwritten family stories from generation to generation, especially by means of oral communication.

Terms to Understand

hy·poth·e·sis - A tentative explanation of an event that can be tested by further investigation; a theory.

THE RESEARCH CYCLE

Certain principles of success operate in the field of family history research. These principles involve customs, geography, and governmental **jurisdictions**, to name but a few. One of these principles is the process which will be used over and over in your research: we call it the *Research Cycle*. It naturally produces success again and again. Successful genealogists use this cycle because it stresses:

1. The critical step of reorganization of data in light of new findings; and

2. **Evaluation** of the new information in context with all of the information you have available.

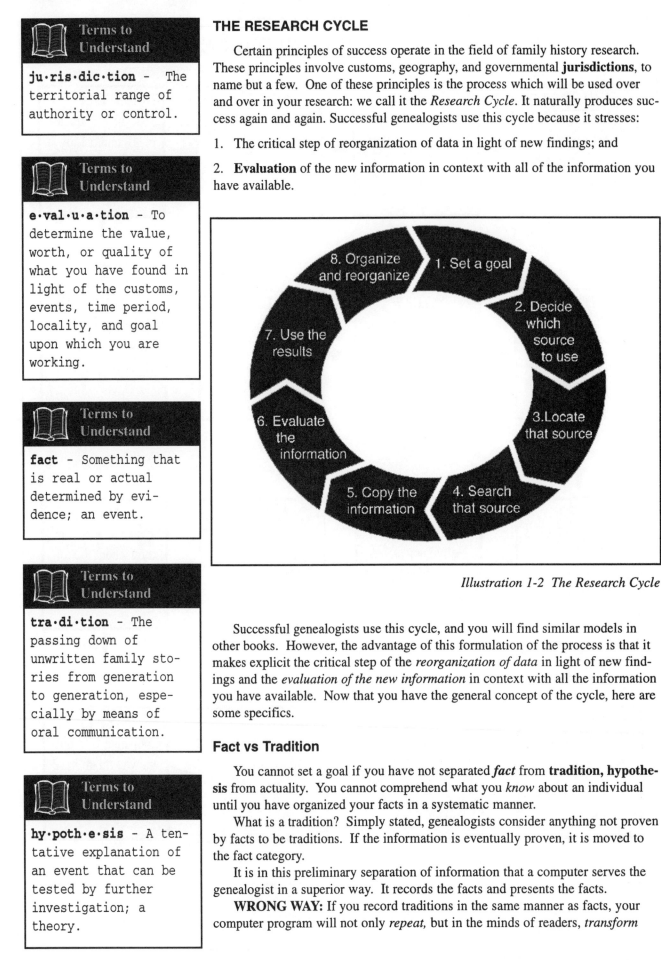

Illustration 1-2 The Research Cycle

Successful genealogists use this cycle, and you will find similar models in other books. However, the advantage of this formulation of the process is that it makes explicit the critical step of the *reorganization of data* in light of new findings and the *evaluation of the new information* in context with all the information you have available. Now that you have the general concept of the cycle, here are some specifics.

Fact vs Tradition

You cannot set a goal if you have not separated *fact* from **tradition, hypothesis** from actuality. You cannot comprehend what you *know* about an individual until you have organized your facts in a systematic manner.

What is a tradition? Simply stated, genealogists consider anything not proven by facts to be traditions. If the information is eventually proven, it is moved to the fact category.

It is in this preliminary separation of information that a computer serves the genealogist in a superior way. It records the facts and presents the facts.

WRONG WAY: If you record traditions in the same manner as facts, your computer program will not only *repeat,* but in the minds of readers, *transform*

FACT   **vs**   **TRADITION**

traditions into facts. This could launch your research into a totally erroneous direction. There is a proper way to record both facts and traditions, actuality and hypothesis. These methods will be explained in depth later, but basically:

- If information based on primary documentation is fact, then documentation must be listed.

- If information based on hearsay is tradition, it must be kept separated with a note to that effect, such as "TRADITION" in capital letters.

- There must also be a place for the researcher's evaluation of the documentation gathered, because *all evidence is not equal.*

DANGER

WRONG WAY

If you record traditions in the same manner as facts, your computer program will not only *repeat*, but in the minds of readers, *transform traditions into facts.* This could launch your research into a totally erroneous direction.

YOUR TURN

Look at the example on the next page ("From Your Computer Screen"). Watch for differences between the actual records and what was said in the traditions. Then answer the question below.

What discrepancies do you see between what was found in the records and what was stated by the tradition?

1.

2.

3.

(Compare your answers with those provided at the end of the chapter.)

YOUR TURN

Facts

Tradition

From Your Computer Screen

```
FACTS - - - - - - - - - - - - - - - - - - - - - - - - - -

1893 CHURCH:  Alexsis Nicholi Lehtonen entry, Rymattala,
Turku-Pori, Finland Christening Records, microfilm no.
0098764, item 4, Family History Library (FHL), Salt Lake
City, Utah.

[Translation] Alexsis Nicholi, the son of Johan Mattss.
Lehtonen, a tenant farmer, and Maria Henriksdr, was born 23
Mar 1893, in Rymattala.

1906 CHURCH:  Alexsis Nicholi Lehtonen entry, Rymattala,
Turku-Pori, Finland Christening Records, microfilm no.
0098764, item 6, Family History Library (FHL), Salt Lake
City, Utah.

Alexsis Nicholi Lehtonen attended communion classes, 25 Aug
1906.

1915 MARRIAGE:  Alex Lehtonen entry, Rymattala, Turku-Pori,
Finland Marriage Records, microfilm no. 0098765, item 2,
Family History Library (FHL), Salt Lake City, Utah.

Alex Lehtonen married Sophia Johansdr, May 15, 1915,
Rymattala.

TRADITION - - - - - - - - - - - - - - - - - - - - - - - -

TRADITION:  From Lempi Lehtonen, daughter of Alex Lehtonen,
my mother, on Sept 5, 1985:

"Alex was the son of a wealthy carriage driver who owned
several carriages near the coast of Finland and transported
tourists.  He ran away from home because of a mean older
sister.  He was a cabin boy and came to America about age 12
and never returned.  By running away he lost his inheritance.
There is probably money in Finland waiting to be collected."
```

After more research was conducted on this family, it was discovered that part of the tradition was true. Alex had worked on a ship, not as a cabin boy, but as a regular worker. He ran away, not from his inheritance, but from the Russian draft. He did have money waiting for him due to his wages from working on the ship, not due to an inheritance.

Had the tradition not been separated from the facts, later information about Alex Lehtonen would have been disregarded in the search.

Your Turn

List some facts and traditions in the spaces provided at the left about an **ancestor** you are interested in locating.

Summary

The first step in setting a goal is to separate all facts from traditions. This will necessitate documenting all of the dates, localities, and relationships you have located.

STEP 1: SET A GOAL

Once you have separated facts from traditions, you can select a goal. Limit your goal to a single, clearly-defined objective. Include in that goal the full name, a time period, a location, and what you hope to find.

YOUR TURN

Here are three goals. Which meets the criteria for being a single, clearly-defined objective?

1. Find the birth date of Grandpa John Thornton Hansen, born about 1890/1895 in Ohio.   Yes   No

2. Track the ancestry of my Hansen line.   Yes   No

3. Write a book on my family.   Yes   No

(Compare your answers with those at the end of this chapter.)

YOUR TURN

Now, try writing a clearly-defined goal of your own.

My Goal:

Summary

Setting clearly-defined goals is very important if you wish to find clearly-defined results. Remember to record each goal separately as you set about to trace your family.

STEP 2: DECIDE WHICH SOURCE TO USE

Once a goal has been selected, you must learn what **sources** are available to reach that goal. Each goal you select requires specialized sources to prove a fact, but you will have a difficult time determining which to select if you are unaware of the many sources available to solve problems within each locality and time period. In addition, sources are being discovered constantly to aid the family historian. Although you may never learn about all of the sources available to genealogists, you should know those which are most successful and which pertain to your problem. Get the latest edition of Val Greenwood's *The Researcher's Guide to American Genealogy* for supplemental reading. Other excellent books that can aid in your source selections will be introduced in this text and in the chapter bibliographies as well.

The most basic genealogical sources include vital records such as the **civil registration** of birth, marriage, and death records; federal and state **census** records; and obituaries.

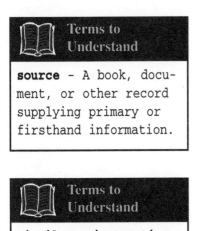

source - A book, document, or other record supplying primary or firsthand information.

ci·vil reg·is·tra·tion- Of, or pertaining to, citizens and their relations with one another or with the state.

YOUR TURN

List three sources you have used.

1.

2.

3.

Summary

There are innumerable sources which aid genealogists in answering their questions, but some sources are better than others for solving family puzzles during different time periods and localities. We will cover sources in several chapters starting with Chapter 7.

STEP 3: LOCATE THE SOURCE (REPOSITORIES)

Next, you must know what **repositories** contain which records, the addresses of the repositories, their availability, and how to use them. Step-by-step guides will be given in this book to aid you in the selection of the repositories that fit your needs. Examples of typical repositories containing genealogical information include:

1. Public Libraries

2. Courthouses

3. Family History Centers

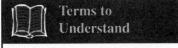

cen·sus - An official, usually periodic, enumeration of a population.

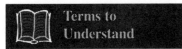

re·pos·i·to·ry - A place, such as a library or an archive, where things may be put for safe-keeping.

4. State and Federal Archives

5. State Libraries.

RECORD REPOSITORY

YOUR TURN

List three repositories you have used.

1.

2.

3.

Summary

Records are stored in different facilities throughout the world. In order to do research effectively, it is necessary to locate the correct repository for the type of record desired. We will cover repositories in depth in Chapters 9 through 13.

Illustration 1-3 Researchers at a Record Repository

STEP 4: SEARCH THE SOURCE

4. Search that source

There are numerous ways to search a source, and there are shortcuts you can learn to use. For example, even in an unindexed source, it is not necessary to read from cover to cover. There are methods to shorten the process, thus helping you to use your time more wisely. The "Your Turn" assignment which follows provides typical situations you'll encounter in your research.

There are numerous ways to search a source.

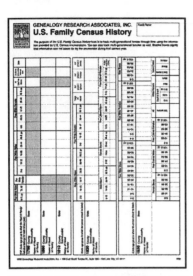

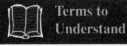

Make accurate copies of
your sources!

tran·scribe - To write
or type a copy of a
given text.

ab·stract - To summa-
rize the important
points of a given
text.

Terms to
Understand

ex·tract - To remove
(a written passage,
for example) for sepa-
rate consideration or
publication.

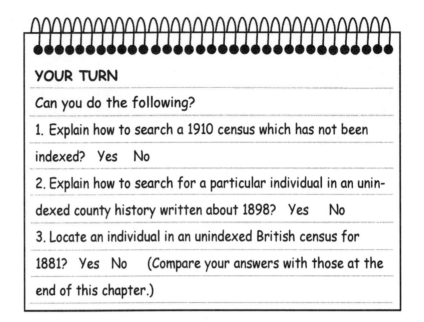

YOUR TURN

Can you do the following?

1. Explain how to search a 1910 census which has not been indexed?   Yes   No

2. Explain how to search for a particular individual in an unin-dexed county history written about 1898?   Yes   No

3. Locate an individual in an unindexed British census for 1881? Yes No   (Compare your answers with those at the end of this chapter.)

STEP 5: COPY THE INFORMATION

It's common for beginning researchers to neglect to make an accurate copy of a source the first time they find it.

YOUR TURN

Ask yourself if you have ever done the following:

1. Have you forgotten to photocopy the author/title page when you've photocopied other information from a book? Yes No

2. Have you neglected to copy the complete source rather than just the date and name of the parties on an 1900 census, or copied only the Soundex (index) card, not the actual record? Yes No

3. Have you ignored the names of the witnesses to an event for clues of possible kinship?   Yes No

Summary

Even though copying information appears to be an easy thing to do, it is very wise for the beginning genealogist to make a photocopy of the entire document until they learn what is important to **transcribe, abstract** or **extract** from it.

STEP 6: EVALUATE THE INFORMATION

The next step is often the most neglected in the process: *evaluating the information.* When we locate a record, our excitement over the obvious might prevent a meticulous evaluation of the less obvious clues. Questions we should always ask ourselves are:

- What else is this record telling me?

- Can more information be obtained if I search this same source using **collateral** lines?

- Am I reading the old handwriting correctly?

- Should I ask someone for help?

- Have I looked at the front of the book for clues the author discovered when he or she compiled the source?

Terms to Understand

col·lat·er·al - Having an ancestor in common, but descended from a different line.

YOUR TURN

In the example below, you have located the birth of an ancestor in the International Genealogical Index (IGI).

In addition to the birth date on this *IGI* sample, list three more pieces of information this record gives.

1.

2.

3.

```
International Genealogical Index (R) - Main File - Version 4.01                    British Isles

                              INDIVIDUAL RECORD

16 FEB 1999                                                           Page 1
===========================================================================
NAME: YEARLEY, James Chalmers
---------------------------------------------------------------------------
SEX:  M

EVENT: Christening
       3 Feb 1836
       Perth, Perth, Scotland
FATHER: John YEARLEY
MOTHER: Jane DEIGHTON

===========================================================================
SOURCE INFORMATION
===========================================================================

Extracted birth and/or christening record for:
  Perth, Perth County, Scotland
Usually arranged chronologically by the birth/christening date.
```

Batch	Dates	Source Call No.	Type	Printout Call No. Type
C119485	1834-1840	1040162	Film	NONE

Illustration 1-4 Individual Record Printout from the IGI

Perhaps you remarked, "What is the *International Genealogical Index?*" You will learn all about it in Chapter 11.

- page 5 -

Mary Morrison was found in a 23 March 1860 Clermont County, Ohio marriage record as a 21 year old woman born in New York the daughter of Joseph Smithwick and Susan Chambers. She was a resident of Clermont County and her husband was listed as Moses Masterson, age 25, born in Ohio the son of J. M. Masterson and Martha Weems of Massachusetts. Moses was a canal worker of Clermont County.

See you next month at the reunion.

Love, Aunt Millie

Summary

Take as much time as is necessary to ask yourself many questions about each source that you locate. As you answer your own questions, you will be guided to more clues for solving your ultimate problem.

STEP 7: USE THE RESULTS

7. Use the results

Once you have searched a source and found your ancestor, you usually discover more clues. For example, finding John Wilkinson in the Arkansas 1880 federal census as an 80-year-old, born in Georgia, with his parents born in North Carolina and a younger brother living with him, age 59, born in South Carolina provides these new clues:

- Birth year of John Wilkinson is 1800.
- Birthplace of John Wilkinson is Georgia.
- Birthplace of John Wilkinson's father is North Carolina.
- Birthplace of John Wilkinson's mother is North Carolina.
- Birthplace of John Wilkinson's brother is South Carolina.
- The family will probably be found in the 1820 federal census of South Carolina, since the brother was born there. This could lead to new county records to search.
- The published surname collections for Arkansas, South Carolina, and North Carolina should be searched for the surname "Wilkinson."

YOUR TURN

Your great-aunt Milly wrote a letter (above left) to your mother long ago, describing information she found in a marriage record of her parents. You are excited because you know nothing more about Aunt Milly's parents other than their names. List the new information you discovered from reading Aunt Milly's letter:

1.

2.

3.

4.

5.

6.

7.

8.

9.

10.

11.

12.

The Complete Beginner's Guide

Summary

Using the results of one search will guide you to more searches. Once you have determined just what new information you have, you can set about considering new sources for extending your family lines further.

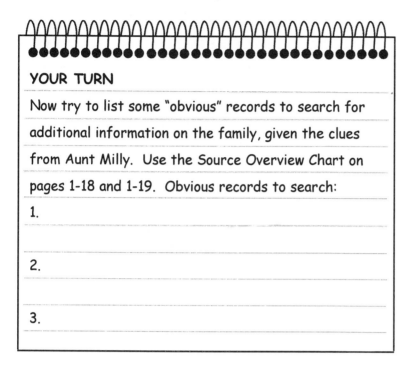

YOUR TURN

Now try to list some "obvious" records to search for additional information on the family, given the clues from Aunt Milly. Use the Source Overview Chart on pages 1-18 and 1-19. Obvious records to search:

1.

2.

3.

Terms to Understand

con·text - The circumstances in which a particular event occurs.

Terms to Understand

chro·nol·o·gy - The arrangement of items in the order of occurrence.

Terms to Understand

doc·u·men·ta·tion - The supplying of documents or supporting references or records.

STEP 8: ORGANIZE AND REORGANIZE

Finally, to benefit from this new information, you must place it in **context** with all the other facts. This is most simply accomplished by using a computer, because you can insert new information at the appropriate point in the **chronology** without retyping **documentation** and research notes. Then you can "reorganize the information" based on new information.

For example, **data fields** can also be quickly updated to allow for such things as corrected dates, places and family connections from your family letters or cen-

Terms to Understand

da·ta fields - a computer term for places to "type in" birth, marriage, and death dates and places.

Organizing family information

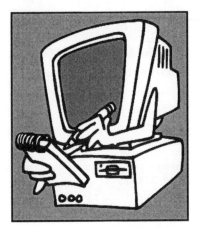

sus findings. A good genealogy computer program also aids in your analysis because it can search all notes for elusive clues such as, "Was the man listed as a witness also listed as a neighbor in a previous state, or later as a spouse of a direct, or collateral line person?"

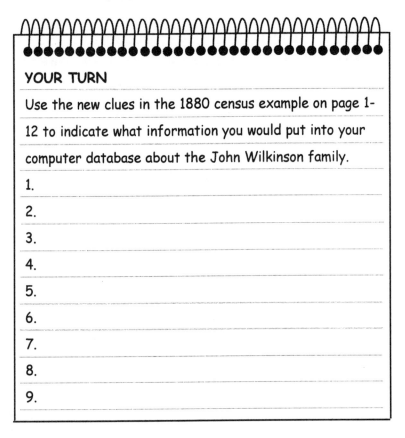

YOUR TURN

Use the new clues in the 1880 census example on page 1-12 to indicate what information you would put into your computer database about the John Wilkinson family.

1.

2.

3.

4.

5.

6.

7.

8.

9.

Your "great ancestral hunt" should begin in your own home.

Summary

Setting a new goal will require another cycle of knowing what sources are available to obtain a goal, which sources to use due to availability and usability, and how to go about obtaining the sources.

PREASSESSMENT

The "Your Turn" self tests you have completed thus far in this chapter will help to preassess your previous genealogical experience. Circle one point for each correct answer given to the questions in the "Your Turn" self test (next page). On the six "Your Turn" assignments given previously, how did you rate?

You could also be at one level of expertise in genealogy and another in computer usage. Use the chart (Illustration 1-5) as well as the level statements (on the next page) to place yourself in one level as far as genealogy research is concerned, and another level as far as computer usage is concerned. Now you have an idea of where you stand in relation to others doing genealogy research.

To those of you who are Level Five in both categories, thanks for reading this book but you really should move on to the next level. If you are enjoying this book for little tidbits you might find herein, may you find what you are seeking.

GATHER FAMILY RECORDS

If you are working on your family history for the first time, you might find yourself with materials all over the house. There could be pictures in a drawer, certificates in a file, family albums on a bookshelf, counted-cross stitched pictures in the attic, a Civil War sword in a trunk in the basement, and obituaries in a

YOUR TURN Self Test (Circle one point for each correct answer.)			
Fact versus Tradition, p. 1-5	1	2	3
Goal Setting, p. 1-7	1	2	3
Sources to Use, p. 1-8	1	2	3
Repositories Used, p. 1-9	1	2	3
Search the Source (subtract 1 point), p. 1-10	1	2	3
Copy the Information, p. 1-10	1	2	3
Evaluate the Information, p. 1-11	1	2	3
Organize and Reorganize, p.1-12 (1/3 pt for each)	1	2	3
Use the Results, p. 1-13, 1-14 (1 pt for each)	1	2	3

GENEALOGICAL LEVEL		Correct Answers
LEVEL ONE	L-1	0-1
LEVEL TWO	L-2	2-6
LEVEL THREE	L-3	7-16
LEVEL FOUR	L-4	17-20
LEVEL FIVE	L-5	21-24

desk drawer somewhere. Use the charts entitled Source Overview (Illustrations 1-8a and 1-8b) to help you find other sources in your home.

Then, place a large box at the entrance of your most frequently used family bathroom. Don't use that room unless you have something pertaining to your family history to deposit in the box. Somehow, either the urgency of using that room requires the collection to mount quickly, or your innate neatness persuades you to spend a whole day gathering everything together.

If, on the other hand, you have been dabbling in family history for years and you have determined to go about it more systematically than in the past, you might have oodles of wonderful odds and ends. I have a friend whose husband's job takes him away for several months at a time. She had always used his side of the bed to store her family history "hobby" while he was away. One time he returned early and she nearly broke her back finding a place for everything. Things fell over, and got out of order, so she joined my classes in order to get organized and stay that way before her husband decided never to return.

Whether you have one box or thirty, they must be organized, analyzed, and filed in order to discover what you already know. If you believe others in your family have submitted information to the LDS Church's *Ancestral File*™ or put information onto the Internet, you could save yourself hours of data entry by locating that information and copying it to your own family records at this point. You could then locate the sources of that information by contacting the submitters and supplementing their sources with your own personal research. If corrections need to be made, you should set goals to do so (this will be covered in Chapter 11).

Preserve original documents by placing them in separate vertical files or into clear, acrylic, archival-quality protectors. Make copies of originals for data input if they are not filed with other records. Notes on small pieces of paper are easily lost, so copy them to full-size sheets. Oversized documents are usually reduced to a standard size to make filing and retrieval more efficient. Oversized copies may be torn, so use the special way to fold legal documents shown in Illustration 1-6.

If the documentation you need to preserve is an entire bound book, make a **bibliographic notation** and place it on a full-size (8 1/2 x 11 inch) sheet in the surname file portion of your notebook (this will be covered in Chapter 6).

Terms to Understand

An·ces·tral File - A lineage-linked, surname-indexed data base of Pedigrees and Family Group Records submitted to the LDS Church since 1980 by researchers all over the world.

Terms to Understand

bib·li·o·graph·ic no·ta·tion - Refers to the written description and identification of the editions, dates of issue, authorship, and typography of books or other written material.

GENEALOGY LEVEL	COMPUTER LEVEL
Level One I've never done genealogy.	**Level One** I've never used a computer.
Level Two I've put together Pedigree Charts and Family Group Records using information provided by others.	**Level Two** I've used a computer, but never a computer genealogy program.
Level Three I have used census records, can calculate a Soundex code, have used the IGI, FHLC, the FamilySearch™ Ancestral File™, Military Index, and Social Security files, as well as the items above. (All must be marked for credit.)	**Level Three** I've used a computer program to enter families from family records, and to organize the information, but I have not used the computer program as a research tool.
Level Four I've visited and used a Family History Center or major genealogy library for at least 250 hours, compiled Family Group Records and Pedigree Charts from original research, filled out at least 25 Research Planners or Logs recording both positive and negative searches and successfully taken a family back one generation through personal research, as well as the items above.	**Level Four** I have used the PAF program to enter original research materials; cited all documentation, including searches which were negative on the lines yet to be completed; made GEDCOM transfers from my Family Records Data to send to others; successfully produced a variety of alphabetical and numerical indexes to aid in the organization of family data; and put together a notebook of materials on my family's history.
Level Five I've visited at least 10 different repositories; used a Family History Center, FHL or other major genealogy library for at least 1000 hours; searched original probate, land and property, military service, pension, and bounty land records; attended at least two workshops or classes taught by professional researchers; and produced a family history, as well as all items above.	**Level Five** I've done all the above and made GEDCOM transfers from the FamilySearch program into the Family Records program, and I have developed research strategies using advanced research tools in the computer program I am using (i.e., in PAF, the Focus and Design Features, as well as Match/Merge features). I have helped others on their research and put together a book on someone else's line.

Illustration 1-5 Genealogy Level/Computer Level Chart

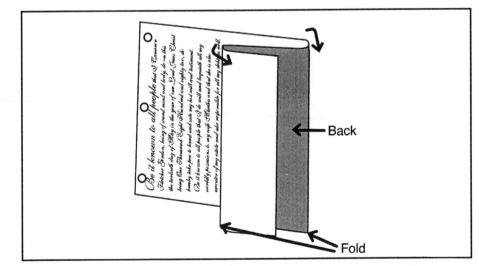

Illustration 1-6 A Special Way to Fold Legal Documents

CONCLUSION: A PROVEN FORMULA

There is a proven formula for success in family history studies: Combine a willingness to try new things (such as basic sources, techniques, and new repositories) with an ability to organize information. Then take that new information and use it wisely with the guidance of knowledgeable and experienced researchers as shown in Illustration 1-7.

Let us now apply this formula. First, it's obvious that you have a willingness to learn new things: we call this "a curious mind" (because you've read this far and haven't run away screaming)—this is a vital ingredient!

Second, you have a copy of this book, in which the bibliographies and assignments will guide you to good source books. You'll need to discover your own nearby public library, research repository, or Family History Center. There are good genealogy computer programs available via the Internet or your local book store. Now you have all of the ingredients to begin your own great adventure.

Start with the assignments on the next page so you can be prepared to learn the "tools of the trade" for organizing and demonstrating your facts—the Pedigree Chart and the Family Group Record, which will be explained in Chapter 2.

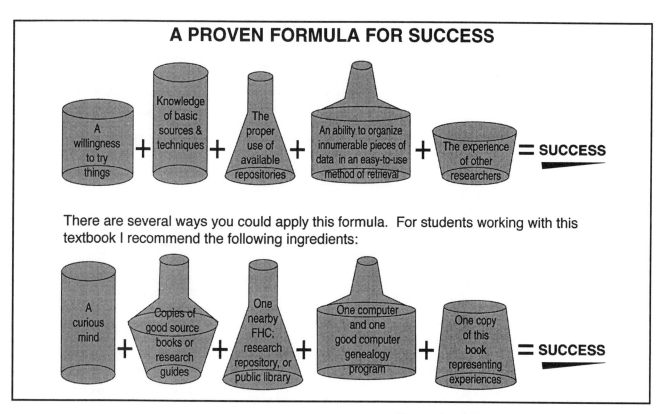

Illustration 1-7 "A Proven Success Formula"

GENEALOGY RESEARCH ASSOCIATES, INC.
Genealogical Source Overview & Checklist

This checklist has been designed to prompt genealogists for information from a wide variety of sources. Check the sources you have acquired or have investigated. Every clue you can uncover will speed up your research and save you time and money.

Family or individual _____   Identification numbers _____

HOME AND FAMILY SOURCES

Personal Records
- ❑ Scrapbooks
- ❑ Heirlooms
- ❑ Journals/Diaries
- ❑ Oral Histories
- ❑ Personal Histories
- ❑ Family Histories
- ❑ Diaries
- ❑ Personal Correspondence
- ❑ Photographs
- ❑ Funeral Cards
- ❑ Obituaries
- ❑ Medical Records
- ❑ Military Records
- ❑ Employment Records
- ❑ Social Security
- ❑ Social Security Application Forms
- ❑ Social Security Recipient Forms
- ❑ Social Security Cards
- ❑ Labels or Tags on Trunks or Baggage
- ❑ Films, Slides and Videos
- ❑ Tombstone Photos
- ❑ Autograph Books

Certificates
- ❑ Birth

- ❑ Military Discharge
- ❑ School Achievement
- ❑ Marriage
- ❑ Death
- ❑ Adoption
- ❑ Graduation
- ❑ Divorce
- ❑ Citizenship
- ❑ Manumission (Liberation/ Emancipation)

School Records
- ❑ Elementary
- ❑ Secondary
- ❑ Vocational, Trade
- ❑ College
- ❑ University
- ❑ Arts
- ❑ Private
- ❑ Ladies Finishing
- ❑ Correspondence Schools
- ❑ Yearbooks

Insurance
- ❑ Life
- ❑ Fire
- ❑ Accident
- ❑ Health
- ❑ Other

Business/Legal Records
- ❑ Accounting Books
- ❑ Bills
- ❑ Receipts
- ❑ Correspondence
- ❑ Credit Applications
- ❑ Citizenship Papers
- ❑ Passports and Visas
- ❑ Mortgage Records
- ❑ Deeds
- ❑ Property Titles
- ❑ Rental Agreements
- ❑ Bank Applications/Forms
- ❑ Bank Statements
- ❑ Wills
- ❑ Probate Papers
- ❑ Intestate Court Papers
- ❑ Legal Briefs
- ❑ Adoption Papers
- ❑ Court Orders

Religious Records
- ❑ Family Bibles
- ❑ Marriage
- ❑ Baptism
- ❑ Confirmation
- ❑ Christening
- ❑ Religious Office
- ❑ Religious Achievement

- ❑ Missionary Activity
- ❑ Ministerial Papers

Non-Document Record Sources
- ❑ Military Uniforms (insignias of organization, rank, service, awards, etc.)
- ❑ Dish and Glassware (manufacturers location and production insignia/dates)
- ❑ Furniture (manufacturers location and production insignia/dates)
- ❑ Photographs/Portraits (photographer's/artist's location, names and dates)
- ❑ Clothing (hand tailored items showing tailor and location)
- ❑ Quilts and stitchery with names
- ❑ Jewelry (watches, trophies, and hand made items with inscriptions and manufacturers)
- ❑ Luggage (inclusing tags and labels)
- ❑ Objects- such as flags, swords, guns, etc.

SOURCES OF RESEARCH DONE BY OTHERS

Personal Research
- ❑ Pedigree Charts
- ❑ Family Group Records
- ❑ Descendancy Charts
- ❑ Book of Remembrance
- ❑ Research Notes

Family History Library
- ❑ Temple Index Bureau
- ❑ Family Registry

- ❑ Family History Library Catalog (Surname Section for Family Histories Collection)
- ❑ International Genealogical Index (IGI)
- ❑ Family Group Record Archive
- ❑ Ancestral File

Printed Sources
- ❑ Family Histories
- ❑ Biographies
- ❑ Genealogies
- ❑ Pedigrees
- ❑ County/Local Histories
- ❑ State and Territorial Histories
- ❑ City Directories
- ❑ Indexes

Periodicals
- ❑ Genealogies
- ❑ Historical Items
- ❑ Queries
- ❑ Source Extracts
- ❑ Directories
- ❑ Genealogical and Historical Society Publications

CHURCH SOURCES (for Original Research)

Events
(Below, a type of event is listed rather than a specific record. Some events may have more than one type of record.)
- ❑ Birth
- ❑ Christening
- ❑ Circumcision
- ❑ Baptism
- ❑ Confirmation

- ❑ Communion
- ❑ Coming of Age (i.e. Bar Mitzvah)
- ❑ Ordination
- ❑ Primary or Sunday School
- ❑ Seminary
- ❑ Marriage
- ❑ Banns
- ❑ Divorce
- ❑ Annulment

- ❑ Death
- ❑ Burial
- ❑ Admissions
- ❑ Removals
- ❑ Disciplinary Proceedings
- ❑ Subscriptions
- ❑ Membership & Transfers

Records
- ❑ Ministers' Records

- ❑ Mission Reports
- ❑ Church Minutes
- ❑ Contribution Records
- ❑ Bishops' Transcripts (of records of original events)
- ❑ Church/Congregational Histories
- ❑ Historical Event and Anniversary Celebration Records

1999 **Genealogy Research Associates, Inc.** 189 East South Temple, Suite 300, Salt Lake City, UT 84111 *(www.graonline.com)*   7/99

Illustration 1-8a   Genealogical Source Overview & Checklist (page 1)

PRIVATE SOURCES (for Original Research)

Newspapers
- ❑ Indexes
- ❑ Births
- ❑ Marriages
- ❑ Deaths
- ❑ Anniversaries
- ❑ Obituaries
- ❑ Advertisements
- ❑ Local News
- ❑ Unclaimed Mail

Legal Notices
- ❑ Probate
- ❑ Auctions
- ❑ Forced Sales
- ❑ Divorces
- ❑ Elopement
- ❑ Bankruptcies

- ❑ Court Claims
- ❑ Convictions
- ❑ Lawyer Briefs
- ❑ Slavery Records

Employment
- ❑ Indentures
- ❑ Apprenticeships
- ❑ Licenses
- ❑ Pensions
- ❑ Service Awards
- ❑ Personal Files
- ❑ Account Books
- ❑ Retirement Records

Institutional
- ❑ Charities
- ❑ Hospitals
- ❑ Convents

- ❑ Seminaries
- ❑ Libraries
- ❑ Historical Societies
- ❑ Mission Societies
- ❑ Orphan Agencies
- ❑ Reunion Registers
- ❑ Schools
- ❑ Colleges and Universities

Mortuary Records
- ❑ Burial Records
- ❑ Funeral Cards
- ❑ Funeral Books

Collections of Historical Data
- ❑ DAR
- ❑ Oral Histories
- ❑ Personal papers
- ❑ Indexes

- ❑ Correspondence
- ❑ Surname Files
- ❑ Inscriptions
- ❑ Biographies
- ❑ Corporate Histories
- ❑ Histories of Charitable Institutions and Organizations

Organizations
- ❑ Clubs
- ❑ Societies
- ❑ Boy Scouts
- ❑ Girls Scouts
- ❑ Upper Class Society Organizations

PUBLIC SOURCES (for Original Research)

U.S. Federal/State Censuses
- ❑ Federal Census Index 1790
- ❑ Federal Census Index 1800
- ❑ Federal Census Index 1810
- ❑ Federal Census Index 1820
- ❑ Federal Census Index 1830
- ❑ Federal Census Index 1840
- ❑ Federal Census Index 1850
- ❑ Federal Census Index 1860
- ❑ Federal Census Index 1870
- ❑ Federal Census Soundex 1880
- ❑ Federal Census Soundex 1890
- ❑ Federal Census Soundex 1900
- ❑ Federal Census Soundex 1910
- ❑ Federal Census Soundex 1920
- ❑ Federal Census 1790
- ❑ Federal Census 1800
- ❑ Federal Census 1810
- ❑ Federal Census 1820
- ❑ Federal Census 1830
- ❑ Federal Census 1840
- ❑ Federal Census 1850
- ❑ Federal Census 1860
- ❑ Federal Census 1870
- ❑ Federal Census 1880
- ❑ Federal Census 1890
- ❑ Federal Census 1900
- ❑ Federal Census 1910
- ❑ Federal Census 1920
- ❑ Mortality Schedules
- ❑ Revolutionary War Veterans
- ❑ Union Army Veterans
- ❑ Agricultural
- ❑ State Censuses (years vary by state)

Land Records
- ❑ Grantor Index
- ❑ Grantee Index
- ❑ Bounty Warrants
- ❑ Deeds
- ❑ Tract Books

- ❑ Plat Maps
- ❑ Mortgages
- ❑ Grants, patents
- ❑ Homestead papers
- ❑ Surveys
- ❑ Indian Treaties

Court and Legal Records
- ❑ Dockets
- ❑ Minutes
- ❑ Judgements
- ❑ Orders, Decrees
- ❑ Case Files
- ❑ Indexes
- ❑ Sheriff/Police
- ❑ Justice of the Peace
- ❑ Lawyer Briefs
- ❑ Jail Records
- ❑ Poor House Records
- ❑ Jury Records
- ❑ Guardian and Ward
- ❑ Orphan Court Records
- ❑ Bankruptcy Records
- ❑ Certificates
- ❑ Licenses
- ❑ Chancery Court Records
- ❑ Civil/Cominal Court Records
- ❑ Correctional Records

Probate Records
- ❑ Indexes
- ❑ Wills
- ❑ Administrations
- ❑ Estate Records
- ❑ Inventories
- ❑ Bonds
- ❑ Settlements
- ❑ Packets
- ❑ Petitions

Tax Records
- ❑ Personal/Property
- ❑ Real Estate

- ❑ School
- ❑ Poor Rate
- ❑ Tax Exemptions
- ❑ Poll Tax (Voting)
- ❑ Householder's Index

Other Governmental Records
- ❑ Birth Records
- ❑ Marriage Records
- ❑ Death Certification
- ❑ Centennial Celebrations
- ❑ Native American Records
- ❑ Social Security Records

Military Records
- ❑ Service Record Index
- ❑ Pension Index
- ❑ Service Records
- ❑ Unit Correspondence
- ❑ Pension Files
- ❑ Bounty Awards
- ❑ Discharges
- ❑ Muster Rolls
- ❑ Regimental Histories
- ❑ Military Campaign and War History
- ❑ Desertion Records
- ❑ Burials
- ❑ Dependents of Personnel Born Abroad
- ❑ Admiralty Court Records

Immigrant Records
- ❑ Emigration (leaving) Records
- ❑ Passenger Lists
- ❑ Passports
- ❑ Vaccination Certificates
- ❑ Alien Registration
- ❑ Change of Name
- ❑ Oaths of Allegiance
- ❑ Register of Voters
- ❑ Citizenship Papers
- ❑ Naturalization Records

- ❑ Immigrant Aid Societies
- ❑ Custom Records
- ❑ Ship's Logbooks
- ❑ Border Crossings

Cemetery Records
- ❑ Sexton Records
- ❑ Cemetery Indexes
- ❑ Monuments
- ❑ Plat Books
- ❑ Tombstones
- ❑ Memorials
- ❑ Gifts
- ❑ Deeds
- ❑ Perpetual Care Funds

Newspapers
- ❑ Obituaries
- ❑ Biographical Articles
- ❑ News Articles

Histories
- ❑ State
- ❑ County
- ❑ Local
- ❑ Business
- ❑ Biographies
- ❑ Church
- ❑ Occupational/Guild
- ❑ Organizational
- ❑ Society
- ❑ Almanacs

Periodicals
- ❑ Genealogical Societies
- ❑ Historical Societies
- ❑ Military Organizations
- ❑ Military History Societies
- ❑ State/Locality News
- ❑ Family Organizations
- ❑ Surname Societies
- ❑ Local Heritage
- ❑ Heraldic Societies

Illustration 1-8b Genealogical Source Overview & Checklist (page 2)

ASSIGNMENT 1: SORTING YOUR FAMILY MATERIALS

1. Sort your family records by surname and then by individual families; then opt for #2 or #3 below.
   A. Use shallow, empty boxes.
   B. Place a label on the side of each box for every surname.
   C. Place materials relating to a family in its box.

2. The *File Method*: Sort those surname boxes by individual families.
   A. Place individual families in file folders, keeping all documents flat.
   B. Unfold old letters; creases will later tear.
   C. Keep copies of originals in protective sleeves.
   This method sometimes results in the loss of records when things are removed or put out of order, but it does allow for great expansion.

3. The *Binder Method*: Place documents in a binder with index tabs dividing various surnames.
   A. Place individual families behind individual tabs, keeping all documents flat.
   B. Unfold old letters; creases will later tear.
   C. Keep copies of originals in protective sleeves.
   D. Reduce over-sized pages by photocopying to a smaller standard size, and store originals in large flat boxes or drawers, or place them in frames for display.

   This method keeps records in order and prepares the records for later placement in the family notebook by hole punching or placing in protective sleeves.

   Preserve original documents by placing them in separate vertical files or into clear, acrylic, archival-quality protectors. Make copies of originals for data input, if they are not filed with other records. Oversized documents are usually reduced to a standard size to make filing and retrieval more efficient.

   Notes on small pieces of paper are easily lost, so copy them to full-size sheets. Oversized copies may be torn, so use the special way to fold legal sized documents that is shown in Illustration 1-6.

YOUR TURN ANSWERS

Fact versus Tradition

1. Did you notice that the Alex listed under "Facts" was the son of a tenant farmer? He would not be of the same social status as a wealthy carriage owner.

2. Did you notice he was still living in Finland at the age of 16 and also at age 22 at the time of his marriage?

3. Did you observe that he either returned to Finland, left later than the tradition stated, or was a different person?

Decide Which Source to Use

Did you include any of those sources listed on the Source Checklist (Illustrations 1-8a and 1-8b)? As you can tell, sources are available in many varieties and locations.

Locate the Source (Repository)

Did you record any of the repositories listed on pages 1-8 and 1-9? Perhaps you have learned about others you would like to visit.

Search the Source

Although you'll discover more complete answers as you read this book, here are some common strategies you could have indicated for #1. The address could be found from a city directory, vital record, or other census, and the Enumeration District (E.D.) could be found from the address of the individual sought. Then, with the E.D. number, you could look through the actual census. Considering the number of rolls on a major city census, this is a much easier alternative.

For #2, you could locate the individual on a 1900 census, which is very well indexed. On that census, the township and county are listed. Going then to the table of contents in the county history, you could look for the township. With that information, you could locate the individual within the few pages devoted to that township without having to read the entire source.

For #3, you could use the quarterly vital records indexes for Great Britain and find at least one individual in the family born around the time period you are searching. With the address on the vital record, you can search an index by street addresses which will guide you to the proper census roll.

Evaluate the Information

Did you list some of these items:

1. The source of the entry.
2. Whether there is additional information in the original source.
3. Whether there are other family members in the same parish.

Use the Results

1. Moses Masterson and Mary Morrison were married 23 Mar 1860.
2. Moses and Mary Masterson were married in Clermont County, Ohio.
3. Mary Morrison was probably married before, because her surname was different than that of her father or her mother.
4. Mary was born in New York
5. Mary was born in 1839.
6. Mary's maiden name was Smithwick.
7. Mary's father was Joseph Smithwick.
8. Mary's mother was Susan Chambers.
9. Moses Masterson was born in 1835.
10. Moses Masterson was born in Ohio.
11. Moses Masterson's father was J. M. Masterson of Massachusetts.
12. Moses Masterson's mother was Martha Weems of Massachusetts.
13. Moses Masterson's occupation was a canal worker.

Organize and Reorganize

1. Add John Wilkinson's birth year of 1800.
2. Add John Wilkinson's birth state as Georgia.
3. Add John Wilkinson's father's birth state as North Carolina.
4. Add John Wilkinson's father's birth year as about 1765/1775.
5. Add John Wilkinson's mother's birth state as North Carolina.
6. Add John Wilkinson's mother's birth year as about 1765/1775.
7. Add John Wilkinson's brother's name.
8. Add John Wilkinson's brother's birth year as about 1821.
9. Add John Wilkinson's brother's birthplace as South Carolina.

COMPUTER CHECKLIST #1

1. Which of the following statements apply to you?

   a. I don't know how to use a typewriter or computer keyboard.

   b. I have never used a personal computer to locate or record information.

   c. I don't have access to a computer, and I can't afford to purchase one.

   d. I don't know where to go for help in learning how to use the computer.

   e. I get hives just thinking about computers.

   f. I am familiar with computers.

2. What kind of computer operating system do you have? Some genealogy computer programs only work in one operating system.

   a. DOS

   b. Macintosh

   c. Windows 3.1

   d. Windows 95

   e. Windows 98

   f. Other

WEB SITE

http:// www.GRAonline.com

The Genealogy Research Associates site contains supplemental materials which complement this book by allowing information to be included which requires frequent updating. For instance, comparisons of various genealogy computer programs can be found in these supplemental Web materials. Individual features of each program are taught and personal applications suggested which allow you to evaluate which program(s) best meet your needs. Free genealogy classes expand upon topics covered in this book and guide you to other Web sites on the Internet. Record look-up services are offered for a fee if you are unable to obtain copies of original documents (such as census records, vital records, or military records), book pages (from books not currently microfilmed or microfiched), or manuscripts you seek.

BIBLIOGRAPHY

Greenwood, Val D. *The Researcher's Guide to American Genealogy.* 3rd ed.
Baltimore: Genealogical Publishing Co., 2000.

Meyerink, Kory L. *Printed Sources: A Guide to Published Genealogical
Records.* Salt Lake City: Ancestry Inc., 1998.

Szucs, Loretto Dennis and Sandra Hargreaves Luebking, Editors. *The Source: A
Guidebook of American Genealogy.* Revised ed. Salt Lake City: Ancestry Inc.,
1997.

CHAPTER 2

Organizing Family Information

"All things began in order, so shall they end, and so shall they begin again; according to the ordainer of order and mystical mathematics of the city of heaven."

—Sir Thomas Browne

BEFORE THE BEGINNING... there is usually chaos

When you began to look for your family data, you may have discovered that you had genealogical clues all over your home. Or perhaps the information was at someone else's home or in someone else's head. And now that you have gathered up the scattered facts, photos, letters, scribbled notes and documents, you may feel somewhat overwhelmed. In fact, you might even have laughed when you saw the heading for this chapter, "Organizing Family Information."

But don't despair! The purpose of this chapter is to help in that organizing process by showing you the charts and forms which are the foundation for building your family's tree, and which will make continued success easier both for you and for those who want to help you. Once information has been placed onto correct charts and forms, others can assimilate the data, assess the problems and offer suggestions more quickly. These charts and forms are the standard "tools of the trade."

THE PEDIGREE CHART

The **Pedigree** Chart gives the basic, **direct-line** "skeleton" of one's family tree. It gives only basic, necessary information because *its job is to show the direct line only.* It is the "map" or "table of contents" to your family tree. To see a filled-out sample Pedigree Chart, turn to page 2-7.

A Pedigree Chart usually begins with the person on whom you want to focus your attention; usually, family researchers begin with themselves and then include their direct ancestors for as many **generations** as they have information. However, you may want to have a Pedigree Chart which starts with your father or mother, if you decide that you want to separate the two sides of your family. From that first person, the chart continues up the direct line, showing only the

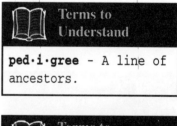

Terms to Understand

ped·i·gree - A line of ancestors.

Terms to Understand

di·rect line - The ancestral line of an individual.

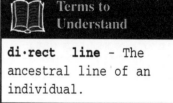

Terms to Understand

gen·er·a·tion - A body of people constituting a single step in the line of descent from an ancestor.

Terms to Understand

sib·lings - One of two or more persons having one or especially both parents in common, e.g., a brother and a sister.

Terms to Understand

char·ac·ter - A symbol or mark used in a writing system, such as a letter of the alphabet.

Terms to Understand

field - A delineated area in a computer database in which a narrowly defined type of information may be entered.

Terms to Understand

da·ta en·try - The typing of information into a computer database.

Terms to Understand

trun·cate - To shorten by cutting off.

parents of each individual.   Other family members, such as **siblings,** aunts, uncles and cousins, do not appear on a Pedigree Chart.

As you can probably guess from looking at the sample in Illustration 2-3, Pedigree Charts have room only for limited information. They are not the place for all the whys and wherefores of a family's history; those come later. Throughout this text, too, you'll notice that I refer to four-generation Pedigree Charts in the visuals. I prefer these charts over the five, six, or seven-generation charts, which are also available via computer printout, because there is more room for the complete locality to be printed. Your computer genealogy program is limited to a designated number of **characters** per **field** in the Pedigree Chart's spaces for the places of birth, death and marriage. Other charts, such as Family Group Records, allow for the entire locality entry.

The above reasoning is also why I choose to use two-letter state abbreviations over typing out the full state name as I do **data entry**. I want to be able to read

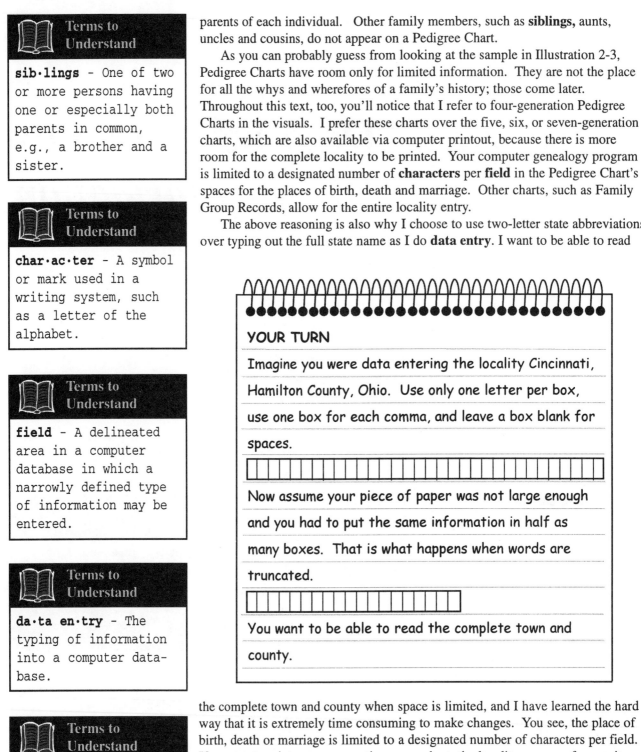

YOUR TURN

Imagine you were data entering the locality Cincinnati, Hamilton County, Ohio. Use only one letter per box, use one box for each comma, and leave a box blank for spaces.

Now assume your piece of paper was not large enough and you had to put the same information in half as many boxes. That is what happens when words are truncated.

You want to be able to read the complete town and county.

the complete town and county when space is limited, and I have learned the hard way that it is extremely time consuming to make changes. You see, the place of birth, death or marriage is limited to a designated number of characters per field. If you try to print seven generations on a chart, the locality names, of necessity, will be **truncated** by your program in order for the type font to remain the same size and still keep everything on the page. While Family Group Records allow for the entire locality entry to be printed, Pedigree Charts may only give abbreviated information.   What is important is that you are consistent in your own data-

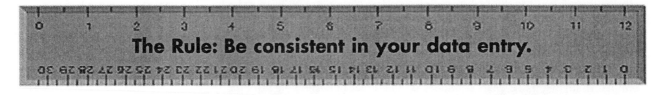

The Rule: Be consistent in your data entry.

entry work. It's easy to make changes in **databases** which are consistent if you later change your mind.

Pedigree Charts list, in order, the parents, grandparents, great-grandparents, etc., as far back as is known for the person listed as #1 on Pedigree Chart #1. Many researchers prefer genealogy computer programs where every person on the chart is given a chart number to the left of the person's name. So person #1's maternal grandfather would be #6. Person #1's father would be #2. The chart, pre-numbered, would look like Illustration 2-1.

Terms to Understand

da·ta·base – Information that is collected, usually on a computer, which fits into a narrowly defined set of parameters; once collected, this information can be sorted and analyzed to reach one or more conclusions.

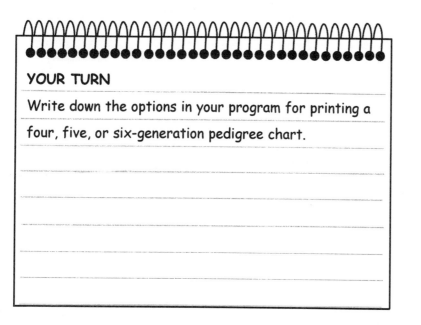

YOUR TURN

Write down the options in your program for printing a four, five, or six-generation pedigree chart.

THE FAMILY GROUP RECORD

For each set of parents on a Pedigree Chart, there needs to be a Family Group Record. All of the information and documentation about the family is recorded on this form. It seems much less intimidating if you refer to it as the "fill in the blanks" form. A good Family Group Record will have a place to record each piece of vital information needed for each person. By filling in the blanks (or fields, in computer terminology), information is recorded in a standard format. Working from a standard form is much easier than a sheet of paper (or several sheets) covered with miscellaneous notes.

There are just three basic style rules for entering information on these two forms:

1. NAMES: Put the surname in capital letters: John TODD.

In order to prevent confusion between surnames and given names, the surname, when handwritten, should be written all in capital letters. In the *Personal*

YOUR TURN

Print this person's name the way you should when you hand-enter it onto a form:

George Washington Johnson

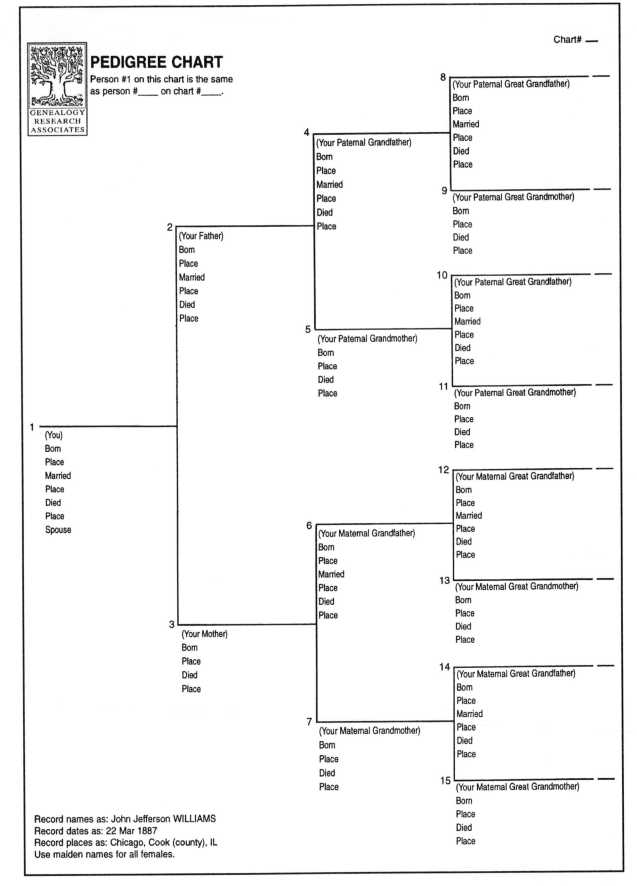

PEDIGREE CHART

Person #1 on this chart is the same
as person #____ on chart #____.

GENEALOGY
RESEARCH
ASSOCIATES

Chart# ___

8 (Your Paternal Great Grandfather)
Born
Place
Married
Place
Died
Place

4 (Your Paternal Grandfather)
Born
Place
Married
Place
Died
Place

9 (Your Paternal Great Grandmother)
Born
Place
Died
Place

2 (Your Father)
Born
Place
Married
Place
Died
Place

10 (Your Paternal Great Grandfather)
Born
Place
Married
Place
Died
Place

5 (Your Paternal Grandmother)
Born
Place
Died
Place

11 (Your Paternal Great Grandmother)
Born
Place
Died
Place

1 (You)
Born
Place
Married
Place
Died
Place
Spouse

12 (Your Maternal Great Grandfather)
Born
Place
Married
Place
Died
Place

6 (Your Maternal Grandfather)
Born
Place
Married
Place
Died
Place

13 (Your Maternal Great Grandmother)
Born
Place
Died
Place

3 (Your Mother)
Born
Place
Died
Place

14 (Your Maternal Great Grandfather)
Born
Place
Married
Place
Died
Place

7 (Your Maternal Grandmother)
Born
Place
Died
Place

15 (Your Maternal Great Grandmother)
Born
Place
Died
Place

Record names as: John Jefferson WILLIAMS
Record dates as: 22 Mar 1887
Record places as: Chicago, Cook (county), IL
Use maiden names for all females.

Illustration 2-1 A Blank Pedigree Chart

Ancestral File (PAF) program, it is not necessary to remember to do this as you enter data, since the program automatically knows to convert the surname to all capital letters if you told it to do so during installation of the program, when you set your preferences. When entering other data into the computer, it is best that you not type in all caps, except for state abbreviations, such as OH, IL, MO, etc.

2. DATES: Enter the day, month and year.

In most countries, the month is written after the day, such as 6 February 1946. But in the U.S., the month is written before the day, as in February 6, 1946. In addition, we have become accustomed to dropping the first two digits of the year, as in 2-6-46, since few of the dates we customarily deal with occur in any century but the twentieth. Yet when you think about it, you can see that a date such as 2-6-46 could mean February 6, 1946, June 2, 1946, or even June 2, 1846. Therefore, the rule is to put the day, then the month (it is perfectly fine to use the three-letter abbreviation for the month: 23 Apr 1823), then the year. If you type, April 23, 1823 the computer will probably automatically convert it to 23 Apr 1823.

Illustration 2-2 Learning How to Write Names and Dates

3. PLACES: Town, county, state or country.

While your particular computer genealogy program may not be limited to a designated number of characters per field when you enter the names, printing the information is another matter. Once again, space is limited for localities. In addition, many newer computer genealogy programs do not designate a particular area for various locality **levels.** Places are entered with the smallest jurisdiction or level first (usually town, **township**, or **parish**), followed by the next largest level (county), followed by the next largest (state), and if a foreign country, by the country's name. Snowville Twp, Jackson, MO is a sample of such an entry (see the state abbreviation chart in Illustration 2-6). The word "county" or "Co." is not usually needed if the county is placed consistently in level two, but, if you think that a place name might be misunderstood, then go ahead and put in the designation "Co." for "County." Do not type USA or U.S.A. It is assumed that everything is in the U.S.A., unless otherwise stated.

There are times when all four location levels could change, thus causing a shifting of the levels and destroying the consistency of your data entry, such as when placing a cemetery name in as the burial place. If you were to enter the

---

Terms to Understand

lev·el - A position in the ranking of a locality that is entered into a genealogy database.

Terms to Understand

town·ship - 1. A subdivision of a county in most northeastern and midwestern states, having the status of a unit of local government with varying governmental powers. 2. A public land surveying unit of 36 sections or 36 square miles. 3. An ancient administrative division of a large parish in England.

Terms to Understand

par·ish - In Great Britain, a political division of a county for local civil government, usually corresponding to an ecclesiastical parish. In Louisana, counties are known as parishes.

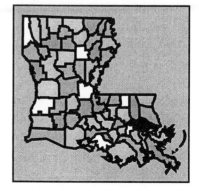

YOUR TURN

1. Write these locations as they should be written on Pedigree Charts and Family Group Records:

A. Born in Mother of Charity Hospital, New York City, New York County, New York State

B. Died in Monterey Community Hospital, Salinas, Monterey County, California

C. Buried at Holy Cross Cemetery, Monterey County, California.

2. Can you find instructions in your genealogy computer program for printing Family Group Records? What are they?

3. Is a definition provided for each of the numbers indicated? What are they?

PEDIGREE CHART

GENEALOGY RESEARCH ASSOCIATES

8 Herman Anterspoika KAMPSULA
(Your Paternal Great Grandfather)
Born   29 Mar 1863
Place   , Ylivieska, Oula, Fin
Married 28 Sep 1884
Place   ,Ylivieska, Oula, Fin.
Died   30 May 1931
Place   New York Mills, Ottertail, MN

4 Andrew KAMPSULA
(Your Paternal Grandfather)
Born   5 Feb 1889
Place   Ishpeming, Marquette, MI
Married 1910
Place   Homstead, OtterTail, MN
Died   13 Dec 1939
Place   Hopewell, Yamhill, OR

9 Hilma Kallentytar WALIMAA
(Your Paternal Great Grandmother)
Born 5 Jun 1862
Place , Ylivieska, Oula, Fin.
Died 8 Sep 1921
Place Brainard, Crowing, MN

2 Bruno Benjamin KAMPSULA
(Your Father)
Born   22 Feb 1924
Place   Homestead, OtterTail, MN
Married 1945 (Div)
Place   Vancouver, Clark, WA
Died   13 Aug 1993
Place   Vancouver, Clark, WA

10 Benjam Juhonpoika TASKINEN
(Your Paternal Great Grandfather)
Born   15 Marr 1867
Place Kivennapa, Viipuri, Fin.
Married 6 Oct 1886
Place Kivennapa, Viipuri, Fin.
Died   18 Oct 1946
Place Portland, Multnomah, OR

5 Ida Maria TASKINEN
(Your Paternal Grandmother)
Born   18 Sep 1887
Place , Kivennapa, Viipuri, Fin.
Died   6 Feb 1949
Place Portland, Multnomah, OR

11 Hilda Maria Nikodemusdotter POLVI
(Your Paternal Great Grandmother)
Born
Place
Died
Place

1 Karen Ann KAMPSULA
(You)
Born   29 July 1953
Place   Milwaukie, Clackamas, OR
Married
Place
Died
Place
Spouse

6 Aleksis Nikolai LEHTONON
(Your Maternal Grandfather)
Born   17 Jul 1895
Place Rymattyla, Turku-Pori, Fin.
Married 1924
Place FtBragg, Mendocino, CA
Died   31 Aug 1941
Place Portland, Multnomah, OR

12 Frans Isaak Isaaksson LEHTONEN
(Your Maternal Great Grandfather)
Born   16 Aug 1862
Place Merimasku, Turku-Pori, Fin.
Married
Place ,,Fin
Died   22 Jun 1928
Place Rymattyla, Turku-Pori, Fin

13 Josefina Justinantytar SAARIS
(Your Maternal Great Grandmother)
Born
Place
Died
Place

3 Lempi Hellena LEHTO
(Your Mother)
Born   31 Jul 1925
Place Cordova, Cordova, Alaska
Died   24 Nov 1979
Place Milwaukie, Clackamas, OR

7 Lempi Lillian KESTI
(Your Maternal Grandmother)
Born   6 Sept 1901
Place Ft Bragg, Mendocino, CA
Died   23 May 1953
Place Longview, Cowlitz, WA

14 Charles Kaarlo Victor KESTI
(Your Maternal Great Grandfather)
Born   4 May 1867
Place   Oulu, Oulu, Fin.
Married 1 Jan 1898 (Div)
Place   Ft Bragg, Mendocino, CA
Died   19 Nov 1942
Place   Ukiah, Mendocino, CA

15 Anna Caisa Johansder POLUS
(Your Maternal Great Grandmother)
Born   21 Jan 1877
Place Limingoja, Pyhajoki, Oulu, Fin.
Died   22 Jan 1946
Place Ft Bragg, Mendocino, CA

Illustration 2-3 Completed Pedigree Chart

HUSBAND	Andrew KAMPSULA		
Born	5 Feb 1889	Place Ishpeming, Marquette, MI	Source
Christened	———	Place	Source
Married	1910	Place Homestead Twp, Otter Tail, MI	Source
Died	13 Dec 1939	Place Hopewell, Yamhill, OR	Source
Buried		Place Portland, Multnomah, OR	Source
Father Herman Anterapoika KAMSULA		Mother Hilma Kallentyter, Walitalo WALIMAA	

WIFE	Ida Maria TASKINEN		
Born	18 Sep 1887	Place , Kivennapa, Viipuri, Fin	Source
Christened	———	Place	Source
Died	6 Feb 1949	Place Portland, Multnomah, OR	Source
Buried	9 Feb 1949	Place Portland, Multnomah, OR	Source
Father Benjamin Juhnopoika TASKINEN		Mother Hilda Maria Nikodemusdotter POLVI	

GENEALOGY RESEARCH ASSOCIATES

FAMILY GROUP RECORD

Husband is same as #___ on pedigree chart #___.
Wife is same as #___ on pedigree chart #___.

CHILDREN (Write under number at left if male [m] or female [f]. List all children in birth order. Mark "X" under number of direct-line child.)

1	Name Andrew Raymond KAMPSULA	Spouse	Source
	Born 14 Jun 1913	Place Homestead Twp, Otter Tail, MN	Source
	Christened	Place	Source
	Married	Place	Source
	Died 5 May 1957	Place Tieton, , WA	Source
	Buried	Place	Source

2	Name Alfred Filmore KAMPSULA	Spouse	Source
	Born 13 Mar 1917	Place New York Mills, Otter Tail, MN	Source
	Christened	Place	Source
	Married	Place	Source
	Died 28 Nov 1985	Place Vancover, Clark, WA	Source
	Buried	Place	Source

3	Name Lilian Victoria KAMPSULA	Spouse Harold Jacob PERALA	Source
	Born 2 Mar 1919	Place Newton, Otter Tail, MN	Source
	Christened	Place	Source
	Married Abt 1937 (div)	Place	Source
	Died 28 Dec 1963	Place , , Idaho	Source
	Buried	Place	Source

4	Name	Spouse	Source
	Born	Place	Source
	Christened	Place	Source
	Married	Place	Source
	Died	Place	Source
	Buried	Place	Source

Key for source abbreviations
PK=Personal knowledge   IF=Information from (name of person or document from which information came)   SE=See enclosed papers

Illustration 2-4 Completed Family Group Record

HUSBAND

Born	Place	Source
Christened	Place	Source
Married	Place	Source
Died	Place	Source
Buried	Place	Source
Father	Mother	Source

WIFE

Born	Place	Source
Christened	Place	Source
Died	Place	Source
Buried	Place	Source
Father	Mother	Source

GENEALOGY RESEARCH ASSOCIATES

FAMILY GROUP RECORD

Husband is same as #___ on pedigree chart #___. **Wife** is same as #___ on pedigree chart #___.

CHILDREN (Write under number at left if male [m] or female [f]. List all children in birth order. Mark "X" under number of direct-line child.)

1

Name	Spouse	Source
Born	Place	Source
Christened	Place	Source
Married	Place	Source
Died	Place	Source
Buried	Place	Source

2

Name	Spouse	Source
Born	Place	Source
Christened	Place	Source
Married	Place	Source
Died	Place	Source
Buried	Place	Source

3

Name	Spouse	Source
Born	Place	Source
Christened	Place	Source
Married	Place	Source
Died	Place	Source
Buried	Place	Source

4

Name	Spouse	Source
Born	Place	Source
Christened	Place	Source
Married	Place	Source
Died	Place	Source
Buried	Place	Source

Key for source abbreviations
PK=Personal knowledge   IF=Information from (name of person or document from which information came)   SE=See enclosed papers

Illustration 2-5 Blank Family Group Record Using PAF 4.0

STATE AND PROVINCE ABBREVIATIONS

United States

Alabama	AL	Montana	MT
Alaska	AK	Nebraska	NE
Arizona	AZ	Nevada	NV
Arkansas	AR	New Hampshire	NH
California	CA	New Jersey	NJ
Canal Zone	CZ	New Mexico	NM
Colorado	CO	New York	NY
Connecticut	CT	North Carolina	NC
Delaware	DE	North Dakota	ND
District of Columbia	DC	Ohio	OH
Florida	FL	Oklahoma	OK
Georgia	GA	Oregon	OR
Guam	GU	Pennsylvania	PA
Hawaii	HI	Puerto Rico	PR
Idaho	ID	Rhode Island	RI
Illinois	IL	South Carolina	SC
Indiana	IN	South Dakota	SD
Iowa	IA	Tennessee	TN
Kansas	KS	Texas	TX
Kentucky	KY	Utah	UT
Louisiana	LA	Vermont	VT
Maine	ME	Virginia	VA
Maryland	MD	Virgin Islands	VI
Massachusetts	MA	Washington	WA
Michigan	MI	West Virginia	WV
Minnesota	MN	Wisconsin	WI
Mississippi	MS	Wyoming	WY
Missouri	MO		

Canada

Alberta	AB	Northwest Territories	NT
British Columbia	BC	Ontario	ON
Manitoba	MB	Prince Edward Island	PE
New Brunswick	NB	Quebec	QC
Newfoundland	NF	Saskatchewan	SK
Nova Scotia	NS	Yukon	YN

Illustration 2-6 State and Province Abbreviations

The Complete Beginner's Guide

cemetery name, then town or township, county, and state, the state would end up in the country level. If you asked your computer program to search by a particular state by entering "TX," it would not find the Texas entries which had been moved to country level. MORAL: Put cemetery names and jurisdictions smaller than the town or parish into your notes, not into your locality levels.

As you can see in the sample PAF-generated Family Group Record in Illustration 2-5, many numbers are provided. These allow for easy cross-referencing to any other record in the collection and make the research phase, the data entry, and the location of materials much easier to handle.

CONCLUSION

Now that you know the basic steps necessary to fill out the principal forms used by genealogists, the next chapter will begin the more detailed process of explaining how to record all facts and how to link each one to the individual to whom it pertains. Chapter 3 will cover some of the details of style, as well as an explanation of using the computer to store your notes. It is also time to begin working on the genealogy computer program you have selected. You will want to learn about how to set the **default preferences** to fit your specific needs. That will be covered under this chapter's Computer Checklist.

> **Terms to Understand**
>
> **de·fault pref·er·ences** - The manner in which your genealogy computer program is set up in advance to react under certain circumstances as you enter and report your genealogical data.

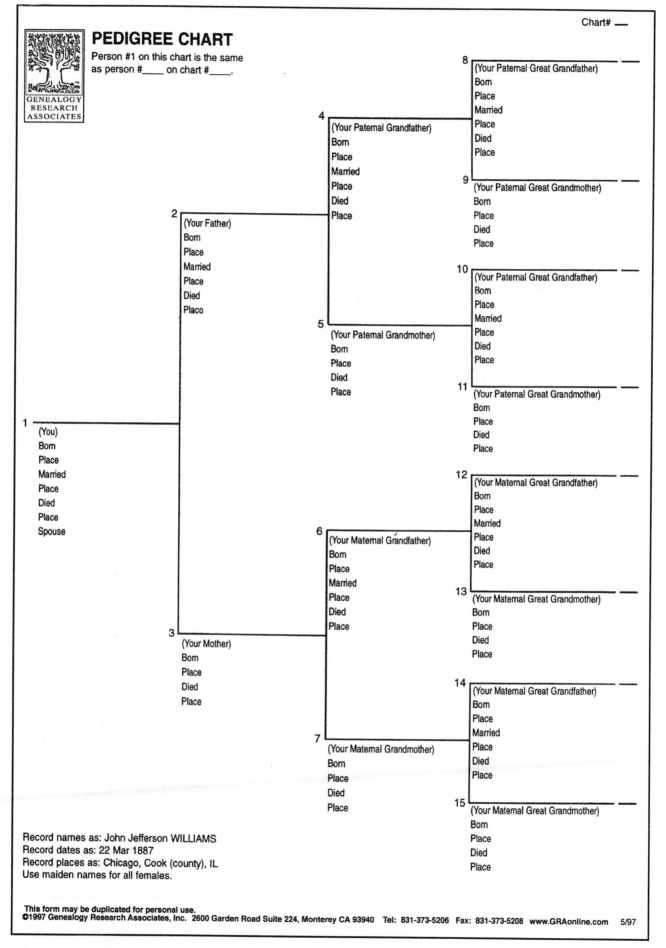

PEDIGREE CHART

Person #1 on this chart is the same as person #____ on chart #____.

Chart# __

GENEALOGY
RESEARCH
ASSOCIATES

8 __
(Your Paternal Great Grandfather)
Born
Place
Married
Place
Died
Place

4
(Your Paternal Grandfather)
Born
Place
Married
Place
Died
Place

9 __
(Your Paternal Great Grandmother)
Born
Place
Died
Place

2
(Your Father)
Born
Place
Married
Place
Died
Place

10 __
(Your Paternal Great Grandfather)
Born
Place
Married
Place
Died
Place

5
(Your Paternal Grandmother)
Born
Place
Died
Place

11 __
(Your Paternal Great Grandmother)
Born
Place
Died
Place

1 __
(You)
Born
Place
Married
Place
Died
Place
Spouse

12 __
(Your Maternal Great Grandfather)
Born
Place
Married
Place
Died
Place

6
(Your Maternal Grandfather)
Born
Place
Married
Place
Died
Place

13 __
(Your Maternal Great Grandmother)
Born
Place
Died
Place

3
(Your Mother)
Born
Place
Died
Place

14 __
(Your Maternal Great Grandfather)
Born
Place
Married
Place
Died
Place

7
(Your Maternal Grandmother)
Born
Place
Died
Place

15 __
(Your Maternal Great Grandmother)
Born
Place
Died
Place

Record names as: John Jefferson WILLIAMS
Record dates as: 22 Mar 1887
Record places as: Chicago, Cook (county), IL
Use maiden names for all females.

This form may be duplicated for personal use.
©1997 Genealogy Research Associates, Inc. 2600 Garden Road Suite 224, Monterey CA 93940 Tel: 831-373-5206 Fax: 831-373-5208 www.GRAonline.com 5/97

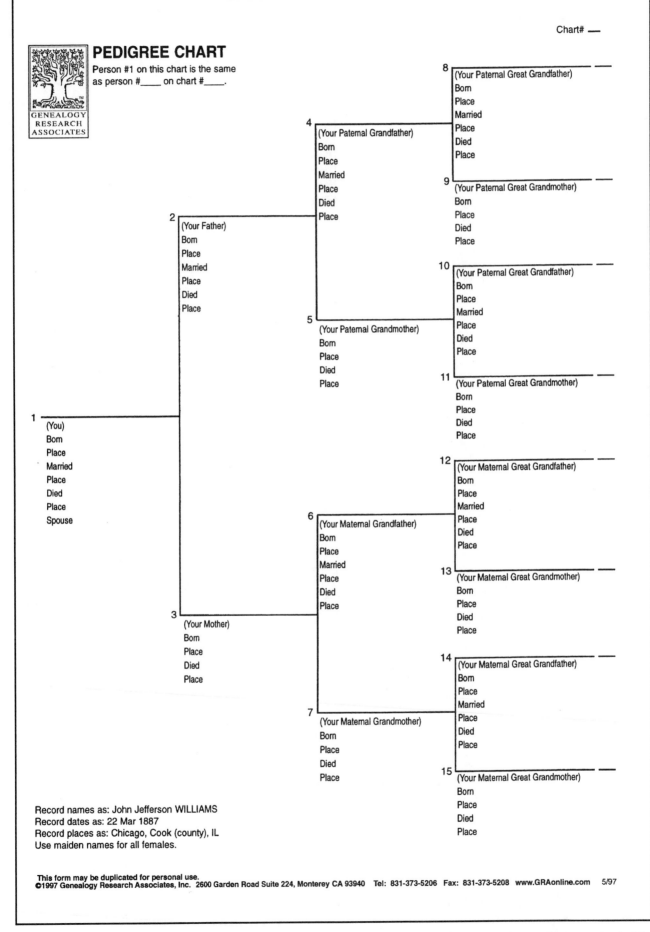

PEDIGREE CHART

Person #1 on this chart is the same
as person #_____ on chart #_____.

GENEALOGY
RESEARCH
ASSOCIATES

8 (Your Paternal Great Grandfather)
Born
Place
Married
Place
Died
Place

4 (Your Paternal Grandfather)
Born
Place
Married
Place
Died
Place

9 (Your Paternal Great Grandmother)
Born
Place
Died
Place

2 (Your Father)
Born
Place
Married
Place
Died
Place

10 (Your Paternal Great Grandfather)
Born
Place
Married
Place
Died
Place

5 (Your Paternal Grandmother)
Born
Place
Died
Place

11 (Your Paternal Great Grandmother)
Born
Place
Died
Place

1 (You)
Born
Place
Married
Place
Died
Place
Spouse

12 (Your Maternal Great Grandfather)
Born
Place
Married
Place
Died
Place

6 (Your Maternal Grandfather)
Born
Place
Married
Place
Died
Place

13 (Your Maternal Great Grandmother)
Born
Place
Died
Place

3 (Your Mother)
Born
Place
Died
Place

14 (Your Maternal Great Grandfather)
Born
Place
Married
Place
Died
Place

7 (Your Maternal Grandmother)
Born
Place
Died
Place

15 (Your Maternal Great Grandmother)
Born
Place
Died
Place

Record names as: John Jefferson WILLIAMS
Record dates as: 22 Mar 1887
Record places as: Chicago, Cook (county), IL
Use maiden names for all females.

HUSBAND

Born	Place	Source
Christened	Place	Source
Married	Place	Source
Died	Place	Source
Buried	Place	Source
Father	Mother	

GENEALOGY RESEARCH ASSOCIATES

FAMILY GROUP RECORD

WIFE

Born	Place	Source
Christened	Place	Source
Died	Place	Source
Buried	Place	Source
Father	Mother	Source

Husband is same as #___ on pedigree chart #___

Wife is same as #___ on pedigree chart #___.

CHILDREN (Write under number at left if male [m] or female [f]. List all children in birth order. Mark "X" under number of direct-line child)

1	Name	Spouse	Source
	Born	Place	Source
	Christened	Place	Source
	Married	Place	Source
	Died	Place	Source
	Buried	Place	Source

2	Name	Spouse	Source
	Born	Place	Source
	Christened	Place	Source
	Married	Place	Source
	Died	Place	Source
	Buried	Place	Source

3	Name	Spouse	Source
	Born	Place	Source
	Christened	Place	Source
	Married	Place	Source
	Died	Place	Source
	Buried	Place	Source

4	Name	Spouse	Source
	Born	Place	Source
	Christened	Place	Source
	Married	Place	Source
	Died	Place	Source
	Buried	Place	Source

Key for source abbreviations

PK = Personal knowledge   **IF** = Information from (name of person or document from which information came)   **SE** = See enclosed papers

CHILDREN CONTINUED (Write under number at left if male [m] or female [f]. List all children in birth order. Mark "X" under number of direct-line child.)

5	Name		Spouse	Source
	Born	Place		Source
	Christened	Place		Source
	Married	Place		Source
	Died	Place		Source
	Buried	Place		Source

6	Name		Spouse	Source
	Born	Place		Source
	Christened	Place		Source
	Married	Place		Source
	Died	Place		Source
	Buried	Place		Source

7	Name		Spouse	Source
	Born	Place		Source
	Christened	Place		Source
	Married	Place		Source
	Died	Place		Source
	Buried	Place		Source

8	Name		Spouse	Source
	Born	Place		Source
	Christened	Place		Source
	Married	Place		Source
	Died	Place		Source
	Buried	Place		Source

9	Name		Spouse	Source
	Born	Place		Source
	Christened	Place		Source
	Married	Place		Source
	Died	Place		Source
	Buried	Place		Source

10	Name		Spouse	Source
	Born	Place		Source
	Christened	Place		Source
	Married	Place		Source
	Died	Place		Source
	Buried	Place		Source

5/97

HUSBAND

Born	Place	Source
Christened	Place	Source
Married	Place	Source
Died	Place	Source
Buried	Place	Source
Father	Mother	

GENEALOGY RESEARCH ASSOCIATES

FAMILY GROUP RECORD

WIFE

Born	Place	Source
Christened	Place	Source
Died	Place	Source
Buried	Place	Source
Father	Mother	Source

Husband is same as #___ on pedigree chart #___

Wife is same as #___ on pedigree chart #___.

CHILDREN (Write under number at left if male [m] or female [f]. List all children in birth order. Mark "X" under number of direct-line child)

1	Name	Spouse	Source
	Born	Place	Source
	Christened	Place	Source
	Married	Place	Source
	Died	Place	Source
	Buried	Place	Source
2	Name	Spouse	Source
	Born	Place	Source
	Christened	Place	Source
	Married	Place	Source
	Died	Place	Source
	Buried	Place	Source
3	Name	Spouse	Source
	Born	Place	Source
	Christened	Place	Source
	Married	Place	Source
	Died	Place	Source
	Buried	Place	Source
4	Name	Spouse	Source
	Born	Place	Source
	Christened	Place	Source
	Married	Place	Source
	Died	Place	Source
	Buried	Place	Source

Key for source abbreviations

PK = Personal knowledge   **IF** = Information from (name of person or document from which information came)   **SE** = See enclosed papers

CHILDREN CONTINUED (Write under number at left if male [m] or female [f]. List all children in birth order. Mark "X" under number of direct-line child.)

5	Name	Spouse	Source
	Born	Place	Source
	Christened	Place	Source
	Married	Place	Source
	Died	Place	Source
	Buried	Place	Source

6	Name	Spouse	Source
	Born	Place	Source
	Christened	Place	Source
	Married	Place	Source
	Died	Place	Source
	Buried	Place	Source

7	Name	Spouse	Source
	Born	Place	Source
	Christened	Place	Source
	Married	Place	Source
	Died	Place	Source
	Buried	Place	Source

8	Name	Spouse	Source
	Born	Place	Source
	Christened	Place	Source
	Married	Place	Source
	Died	Place	Source
	Buried	Place	Source

9	Name	Spouse	Source
	Born	Place	Source
	Christened	Place	Source
	Married	Place	Source
	Died	Place	Source
	Buried	Place	Source

10	Name	Spouse	Source
	Born	Place	Source
	Christened	Place	Source
	Married	Place	Source
	Died	Place	Source
	Buried	Place	Source

HUSBAND

Born	Place		Source
Christened	Place		Source
Married	Place		Source
Died	Place		Source
Buried	Place		Source
Father		Mother	

GENEALOGY RESEARCH ASSOCIATES

FAMILY GROUP RECORD

Husband is same as #___ on pedigree chart #___

Wife is same as #___ on pedigree chart #___.

WIFE

Born	Place		Source
Christened	Place		Source
Died	Place		Source
Buried	Place		Source
Father		Mother	Source

CHILDREN (Write under number at left if male [m] or female [f]. List all children in birth order. Mark "X" under number of direct-line child)

1 | Name | | Spouse | | Source

Born	Place	Source
Christened	Place	Source
Married	Place	Source
Died	Place	Source
Buried	Place	Source

2 | Name | | Spouse | | Source

Born	Place	Source
Christened	Place	Source
Married	Place	Source
Died	Place	Source
Buried	Place	Source

3 | Name | | Spouse | | Source

Born	Place	Source
Christened	Place	Source
Married	Place	Source
Died	Place	Source
Buried	Place	Source

4 | Name | | Spouse | | Source

Born	Place	Source
Christened	Place	Source
Married	Place	Source
Died	Place	Source
Buried	Place	Source

Key for source abbreviations

PK = Personal knowledge   **IF** = Information from (name of person or document from which information came)   **SE** = See enclosed papers

CHILDREN CONTINUED (Write under number at left if male [m] or female [f]. List all children in birth order. Mark "X" under number of direct-line child.)

5	Name		Spouse	Source
	Born	Place		Source
	Christened	Place		Source
	Married	Place		Source
	Died	Place		Source
	Buried	Place		Source

6	Name		Spouse	Source
	Born	Place		Source
	Christened	Place		Source
	Married	Place		Source
	Died	Place		Source
	Buried	Place		Source

7	Name		Spouse	Source
	Born	Place		Source
	Christened	Place		Source
	Married	Place		Source
	Died	Place		Source
	Buried	Place		Source

8	Name		Spouse	Source
	Born	Place		Source
	Christened	Place		Source
	Married	Place		Source
	Died	Place		Source
	Buried	Place		Source

9	Name		Spouse	Source
	Born	Place		Source
	Christened	Place		Source
	Married	Place		Source
	Died	Place		Source
	Buried	Place		Source

10	Name		Spouse	Source
	Born	Place		Source
	Christened	Place		Source
	Married	Place		Source
	Died	Place		Source
	Buried	Place		Source

5/97

HUSBAND

Born	Place	Source
Christened	Place	Source
Married	Place	Source
Died	Place	Source
Buried	Place	Source
Father	Mother	

GENEALOGY RESEARCH ASSOCIATES

FAMILY GROUP RECORD

WIFE

Born	Place	Source
Christened	Place	Source
Died	Place	Source
Buried	Place	Source
Father	Mother	Source

Husband is same as #___ on pedigree chart #___

Wife is same as #___ on pedigree chart #___.

CHILDREN (Write under number at left if male [m] or female [f]. List all children in birth order. Mark "X" under number of direct-line child)

1

Name	Spouse	Source
Born	Place	Source
Christened	Place	Source
Married	Place	Source
Died	Place	Source
Buried	Place	Source

2

Name	Spouse	Source
Born	Place	Source
Christened	Place	Source
Married	Place	Source
Died	Place	Source
Buried	Place	Source

3

Name	Spouse	Source
Born	Place	Source
Christened	Place	Source
Married	Place	Source
Died	Place	Source
Buried	Place	Source

4

Name	Spouse	Source
Born	Place	Source
Christened	Place	Source
Married	Place	Source
Died	Place	Source
Buried	Place	Source

Key for source abbreviations

PK = Personal knowledge   **IF** = Information from (name of person or document from which information came)   **SE** = See enclosed papers

CHILDREN CONTINUED (Write under number at left if male [m] or female [f]. List all children in birth order. Mark "X" under number of direct-line child.)

5	Name		Spouse	Source
	Born	Place		Source
	Christened	Place		Source
	Married	Place		Source
	Died	Place		Source
	Buried	Place		Source

6	Name		Spouse	Source
	Born	Place		Source
	Christened	Place		Source
	Married	Place		Source
	Died	Place		Source
	Buried	Place		Source

7	Name		Spouse	Source
	Born	Place		Source
	Christened	Place		Source
	Married	Place		Source
	Died	Place		Source
	Buried	Place		Source

8	Name		Spouse	Source
	Born	Place		Source
	Christened	Place		Source
	Married	Place		Source
	Died	Place		Source
	Buried	Place		Source

9	Name		Spouse	Source
	Born	Place		Source
	Christened	Place		Source
	Married	Place		Source
	Died	Place		Source
	Buried	Place		Source

10	Name		Spouse	Source
	Born	Place		Source
	Christened	Place		Source
	Married	Place		Source
	Died	Place		Source
	Buried	Place		Source

5/97

HUSBAND

Born	Place	Source
Christened	Place	Source
Married	Place	Source
Died	Place	Source
Buried	Place	Source
Father	Mother	

GENEALOGY RESEARCH ASSOCIATES

FAMILY GROUP RECORD

WIFE

Born	Place	Source
Christened	Place	Source
Died	Place	Source
Buried	Place	Source
Father	Mother	Source

Husband is same as #___ on pedigree chart #___

Wife is same as #___ on pedigree chart #___.

CHILDREN (Write under number at left if male [m] or female [f]. List all children in birth order. Mark "X" under number of direct-line child)

1
Name	Spouse	Source
Born	Place	Source
Christened	Place	Source
Married	Place	Source
Died	Place	Source
Buried	Place	Source

2
Name	Spouse	Source
Born	Place	Source
Christened	Place	Source
Married	Place	Source
Died	Place	Source
Buried	Place	Source

3
Name	Spouse	Source
Born	Place	Source
Christened	Place	Source
Married	Place	Source
Died	Place	Source
Buried	Place	Source

4
Name	Spouse	Source
Born	Place	Source
Christened	Place	Source
Married	Place	Source
Died	Place	Source
Buried	Place	Source

Key for source abbreviations

PK = Personal knowledge   **IF** = Information from (name of person or document from which information came)   **SE** = See enclosed papers

CHILDREN CONTINUED (Write under number at left if male [m] or female [f]. List all children in birth order. Mark "X" under number of direct-line child.)

5	Name		Spouse	Source
	Born	Place		Source
	Christened	Place		Source
	Married	Place		Source
	Died	Place		Source
	Buried	Place		Source

6	Name		Spouse	Source
	Born	Place		Source
	Christened	Place		Source
	Married	Place		Source
	Died	Place		Source
	Buried	Place		Source

7	Name		Spouse	Source
	Born	Place		Source
	Christened	Place		Source
	Married	Place		Source
	Died	Place		Source
	Buried	Place		Source

8	Name		Spouse	Source
	Born	Place		Source
	Christened	Place		Source
	Married	Place		Source
	Died	Place		Source
	Buried	Place		Source

9	Name		Spouse	Source
	Born	Place		Source
	Christened	Place		Source
	Married	Place		Source
	Died	Place		Source
	Buried	Place		Source

10	Name		Spouse	Source
	Born	Place		Source
	Christened	Place		Source
	Married	Place		Source
	Died	Place		Source
	Buried	Place		Source

5/97

HUSBAND

Born	Place	Source
Christened	Place	Source
Married	Place	Source
Died	Place	Source
Buried	Place	Source
Father	Mother	

GENEALOGY RESEARCH ASSOCIATES

FAMILY GROUP RECORD

Husband is same as #___ on pedigree chart #___

Wife is same as #___ on pedigree chart #___.

WIFE

Born	Place	Source
Christened	Place	Source
Died	Place	Source
Buried	Place	Source
Father	Mother	Source

CHILDREN (Write under number at left if male [m] or female [f]. List all children in birth order. Mark "X" under number of direct-line child)

1 | Name | Spouse | Source

Born	Place	Source
Christened	Place	Source
Married	Place	Source
Died	Place	Source
Buried	Place	Source

2 | Name | Spouse | Source

Born	Place	Source
Christened	Place	Source
Married	Place	Source
Died	Place	Source
Buried	Place	Source

3 | Name | Spouse | Source

Born	Place	Source
Christened	Place	Source
Married	Place	Source
Died	Place	Source
Buried	Place	Source

4 | Name | Spouse | Source

Born	Place	Source
Christened	Place	Source
Married	Place	Source
Died	Place	Source
Buried	Place	Source

Key for source abbreviations

PK = Personal knowledge   **IF** = Information from (name of person or document from which information came)   **SE** = See enclosed papers

CHILDREN CONTINUED (Write under number at left if male [m] or female [f]. List all children in birth order. Mark "X" under number of direct-line child.)

5	Name		Spouse	Source
	Born	Place		Source
	Christened	Place		Source
	Married	Place		Source
	Died	Place		Source
	Buried	Place		Source

6	Name		Spouse	Source
	Born	Place		Source
	Christened	Place		Source
	Married	Place		Source
	Died	Place		Source
	Buried	Place		Source

7	Name		Spouse	Source
	Born	Place		Source
	Christened	Place		Source
	Married	Place		Source
	Died	Place		Source
	Buried	Place		Source

8	Name		Spouse	Source
	Born	Place		Source
	Christened	Place		Source
	Married	Place		Source
	Died	Place		Source
	Buried	Place		Source

9	Name		Spouse	Source
	Born	Place		Source
	Christened	Place		Source
	Married	Place		Source
	Died	Place		Source
	Buried	Place		Source

10	Name		Spouse	Source
	Born	Place		Source
	Christened	Place		Source
	Married	Place		Source
	Died	Place		Source
	Buried	Place		Source

The Complete Beginner's Guide

HUSBAND

Born	Place		Source
Christened	Place		Source
Married	Place		Source
Died	Place		Source
Buried	Place		Source
Father		Mother	

GENEALOGY RESEARCH ASSOCIATES

FAMILY GROUP RECORD

WIFE

Born	Place		Source
Christened	Place		Source
Died	Place		Source
Buried	Place		Source
Father		Mother	Source

Husband is same as #___ on pedigree chart #___

Wife is same as #___ on pedigree chart #___.

CHILDREN (Write under number at left if male [m] or female [f]. List all children in birth order. Mark "X" under number of direct-line child)

1

Name	Spouse	Source
Born	Place	Source
Christened	Place	Source
Married	Place	Source
Died	Place	Source
Buried	Place	Source

2

Name	Spouse	Source
Born	Place	Source
Christened	Place	Source
Married	Place	Source
Died	Place	Source
Buried	Place	Source

3

Name	Spouse	Source
Born	Place	Source
Christened	Place	Source
Married	Place	Source
Died	Place	Source
Buried	Place	Source

4

Name	Spouse	Source
Born	Place	Source
Christened	Place	Source
Married	Place	Source
Died	Place	Source
Buried	Place	Source

Key for source abbreviations

PK = Personal knowledge   **IF** = Information from (name of person or document from which information came)   **SE** = See enclosed papers

CHILDREN CONTINUED (Write under number at left if male [m] or female [f]. List all children in birth order. Mark "X" under number of direct-line child.)

5	Name		Spouse	Source
	Born	Place		Source
	Christened	Place		Source
	Married	Place		Source
	Died	Place		Source
	Buried	Place		Source

6	Name		Spouse	Source
	Born	Place		Source
	Christened	Place		Source
	Married	Place		Source
	Died	Place		Source
	Buried	Place		Source

7	Name		Spouse	Source
	Born	Place		Source
	Christened	Place		Source
	Married	Place		Source
	Died	Place		Source
	Buried	Place		Source

8	Name		Spouse	Source
	Born	Place		Source
	Christened	Place		Source
	Married	Place		Source
	Died	Place		Source
	Buried	Place		Source

9	Name		Spouse	Source
	Born	Place		Source
	Christened	Place		Source
	Married	Place		Source
	Died	Place		Source
	Buried	Place		Source

10	Name		Spouse	Source
	Born	Place		Source
	Christened	Place		Source
	Married	Place		Source
	Died	Place		Source
	Buried	Place		Source

HUSBAND

Born	Place	Source
Christened	Place	Source
Married	Place	Source
Died	Place	Source
Buried	Place	Source
Father	Mother	

FAMILY GROUP RECORD

GENEALOGY RESEARCH ASSOCIATES

WIFE

Born	Place	Source
Christened	Place	Source
Died	Place	Source
Buried	Place	Source
Father	Mother	Source

Husband is same as #___ on pedigree chart #___

Wife is same as #___ on pedigree chart #___.

CHILDREN (Write under number at left if male [m] or female [f]. List all children in birth order. Mark "X" under number of direct-line child)

1 Name | Spouse | Source
Born	Place	Source
Christened	Place	Source
Married	Place	Source
Died	Place	Source
Buried	Place	Source

2 Name | Spouse | Source
Born	Place	Source
Christened	Place	Source
Married	Place	Source
Died	Place	Source
Buried	Place	Source

3 Name | Spouse | Source
Born	Place	Source
Christened	Place	Source
Married	Place	Source
Died	Place	Source
Buried	Place	Source

4 Name | Spouse | Source
Born	Place	Source
Christened	Place	Source
Married	Place	Source
Died	Place	Source
Buried	Place	Source

Key for source abbreviations

PK = Personal knowledge   **IF** = Information from (name of person or document from which information came)   **SE** = See enclosed papers

CHILDREN CONTINUED (Write under number at left if male [m] or female [f]. List all children in birth order. Mark "X" under number of direct-line child.)

5	Name		Spouse	Source
	Born	Place		Source
	Christened	Place		Source
	Married	Place		Source
	Died	Place		Source
	Buried	Place		Source
6	Name		Spouse	Source
	Born	Place		Source
	Christened	Place		Source
	Married	Place		Source
	Died	Place		Source
	Buried	Place		Source
7	Name		Spouse	Source
	Born	Place		Source
	Christened	Place		Source
	Married	Place		Source
	Died	Place		Source
	Buried	Place		Source
8	Name		Spouse	Source
	Born	Place		Source
	Christened	Place		Source
	Married	Place		Source
	Died	Place		Source
	Buried	Place		Source
9	Name		Spouse	Source
	Born	Place		Source
	Christened	Place		Source
	Married	Place		Source
	Died	Place		Source
	Buried	Place		Source
10	Name		Spouse	Source
	Born	Place		Source
	Christened	Place		Source
	Married	Place		Source
	Died	Place		Source
	Buried	Place		Source

This form may be duplicated for personal use.
©1997 Genealogy Research Associates, Inc. 2600 Garden Road Suite 224, Monterey CA 93940 Tel: 831-373-5206 Fax: 831-373-5208 www.GRAonline.com

5/97

ASSIGNMENT 2: FILLING IN CHARTS AND FORMS

The following exercise will help you determine specifically what you need to learn about your own family by completing the two basic forms used by genealogy researchers.

1. In pencil, fill in the blank Pedigree Chart (page 2-13) generated from the PAF program. At this point, try to remember the "rules" that you learned in this chapter for entering names, dates, and places. See how many generations you can enter from memory.

2. Complete the blank Family Group Records (pages 2-15 through 2-30). Do one record where you appear as a child with your parents. Then do one for each of your parents and grandparents, in which each appears as a child with his or her parents.

SELF-EVALUATION: Filling Out Basic Charts and Forms

How well did you do in filling out the Pedigree Chart and Family Group Records? Did you:

1. Capitalize the surname?

2. Write the dates in day-month-year format?

3. Include the name of the county for every location and enter the places with the smallest area designation first?

If you forgot about some of these, this little pre-exercise will remind you to be aware of these good research habits. Another good research habit to learn from the very beginning is to keep excellent records of all notes and to link them to the individuals to whom they belong. That is the subject of Chapter 4.

YOUR TURN ANSWERS

The Pedigree Chart

Imagine you were entering the locality "Cincinnati, Hamilton County, Ohio." Use only one letter per box; use one box for each comma, and leave a box blank for spaces.

| C | i | n | c | i | n | n | a | t | i | , | | H | a | m | i | l | t | o | n | , | | O | h | i | o | | | | | | |

Now assume that your sheet of paper was not large enough and you had to put the same information into half as many boxes. That is what happens when words are truncated.

| C | i | n | c | i | n | n | a | t | i | , | | H | a | m | i | l | t | o |

Of course, you want to be able to read the complete town and county. Most computer programs ask you if you want to eliminate the first part or the last part of the locality. If you eliminate the first part, you lose the town. If you eliminate the last part, you lose the state. Some programs eliminate what is in the middle, causing you to lose the county.

Recording Names

Print this person's name the way you should when you hand-enter onto a form: George Washington Johnson.

JOHNSON, George Washington

Recording Dates

Write these dates in the correct format for genealogical forms:

A. June 1, 1967   1 Jun 1967

B. April 7, 1899.   7 Apr 1899

C. May 23, 1776.   23 May 1776

Recording Places

Write these locations as they should be written on Pedigree Charts or Family Group Records.

A. Born in Mother of Charity Hospital, New York City, New York County, New York.

    New York City, New York, NY

B. Died in Natividad Hospital, Salinas, Monterey County, California.

    Salinas, Monterey, CA   (Put the name of the hospital in the notes.)

C. Buried at Holy Cross Cemetery, Monterey, Monterey County, California.

    Monterey, Monterey, CA   (Put the name of the cemetery in the notes.)

COMPUTER CHECKLIST #2

1. Check the "Preferences" option on your computer genealogy program. List here all of the preference options you have available.

2. Which options have you selected, and why?

WEB SITE

http://www.cyndislist.com
An alphabetical listing of genealogy Internet sites by topic.

BIBLIOGRAPHY

Rubincam, Milton, Editor. "Genealogy and Chronology." *Genealogical Research: Methods and Sources*. Rev. ed. Vol. 1. The American Society of Genealogists: Washington, D.C., 1980: 27-37.

Westin, Jeane Eddy. "First Step Backward: How to Take A Family History and Gather Available Records." *Finding Your Roots*. New York: Ballantine Books, 1990: 43-63.

CHAPTER 3

Becoming Acquainted with Your Genealogy Program

"Pursuing a research goal in genealogy is like a journey toward a distant horizon. The progress you've made isn't apparent until you look back and see how far you've come."

—*Ray T. Clifford*

So far, you have been introduced to the principal techniques for successful family history research, including the Research Cycle. You have been instructed in ways to manually organize whatever family history information you could locate in family documents and among your relatives. Finally, you were asked to fill out a Pedigree Chart and Family Group Record on your own family. Another way to make your work more effective is through the use of a good genealogy computer program.

This chapter aims to demonstrate the effectiveness of using a computer to accomplish the above tasks, but since each of you may own a different program, this book will ask you to experiment as you go along. In addition, specific suggestions for using the various programs will be made available at our Web site, *http://www.GRAonline.com,* if you feel you cannot find a way to accomplish a specific assignment. This Web site "appendix," as we might call it, allows us to update your program's features as they are modified, due to the constant changes in genealogy computer programs, and to make specific suggestions pertinent to genealogy research.

ENTERING FAMILY INFORMATION

The first thing you want to do with any genealogical software program is to enter your own family information. Information for each individual in the family will include those vital records that uniquely identify his or her life. This includes information about birth, marriage(s), and death. Once an individual's information has been entered into the computer, you can **edit** or make changes to it at any time. In addition to this "vital records" information, you can enter sources and notes that will verify, or "document," the dates and places that you have entered—a very important part of good record keeping.

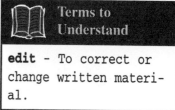

Terms to Understand

edit - To correct or change written material.

But entering dates and locations is only part of the value of a good genealogy computer program. This chapter will also help you to identify the features which are desirable in any good genealogy computer program.

EXCITING FEATURES OF GOOD GENEALOGY COMPUTER PROGRAMS

Using such a program aids in both organizing your information and in doing research. As we list some of the benefits, determine if the program you use can accomplish the tasks listed below:

1. As you enter vital records, you will internalize the information and begin to notice discrepancies in information.

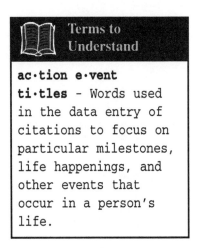

Terms to Understand

ac·tion e·vent ti·tles - Words used in the data entry of citations to focus on particular milestones, life happenings, and other events that occur in a person's life.

YOUR TURN

Does your genealogy computer program have a place to capture wrong or missing data? Does it provide a quick way to find notes you have made about discrepancies? How is that done?

---

2. As you link documentation to individuals you are entering, clues are revealed. Clues can be flagged with **action event titles,** such as "MIGRATION," to alert the researcher of movements to new areas where records may be kept. You might want to call them "new jurisdictions for records" in your notes.

YOUR TURN

Where would you enter migration clues into your genealogy computer program?

---

3. The program acts like a handy notepad and pencil where you can jot down any ideas that come to you, such as:

   A. Where was Uncle Joe buried?
   B. When did Aunt Mary and Uncle Jim marry? Where did they marry?
   C. Cousin Marvin might have a copy of this obituary. I need to ask him.

These ideas can be flagged with action event titles, such as "TO DO," to indicate that work needs to be done, perhaps at a local **Family History Center**. Then either you, or those who will use your research after you are gone, can continue.

YOUR TURN

Where would you enter "TO DO" lists in your genealogy computer program?

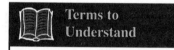

> **Terms to Understand**
>
> **Family History Centers** - Genealogy research centers operated by The Church of Jesus Christ of Latter-day Saints in locations throughout the world, where individuals can search the center's own holdings, order genealogy materials on microfilm and microfiche through a loan program, and access a variety of genealogy databases.

4. Genealogy computer programs which automatically assign an ID number to every individual and Family Group Record ease the research and filing process. These same ID numbers can then be written in the upper right-hand corner of documents for ease in filing, since a number is faster to write and easier to keep track of than a complete name. Each number in your database is unique, while families often use the same names over and over again.

YOUR TURN

Determine whether your computer program assigns ID numbers for individuals and families. If it doesn't automatically do so, look at your genealogy computer program "preferences" options to see if you can assign ID numbers. How do you do it on your program?

> **Terms to Understand**
>
> **da·ta** - 1. Information organized for analysis or decision-making. 2. Information suitable for computer processing.

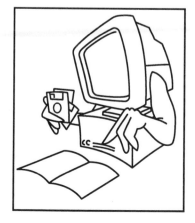

5. Good genealogy computer programs allow you to copy notes from one person to another to avoid excessive **data** entry.

Terms to Understand

GEDCOM - Acronym for Genealogical Data Communication, which is the standard protocol for transferring data from one genealogy program to another. It was originally written to enable home users to receive data from the largest genealogical databases in the world maintained by The Church of Jesus Christ of Latter-day Saints, which is constantly being updated. It has now become a standard transfer protocol for all major genealogy computer programs. GEDCOM files may also be submitted via the Internet at www.familysearch.org.

Terms to Understand

down·load - To transfer or copy data from one computer to another, or to a disk or peripheral device, or to be transferred or copied in this way.

6. Good genealogy programs have the ability to accept information data entered by others. Those programs which are **GEDCOM**-compatible can save typing time and typing errors by **downloading** information from others (such as

YOUR TURN

Read the instruction manual that came with your genealogy computer program to learn about the kinds of information it can accept and transmit to other programs. Briefly summarize what you learned.

information from *FamilySearch* at local Family History Centers or *World Family Tree*™ CDs).

7. Computer programs create Pedigree Charts, Family Group Records, descendancy charts, and other handy aids, both for visualizing the family history and for extending the research.

YOUR TURN

1. Find the surname index in your program. Where is it located on the screen? What happens when you type in a name at the blinking cursor located at the top of the index?

2. Find out if you have a locality index. How do you use it?

YOUR TURN

What other kinds of charts does your program provide? List them.

8. Computer programs alphabetize and create multiple indexes, such as:

   A. Surname indexes in many varieties
   B. Record ID Number (RIN) or Marriage Record ID Number (MRIN) indexes
   C. Locality indexes by event
   D. Event indexes.

9. Additions or corrections made in one area can be carried over to other charts referring to that same person, eliminating hours of typing.

YOUR TURN

How do you make corrections to existing individuals and families in your genealogy computer program?

YOUR TURN

Do you have a "cut and paste," "copy," or "ditto" feature in your genealogy computer program? Which one(s)?

Terms to Understand

up·load - To transfer data or programs to a central computer on the Internet (or storage medium) to another computer.

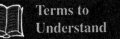

Terms to Understand

FamilySearch - The umbrella name for the various records and research aids developed by The Church of Jesus Christ of Latter-day Saints. Many separate segments are included such as the Ancestral File™, the International Genealogical Index™, the Social Security Death Index, the Military Index (U.S. only), and several others.

Terms to Understand

World Family Tree - A collection of actual family trees submitted by users of the Family Tree Maker genealogy computer program. Many trees contain documented sources which are very helpful for continuing research. The contributors may be contacted.

10. Good genealogy computer programs have the ability to send information (**upload**) to databases (such as information to *FamilySearch*™ at local Family History Centers, or *World Family Tree*™).

11. Good genealogy computer programs have the ability to search all notes for a particular word or string of words, in order to look for an elusive clue that could tie two families together.

YOUR TURN

Is your genealogy computer program able to convert files completely? Yes No

Is it considered 100% GEDCOM compatible? Yes No

YOUR TURN

Can you locate a function in your genealogy computer program which will allow you to search and locate any word you have entered into your database for elusive clues you might have entered? Explain how this works in your program.

12. Good genealogy computer programs alert you when you make obvious errors, such as typing 1780 for 1980 or misspelling a name.

13. Good genealogy computer programs repeat places, dates and localities, when they are used more than once, to save typing time.

These are just some of the exciting features of a good genealogy computer program. They can be a great boost for the genealogist--especially for one who does not type very fast, or who finds writing by hand uncomfortable or slow. In addition, once you have entered your family data into a genealogy computer program, you can be assured that it will be printed out or transmitted in a neat, legible form.

YOUR TURN

Try typing in the birth date of 1980 for someone, and then entering the death date as 1780. Does your program warn you of a potential error?

Yes No

Type in the name "George." Now in another field type in the name "Goerge." Did your program warn you that you had made an error in spelling?   Yes No

There are other reasons why computers are so popular today: they are fast, accurate and perform repetitive tasks very well. It is even possible to scan a typed manuscript directly into a computer through a separate scanning program, and then "cut and paste" the information into your genealogy computer program so that its database can index it for you.

YOUR TURN

Type in a locality under the birthplace of an individual. Now enter that same location as the birthplace of another individual. Can you locate a function key or a drop down list of localities which will duplicate the entry you just made so you don't have to retype it? Or does your program automatically complete the location's name after you have typed in a few letters?

This chapter will get you started with your favorite genealogy computer program. If you have never used a genealogical software program, you may wish to choose one to begin with, then follow the tutorials given in this book and at our Web site *www.GRAonline.com*. As you become familiar with one program, you can expand your knowledge to other programs, and this will add to your capabilities. For now, you will be surprised to discover that, working with this text, you can learn how to use a genealogy computer program very quickly!

The charts on the following pages will cover the basics of using a genealogy computer program.

Just a Reminder

Before you begin entering your materials on a computer, be aware of their frailties as well as their possibilities. Unfortunately, many beginning genealogists fail to protect their investment of time by:

1. Not making proper back-ups of programs or copies of disks;
2. Not storing their disks properly;
3. Mishandling disks; or
4. Not checking their data if their genealogy computer program asks them to check it. (If you do not, your copy will be just as "flawed" as the original. Many programs today do not require this step.)

CONCLUSION

Now that you have become familiar with your own genealogy computer program, you will be given an assignment to put together the "skeleton" for your family into that program. This includes data entering the names, dates, and places. The next chapter will show you how to document the sources of your information and, if possible, to record every clue as you go back in time, in order to add "flesh" to that "skeleton."

Illustration 3-1
3 1/2" diskette

THE MOST COMMON MISTAKES OF NEW COMPUTER USERS

1. Neglecting to take seriously the basics of disk care:

Disks are fragile and can be damaged by excessive heat, direct sunlight, moisture, dust, and strong magnetic fields. Avoid placing them on dusty surfaces. Don't set them on top of other electronic devices, as the data can be altered. And remember to take them with you when you leave your car. Disks can be damaged by contact with car radio stereo units, by the sunlight from the back window, and from the heat in the glove compartment. *FOR GOOD DISK CARE:* Store the disk in a dust-free container which also protects it from pressure.

Remember: Even if your disk "looks" fine, the data can be corrupted if it is not treated carefully. If this happens, you might not even realize that the information about third-Great-Aunt Hortense has been altered or lost due to such damage.

2. Inserting disk into drive incorrectly:

Never force the disk in. If it does not go in smoothly, pull it out and try again. When information, or data, is being read from the disk or copied onto it, the light on the drive will be on. You may also hear a whirring, grinding sound, which is normal. As a general rule: NEVER OPEN A DISK DRIVE WHILE THE LIGHT IS ON, and NEVER remove a disk during an operation (there are exceptions to this, but it's not worth the risk unless you know your program acts differently). If you do remove the disk before it has finished its work, the information may become lost or garbled.

3. Not understanding the differences between typewriter keyboards and computer keyboards:

In some ways, computer and typewriter keyboards look alike, but soon you will learn that they have differences.

Illustration 3-2 The Most Common Mistakes of New Computer Users

A disk left in the sun   A "bad," mishandled disk

HOW COMPUTER AND TYPEWRITER KEYBOARDS ARE ALIKE

The character keys are generally the same, but a cursor (a small, solid rectangle or flashing underline) shows you where on the screen the character will appear. The [Shift] key works like the shift key on a typewriter. When you hold it down while you press a character key, the upper character or uppercase (capital) letter will appear. The [Caps Lock] key will allow you to use all capital letters. You will still have to use the [Shift] key to display the top character on a number or symbol key. The [Enter] key and [Tab] keys on several programs are the same, in that they both start a new line of text or move you from field to field in the data entry portions of your program.

HOW THE COMPUTER KEYBOARD IS DIFFERENT

There is a distinct difference between the number 1 and the letter l, as well as the number 0 [zero] and the letter O. On the computer screen, the zero often has a line through it, making it look a little like the number eight. Using the lowercase L instead of a number 1 in a date like 1936 will cause the program to give you an error message, and it won't continue until you correct it.

The *Space Bar* on the computer does more than move across text. It can erase the letters or characters in front of it, if it is not in "Insert" mode. The [Ins] (*Insert*) key lets you add characters to the left of the cursor. It pushes the rest of the characters forward.

Speaking of "spaces," these are very important on the computer. To the computer, there is as much difference between two spaces between words as putting three t's in the word PUTTTING. If you were to type in a surname field "_ _ Johnson," placing two spaces in front of the word, the computer would not alphabetize the word under Js but at the top of the entire surname list, because spaces come before the letter "A."

The [Ctrl] (*Control*) key is used, in conjunction with one or two other keys, in order to perform a specific function. It must be held down while the other key is pressed.

Computers are fast and accurate but they do not think for you. The only way they know you are finished with a task is for you to press the [Enter] key.

The [Backspace] key erases words as the cursor passes over them. The [Del] (*Delete*) key will erase the character under the cursor and move the remaining characters on the line one space backward. One character is erased each time you press the key.

Arrow keys (see Illustration 3-4) allow you to move the cursor around the screen without erasing information. See the illustration at the left.

Function keys do not put a character on the screen, but they do cause an internal operation to take place. The [F1] function key is often used to save changes, and then exit.

Most screens are like forms with fill-in blanks added. Pressing the [Enter] or [Tab] key will move you from one blank, or field, to another. *Up* and *down*, *left* and *right* arrow keys will move you from one field to another on the screen.

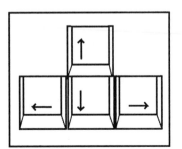

Illustration 3-4 Arrow Keys

Illustration 3-3 How Computer and Typewriter Keyboards are Alike

ASSIGNMENT 3: ENTERING YOUR OWN FAMILY INFORMATION

You will need plenty of time to enter all the information you currently have on all of your family that you are interested in studying. Enter at least your parents, grandparents and, if possible, your great-grandparents.

Using the handwritten charts you filled out in Chapter 2, data enter your family information into your genealogy computer program. Remember the rules that you learned regarding surname capitalization, how to enter dates, and how to enter localities. Enter as many names as you have on all of your lines for at least four generations.

YOUR TURN ANSWERS

Personal preferences are allowed on all Chapter 3 responses.

COMPUTER CHECKLIST #3

1. Note that some programs automatically capitalize surnames. If not, you may set the preference for doing so. If you set the program to capitalize surnames for you, and then you also capitalize another kind of word, that word may be capitalized elsewhere when you don't want it to be. For example, the name BROWN, if capitalized, as a surname, might also end up capitalized when used as Brown County, Kansas.

2. Enter your name and dates into your genealogy computer program.

    A. Did you enter the birth date correctly, i.e. 1946 instead of 46?

    B. Did you enter the location correctly, i.e., city, county, state. If you know the hospital, put that information into notes. You want to maintain the consistency of three fields, for locations, not four fields, which is what would happen if you put the hospital before the city. This also would not allow you enough space on your pedigree chart for all the locations you need to continue your research.

3. What is necessary to "save" the information you just entered?

3. What must you do to link an individual to a family? CAUTION: You should never be required to enter the same person twice.

4. How can you look at a listing of everyone you have entered so far?

WEB SITES

http://www.FamilyTreeMaker.com; also *genealogy.com*
Information on the Family Tree Maker™ program. Commercial site.

http://www.Ancestry.com; also *FamilyHistory.com* and *MyFamily.com*
Commercial site.

BIBLIOGRAPHY

Ancestral Quest. For Windows. Hope Foundation, Salt Lake City, Utah, 1999.

Family Origins. For Windows. Parsons Technology, Inc., Hiawatha, Iowa, 1999.

Family Tree Maker Version 8.0. For Windows. Genealogy.com, Fremont, California, 2000.

Genelines. For Windows. Progeny Software & Progeny Publishing, Inc., Buffalo, New York 2000.

Generations Family Tree Software, Beginner's Edition. For Windows. Sierra Home, Inc., Bellevue, Washington, 2000.

Legacy Family Tree. For Windows. Millennia Corporation, Duvall, Washington, 2000.

The Master Genealogist, Gold Edition, Version 4. For Windows. Wholly Genes, Inc., Elk Ridge, Maryland, 2000.

PAF Mate: Charts and Reports for PAF. For Windows. Progeny Publishing, Inc., Buffalo, New York 2000.

Personal Ancestral File 4.0.4. For Windows. The Church of Jesus Christ of Latter-day Saints, Salt Lake City, Utah, 2000.

Reunion: The Family Tree Software. For Macintosh. Leister Productions, Inc., Mechanicsburg, Pennsylvania, 1999.

CHAPTER 4

Why Document?

There is no life of a man, faithfully recorded, but is a heroic poem of its sort, rhymed or unrhymed.

—Thomas Carlyle

Have you ever said, "If I could only find that clue that led me to believe that. . . " or, "I wonder if I have already searched this book for the wife's side of the family, or did I only look for the husband's side?" For these reasons and others which follow, it is important to record the sources you use as you are searching for your family, by providing complete **citations**, **documents** and evaluations. The purpose of this chapter is to help you understand the great significance of this aspect of family research.

YOU'LL WANT TO DOCUMENT BECAUSE

- It saves time and helps you to avoid duplication of research.

- Your work is accepted as credible.

- Others who follow your lead will seek out, or provide, new resources you lack because they know where you have traveled.

- You are able to **synthesize** an abundance of information more readily when it is organized and linked to the individual or family to whom it belongs.

- If your documentation has been appropriately entered from the beginning, you will need to do very little editing when you decide to publish a book on your family.

Today's computer genealogy programs can help you document your sources as you enter your family's vital statistics, and they even enable you to attach sources to the events to which they refer. Although it is possible to do research without the aid of a computer, keeping track of documentation is the greatest benefit of a good genealogy computer program.

Terms to Understand

ci·ta·tion - A polished reference to a particular authority; or a quoting of an authoritative source for substantiation.

Terms to Understand

doc·u·ment - A written or printed paper that bears the original, official, or legal form of something and can be used to furnish decisive evidence or information.

Terms to Understand

syn·the·size - To study all the facts and combine the information in your mind to form a new, more complex idea.

There are many ways to data enter documentation into your computer genealogy program, and it's important that you learn the methods and strategies that will work best for you. Remember, you're providing an important "paper trail," not only for yourself, but for those who will follow your work. Consequently, just as you will hope to find sources which will give you the information you need, you should provide the same courtesy to others by supplying:

- Complete citations, so that you or those who read your information can track down the original sources for other clues.

- What you found and what you did not find, so that you and others won't need to spend time searching irrelevant sources.

- Your evaluation of the materials, as well as the evaluation of others, so that you and others can see if your opinions agree.

- Suggestions of what to do next, in case you or others might want to continue the quest.

THE ELEMENTS OF A COMPLETE CITATION

Experienced researchers can think back to the information they hoped to receive when they were doing research. They wanted to know who wrote or gathered the information, what the information contained, when it was gathered or written, where it can be found in its original form, how it was put together, what information the document itself contained, and an evaluation of the materials based on previous research or experience. Imagine how much further along we would all be if all of these questions had been made available in the genealogies that have already been published. Such information would have streamlined the process

Items covered	Description of items covered
WHO?	The author, compiler, publisher and/or provider of the information.
WHAT?	A description of the source: the title of the book, a description of the collection, or an index to other records.
WHEN?	A specific date or span of time covered by the source, whether it is a records collection, book, film, or fiche. Example: Wills, 1834-1910.
WHERE?	The places covered by the source, as well as the addresses of the publisher, the person providing information, or the repository where the information is stored.
HOW?	The format of the source, e.g., book, film, fiche, electronic media.
THE DOCUMENT	Whether the document you used is a photocopy, scanned copy, transcript, abstract or extract.
WHY?	The researcher's evaluation, the historical background, and societal customs, all of which may provide the evidence to prove a point.

Illustration 4-1 Important Items to Include

for all of us, permitting us to move on and discover the answers to new questions, instead of having to verify the information left by others.

In the past, not only was information less readily available than it is today, but the space available to record information was limited on Family Group Record forms. Because of this, little information regarding sources was provided. With today's technology, however, we can pretty much put in all the information we need in order to adequately document our sources. The most important items we should include in any records we produce in our genealogy computer programs are those you see listed in Illustration 4-1.

Illustration 4.1 indicates various parts of your documentary **evidence** and **analysis.** The who, what, when, where, and how describe the location, condition, format, and provider of the information. The next area is lightly shaded to refer to the act of capturing the actual document itself. Whether we make a photocopy, **extract, abstract, transcription** or scanned image of the document, we need to preserve the information in some way in order to evaluate this piece of evidence. But the last and most important item (shaded the most in Illustration 4.1) is our evaluation of the information. Why do we think that this document has solved or guided us to a conclusion in our research? What does it guide us to?

MAKING YOUR RESEARCH MORE EFFECTIVE

Record What You Have Done to Avoid Duplication of Research

Documenting your sources includes more than indicating the citations for the materials found. Your documentation should also include what was searched and not found. When you are recording your documentation, you can use a variety of places in your computer program to record what you have searched and what you have done. The locations preferred by most researchers include:

- Research planners or calendars (a sample research planner is reproduced on pages 4-5).
- Written reports.
- The "Notes" field of the computer genealogy program.

Research planners or calendars are filled out in advance of the work. They record what we "hope" to locate as we travel to various repositories. When, finally, we are able to look at the sources we have recorded on our planners, it's important to record the date of the search and the extract number; once we have done this, the planner then becomes a "table of contents" to the copies of our notes about the records we have gathered. Our research planner can also be the place where we record the code to the repository, the call numbers for the sources, the name of the individual or family for whom we're searching, what we want to find, and where we should record that information (such as under a Family Group Record) after we return home.

Document "As You Go"

Experienced genealogists will tell you that you can simplify your work if you will take the time to document each source as you record its information. And as you begin to amass information from a variety of sources, you will discover that each piece of documented information adds to every other piece, helping you to put together a much more complete picture than you thought possible.

While there is not, as yet, a universally accepted, "standard" documentation format, certain elements should always be included, such as those indicated in Illustration 4-1. Ideally, all facts and clues pertaining to an individual would be recorded with that individual as well.

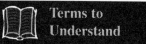

Terms to Understand

ev·i·dence - Some documentary or oral statements or material objects helpful to forming a conclusion or judgment.

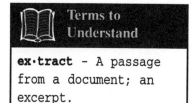

Terms to Understand

a·nal·y·sis - The separation of an intellectual whole into its constituent parts for individual study.

Terms to Understand

ex·tract - A passage from a document; an excerpt.

Terms to Understand

ab·stract - A written summary of the most important parts of a document.

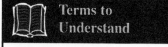

Terms to Understand

tran·scrip·tion - A written or typewritten copy of materials, as from notes or archived documents.

YOUR TURN

Imagine, for example, that everything you knew about your grandfather, James, was recorded, as in Illustration 4-2. In your family he had always been known as James "M." Nelson, but no one knew what his middle initial represented. What does the following documentation tell you?

COMPUTER DOCUMENTATION SAMPLE

1897 BIRTH: WI, Milwaukee Co., James M. Nelson entry, Milwaukee County Births, Vol. 1, page 346, microfilm no. 1275678, item 2, Family History Library [FHL], Salt Lake City, Utah.

James M. Nelson, son of George O. and Mary Elizabeth Nelson, of Milwaukee Heights, born 4 May 1897.

1900 CENSUS: WI, Green Co., Monroe Twp, George O. Nelson household, 1900 U.S. census, Greene County, Wisconsin, population schedule, township of Monroe, enumeration district [ED] 43, supervisor's district [SD] 1, sheet 13A, line 14; National Archives micropublication T00, roll 32.

George O. Nelson, white, male, 40 years old, born Jun 1860 OH, father born OH, mother born NY, can read and write, owns home freely, occupation farmer; Ellie [Mary Elizabeth's nickname was Ellie], white, female, wife, age 38, born Sep 1862 Canada, parents born NY, housekeeper, can read and write; George, 18, born Nov 1882 OH, father born OH, mother born NY, farmer laborer, can read and write; Mary, 16, born Oct 1884 IL, father b. OH, mother b. NY, going to school . . . Monroe, son, age 3, born May 1897 WI, father b. OH, mother born Canada.

1905 LETTER: Letter from George O. Nelson to his wife, dated 14 June 1905 from Medicine Lodge, Kansas. Copy in possession of Mr. John Browning, 12566 How'd He Do It Drive, Hoe, CA 98435:

". . . Sweetheart, found a wonderful new farm outside of Medicine Lodge...will be there in two weeks with the boys to pick up the household goods . . . Jim Boy can even have a swing in the big tree we've found for him here . . . love George."

1920 MARRIAGE: CA, Monterey Co., Salinas, James Monroe Nelson, State File Number 45723, California Department of Health Services, State Registrar of Vital Statistics, Sacramento, California:

James Monroe Nelson, age 22, and Sarah Marie Brown, age 19, both of Salinas, were married at the home of the bride, on 14 February 1920.

Illustration 4-2 Computer Documentation Sample

Research Planner

Remember to have only *one goal* per Research Planner.

Goal _____

_____

Surname/Subject _____   Researcher _____

Area _____   Client _____

Source Location		Description of Source	Object	Time	Remarks		
Date source searched	Library or repository & call #	(State, county, type of record, and time period of record)	(Person's name or what is sought)	(Person's age or date of event)	Comment or ID # of family	Index	File

Genealogy Research Associates, Inc. 139 East South Temple, Suite #300 Salt Lake City, UT 84111 Phone (801) 363-3464

Illustration 4-3 Research Planner

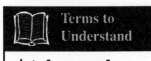

Terms to Understand

vi·tal re·cords - Documents which contain information about births, marriages, and deaths.

Terms to Understand

chron·o·log·i·cal or·der - Events arranged in order of time of occurrence.

Terms to Understand

time·line - A linear representation of significant events shown in chronological order.

Answers

Did you notice that:

- James was born in Milwaukee, Wisconsin on the 4th of May 1897, and lived in Milwaukee Heights.

- His family moved to Greene County, Wisconsin when he was 3 years old.

- James had two older siblings who were from a different mother. Their mother was born in New York, and his mother was born in Canada.

- His father was born in Ohio, and his paternal grandparents were born in Ohio and New York.

- His father could read and write and was financially secure, for he owned his own farm. His mother, Ellie, was born September 1862 in Canada, but her parents were born in New York.

- James had a middle name, Monroe. When James Monroe was eight years old, his family moved to Kansas. He was called "Jim Boy" and obviously liked to swing.

- By the time James Monroe was twenty-two years old, he had moved to California.

- He married Sarah Marie Brown at her home in Salinas, Monterey County, California, where he, too, was a resident in 1920.

You can see that more can be discovered about a person's life once you have recorded the full documentation, rather than simply saying, "Oh, I found him in the **vital records**, on a census, and in family correspondence."

Another miracle happens when we data enter our materials into a computer. We think of other things we could be doing to solve our problem. If we keep track of ideas and unanswered questions which evolve as we enter our documentation, the next phase of our research will be clearly mapped out.

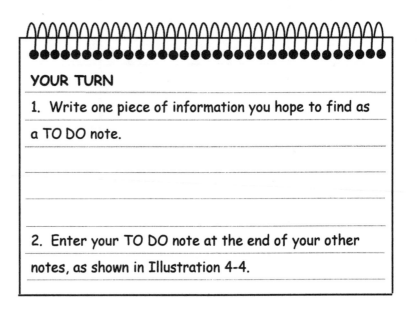

YOUR TURN

1. Write one piece of information you hope to find as a TO DO note.

2. Enter your TO DO note at the end of your other notes, as shown in Illustration 4-4.

A Tip About Chronology

Notes entered in **chronological order** are most effective in the research process. The sequence may be a simple chronology or a complicated sequence of cause and effect. Such **timelines** help us to understand and remember

sequential relationships; they act as visual aids to promote the mental arrangement of events in their proper order; and they help us to reconstruct history. When our family timelines are accurate, they provide the maximum amount of information in the minimum amount of time. They reduce the critical elements necessary for family history—events, times and places—to an understandable conclusion.

A tip about evaluating the source: If a document is torn, difficult to read, missing parts, or in some way different from others in the same series, that fact should be noted as well. Many computer genealogy programs today allow an area to make a comment about the quality of the source, as well as what the source contained.

IMPORTANT: To be most effective as a research tool, as well as a register, notes should be comprised of source citations of the original document and complete abstracts of what information was included in those original documents.

TO DO:

1. Order death certificate in California, perhaps Monterey County, for James Monroe Nelson. Maybe it will tell the year he moved to California.

2. Search the 1910 census index for California and/or Kansas for James Monroe Nelson, via his father, George.

3. The 1920 census would give Sarah's birthplace. Maybe her obituary, in Mom's scrapbook, would tell me more. Ask Mom to read it to me over the phone.

4. What happened to the brother and sister of James Monroe? They were quite a bit older than he was, and the census says their mother was born in New York, and that James' mother was born in Canada. Did his father marry once before, in Kansas?

Illustration 4-4 TO DO notes

Terms to Understand

cite - To quote as an authority or example, to mention or bring forward as support, illustration or proof.

TRANSCRIBING AND ABSTRACTING

The beginning genealogist is often surprised to find that a source citation is not enough to document a family history. While it was customary, in genealogies written in the past, to include a minimum of information, technology has changed all that. In electronic formats, the space limitations are not nearly as restrictive as the short forms of the past. We are not only able to **cite** sources, but we can also transcribe or abstract text, keep track of the sources we have searched, and include our individual skill, knowledge and experience in a personal interpretation of the materials within our documentation.

All of this should be entered in a format which would keep all three parts distinct: the citation, the document itself (in whatever format it is recorded), and the researcher's evaluation. Transcripts, abstracts and interpretations of the record should be part of the documentation, along with the citation. Abstracting, extracting, transcribing or copying the record that you have cited into your computer genealogy program provides a valuable service for the reader or researcher who is building on your work.

Fortunately, there are guidelines to help you avoid pitfalls when you are data entering this aspect of a complete documentation reference. For example, when you are extracting the essential information, remove only the extraneous, redundant words, but keep all of the essential Who, What, When, Where, Why, and

Terms to Understand

au·thor·i·ta·tive - Of acknowledged accuracy or reliability.

Terms to Understand

un·a·bridged - Containing the original content; not condensed.

How elements. If you encounter something unusual, record it as you find it. Important: Never "correct" names, dates, signatures, spelling or punctuation; you must copy the record as you see it. You can then add any necessary explanatory remarks in brackets, which look like this: [ ]. For example, if the spelling of a word or name is unusual, or if the grammar is out of the ordinary, you may follow the word or phrase with the Latin term *sic* in brackets, signaling the reader, "I see that this is not usual, and I am noting the fact."

Ellipses

Use ellipses (three periods, with spaces between) to indicate that part of the original text is being omitted. The ellipses will indicate to any other reader that you have left out non-essential information, such as legal verbiage or redundant sentences. An example of this is found in Illustration 4-2, above, where the entire letter is not transcribed, only those parts pertaining to Jim Boy and his dad:

... Sweetheart, found a wonderful new farm outside of Medicine Lodge ... will be there in two weeks with the boys to pick up the household goods ... Jim Boy can even have a swing in the big tree we've found for him here ... love George.

Brackets

Brackets are used to signify that material not found in the original is being added, such as a point of clarification or an alternative transcription of a hard-to-read word. A point of clarification was added to a nickname given to Mary Elizabeth in this census record from Illustration 4-2.

George O. Nelson, white, male, 40 years old, born Jun 1860 OH, father born OH, mother born NY, can read and write, owns home freely, occupation farmer; Ellie [Mary Elizabeth's nickname was Ellie], white, female, wife ...

Evaluations, Impressions, Insights and Working Notes

Besides including basic sources to substantiate the vital information entered into individual data fields, you can use the "Notes" field as a place to enter impressions about what records to search the next time you have an opportunity to go to a repository, or to identify conflicting or missing information.

The evaluation of any document, in light of the objective or goal for using that particular document to prove a point, requires that the interpretation of data be placed either in a separate report or in a separate area of the note field in order to prevent confusion with the original document. The original document, as well as the evaluation, is likely to be used by others who will rely on your work. You could also put this information in brackets if the genealogy computer program you are using does not have a separate place to record the researcher's evaluation notes.

Because social customs and terminology have changed over time, a proper explanation of terms used in documents would be helpful. By consulting **author-itative** sources, such as *Black's Law Dictionary*, or by referring to historical information in order to understand how the definitions of phrases have shifted over time, or by examining **unabridged** dictionaries for multiple definitions, you can more accurately verify relationships and events, placing them in the context of the times in which they occurred.

Not only will citations and abstracts help others, once they are listed in their entirety, they will guide you and future researchers to other sources and lead to additional clues. As sources are constantly coming to light with the help of computer-aided inventory processes, electronic copying technologies, heightened public awareness of genealogy, involvement by businesses in disseminating information, and faster and more efficient preservation methods, many of these new sources require new citation guidelines. There are, however, certain basics with regard to source citations—the Who, What, When, Where, Why guidelines you learned about earlier in the chapter—that are unlikely to change, no matter what source or medium you use.

GENEALOGY DOCUMENTATION GUIDELINES

Several genealogy documentation guides are included in the closing bibliography. But we should remember that documentation can vary according to the medium in which it is being written (e.g., pen, typewriter, or computer), as well as the type of computer genealogy program being used (i.e., the program's features). Documentation requirements may also vary, depending on whether the information is to be published in an article, book, or electronic database, and it can vary depending on our current purposes. Often, what we start out doing (e.g., having fun entering our family into a computer program for Christmas), is not what we end up doing (publishing a history for a family reunion), and you will discover that information you prepared for one purpose is often needed for another medium or publication format.

Since this is the case, it would be extremely helpful if we could have a couple of basic sample formats for entering our sources. However, to be sure the format is what we have in mind, it's also important for us to know how the information will look when it is printed out. For example, do you want your sources to be printed directly below the individual to whom they apply, including all the source elements (the citation, the abstracted information, and the researcher's evaluation notes), or would you prefer that the citation for a major event be given as a footnote or endnote?

The Documentation Guideline forms which follow will allow you to practice in pen or pencil the recording of the information that you can eventually put into your computer program. The form entitled *Documentation Guidelines for Notes* (Illustration 4-5) is used to practice the free-form method. This would print out like the examples shown in our James Monroe Nelson example, Illustration 4-2, earlier in this chapter.

The *Documentation Guidelines for Source Entries* (Illustration 4-6) provides you with a chance to practice entering sources which would be picked up as abbreviated footnotes or endnotes. Each genealogy computer program has its own formats for printing these items, but they are always linked to an event (such as birth date, birthplace, marriage date, marriage place, death date, death place, burial date, burial place, name, etc.). Rarely will a genealogy computer program allow you to include more than a few sentences under the "Comments" field, but they do allow entry for your own cautions or warning about a record. Each user will need to decide for him/herself which is best.

Whether you use a free program downloaded from the Internet, or a more robust Windows program, ranging in price from $99 to $150, you should be sure that it contains the basic elements necessary to document sources properly.

In the general notes area, you should have the flexibility of recording your notes in any way you want. This option, however, has its good and bad points. If you enter your notes every which way:

- your final report will not be orderly;

- it won't be easy for others to read;

- you will have difficulty finding information; and

- if you change computer programs, it will be difficult to transfer your sources.

From Your Computer Screen

1897 BIRTH: WI, Milwaukee Co., James M. Nelson entry, Milwaukee County Births, Vol. 1, page 346, microfilm no. 1275678, item 2, Family History Library [FHL], Salt Lake City, Utah.

James M. Nelson, son of George O. and Mary Elizabeth Nelson, of Milwaukee Heights, born 4 May 1897.

1900 CENSUS: WI, Green Co., Monroe Twp, George O. Nelson household, 1900 U.S. census, Greene County, Wisconsin, population schedule, township of Monroe, enumeration district [ED] 43, supervisor's district [SD] 1, sheet 13A, line 14; National Archives micropublication T00, roll 32.

George O. Nelson, white, male, 40 years old, born Jun 1860 OH, father born OH, mother born NY, can read and write, owns home freely, occupation farmer; Ellie [Mary Elizabeth's nickname was Ellie], white, female, wife, age 38, born Sep 1862 Canada, parents born NY, housekeeper, can read and write; George, 18, born Nov 1882 OH, father born OH, mother born NY, farmer laborer, can read and write; Mary, 16, born Oct 1884 IL, father b. OH, mother b. NY, going to school . . . Monroe, son, age 3, born May 1897 WI, father b. OH, mother born Canada.

1905 LETTER: Letter from George O. Nelson to his wife, dated 14 June 1905 from Medicine Lodge, Kansas. Copy in possession of Mr. John Browning, 12566 How'd He Do It Drive, Hoe, UT 94835:

"... Sweetheart, found a wonderful new farm outside of Medicine Lodge...will be there in two weeks with the boys to pick up the household goods . . . Jim Boy can even have a swing in the big tree we've found for him here . . . love George."

1920 MARRIAGE: CA, Monterey Co., Salinas, James Monroe Nelson, State File Number 45723, California Department of Health Services, State Registrar of Vital Statistics, Sacramento, California:

James Monroe Nelson, age 22, and Sarah Marie Brown, age 19, both of Salinas, were married at the home of the bride, on 14 February 1920.

TO DO:

1. Order death certificate in California, perhaps Monterey County, for James Monroe Nelson. Maybe it will tell the year he moved to California.

2. Search the 1910 census index for California and/or Kansas for James Monroe Nelson, via his father, George.

3. The 1920 census would give Sarah's birth place. Maybe her obituary, in Mom's scrapbook, would tell me more. Ask Mom to read it to me over the phone.

4. What happened to the brother and sister of James Monroe? They were quite a bit older than he was, and they said their mother was born in New York, while James stated his mother was born in Canada. Did his father marry once before, in Kansas?

General Notes Free-form Style
(see Illustrations 4-2 and 4-4)

Source Notes Step 1

Source Notes Step 2

Documentation Guidelines for Notes

Event Year	Event	Foreign Country	State/Shire
County		Town/Parish	

Title of Source

Author	Publisher	Copyright Date

Vol., Folio or ED.	Page #, House or Line #	Repository Address or Person:
Call #	Item #	

Abstract/Extract/Transcript/Scanned Image:

Evaluation of Materials

Illustration 4-5 Documentation Guidelines for Notes

Documentation Guidelines for Source Entries

Source Title

Author | Publication Information

Copyright Date   Source Call #

Repository (address and telephone or person)

Individual Reference (certificate #, volume or page)

Date of Entry

Actual Text (Abstract/Extract/Transcript/Scanned Image)

Comments (Evaluation of Material)

Illustration 4-6 Documentation Guidelines for Source Entries

On the positive side, if you know the rules of good notes entry, this open option allows you to:

- enter your notes in chronological order;

- indicate locations and dates in a way that is required for research purposes;

- cut and paste blocks of information from one individual to another;

- cut and paste blocks of information from one program to another; and

- create a place to data enter information that applies to more than one person since these notes are printed below the individual in the body of the text.

Why, then, do computer genealogy programs provide two places to cite sources? The most obvious reason is that individuals are unique and desire a variety of choices. But this is coupled with the possibilities available when source "fields" are set up for information. Fields can be sorted and linked to other items, as technology improves. Once information is entered into a field, it can be duplicated in other fields without more data entry. This also allows for limited standardization of sources, so that they can be brought into other programs more easily.

Therefore, once a repository such as the Oregon State Board of Health, with its appropriate addresses and phone numbers, is data-entered, it will never need to be entered again. Likewise, once a film obtained from the Family History Library containing the vital records of the parish of Viipuri, Finland is entered, it will not need to be entered again except to change the page number or the content.

All of these labor-saving features are welcome, but as you begin your family research, be sure that whatever program you select has a place for unlimited note-keeping abilities and that your notes and family vital record data can be transferred to more sophisticated programs as you move along. The most common transfer program in genealogy is called GEDCOM, and you will want to look for 100% GEDCOM compatibility in any genealogy computer program you use. In this way, the source citations that prove the vital information in your family lines, and the family data you have worked so hard to collect and record, can be automatically transferred to more advanced programs and large databases of shared information, either on disk or through the Internet.

What if you want to be able to scan your documents and pictures into your computer genealogy program? Are there programs to do that as well? Absolutely. But because most programs link their data files directly to their image files, scanned images will quickly fill up your computer's hard drive and limit the pure research you can record and document. I suggest that you save those scanned images in a separate file that can later be copied into your computer genealogy program. For now, don't mix the two, because you will need plenty of computer working space to download and match text files.

The time will come very quickly when we can take those saved, scanned images and link them directly to the person they involve. Since this will add to our overall understanding of an individual, it's no wonder that we want to use greater technology to capture all that we know about those we are researching, and that we will want to standardize our documentation methods in order to produce the best possible results from our research and in our reporting. We just need to be patient for a while, in order to take advantage of the resources we currently have, or until we have the money for unlimited storage space on the computer.

A GUARANTEED GUIDE FOR EXCELLENT DOCUMENTATION

The steps that follow will help you to keep your documentation succinct, yet inclusive, of all pertinent information (whether you enter it at first by hand, or directly into your computer):

Steps for Computer Entry

1. Place documentation in chronological order, based on the date of the information contained within each transcript, abstract or extract--not the date of publication. So your first entry for an item should be the date. For example, if your goal is to verify the birth year of an individual, and a marriage certificate indicates that this person was born in 1847, you should begin the citation with the year of birth, not the year of the marriage certificate. Remember: the purpose for this entry is to prove documentation for the birth year.

EXAMPLE: 1847

2. Give each event a one-word **event title** (if possible), to quickly pinpoint what events are included and what events have yet to be found (e.g., those not having a title). Again, this word should describe the event, not the source from which it originated.

EXAMPLE: 1847 BIRTH

3. Next, show the **geographical** location in this order: the country (if outside the U.S.), state (two-letter postal abbreviation since these can be changed automatically by the computer later to full state names), county (with the word "county," abbreviate the letters to "Co."), and town/parish/township, post office, river courses or other geographical designations. In other words, go from the largest jurisdiction down to the smallest (this is exactly the opposite of the way that information is entered into the individual entry fields in most genealogy programs).

EXAMPLE:

1847 BIRTH: OH, Hamilton Co., Cincinnati, California Twp.

1850 CENSUS: KY, Jefferson Co., Louisville, District 2.

1860 CENSUS: IN, Vanderburgh Co., Evansville, Evansville P.O.

The purpose of entering the data in this manner is to make it as easy as possible to interpret the chronological life events of an individual. The examples (which include only part of the citation portion of a complete, three-part documentation) demonstrate the ease with which a researcher may see both the years and the movement within a county, from state to state, or from country to country.

Can you see, in the example above, how the available collected notes on one individual lists a movement pattern from Ohio to Kentucky, and finally Indiana?

> **Terms to Understand**
>
> **e·vent ti·tle** - A brief introductory word or two to signify an important milestone or occurrence in an individual's life (see Illustration 4-8).

> **Terms to Understand**
>
> **ge·o·graph·i·cal** - Relating to the topography of a specific region, or to the study of physical features of the earth's surface.

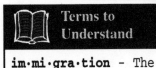

Terms to Understand

im·mi·gra·tion - The act of entering a country to which one is not a native, to settle permanently.

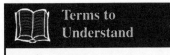

Terms to Understand

nat·u·ral·i·za·tion - To grant full citizenship to one of foreign birth.

PRIVATE INVESTIGATOR

YOUR TURN

What pattern does this example demonstrate?

1835 BIRTH: England, Wiltshire, Salisbury

1862 MARRIAGE: England, Wiltshire, Salisbury

1863 BIRTH OF SON: UT, Great Salt Lake Co., Parley's Canyon

1914 DEATH: UT, Salt Lake Co., Mill Creek

Answers

Did you recognize that the "Your Turn" example portrays the movement of an individual from England to Utah, all taken from the collected notes of that person?

Calling Sherlock Holmes . . .

Notes listed in chronological order can also help you determine what sources were not searched. The next example shows you how a quick glance can suggest to a researcher other, unused, easy-to-acquire resources which should be searched to contribute evidence regarding children, dates of **immigration** and **naturalization,** previous marriages, etc.

EXAMPLE 3:

1835 BIRTH: England, Wiltshire, Salisbury

<u>1841 CENSUS: England</u>

<u>1851 CENSUS: England</u>

<u>1861 CENSUS: England</u>

1862 MARRIAGE: England, Wiltshire, Salisbury

1863 BIRTH OF SON: UT, Great Salt Lake Co., Parley's Canyon

<u>1870 CENSUS: UT</u>

<u>1880 CENSUS: UT</u>

<u>1900 CENSUS: UT</u>

<u>1910 CENSUS: UT</u>

1914 DEATH: UT, Salt Lake Co., Mill Creek

The underlined type illustrates the sources which you can research for further information. (We are not suggesting that these be entered into their appropriate place until they have actually been researched; this is only to show you how to go about discovering missing information.)

YOUR TURN

Can you tell that the underlined items suggest that the researcher look at the 1910, 1900, 1880, and 1870 federal census records of Utah? What records should be searched in England from this brief list?

Terms to Understand

fiche - A microfiche, or a card or sheet of microfilm capable of preserving a considerable number of printed pages in reduced form.

Did you also notice that a full location citation, such as "UT, Great Salt Lake Co., Parley's Canyon," is more descriptive than just Salt Lake County? Which records would permit you to search for the precise location where the individual you're researching lived?

We must learn to list the major parts of the citation, using one of the major guidelines for bibliographical formats (see the bibliography at the end of this chapter, or use as a guideline the methods of an experienced researcher). In Illustration 4-1, "Items Covered in Documentation," the various segments of the citation were described. Each one attempts to answer one of the following questions: Who? (the author, compiler, etc.); What? (description of the source which may be the title of a book, the description of a collection, or an index to other records); When? (a specific date, a span of time for this record collection—but not the event year); Where? (the places covered by this book, collection, or item, which may include a geographical location, as well as the actual repository for the item being used); and How? (book, film, **fiche,** electronic media, etc.).

Evaluate, Evaluate . . .

The "why" question is part of the evaluation process, and it is the most neglected aspect of the research process. Begin now to develop the habit of evaluating each document in light of your objective or goal; your use of that document should be included in the data entry process. Although not every item you data enter will require an evaluation statement (a marriage document obviously gives the marriage date), other entries will need an explanation (that same marriage document may list the witnesses to the ceremony, which may provide important clues to family members or close friends).

Other Helpful Tips

- All facts and clues pertaining to an individual should be recorded with that individual. (When you keep notes on different individuals, be sure to use separate sheets of paper; don't combine surnames on one page. If you have three names on one sheet of paper, under which name will you file it?)

- Keep track of ideas and unanswered questions which evolve as you record what you have found. (Use the same term again and again, such as TO DO!)

PROBLEM TO OVERCOME	POSSIBLE SOLUTION
Something unusual is found (misspelled name, wrong date, etc.)	Record the entry as you find it. Names, dates, signatures and punctuation are never corrected. Put needed explanatory remarks in brackets [ ]. *Example: "John Moore" [sic: transcription error; should be Moon]*
Document is torn, difficult to read, or has missing parts	Record the entry as you find it. Put explanatory remarks, or added material not found in the original, in brackets [ ]. *Example: "Th[omas]" or [court date was torn but the document was placed between others in the court ledger dated 1794].*
Interpretation of the data is necessary	Separate the interpretation from the actual document by entering the interpretation below the document, either all in capital letters or in a separate paragraph surrounded by brackets. Consult authoritative sources to interpret the meaning of phrases, terms of relationship, or legal terms. *Example: [The term son-in-law in his will does not mean his daughter's husband, but rather his stepson, or son "by" law, which was a meaning of the word during this time period. See Webster's Unabridged Dictionary, p. 1678 (. . . include full citation . . .). Further evidence: He stated he had no daughters in his pension papers].*
Document is full of redundant legal verbiage	Use ellipses . . . (three dots, with spaces between to signify that part of the original text or title is not being cited). *See sample above.*

Illustration 4-7 Rules for Entering Evaluation Comments in the Computer

- Give each Family Group Record its own ID number. You won't have to worry about this last detail if you are using the PAF program. The program automatically assigns a Family Group Record number, called an MRIN (Marriage Record Identification Number), each time you enter a family. That number appears at the center top of the record when you print information on your families, and it is titled "Family Group Record #." You should also use this number to identify items you have entered onto your research planner.

- When I return from a research trip, I place Post-It notes, with MRIN numbers, on the documents I have brought back, in order to remind myself where I should enter them. Once they are entered, I jot down, LIGHTLY IN PENCIL somewhere on the actual document (usually the upper right-hand corner), the Family Group Record (FGR/MRIN) number where I entered the data. This aids in filing the document later.

Remember to Analyze the Information You Have Gathered

- Notes listed in chronological order can help you to determine *what sources were not searched*, as well as which sources were located.

- Evaluation of the document, in light of the objective or goal (the purpose for which you searched for and copied the document), should now be undertaken.

- Although an evaluation statement is not necessary with every item that has been data entered, some documents require explanation.

SAMPLE EVENT TITLES

BIRTH	EDUCATION	OCCUPATION
BURIAL	IMMIGRATION	PROBATE
CENSUS	LAND	RELIGIOUS ACTIVITIES
CHRISTENING	LIFE EVENTS	RESIDENCE/MIGRATION
CITIZENSHIP/NATURALIZATION	MARRIAGE	TAX
COURT	MEMBERSHIP	
DEATH	MILITARY	

Illustration 4-8 Sample Event Titles

ASSIGNMENT 4: FILLING OUT DOCUMENTATION GUIDELINE FORMS

1. Use the Documentation Guideline for Notes form on page 4-10 to record, in pencil or ink, one of the sources listed below.

   A. First as a citation;
   B. Then as an abstract of the actual document;
   C. Finally, evaluate or interpret the information you have recorded.

   The repository you visited:
   Family History Library
   35 North West Temple Street
   Salt Lake City, Utah 84150

   The individual you were looking for and the record you found:
   John Bassett, age 43, male, white, farmer, real estate $ 1500, personal $ 100, born VA; Nancy, 33, f, w, keeping house, b VA; Joshua, 7, w, m, at home, b VA; Mary, 5, f, w, at home, b VA; John D., 2, m, w, at home, b VA; Charles A., 1, m, w, at home, b VA.

   The individual you were looking for and the record you found:
   Elijah D. Hundley, found in a book by George Calvin Waldrep called *Halifax County Cemeteries*. Published Nathalie, Va.: Clarkton Press, 1984. A three-volume collection. He was found in volume 1, page 188.

   Hundley Family Cemetery (Old Christ Episcopal Church). This cemetery, located on Rt. 736 north of Clover, VA, was part of Christ Episcopal Church. The graves, about 75, are unmarked, with the exception of the Carringtons. The Hundleys are in a fenced plot on the cemetery lot. "Elijah D. Hundley, B. 4 Sept 1798, D. 1 Jan 1873."

   Repository you visited:
   You were driving in Henry County, Virginia when you found a cemetery which you were later told was the Vaughn-Philpott-Morris Cemetery.

   Individual you were looking for and the record you found:
   Tombstone for Benjamin R. Wells, found in the Vaughn-Philpott-Morris Cemetery, Henry County, Virginia.

   "Benjamin R. Wells b. 20 Aug 1897, d. 8 Sept 1898."

2. Enter source notes and free-form notes under at least three different individuals in your family file.

3. Go into the general notes area for one person you are working on. Start a line with the words TO DO. Now enter a note to make a phone call, in order to ask a relative for information, or a reminder regarding a repository you heard about that might have information on this person, or some other information you want to remember.

YOUR TURN ANSWERS

Those pages not listed below are appropriate for personal preference responses.

What does Illustration 4.2 tell you about the middle initial of James M. Nelson?

The 1900 census indicates that the initial stood for Monroe because the 3-year-old boy born in May agreed with the May 1897 birth date in the birth record. The 1920 marriage certificate substantiated the census record when the groom was listed as James Monroe Nelson.

What pattern does this example demonstrate?

It indicates a movement of the family from Wiltshire, England to Salt Lake County, Utah.

What records should be searched in England from this brief list?

The 1861, 1851, and 1841 British census records for Salisbury, Wiltshire, England.

COMPUTER CHECKLIST #4

1. What keystrokes are necessary to enter "source notes" for events in your program?

2. What keystrokes are necessary to enter "general notes" for individuals in your program?

WEB SITES

http://www.msoe.edu/gen_st/style/stylguid.html
This Web site provides guidelines which follow the *Chicago Manual of Style.*

http://www.mla.org/set_stl.htm
This Web site provides guidelines for the *MLA Style Manual.*

http://www.columbia.edu/cu/cup/cgos/idx_basic.html
This Web site provides guidelines for the *The Columbia Guide to Online Style.*

BIBLIOGRAPHY

Chicago Manual of Style. 14th ed. Chicago: University of Chicago Press, 1993.

Gibaldi, Joseph. *MLA Style Manual.* 2nd ed. New York: The Modern Language Association of America, 1999.

Mills, Elizabeth Shown. *Evidence! Citation & Analysis for the Family Historian.* Baltimore: Genealogical Publishing Co., 1997.

Turabian, Kate L., John Grossman and Alice Bennett. *A Manual for Writers of Term Papers, Theses, and Dissertations.* 6th ed. Chicago: University of Chicago Press, 1996.

Walker, Janice R. and Todd Taylor. *The Columbia Guide to Online Style.* New York: Columbia University Press, 1998.

Wylie, John Vincent. "Richard Lackey Died Too Soon: How to Document Modern Media and Online Sources." *In Your Ancestors' Image.* The Federation of Genealogical Societies and The Rochester Genealogical Society, 14-17 August, 1996; Rochester, New York, F-80.

Printing Your Records

Hold fast the form of sound words.

—*2 Timothy:13*

Now that you have entered the individuals in your direct line, their spouses and children, and you have started your documentation, you are ready to print your materials. In this way you can determine if your notes are printing out the way you want them to, you can correct your information, and you can begin to assemble your notebook. Certainly, one of the real miracles of keeping your family records and genealogical information in a good genealogy computer program is in the many kinds of reports that can be printed.

BEFORE YOU PRINT

Do you want one of those nifty-looking family trees you've always associated with genealogical reports? It can be yours at the press of a button. How about a fancy fan-style chart that looks good enough to frame? You can have that, too. Or do you want a business-like genealogical report, including notes and sources, that you can send off to a **family association**, **genealogical society** or **fraternal** organization? It's all yours, as long as you've entered the information into your computer program. But as you will see, there are basic questions to consider before printing any report.

Many different types of charts and reports can be printed using your family records. The basic questions to consider before printing any report include the following:

1. What is my purpose in creating a report?
2. Who will see this report? What information do they need?
3. How do I want the report to look when it's printed?
4. What information should be included? Just names? Dates and locations? Notes and sources?
5. Do I want to print the report on paper, display it on screen, or save it to disk?

Terms to Understand

fam·i·ly as·so·ci·a·tion - An organization of individuals who study and research a particular family or families. Such organizations often produce newsletters and published histories, organize "family reunions," and promote the gathering of information on their particular lines.

Terms to Understand

ge·ne·a·lo·gi·cal so·ci·e·ty - An organization of individuals who gather to promote family history research within their locality, among a particular ethnic group, or focused on a particular subject.

Terms to Understand

fra·ter·nal - Brotherly, benevolent.

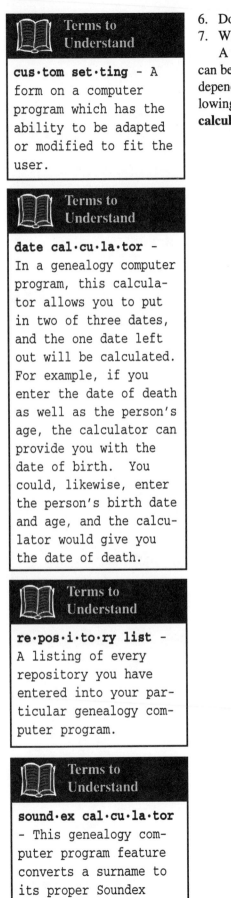

Terms to Understand

cus·tom set·ting - A form on a computer program which has the ability to be adapted or modified to fit the user.

Terms to Understand

date cal·cu·la·tor - In a genealogy computer program, this calculator allows you to put in two of three dates, and the one date left out will be calculated. For example, if you enter the date of death as well as the person's age, the calculator can provide you with the date of birth. You could, likewise, enter the person's birth date and age, and the calculator would give you the date of death.

Terms to Understand

re·pos·i·to·ry list - A listing of every repository you have entered into your particular genealogy computer program.

Terms to Understand

sound·ex cal·cu·la·tor - This genealogy computer program feature converts a surname to its proper Soundex equivalent (see Chapter 14).

6. Do I want to print all of the pages of the report or only selected pages?
7. What **custom settings** do I want to add before printing?

A wide variety of reports in the form of charts, trees, lists, and research tools can be produced using your specific genealogy computer program (these vary, depending on the program you are using, but they may include some of the following: **date calculators**, birthplace distribution lists, **repository lists**, **soundex calculators**, data errors lists, etc.).

YOUR TURN

Explain the various keystrokes for producing the following using your genealogy computer program:

1. Pedigree Charts

2. Family Group Records

3. Descendant Charts or Trees

4. Lists

5. Research Tools

6. Custom Reports

PEDIGREE CHARTS

Pedigree Charts can be printed singly, in groups, or for the entire data file. In addition, you can determine how many generations to include, as well as how many generations per page – 4, 5, or 6. (Note: six generations per page can present problems for some printers.) Other options include whether to print a RIN for each individual; whether to print a Pedigree Index (an alphabetical list of each person on the selected Pedigree Charts); and whether to include **LDS ordinance** information. You can also opt to print Family Group Records which will correspond to the Pedigree Chart(s) being printed. Similar charts are labeled differently by different programs. See Illustration 5-1, which explains similar charts under different headings.

Pedigree Family Group Records Only. This option will print only Family Group Records within a selected pedigree **range**–for example, from your Great-Grandfather Anderson to your own grandchildren. You simply stipulate how many generations you want, beginning with a specific individual. This option will not print the entire Pedigree Chart(s), it will only print Family Group Records, and it includes many of the features available on Family Group Records. No Family Group Records would be printed for siblings, aunts and uncles, however.

Pedigree Index Only. This prints an alphabetical list of each person within a selected pedigree range. You specify how many generations, beginning with a specific individual.

Blank Pedigree Chart. The Pedigree Chart is printed without family records data. It is just a blank form for hand-entering information.

Ancestry Chart. This is just another name for a Pedigree Chart. Larger versions of a Pedigree Chart or Ancestry Chart can be printed to run vertically on a standard page size, or it can be printed on a larger scale (pages must be taped together after printing).

At this point in the evolution of genealogy programs, the appearance of charts and reports differ, depending on the program. Some programs offer boxes around each individual name/date/location area, as well as around the charts themselves. Other programs provide the option of shading within the boxes that contain names, or other ways to make charts more attractive. Some, like *PAF 3.0,* have programs to enhance the appearance of printed charts and reports. *PAF Companion,* for example, converts data from an MS-DOS format to a Windows format for more attractive printouts. It also provides more printing options for *PAF 4.0* and higher.

Fan Charts. A fan chart is a kind of Pedigree Chart which, because of its configuration, allows many more generations of a family to be viewed at once.

FAMILY GROUP RECORDS

The Family Group Record is at the heart of every genealogical report. Without the nuclear family—father, mother and children—there is no genealogy. And if the information for that family is not accurate or complete, the genealogy as a whole cannot be accurate or complete. So it's crucial that you keep careful track of every family in your database by printing out current copies of Family Group Records for your files. When you print a Family Group Record, it may also include the following custom options:

Print spaces for additional children. If selected, this option allows the Family Group Record to be printed with empty children's sections (these fill the remainder of the page), making it possible for you to fill in "newly discovered" children, by hand, as you do subsequent research.

Other marriages listed in notes. If an individual has multiple marriages, the other spouses can be included in the "Notes" section.

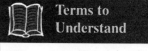

Terms to Understand

LDS - An abbreviation for The Church of Jesus Christ of Latter-day Saints.

Terms to Understand

or·di·nance - Refers to baptisms, endowments, and sealings, as mentioned in Matthew 16:19, performed for deceased relatives by members of The Church of Jesus Christ of Latter-day Saints with the purpose of identifying and linking one's entire family. When used in the phrase "LDS ordinance field," it means those computer fields which record the dates of the ordinances.

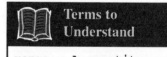

Terms to Understand

range - A quantity or specific order of something, e.g., a range of MRINs would include only those MRINs selected by an individual.

The Master Genealogist 3.5	Personal Ancestral File 4.0	Family Tree Maker 7.0
Family Group Sheets	Family Group Sheets	Family Group Sheets
	Ancestry Charts	Ancestor Trees
Pedigree Charts	Pedigree Charts	
Descendant Trees	Descendant Charts	Descendant Trees
Descendancy Narratives		
		Descendancy Outlines
	Descendancy Lists	
Genealogy (Journal Format)		Genealogy Report
Ahnentafel (standard & linear)	Ahnentafel	
	Modified Register	
Individual Detail	Individual Summary	
Individual Narrative		
Kinship Reports		Kinship Reports
		Kinship - canon & civil
Relationship Charts	Relationship Calculator	
Marriages	Marriages	Marriages
		Parentage
Birthdates	Birthdates	Birthdates
	Anniversaries	
Witnesses		
Events		Documented Events
		Alternate Facts
	Date Calculator	
		Timeline
		Medical Information
Distribution by Birthplace		
	Family Reunion Contacts	
		Addresses
Repositories	Repositories	
Sources	Sources	
Endnotes Lists		
Bibliography		
Citations		
People		
Places		
	Soundex Calculator	
	RIN/MRIN Lists of Individuals	
	Unlinked Individuals Lists	
	Duplicate Individuals Lists	
	End of Line Individuals Lists	
	Alphabetical Lists of Individuals	
		Data Errors Lists
	Possible Problems Lists	
Statistical Report		
Tag Type Lists		
Task Lists		To Do Lists
Custom Reports	Custom Reports	Custom Reports
Data Set Information		

Illustration 5-1 Genealogy Computer Program Comparison Chart

MRIN (Marriage Record Identification Number)

Family Group Record- 4

Page 1 of 2

Husband	**Andrew KAMPSULA-8**		
Born	5 Feb 1889	Place	Ishpeming, Marquette, Michigan
Died	13 Dec 1939	Place	Hopewell, Yamhill, Oregon
Buried		Place	Portland, Multnomah, Oregon
Married	1910	Place	Homestead Twp, Otter Tail, Minnesota
Husband's father	Herman Anterspoika KAMSULA-21		
Husband's mother	Hilma Kallentytar Walitalo WALIMAA-22		

How many pages in this particular Family Group Record

MRIN: 8

MRIN of Husband's Parents

Wife	**Ida Maria TASKINEN-116**		
Born	18 Sep 1887	Place	, Kivennapa, Viipuri, Finland
Died	6 Feb 1949	Place	Portland, Multnomah, OR
Buried	9 Feb 1949	Place	Portland, Multnomah, OR
Wife's father	Benjam Juhonpoika TASKINEN-36		
Wife's mother	Hilda Maria Nikodemusdotter POLVI-37		

MRIN of Wife's Parents

MRIN: 32

Children	List each child in order of birth.		

1 M Andrew Raymond KAMPSULA-9

Born	14 Jun 1913	Place	Homestead Twp, Otter Tail, Minnesota
Died	5 May 1957	Place	Ticton, , Washington
Buried		Place	Terrace Heights, Yakima, WA

2 M Alfred Filmore KAMPSULA-11

Born	13 Mar 1917	Place	New York Mills, Ottertail, Minnesota
Died	28 Nov 1985	Place	Vancouver, Clark, Washington
Buried	3 Dec 1985	Place	Woodland, Cowlitz, Washington

Child's position in this family

3 F Lilian Victoria KAMPSULA-12

Born	2 Mar 1919	Place	Newton, Otter Tail, Minnesota
	28 Dec 1963	Place	, , Idaho
	Jan 1964	Place	New York Mills, Otter Tail, Minnesota
	Harold Jacob PERALA-177		
Married	Abt 1937 (Div)	Place	, , MN

MRIN: 10

RIN (Record Identification Number)

4 F Edla Veneda KAMPSULA-13

Born	2 May 1921	Place	Homestead Twp, Otter Tail, Minnesota
Died	25 Jan 1963	Place	Homestead Twp, Otter Tail, Minnesota
Buried	1963	Place	Homestead Twp, Otter Tail, Minnesota
Spouse	Wayne Waino Arnold KUUKAS-122		
Married	22 Jun 1945	Place	, Ottertail, MN

MRIN: 13

5 M Bruno Benjamin KAMPSULA-2

Born	22 Feb 1924	Place	Homestead Twp, Otter Tail, Minnesota
Died	13 Aug 1993	Place	Vancouver, Clark, WA
Spouse	Lempi Hellena LEHTO-3		
Married	1945 (Div)	Place	Vancouver, Clark, Washington

MRIN of this child and his spouse

MRIN: 2

Name, address and phone number of family representative

Prepared by	John Smith	Address	1234 Some Road
Phone	555-111-4444		Any City, GA 23423
Date prepared	02 Aug 1999		

Illustration 5-2 Completed Family Group Record Printed from PAF 4.0

Terms to Understand

MRIN - An abbreviation for Marriage Record Identification Number.

 **Terms to Understand**

de·scen·dant - The offspring of a particular individual.

Record Identification Numbers (RINs). These can be included in any of your printouts, if your program is capable of providing RINs.

Notes to Print. In most programs, you can choose to print: 1) all notes in a record (the default setting), 2) only specific notes, or 3) no notes.

Sources to Print. If sources are included in the documentation, some programs allow you to choose to cite: 1) the the full source, 2) part of the source, or 3) no sources. If you include the full source, you may be able to select whether to include all comments, some comments, or none.

Print LDS Ordinance Information. The LDS ordinance information can be included or omitted on the record.

Pedigree Chart Reference Number. This option is used only if you wish to print a reference chart and position number (e.g., Chart #1, Position #8) to cross-reference Family Group Records and Pedigree Charts.

Pages to Print. You can choose to print selected pages or all of the pages of a record.

Range of Family Group Records. If you wish to print more than one Family Group Record, you may enter a range of **MRINs** that will be printed automatically.

Blank Family Group Records. You can print these blank Family Group Records with or without LDS ordinance fields, so that you can fill them in by hand when a computer is not available (e.g., when you're doing research in a library).

Notes for Range of Marriages. This feature is helpful if you wish to print only the notes for several families. The options include printing all notes and sources, or only selected notes and sources. You can also choose to include or omit LDS ordinances, and you can select the pages you wish to print.

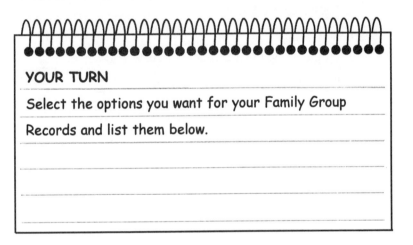

YOUR TURN

Select the options you want for your Family Group

Records and list them below.

OTHER CHARTS AND FORMS

Descendancy Chart

A Descendancy Chart shows all of the **descendants** of a selected individual for the number of generations that you choose. RINs and MRINs can also be displayed, but this feature can be changed or omitted. You can also choose to print an Index of Descendants (this might be helpful for a lengthy descendancy report).

Individual Reports

This report includes an individual's name and information found in his or her Individual Report and Marriage Record, as well as all of the notes and sources pertaining to that individual. You can choose to print one or more Individual Reports, or you can choose to print only the notes when you use this option.

Printed Lists

Your computer genealogy program can generate many kinds of lists, but since each program offers a slightly different variety, it's important for you to explore what lists are available to you.

The best way to find out what each list offers is to print them out, using your own family file. In addition, many of these lists offer the same customizing options available with Pedigree Charts and Family Group Records. Following is a sample of the kinds of lists you may find on your computer genealogy program:

Alphabetical, or *Name Sorted List.* This is an alphabetical list of all individuals in a data file. It includes each individual's RIN, birth and/or christening date(s), death and/or burial date(s), parents' MRIN, and the spouse's (or father's) name.

Place Sorted List. This schedule lists all place names included in the data file, alphabetically, by location. Place Sorted Lists can help you check for inconsistencies in place-name formatting (e.g. Los Angeles, L.A., LA, etc.), though many programs handle formatting automatically. A Place Sorted List also provides a key to the locations of vital events for all individuals in the data file. This feature is not available on all programs.

Source List. This permits you to print all of the sources you have cited in your data file.

ID Sorted List. If your computer genealogy program provides identification numbers, you can list all records in your data file by their ID numbers.

Possible Record Problems or **data error lists** can be very helpful, pointing out possible conflicts within your records, such as a death date that occurs before the birth date, or a child's birth date which comes before the mother's birth date. You should check this feature periodically, as you add new records to your file. Some programs automatically catch the most common types of errors as they are entered.

Research Tools and Forms. Genealogy programs include many other features, such as blank forms, correspondence **logs**, research logs, relationship charts and research process forms—all helpful in keeping your research organized and written down. For example, the **relationship chart** can be used to determine the family relationships between two individuals, such as first cousins, second cousins, aunts, uncles, etc.

Custom Reports. Several programs allow you to create custom reports that you would like to have, such as one which permits you to include additional information, or to change **fonts**, or to change frames around boxes, etc.

PRINT DESTINATION

When printing forms or reports, you always have the option to "print" to:

1. various printers,
2. the screen,
3. a diskette or file.

When you want your materials organized in a manner that will help you analyze connections, but you don't have a printer available, **screen printing** in MS-DOS programs or print preview in Windows programs works well. This is also particularly helpful when you want to evaluate how a new chart or form will look without wasting paper.

NOTE: When printing to the screen or preview, some charts and reports may only appear in pieces, because the monitor cannot display the entire report at one time. Use the arrow keys to view the remainder of the report.

Terms to Understand

data er·ror list - A grouping of mistaken entries put into your particular genealogy program.

Terms to Understand

log - A list of resources usually recorded after they have been searched.

Terms to Understand

re·la·tion·ship chart - A genealogy diagram which describes the familial connections between individuals.

Terms to Understand

fonts - The various typefaces, or type styles, produced by your computer program.

Terms to Understand

screen print·ing - The ability of a computer program to produce a report on the screen rather than on paper.

Terms to Understand

re·trieve - To open a file in a computer program, whether it was saved in that program or in a different program.

Printing to file or diskette in *PAF* allows you to print and save your notes into an electronic format, saving the data to a diskette, or to a folder in Windows. This then allows you to **retrieve** the notes into a "spell check" program to correct spelling errors and/or rearrange data which can then be cut and pasted back into your genealogy computer program. This is also a handy feature for pulling reports into another word processing document. However in other Windows programs, such as Family Tree Maker, if you print to file, your file will have an ending of ".prn" which can only be utilized by a printer (and not a program).

It is also a good idea to learn how to interrupt a print job, in case you find that you have opted to print 500 pages and you only wanted five! Don't worry: the printer may take a minute or two in order to finish printing what was already stored in its memory, so it probably won't stop right away. But it will stop.

CONCLUSION

As you will soon discover, various report formats help you analyze your family history data more effectively in preparation for setting good research goals. Reports containing partial localities alert you that preliminary work needs to be done to determine the full names of places at which events occurred. Problem lists can alert you to erroneous dates in your program, which may require research to locate the proper answers. Approximate dates warn you that research is needed to locate the actual date of the event. Therefore, you should practice the various print options available while you have a small number of names in your computer genealogy program and can more easily understand the reports. You'll then be prepared to use these reports, as necessary, throughout your research experiences.

ASSIGNMENT 5: PRINTING YOUR OWN FAMILY INFORMATION

1. Using the source notes and free-form notes you entered in Assignment 4, print out a Family Group Record, including all notes.

2. Print a copy of your Pedigree Chart.

3. Print an alphabetical list of all individuals in your family database.

YOUR TURN ANSWERS

Personal preferences are appropriate for all answers in this chapter.

COMPUTER CHECKLIST #5

1. Did you find all of the reports listed below, under #2, in your program? Make a list of the reports that are available in your program, in addition to those named under question #2.

2. For each report you have named in response to question #1, write down the computer command(s) necessary to access it.

   Pedigree Charts

   Family Group Sheets

   Descendant Charts or Trees

   Lists

   Research Tools (these vary greatly, depending on the program you are using, but they may include some of the following: date calculators, birthplace distribution lists, repository lists, soundex calculators, data error lists, etc.).

   Custom Reports

3. Locate the options in your program for printing to screen. What keystrokes must you use?

4. Locate the options in your program for printing to a disk or file. What key strokes must you use?

5. Locate the options in your program for printing to paper. What keystrokes must you use?

6. Can you change the font sizes? How do you do that?

7. What other reports can you print with your program? List them all.

WEB SITES

http://www.legacyfamilytree.com
This Web site provides information on the *Legacy*™ genealogy computer program.

http://www.parsonstech.com
This Web site provides information on the *Family Origins 8.0 Deluxe*™ genealogy computer program.

BIBLIOGRAPHY

Rodgers, Maxine. "Writing and Publishing Family Histories." *Genealogical Journal* 15, no. 2 (1987): 50-66.

Check the manuals for the computer programs listed in the Bibliography at the end of Chapter 3.

CHAPTER 6

Your Family History Notebook

Rejoice, ye dead, where'er your spirits dwell,
Rejoice that yet on earth your fame is bright,
And that your names, remembered day and night,
Live on the lips of those who love you well.

—Robert Bridges

Now that you have printed out the materials from your first data-entry work, you will need a place to **archive** your personal family history materials. A simple three-ring binder system is quick and easy to put together and allows you to find anything in a matter of minutes if you are consistent in your filing strategies.

The purpose of this chapter is to instruct you on a unique filing system that caters to genealogy computer users who can have **RIN** numbers printed on their pages. Filing pages in numerical order is much faster than filing families (often with duplicate surnames and given names) in alphabetical order. Plus, each Family Group Record acts as a cross-index to other pages in the notebook as shown in Illustration 6-5, and the Pedigree Chart acts as a table of contents because of cross-referenced numbers printed on them (see Illustration 6-6).

YOUR FAMILY HISTORY NOTEBOOK AND FILING SYSTEM

You can easily create a Family History Notebook by following these simple steps:

Materials Needed

(How many you need will be determined by how much information you have gathered.) Begin by purchasing the following:

1 or 2 - Two-inch, three-ring binders with see-through covers
2 or 3 - Packages of colored index tabs (8 per package)
4 to 8 - Packages of clear index tabs (8 per package)

Terms to Understand

ar·chive - A place or collection containing records, documents, or other materials of historical interest; a repository for stored memories or information.

Terms to Understand

RIN - An abbreviation for Record Identification Number used in computer programs (e.g. *Personal Ancestral File*).

Illustration 6-1 Document Protectors

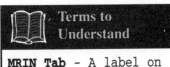
Terms to Understand

MRIN Tab - A label on a notebook separator used to divide one Family Group Record from another. Family Group Record Numbers are also called MRINs or Marriage Record Identification Numbers in genealogy computer programs.

In addition, you will need clear sheet protectors suitable for the three-ring binders to store documents. A three-hole punch will also facilitate the filing process.

YOUR TURN

1. Open the two-inch, three-ring binder.

2. Make a basic set of dividers using one package of colored index tabs. (As you need others you may add them, but A-E below provide a basic guide to your notebook(s) which will expand over the years.) Label them as follows:

   A. Research Planners (placed as a reminder to do them)

   B. Pedigree Charts

   C. Pedigree Chart Index

   D. Alphabetical Index (on some programs known as a Family Group Index)

   E. Descendancy Charts

3. Using clear index tab dividers, label them starting with the number 1 and going to at least the number 20.

You may soon have hundreds of Family Group Record (**MRIN**) **tabs**. CAUTION: *Do not try to outdo your computer program by trying to force these numbers to match a particular surname.* Just file the Family Group Record you have printed behind the MRIN tab to which it applies. (MRIN or Family Group Record 3 would be filed behind Tab 3.) You will have many more clear dividers than colored ones.

NOTE: *PAF* 4.0 no longer maintains the same MRIN numbers when you transfer data or upgrade. It is suggested that if you use this method of filing, you use the ID field to record the family MRIN.

A RULE OF THUMB

Break down documentation whenever you cannot find something quickly.

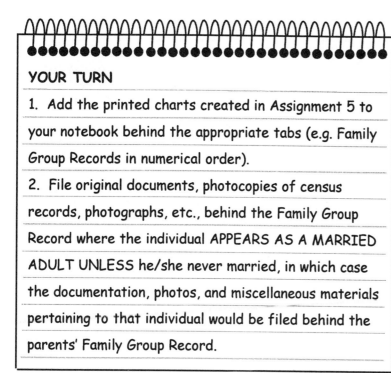

YOUR TURN

1. Add the printed charts created in Assignment 5 to your notebook behind the appropriate tabs (e.g. Family Group Records in numerical order).

2. File original documents, photocopies of census records, photographs, etc., behind the Family Group Record where the individual APPEARS AS A MARRIED ADULT UNLESS he/she never married, in which case the documentation, photos, and miscellaneous materials pertaining to that individual would be filed behind the parents' Family Group Record.

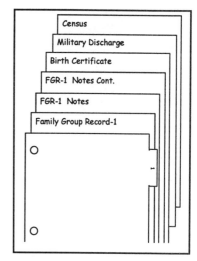

Illustration 6-2 Example of Pages Filed Behind an MRIN Tab

Miscellaneous completed Research Planners, abstracts, notes, copies, etc., that do *not* tie in at the moment to a specific Family Group Record, are filed under colored tabs behind the clear numbered tabs or in a separate three-ring notebook as your records expand. They are filed under surname tabs or locality subdivisions if there are too many to place under one surname. For example, a hundred pages of notes on CANNON families (some from Montgomery County, Virginia; some from Henry County, Virginia; and some Virginia with no county as yet known), could be filed behind tabs labeled *Cannon, Montgomery, VA; Cannon, Henry, VA;* and *Cannon, Virginia. Rule of thumb: break down documentation whenever you cannot find something quickly.*

Mixed surnames on the same page of a compiled history, a census or book index, and other combined locality sources would be kept under tabs by locality (e.g. NC, Hyde Co, Histories). Once an item has been determined to apply solely to one Family Group Record, however, file it behind that record so you can find the information on each person quickly.

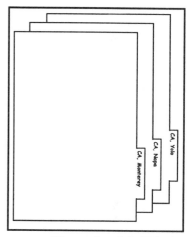

Illustration 6-3 Tabs by Counties Filed Behind MRIN Tabs or . . .

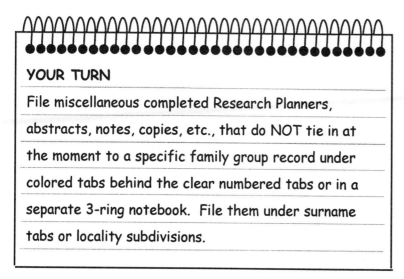

YOUR TURN

File miscellaneous completed Research Planners, abstracts, notes, copies, etc., that do NOT tie in at the moment to a specific family group record under colored tabs behind the clear numbered tabs or in a separate 3-ring notebook. File them under surname tabs or locality subdivisions.

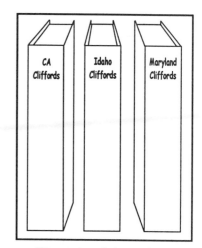

Illustration 6-4 . . . Separate Notebooks for Miscellaneous Papers

Terms to Understand

Name Sort·ed Lists - Groups of individuals arranged in various ways by given name or surname, in order to accomplish some purpose such as locating and separating into two groups a similar surname. For example, all the American-born side of the family called themselves Kampsula, while the Finnish-born side called themselves Kamsula (see Illustrations 6-5 and 6-6).

A computer-generated family history notebook is arranged so that you can quickly locate not only direct-line families but collateral lines and those not related (as yet) individuals who are in the process of being researched. *Your computer program cannot assist in your analysis if it doesn't have all the facts.* Therefore, don't forget to add everyone to your database from your family materials.

The reports filed behind the first five colored tabs act as a guide to all family groups in your Family History. As thousands of names are added to the Family History, you will find that many people have the same names. This is why it is so helpful for the computer to automatically assign the RIN to each person. (The RIN number is to the right of the individual's name in *PAF*.) The program can also produce **Name Sorted Lists** to help you keep track of the individuals you have entered into your program, their birth and death years, and their spouse or parents' names.

Also, as people are connected to families, an MRIN is assigned to each family. This number becomes the Family Group Record number as well. The families in your notebook are in numerical order, according to their Family Group Record (also known as MRIN). This MRIN number is given directly to the right of the marriage date in the Pedigree Chart in *PAF* (see Illustration 6-6). So, for example, if you wish to locate the brothers or sisters of any direct-line individual, all you need to do is turn to the clear tab which has the same number as that listed across from the marriage date on the Pedigree Chart.

YOUR TURN

File the appropriate forms behind the appropriate tabs (e.g., Pedigree Charts behind the colored Pedigree Chart tab).

A. Research Planners

B. Pedigree Charts

C. Pedigree Chart Index

D. Alphabetical Index

E. Descendancy Charts

PEDIGREE CHARTS

Pedigree Charts list in order the parents, grandparents, great-grandparents, etc., as far as is known for the person listed as #1 (to the left of the name) on Pedigree Chart #1. See Illustration 6-7.

Every person on the chart is given a chart number, which is to the left of the person's name. So person #1's maternal grandfather would be 6. Person #1's father would be 2. The blank chart, prenumbered, would look like Illustration 6-7.

As individual families go beyond the four generations found on the standard Pedigree Chart (or in other words, beyond #1's great-grandparents), a new chart is assigned for each great-grandparent. Now person #8 will be found on Chart No. 2, person #9 on Chart No. 3, etc. The chart number is indicated in the upper right-hand corner.

MRIN (Marriage Record Identification Number)

Family Group Record- 4

Page 1 of 2

Husband	**Andrew KAMPSULA-8**		
Born	5 Feb 1889	Place	Ishpeming, Marquette, Michigan
Died	13 Dec 1939	Place	Hopewell, Yamhill, Oregon
Buried		Place	Portland, Multnomah, Oregon
Married	1910	Place	Homestead Twp, Otter Tail, Minnesota
Husband's father	Herman Anterspoika KAMSULA-21		
Husband's mother	Hilma Kallentytar Walitalo WALIMAA-22		

How many pages in this particular Family Group Record

MRIN of Husband's Parents

MRIN: 8

Wife	**Ida Maria TASKINEN-116**		
Born	18 Sep 1887	Place	, Kivennapa, Viipuri, Finland
Died	6 Feb 1949	Place	Portland, Multnomah, OR
Buried	9 Feb 1949	Place	Portland, Multnomah, OR
Wife's father	Benjam Juhonpoika TASKINEN-36		
Wife's mother	Hilda Maria Nikodemusdotter POLVI-37		

MRIN of Wife's Parents

MRIN: 32

Children   List each child in order of birth.

1	M	**Andrew Raymond KAMPSULA-9**		
	Born	14 Jun 1913	Place	Homestead Twp, Otter Tail, Minnesota
	Died	5 May 1957	Place	Tieton, , Washington
	Buried		Place	Terrace Heights, Yakima, WA

2	M	**Alfred Filmore KAMPSULA-11**		
	Born	13 Mar 1917	Place	New York Mills, Ottertail, Minnesota
	Died	28 Nov 1985	Place	Vancouver, Clark, Washington
	Buried	3 Dec 1985	Place	Woodland, Cowlitz, Washington

3	F	**Lilian Victoria KAMPSULA-12**		
	Born	2 Mar 1919	Place	Newton, Otter Tail, Minnesota
	Died	28 Dec 1963	Place	, , Idaho
	Buried	Jan 1964	Place	New York Mills, Otter Tail, Minnesota
		Harold Jacob PERALA-177		
	Married	Abt 1937 (Div)	Place	, , MN

Child's position in this family

MRIN: 10

RIN (Record Identification Number)

4	F	**Edla Veneda KAMPSULA-13**		
	Born	2 May 1921	Place	Homestead Twp, Otter Tail, Minnesota
	Died	25 Jan 1963	Place	Homestead Twp, Otter Tail, Minnesota
	Buried	1963	Place	Homestead Twp, Otter Tail, Minnesota
	Spouse	Wayne Waino Arnold KUUKAS-122		
	Married	22 Jun 1945	Place	, Ottertail, MN

MRIN: 13

5	M	**Bruno Benjamin KAMPSULA-2**		
	Born	22 Feb 1924	Place	Homestead Twp, Otter Tail, Minnesota
	Died	13 Aug 1993	Place	Vancouver, Clark, WA
	Spouse	Lempi Hellena LEHTO-3		
	Married	1945 (Div)	Place	Vancouver, Clark, Washington

MRIN of this child and his spouse

MRIN: 2

Name, address and phone number of family representative

Prepared by	John Smith	Address	1234 Some Road
Phone	555-111-4444		Any City, GA 23423
Date prepared	02 Aug 1999		

Illustration 6-5 Completed Family Group Record Using PAF 4.0

Pedigree Chart

Chart no. 1

8 Anders Johansson R KAMSULA-32
B: 26 Oct 1840
P: , Ylivieska, Oulu, Finland
M: 30 Dec 1862 - 22
P: , Ylivieska, Oulu, Finland
D:
P:

4 Herman Anterspoika KAMSULA-21
B: 29 Mar 1863
P: , Ylivieska, Oulu, Finland
M: 28 Sep 1884 - 8
P: Ylivieska, Oulu, Fnln
D: 30 May 1931
P: New York Mills, Ottertail, Minnesota

9 Gustava Henriksdr K KNUUTILA-33
B: 16 Aug 1844
P: , Ylivieska, Oulu, Finland
D:
P:

2 Andrew KAMPSULA-8
B: 5 Feb 1889
P: Ishpeming, Marquette, Michigan
M: 1910 - 4
P: Homestead Twp, Otter Tail, Minnesota
D: 13 Dec 1939
P: Hopewell, Yamhill, Oregon

10 Kalle Kallenpoika H WALITALO-147
B: 25 Aug 1833
P: , Ylivieska, Oulu, Finland
M: Abt 1854 - 23
P: Ylivieska, Oulu, Fnln
D: 28 Dec 1882
P: , Ylivieska, Oulu, Finland

5 Hilma Kallentytar W WALIMAA-22
B: 5 Jun 1862
P: , Ylivieska, Oulu, Finland
D: 8 Sep 1921
P: Brainard, Crow Wing, Minnesota

11 Johanna Gustafva HENRIKSDR-148
B: 29 Jul 1834
P: , Ylivieska, Oulu, Finland
D: 26 Jul 1885
P: , Ylivieska, Oulu, Finland

1 Alfred Filmore KAMPSULA-11
B: 13 Mar 1917
P: New York Mills, Ottertail, Minnesota
M:
P:
D: 28 Nov 1985
P: Vancouver, Clark, Washington

(Spouse of no. 1)

12 Johan Thomasson TASKINEN-67
B: 9 Jun 1844
P: Terijoki No 4, Kivennapa, Viipuri, Finland
M: 1863 - 33
P: Terijoki, Kivennapa, Viipuri, Finland
D:
P:

6 Benjam Juhonpoika TASKINEN-36
B: 15 Mar 1867
P: Kivennapa, Viipuri, Finland
M: 16 Oct 1886 - 32
P: Kivennapa, Viipuri, Finland
D: 18 Oct 1946
P: Portland, Multnomah, OR

13 Lovisa Johansdotter KORKKINEN-68
B: 21 Aug 1843
P: , Oulu, Finland
D:
P:

3 Ida Maria TASKINEN-116
B: 18 Sep 1887
P: , Kivennapa, Viipuri, Finland
D: 6 Feb 1949
P: Portland, Multnomah, OR

14 Nikodemus Henriksson K POLVI-72
B: 3 Mar 1842
P: Ojakyla, Ylivieska, Oulu, Finland
M: 17 Oct 1862 - 34
P: Ylivieska, Oulu, Fnln
D:
P: , Ylivieska, Oulu, Finland

7 Hilda Maria Nikodemusdotter POLVI-37
B: 5 Jun 1869
P: Ylivieska, Oulu, Finland
D: 31 Jan 1942
P: Portland, Multnomah, Oregon

15 Brita Maja Eriksdotter SOMEROJA-73
B: 24 Jun 1841
P: Ojakyla, Ylivieska, Oulu, Finland
D:
P:

Prepared by
John Smith
1234 Some Road
Any City, GA   23423

Telephone
555-111-4444

Date prepared
27 Aug 1999

Illustration 6-6 Completed Pedigree Chart Using PAF 4.0

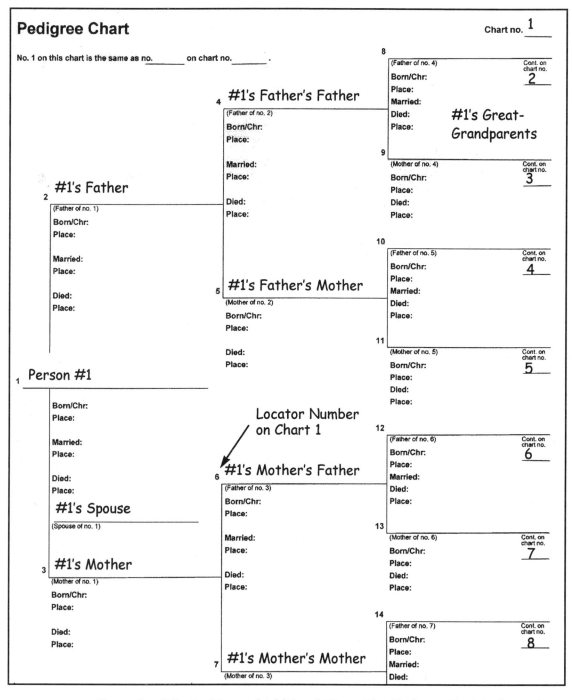

Illustration 6-7   Position and Additional Charts Identified on a Blank Pedigree Chart

PEDIGREE CHART INDEX

By the time you have traced a family back eight generations, there are 135 different surnames on the Pedigree Charts alone. Therefore, the next tab in the Family History is the Pedigree Chart Index. The names are given in alphabetical order on this index, and each Record Identification Number or RIN is shown immediately to the right of each person's name. Also the year they were either born or christened, died or buried is provided to help you select the person you are seeking.

The chart number is then listed, which is the number in the upper right-hand corner, as indicated in Illustrations 6-6 and 6-7. The person's number on that particular chart is then listed. Remember that the chart number appears to the left of the person's name, while the RIN number is to the right of the name.

Finally, the person's parents' Family Group Record number, or MRIN, is given to aid you in locating further information. In some computer programs, such as *PAF 4.0*, the Pedigree Chart default option is set not to print the index. Therefore, it won't even show as an option unless you go into your Report options and change that default.

Name	RIN	Born/ Chr	Died/ Bur	Chart Number	Person Number	Parent MRIN
BROWN, John E.	421	1854	1921	1	5	4
CHATWIN, William	13	1902	1992	1	3	2

Illustration 6-8 Pedigree Chart Index

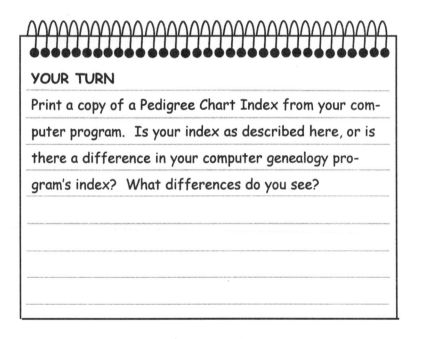

YOUR TURN

Print a copy of a Pedigree Chart Index from your computer program. Is your index as described here, or is there a difference in your computer genealogy program's index? What differences do you see?

ALPHA INDEX OR FAMILY GROUP SORTED LIST

If there are 135 parents and grandparents by the time only eight generations are listed, you can imagine how many aunts, uncles, cousins, brothers, sisters and in-laws are included. Fortunately, an easy-to-use, every-name index is available. It has different names in different programs, such as Alphabetical Index, or Family Group Sorted List.

Since all of your direct-line people, as well as the majority of your collateral lines, will appear on at least two Family Group Records, one as a child and one as a parent, this list can help locate them.

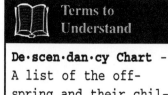

Terms to Understand

De·scen·dan·cy Chart - A list of the off-spring and their children for one particular individual.

YOUR TURN

Print a copy of an Alphabetical Index from your

genealogy computer program.

DESCENDANCY CHART

While Pedigree Charts list everyone from the present person back to the earliest ancestor, **Descendancy Charts** start with the earliest ancestor on a line and go to the present. All related people in the computer files are included, such as nieces, nephews, step-children, etc. On a Descendancy Chart, a person's RIN is given to the right on *PAF 4.0* and those programs using the same option, but the birth, christening, or death date is also given (e.g., PERSON-875 as shown in Illustration 6-9.)

To the left of each name on a Descendancy Chart is a number indicating what generation removed an individual is from the starting ancestor. (Note: The letters "sp" mean "Spouse.") Many of these charts, such as those in the *Family Tree Maker 5.0* (and higher) programs, can be customized to contain as much information (including the birth, marriage, and death dates and locations) as you desire.

```
                    DESCENDANCY CHART

Date Chart Printed                        Page of Chart
---------------------------------------------------------
1-- Oldest PERSON-989 (1669)
   2-- Oldest Person's Eldest SON-877 (1695)
   sp-Oldest Person's Eldest Son's WIFE-876 (1698)
      3-- Oldest Person's GRANDSON-875 (1740)
      sp- Grandson's WIFE-945 (1745)
         4-- Oldest Person's Grandson's DAUGHTER-766 (1771)
         4-- Oldest Person's Grandson's 2nd DAUGHTER-767 (1773)
      3-- Oldest Person's 2nd GRANDSON-876 (1742)
```

Illustration 6-9 Descendancy Chart Printout

(This would continue for as many generations as you wish, or to the end of the computer genealogy program's files.)

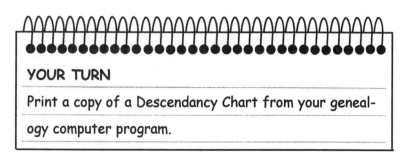

YOUR TURN

Print a copy of a Descendancy Chart from your geneal-

ogy computer program.

Once you have this printed out, it would complete the files to be placed behind the five colored tab indexes at the front of the Family History Notebook (see Illustration 6-11). Let us now look at the Family Group Record layout.

FAMILY GROUP RECORDS

As you can see in Illustration 6-5, Family Group Records contain many numbers. These allow for an easy cross-reference to any other record in the collection. See if you have discovered the key to using the numbers printed on the MRIN records, also known as Family Group Records.

YOUR TURN

Using Illustration 6-5, identify the following:

1. The MRIN for this family is number _____.

2. The Andrew Kampsula, who was born in 1889, has a Record Identification Number of _____.

3. The Andrew Kampsula, who was born in 1889, is the son of _____.

4. The Andrew Kampsula, who was was born in 1889, would be found as a child on MRIN number _____.

5. Ida Maria Taskinen would be found as a child on MRIN _____.

6. Edla Veneda Kampsula, RIN 13, would be found with her husband on MRIN _____.

7. Bruno Benjamin Kampsula, RIN _____, would be found with his wife on MRIN _____.

8. Who is the wife of husband of Edla Veneda Kampsula? _____

Also, you may have noticed that much more room is allowed for each location field so words do not have to be truncated as they might need to be on Pedigree Charts. The biggest advantage to Family Group Records is the opportunity to print out all your source notes, comments, and TO DO lists. (See Illustration 6-10.)

Family Group Record

Husband

ANDREW KAMPSULA

Wife

IDA MARIA TASKINEN

Notes

Andrew Kampsula provided the date and place of his birth on his children's birth certificates. His parents were recent immigrants from Finland when he was born in Ispeming, which is located in the upper peninsula of the state of Michigan, in the county of Marquette. There his father worked in the lumber and mining industries as he waited to become a U.S. citizen so he could apply for a Homestead. His parents were located on the following U.S. federal census records:

1900 CENSUS: Minnesota, Otter Tail Co, Homestead Twp, T-1053-85 Vol 39 Ed 144, line 12, sheet 5:

Andrew Kampsula, son, white, male, born Mar 1890, age 10, single, born Michigan, Fa born Finland, Mo born Finland.

1910 CENSUS: Minnesota, Otter Tail Co, Homestead Twp, ED #9, sheet 3A:

Andrew Kampsula, age 21, single, born Michigan, parents born Finland, occupation farm work, home farmer.

His marriage information came from the personal knowledge of Alma Niemela, Andrew's sister who was present at his wedding in Herman Kampsula's home. They were married by Rev. Nissila. The marriage record is stored in a bank vault in New York Mills, Minnesota, in custody of the Apostolic Lutheran Church, but I have not been able to get permission to look at it.

I wrote the family history of Andrew Kampsula with that of his son, Bruno. But one little glimpse into his life from that book was that Andrew would dance around with Ida, his wife, if she was mad at him to get her over the anger. Ida had a stroke when the children were young which paralyzed her face. She later recovered. Andrew was very mild mannered. Ida did the disciplining. Andrew died of lung cancer in Portland, Oregon, just months after moving there from Minnesota, on the advice of doctors. He was buried at the Lincoln Memorial Cemetery in Portland, where his wife, his daughter-in-law, Helen, and other members of his extended family are also buried.

TO DO

1. Pull in the family history stories from the previously published works into this database.
2. Locate pictures of Ishpeming, Michigan.
3. See if the Lutheran marriage certificate can now be obtained.

Illustration 6-10 A Printout of Family Group Record Notes

ta·ble of con·tents - Provides a listing of the chapters or other divisions at the front of a book, database, or other compilation, along with locator guides, such as page numbers.

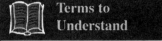

an·ces·try - The people from whom you are descended, i.e., your parents and grandparents.

Terms to Understand

Ahnen·ta·fel Charts - Lists of direct-line ancestors displayed by generation in a basic numbering formula, in which an individual's paternal (father's) lines are two times the number of the child, and the maternal (mother's) lines are two times plus one the number of the child. The word Ahnentafel comes from a German word meaning "Ancestor Table."

OTHER TABS

For research purposes, many other charts and forms are possible, but they may or may not be included in your "**Table of Contents**" in the front of your personal Family History Notebook. Some charts would include:

Ancestry Wall Chart
Ahnentafel Chart
Place Sorted Index
RIN Numbers in Order
MRIN Numbers in Order
Individuals with Notes
End-of-Line Individuals
Possible Data Entry Problems
Duplicate Individuals
Surname Frequencies
Incomplete Ordinance Forms

YOUR TURN

Experiment with your computer program by printing out various formats and filing them, as directed above.

CONCLUSION

There are a great variety of forms which may be created by you, the genealogy computer operator, to help visualize or solve research problems. Also, many documents, lists, notes, letters, etc. contain information that involve many families that are of the same surname, or that are connected to that surname by marriage, geography, religion, etc. These are filed at the back of the last section (or volume, if you have that many family records) behind the Family Group Records (see Illustration 6-11). When necessary, due to the volume of information you have collected, you can break down materials even further into smaller units, such as a particular surname in one state or one county as shown in Illustration 6-4. These surname tabs are also colored, so that you can locate information easily.

This Family History Notebook will be constantly expanding. Not only will it record ancestors long gone, it will record more recent events. It is a good idea to periodically update the information in your binder(s), as people are born, pass away, marry or move. Just pencil the information in as you learn about it and later update your files.

Now, take all the information completed in the YOUR TURN sections and assemble your Family History Notebook, as explained in Assignment 6, and label the spines with the number of MRINs included in that volume as shown in Illustration 6-11 inset.

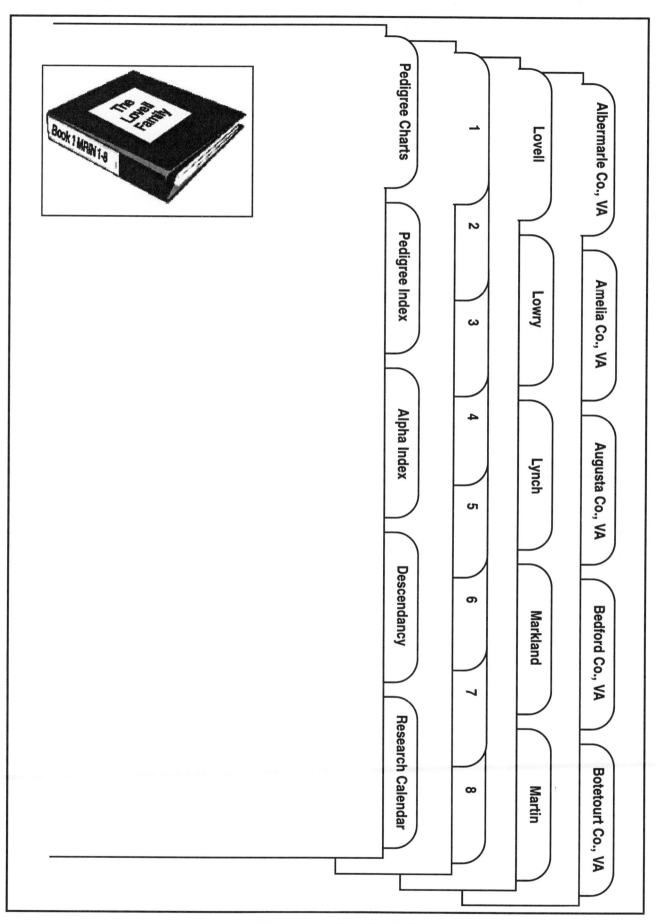

Illustration 6-11 A Family History Notebook (inset) with Labeled Tabs

ASSIGNMENT 6: ASSEMBLING YOUR FAMILY HISTORY NOTEBOOK

1. File your Family Group Records, the documentation pages, copies of documents, pictures, and originals (in acrylic sleeves) behind the appropriate clear Family Group Record tab in the family history notebook according to chapter instructions. Each Family Group Record is filed behind its own MRIN number, which cross-indexes to each other record.

2. File the Pedigree Charts, Pedigree Chart Index, and miscellaneous surname materials, as indicated in Chapter 6, behind their appropriate colored tabs.

3. Make a title page to slip behind the clear cover of the notebook, and then make a spine cover to indicate the Family Group Record series that appear in this notebook. You may be very creative in designing your own personal cover. Don't forget to add your own name as the compiler.

YOUR TURN ANSWERS

Analyzing the Family Group Records

Page 6-10 answers:

1. The MRIN for this family is number 4.
2. The Andrew Kampsula who was born in 1889 has a Record Identification Number of 8.
3. Andrew Kampsula born in 1889 is the son of Herman Anterspoika KAMSULA and Hilma Kallentytar Talitalo WALIMAA.
4. Andrew Kampsula born in 1889 would be found as a child on MRIN 8.
5. Ida Maria Taskinen born in 1887 would be found as a child on MRIN 32.
6. Edla Veneda Kampsula, RIN 13, would be found with her husband on MRIN 13.
7. Bruno Benjamin Kampsula, RIN 2, would be found with his wife on MRIN 2.
8. Who is the husband of Edla Veneda Kampsula? Wayne Waino Arnold KUUKAS.

COMPUTER CHECKLIST #6

1. Computer programs can produce various reports that help in the filing and
    retrieval process. Look at your program for such options, and list them here.

2. Describe how each one can help you.

WEB SITE

http://www.whollygenes.com
This Web site presents information on the genealogy computer program known as
The Master Genealogist.

BIBLIOGRAPHY

Ames, Stanley Richard. *How to Write and Publish Your Family History Using WordPerfect® DOS Versions 5.1 and 6.0.* Interlaken, New York: Heart of the Lakes Publishing, 1994.

CHAPTER 7

Developing a Sense of Our Ancestors' Environment

A normal adult never stops to think about problems of space and time. These are things which he has thought about as a child. But my intellectual development was retarded, as a result of which I began to wonder about space and time only when I had already grown up.

—Albert Einstein

Genealogists, it turns out, also think a lot about space and time. Like Einstein, we continue to wonder about who we are, where we came from, and what forces of time and space came together to create us and our current **environment.** We understand that our lives and the lives of our ancestors are both the creations of our history and the creators of history for the next generation.

In addition, as we learn more about who our ancestors were and how they lived, we come face-to-face with this great truth of history: *history is the product of the relationship between time and events, in sequence.* The challenge for us as genealogists is to uncover that relationship and the way it functions in the lives of our ancestors. And when we begin to follow the clues to our ancestors' lives, we may discover a sequence which is a simple chronology—a puzzle easily solved. On the other hand, those clues may lead us to a complicated cause-effect scenario, complete with genuine mysteries, fascinating stories, and surprises we never dreamed of.

> ### Terms to Understand
>
> **en·vi·ron·ment** - The circumstances and complex social and cultural conditions that surround an individual.

> ### Terms to Understand
>
> **se·quence** - The following of one thing after another; an arrangement that is related or continuous.

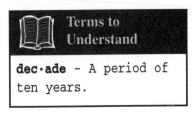

Terms to Understand

dec·ade - A period of ten years.

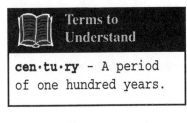

Terms to Understand

cen·tu·ry - A period of one hundred years.

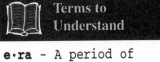

Terms to Understand

e·ra - A period of time as reckoned from a specific date, which serves as the basis of a chronological system.

Terms to Understand

Pre-Rev·o·lu·tion·ar·y per·iod - American history prior to 1776.

Terms to Understand

ma·ter·nal - Related through one's mother.

MAPPING YOUR ANCESTORS' LIVES

Einstein wouldn't be a bit surprised to learn that, in order to discover the events in our ancestors' lives, it is necessary for us to develop two key traits: a sense of historical time and a meaningful knowledge of historical periods.

If you can determine the basic time concepts, such as the year, the **decade,** and the **century** that included the events in your ancestors' lifetime, then capture the historical events of that **era** on paper, you will be able to use this information to help plot, or map, your family's activities.

Such a study is made easier by the fact that certain periods in time are naturally divided by historical events. The most significant of these for U.S. researchers include the **pre-Revolutionary** period, the Westward Movement, the Civil War era, the two world wars, and the Great Depression; in fact, you may already know about the effects of one or more of these events on your own family. Since trade, travel, education, and the price and availability of real estate are affected by great historical events, and each individual family is therefore affected to some degree by these forces, you can see that it's important to understand the events that occurred during the times in which your family was living.

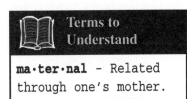

YOUR TURN

In order to make good use of the ideas you jotted down as you did your data entry and to add to your "TO DO" lists, here are examples of the kinds of questions a good researcher should ask.

What do you really know, for example, about the place your **maternal** grandfather was born? You were told he was born in such and such state, but in what town? In fact, what do you know about all of the people who appear on your Pedigree Chart? What has been substantiated in your family history? Begin the process of substantiating the facts in your family history by writing down one thing that you do not know about a geographical locale for one of your ancestors.

The development of such a sense of geography and chronology begins at a very basic level—we must constantly evaluate and re-evaluate our information. For example, think about what you know about the geographic locality of all those ancestors you have entered on your Pedigree Chart. If your answer is "Not much," or "Those details didn't seem very important," then you need to pay particular attention to the next exercises.

Most of the time, records are filed, catalogued and located at the *county level* in the United States with the exception of **independent cities**–such as Richmond, Virginia, and towns within the New England states (Massachusetts, Connecticut, Rhode Island, Vermont, Maine, and New Hampshire.) Therefore, you need to know the county jurisdictions in non-New England states and you need to know the towns in the New England states. Other countries have similar procedures. In the British Isles, Europe, Mexico, South America, and Scandinavia, for example, you must identify a parish or village name because vital records and church records are kept at the local level. Road **atlases,** maps (both current and historical), and **gazetteers** are all methods whereby we can find the names of counties and towns as they exist today.

YOUR TURN

Have you listed the county (or county equivalent, if you are researching in a foreign country) for every locality on your Pedigree Chart? Using an atlas, map, or gazetteer, locate the names of the counties and/or towns where an ancestor's birth, marriage or death event occurred. Use the jurisdiction that existed during the time of the event. What localities have you been able to add?

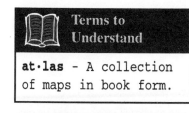

Terms to Understand

in·de·pend·ent cit·ies - Cities which are self-governing and free from affiliation or control by a county jurisdiction.

Terms to Understand

at·las - A collection of maps in book form.

Terms to Understand

gaz·et·teer - A geographical dictionary or index; which contains word descriptions of localities, including population, distance from large towns, how to get there, what the town is known for, etc.

Terms to Understand

post·al di·rec·to·ry - A book containing an alphabetical listing of post offices.

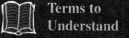

Terms to Understand

ship·ping guide - A book containing an alphabetical listing of places to which items could be transported by wagon, ship, train, etc.

Perhaps the map you consulted does not show the town in question. At times like this, a **postal directory** or **shipping guide** is helpful because they list all of the little localities that are not listed on maps. We must once again re-evaluate the county formation date for the location we have just obtained. For example, if you were to look at a map or gazetteer for a particular locality, published close to the time of the event you are researching (these are also known as historical maps and gazetteers, if they were made to show an earlier time period), you might find that the locality name has changed. This is very common everywhere, and yet records are kept at their original point of creation.

Since many place-names have changed over the years, there are several resources for obtaining the original name for a locality. *The Handy Book for*

YOUR TURN

Were the counties and towns you recorded on your Pedigree Chart actually in existence at the time of the birth, marriage, or death events? List an event (birth, marriage, or death) for one of your grandparents or great grandparents and include the name of the location at the time of that event using the sources just mentioned.

Genealogists, the *Map Guide to the U. S. Federal Censuses, 1790-1920,* and *Ancestry's Red Book* are three basic genealogy books which provide this information.

Once you find the name of the county where an event occurred, you must find out from which other county it may have been formed. This original county is called the "parent" county. If the parent county was formed after the date of the event, then you must look at the county from which that parent was formed and so forth until both the county and date range match. In the documentation area of your genealogy computer program that is connected with the person you are researching, or on a copy of the print-out for that person (to be data entered later), you should enter or write a note about the county's formation, so you will not have to look it up again. If you have no idea where your relative came from, consider who else in your family might have that information and record that information on your "TO DO" list.

YOUR TURN

In the documentation area of your genealogy computer program connected with the person you are researching, enter or write a note about the county's formation for the event in the previous "Your Turn" assignment.

Becoming a Better Family Historian

Have you noticed that the terms "genealogy" and "family history studies" have been used rather interchangeably thus far? Many people do not know the meaning of the word *genealogy* and this can cause a great deal of misunderstanding. The following incident happened a few years ago, but it is a perfect illustration of the kind of thing that can happen.

We had arranged for commercial bus transportation, and the driver had been notified to pick up fifty enthusiastic genealogists at 7:00 a.m. sharp for a field trip to various repositories. Many of these family historians were elderly, and they gingerly stepped aboard the bus with briefcases, totebags, and notebooks in hand. Because they were dressed for speed and efficiency at the repositories we were visiting, some wore cobbler's aprons, some had on sleeve guards, and some sported fanny packs.

Our driver, I later discovered, had misunderstood the communication involving who he was picking up. He thought we were "geologists" and was amazed at the agility of the group of "rock collectors" who boarded his bus, as well as at their attire. But imagine our driver's confusion when he heard, "I hired a professional to eliminate one of my grandparents. He charged me $3,000. One thousand dollars for the report and $2,000 to have it hushed up."

After a chuckle, another "geologist" retorted, "I've been trying unsuccessfully to dig up my great-grandfather for over twenty years. Do you think they'll have him at Sutro Library?" And across the aisle, someone leaned over and asked me, "Karen, if you'll run down the Wheelers, I'll pay you double."

By this point, our driver must have thought he was chauffeuring a busload of desperadoes. After the bus pulled up in front of San Francisco's wonderful Sutro Library, the driver expressed his confusion, and we all had a good laugh over the misunderstanding. But it was quite understandable. There are always new words and phrases when you approach a new field of study.

In Chapter 1, we briefly looked at the distinction between the terms genealogy, with its greatest concern being primarily kinship and matters of descent, and family history, which we consider an extension of genealogy, but with more depth. "Meat on the bones," is what we called it. As you move back in time in your family history studies, you will be continually confronted with terms and localities of which you may not be aware. The personal family historian is interested in all aspects of time and place that affect his subjects. He or she doesn't just identify ancestors. The family historian tries to answer why they did what they did, where they went, what routes they took to get there, the political conditions of the time and place, and other seemingly insignificant aspects of the environment, such as words that were common but are unusual to us (this is why a good dictionary becomes invaluable). You begin to see that people, places, their language and customs really are inseparable. This is why it is so important to obtain an environmental perspective on our ancestors' lives.

YOUR TURN

Look at Illustration 7-1, "Environmental Influences on Research," and ponder the history surrounding the individual you selected to study for the previous two "Your Turn" assignments.

1. What world, national, state, county or local events were impacting upon his or her life?

2. Could these events provide clues to further research? Identify two areas of research that you can add to your TO DO list, as a result.

3. Might these same events have impacted upon his neighbors? How?

4. If one individual's records were lost, could not his neighbor's records provide insights? If so, how?

A GEOGRAPHICAL PERSPECTIVE

While history provides part of the background to a person's life, geography provides an even clearer picture. For example, knowing that rivers were the early "highways" of this nation, and that they were probably one of the ways your ancestors traveled, makes knowing their whereabouts important. Why? Because the records providing clues about your ancestors will be found among the documents originally recorded along the banks of these well-traveled rivers, and such original sources may be only counties removed from where you know your ancestor lived.

ENVIRONMENTAL INFLUENCES ON RESEARCH

	INFLUENCES	IMPLICATION ON RESEARCH
	TOPOGRAPHY Land configurations, waterways, and geographic barriers affected settlement and movement of individuals.	Finding family dwellings and later migrations involves an understanding of specific geographical settings for families being studied.
	JURISDICTION The power, right or authority exercised by an individual or governing body, to legislate, interpret, and apply civil and religious law.	Civil and religious records are maintained by different jurisdictions. Knowing where to find these important genealogical records is half the battle in family history research.
	LIFE EVENTS Occurrences in most individual's lives involving their family, government, religion, social interactions, and private affairs.	Life events took place in specific jurisdictions, during specific time periods in the existence of individuals, and often involved other associates.
	TIME Life events occur during specific time periods. People marry at certain ages, have children soon thereafter, may serve in the military during certain time periods, etc.	Maintaining records chronologically, and comparing the results with history, directs the researcher to jurisdictional events, specific locations, and original records.
	HISTORY Accounts of many individual life events and individual involvement with others constitutes "history."	Studying the history of specific periods of time leads to associations, relatives, motives for movement, involvement in common enterprises, and new sources to search.

Illustration 7-1 Environmental Influences on Research

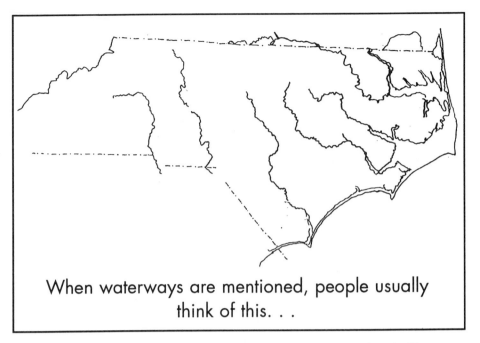

When waterways are mentioned, people usually think of this. . .

Illustration 7-2 Map with Simple Waterways

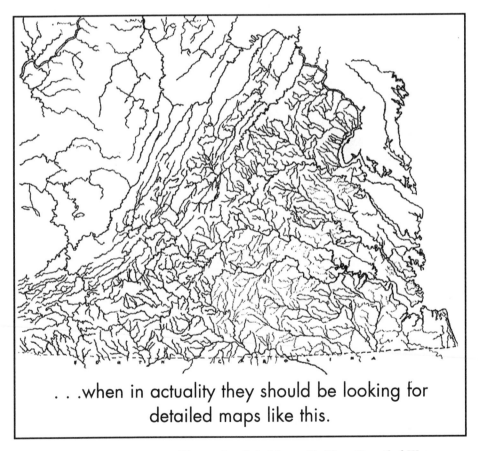

. . .when in actuality they should be looking for detailed maps like this.

Illustration 7-3 Map with More Detailed Waterways

People in the past were not very different from people today. If a town was closer to home, even if it was over the state line, it was probably the place where your ancestors' family shopped, attended church, or even filed property records. Similarly, if a mountain stood between their village and the next, your ancestors may have decided to travel by boat to a church in a neighboring parish, much further in miles, but quicker and easier to reach.

In addition, since people took the path of least resistance to handle their daily chores, these very movements may have contributed to actual jurisdictional changes in county and state boundaries. So while your ancestor may never have moved, his records might be found in several areas depending on the religious or political jurisdictions under which he lived. Consider this example from North Carolina, as described by historian Dr. Adelaide L. Fries, in writing about the Moravian community of Wachovia in North Carolina:

> The Moravians selected their lands in Anson County; they settled in Rowan County; they went through the Revolutionary War in Surry County; they lived through the War of 1812 and the Mexican War in Stokes County; they experienced the Civil War in Forsyth County—and they always stayed where they started! (Extracted from a letter dated April 17, 1941 from Adelaide L. Fries, Archivist, to Mrs. Braun.)

Finally, events played an important part in each person's life. The death of a spouse might cause a movement elsewhere. Wars, fires, floods, drought and hostile neighbors could provide a "push" away, while lower living costs, the promise of free land, or the encouragement of friends might have caused a "pull" to another area.

The Value of Maps

Where our ancestors were, *when* they were in a particular place, and *why* they were there all tell us a great deal about the conditions of their lives. And that is why, as genealogists, we must learn to think not only about time, but also about space. As a consequence, successful genealogists know that it's important to study geographical maps of the areas where our ancestors lived and traveled. Maps often provide us with "the picture that is" worth a thousand words, both in terms of the events and forces that motivated our ancestors.

Maps not only help us to understand movement patterns and interpersonal relationships, but they also help us to recognize the significance of causes and effects, both in terms of geography and in terms of the times in which they were living. But first, you must know what to look for in the maps you are studying, and you must find maps that reflect the period you are interested in.

It's important to look first at a map's **legend** in order to understand the distance between the localities being examined. That information can then be combined with what we know about the modes of travel available at the time, along with a sense of the speed of that travel. As you study maps for clues, be sure to watch for features of the landscape that might also have *facilitated travel*— canals, navigable rivers and railroads, for example. While it may appear at first glance that the Hartmann and Young families couldn't possibly have met in 1852 because one family lived in New York and the other in Ohio, a quick map study will tell you that the two states are actually less than fifty miles apart at one point. In addition, a researcher who consults a map can see at a glance that Ohio and New York are connected by the nineteenth century's version of a freeway--a navigable waterway. And since the Hartmanns lived in the northeast corner of Ohio and the Youngs lived in the far northwest corner of New York, both along the shore of Lake Erie, our researcher would be able to see right away that a meeting between members of the two families was entirely possible.

Terms to Understand

leg·end - Definition of symbols listed on a map.

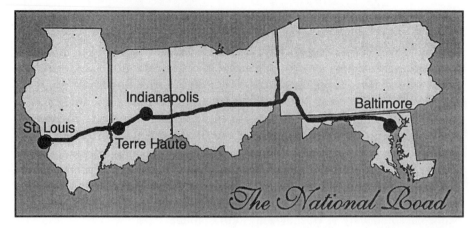

Illustration 7-4   Map of the National Road

Similarly, you will also need to look for mountains, rivers, or other natural *barriers to common travel.* As an example, let's take a look at the Thompsons and Odells whose Western North Carolina villages appear to lie only ten miles apart. In this case, a researcher can't assume that the two families could meet in the middle, since a closer study of the map will reveal a high and densely forested range of mountains between the two villages. As a consequence, travel from the Odells' village to the Thompsons' village would have required a journey *around* the mountains and rivers--over 150 miles.

But our ancestors were not so easily discouraged. When the opportunity to trade or the chance to settle on new land presented itself, people found alternate routes around the obstructions, and this is why information about routes, such as navigable rivers, valleys, mountain passes and coastal routes is important for us to know about. The road to Pittsburgh, for example, became a major artery of travel, and its value to travelers was increased by the easy descent of the Ohio River. And the National Road (also called the Cumberland), which ascended the Potomac in Maryland, extended across southern Ohio and ended at Vandalia, Illinois, provided one of the shortest routes to the west. As a result, the National Road was one of the most heavily traveled routes in the nineteenth century. When it came to travel, then, our hardy ancestors were not very different from people today. They followed the easiest, safest, fastest routes they could find, just as we do, and as a result, most people crowded on to the same rivers and roads, just as we do today.

YOUR TURN

1. On a contemporary map, locate the path of the National Road.

   a. What is it called today?

   b. Through what states does it pass?

2. Locate the Ohio River.

   a. Through what cities does it pass?

   b. Where does it end?

3. What does this tell you about its importance as a major route of travel?

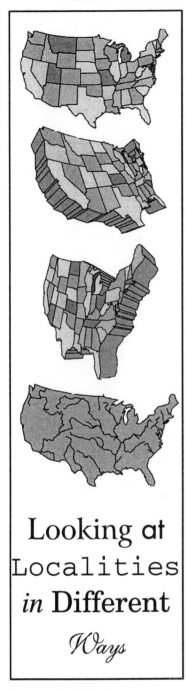

Looking at Localities *in* Different *Ways*

Illustration 7-5 Looking at Localities in Different Ways

On the Hunt for the Vanishing Ancestors . . .

Although each of our ancestors' moves from one place to another presents new challenges, the fact that people traveled the same routes may make it easier to trace their journeys, even across the continent. Let's imagine that your ancestors disappeared from Pennsylvania after one census and turned up on a land record in Illinois, six years later. Knowing this much, you can be pretty sure that they followed a proven route, like the National Road, to reach their goal. So when you're trying to figure out where your ancestors might have been in the years between the Pennsylvania census and the Illinois land purchase, the most likely places to look would be along one of those heavily traveled routes.

The Effectiveness of Maps

One reason maps are so effective is that the information they provide can be more appealing and easier to understand than pages of text. When maps are accurate, they provide a maximum amount of information in a minimum amount of time. Historical maps and atlases are my favorites. They reduce the critical elements necessary for family history--events, time, and place, to an understandable conclusion.

Maps also show features that may have existed during key historical periods, but which no longer exist. An example is the network of canals that existed through much of the eastern U.S. At one time, it was possible to travel, using canals, from upstate New York to Southern Ohio. Yet if you look for those canals on a current map, you won't see them. With the advent of faster and cheaper modes of transportation, travel by canal fell out of favor and the canals fell into disrepair, so that only remnants of this great system remain. A good historical map would tell you about where this canal system was located and even provide the dates it was active. Therefore, information about your ancestors can actually be obtained from maps as they become sources of information as well as devices for understanding events.

Illustration 7-6 Map of New York Canals

Good maps portray changes such as migration, emigration, immigration, transportation, and the growth of towns. They provide an area for research, the shape of the land, and how its topography might affect movement and, thus, the locality of records. So a good map can provide not only a place for your research, but also insights into what that place is like. Since history is time in recorded sequence, maps illustrate an event before it happens and after it happens, and they help us to understand the consequence of various incidents. This is graphically illustrated by looking at the dramatic changes illustrated in a topographical map of Mt. St. Helens, before and after its 1980 eruption.

Some Historical Background

Some of the first maps produced on this continent were of the coastal areas, since ships plying the Atlantic between Europe and America provided the lifeline that kept isolated settlers connected to British and European civilization. In addition to the arrival of new settlers, goods of all kinds were shipped across the Atlantic, and they were paid for by the export of American furs and other natural resources.

Because ships and their cargo were so important to the fragile society in America, shipwrecks were disasters of major proportions, and those on both sides of the Atlantic were anxious to minimize the risks. So map makers were engaged, early in our history, to provide accurate maps to sailors so that ships could arrive safely. Imagine being commissioned to draw the coastline of America with none of the technology we have available today. This is why you may not find old maps of the area you are seeking without considerable, or at least directed, effort.

Away from the coast, early maps served dual purposes: military and political. George Washington, a surveyor himself, understood that accurate maps were important for military campaigns, and he used his knowledge during the Revolutionary War. While military mapping was not pursued with vigor until the Civil War, and while many small, local surveys were quietly being conducted as towns were established and public lands opened up, there were also some noted early survey projects: the Lewis and Clark explorations in 1803, the Zebulon Pike expedition to the Rocky Mountains in 1805, and several geologically-oriented field trips to the Ozark Mountains in the 1830s. In the 1850s, formal surveys for wagon roads, railroad routes to the Pacific and international boundaries were begun. During the Civil War, an unprecedented demand for maps strained the resources of the government. Defense surveys were performed around major northern cities, and they played important roles in Grant's campaign at Vicksburg and Sherman's march to the sea.

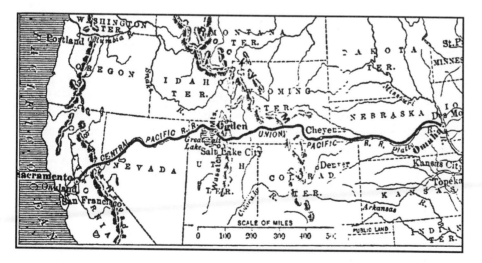

Illustration 7-7 The First Transcontinental Railroad, 1869

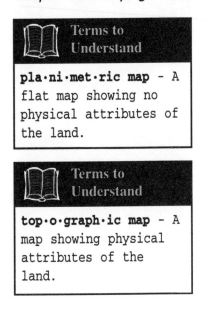

Terms to Understand

pla·ni·met·ric map - A flat map showing no physical attributes of the land.

Terms to Understand

top·o·graph·ic map - A map showing physical attributes of the land.

YOUR TURN

1. Choose a small town where your ancestors settled and write down the town, county, and state.

2. Now locate the town on a U.S. Geological Survey (USGS) or other topographical map. (Many such maps are available on the Internet: go to http://www.usgs.gov.)

3. Either make a photocopy, print it out, or describe in detail, giving the names of features such as lakes, hills, and other towns that are nearby.

Then, because of the westward migration following the Civil War, a great need arose for detailed information about the resources and natural features of the country. And as national, state and county boundaries changed, those, too, had to be mapped. In 1881, Congress authorized and financed a twenty-year program which, over time, became the U.S. Geological Survey. Having relatives engaged in engineering by the government, I've seen the equipment and pictures of the strenuous activities necessary to map this country.

Anyone involved in Tennessee research can tell you about the great changes brought about by the establishment of the Tennessee Valley Authority in 1933. But before those changes were put into effect, the government had to have map coverage of the entire area. **Planimetric** maps of the area, using five-lens aerial photographs and radial-line plotting methods, filled this need. **Topographic** and planimetric maps are very helpful for those doing Tennessee research.

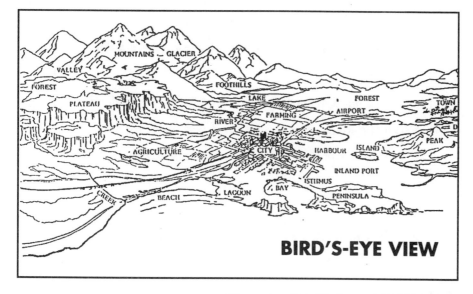

Illustration 7-8 Bird's-eye View Style Map

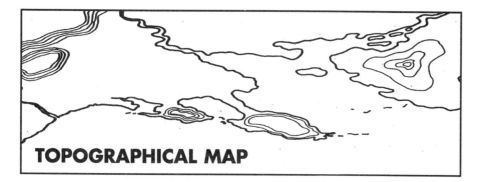

Illustration 7-9 Topographical Map

HOW TO USE MAPS EFFECTIVELY IN YOUR RESEARCH

In this section, we'll explore some of the ways that maps can provide a knowledge of topography, jurisdictions, historical background, and clues to available sources. No map on its own can provide all of the information you need to solve a specific genealogical problem, but your use of maps can become part of a back-and-forth, reciprocal process with original documents. Original documents, such as census, legal and church records, usually provide more substantive information. But maps act as invaluable guides to help us interpret the information we gather, just as our knowledge of the history of the place and era we're researching helps us interpret the information we find in maps.

Before you begin to study a map, *always* read the explanatory information provided about it. If the map has been published in a book, you will often find that information in the book's Foreword or Introduction. If the map is not part of a book, you will find the explanatory information located in one or more corners of the map itself along with the map's legend, scale and list of abbreviations.

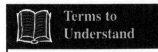

Terms to Understand

dem·o·graph·ic -
Relating to the study of the characteristics of human population, size, growth, density, distribution, and vital statistics.

YOUR TURN

Locate a good map of the United States and record below the kinds of information it provides, such as:

1. What features are shown in the legend?

2. What measures does it use for distance?

3. What other information does it provide?

Often, collections or series of maps cover specific topics, such as religious migrations, the historical background of a region, or occupations. These publications are filled with rich bibliographies of source materials which can aid the family historian in finding information and sources. Some maps are even developed with the help of **demographic** studies, and as part of the information they provide, contemporaries of your ancestors may be listed. Ultimately, *maps relinquish their secrets best to those who are best equipped to appreciate their information,* so the most powerful combination is the use of maps, historical texts, and original documents.

As a researcher, try to establish relationships between what you see on the map and what you know about an event. Make contrasts and comparisons. Seek to establish patterns of sequence and movement.

Maps Most Beneficial to Genealogists

There are several types of maps which are most beneficial to genealogists, including those which:

- depict the topography of the surface of the earth, so that we can understand how geography might have affected the movements of people,

- portray *political jurisdictions* created by government so we know where to find records,

- illustrate *religious boundary divisions* which might be affected by topography, or politics, so we can ascertain the location of church records,

- outline the stage upon which our ancestors played out their lives, including all the above, as well as occupational pursuits, distances from trading posts, and migration trails.

Maps Depicting Topography

Events are easier to understand when the nature of a place is known.
Physiographic maps illustrate with colors and symbols, features such as elevation, population, or rainfall. They indicate why the Rocky Mountains were a formidable barrier to land travel and commerce, and why the deserts had no great concentration of population until air conditioning and water were available. It is not surprising, then, to see the cradle of civilization in our country centered around seacoasts, waterways, valleys, and plains. Favorable environments attracted early settlers.

Terms to Understand

phys·i·o·graph·ic map – A map that uses colors and symbols to illustrate elevation, population, and rainfall.

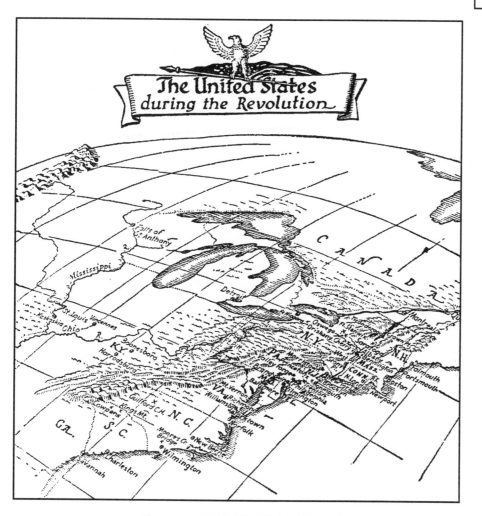

Illustration 7-10 The United States During the Revolution

Maps Depicting Political Jurisdictions

The early sovereigns of Europe possessed confused ideas about the size of this country and the location of its rivers and resources. It is not surprising, therefore, that their patents and grants of land overlapped, causing confusion and conflicts generations later. Seeing the maps that were drawn at the time helps us to understand the disputes that arose. When a map points out the boundary of another country, this guides us to resources in other nations which may solve our research problems.

In the early years of America, as populations grew and people learned more about the land, it was not uncommon for boundaries to shift, place names to change, and one governmental jurisdiction take over for another. The result was that *our ancestors may have thought they were living in one place, while in fact, they were actually in another.* For example, George Campbell and his family lived for some years on a farm in the newly formed county of Schuyler, Illinois. At some point, the county line was shifted slightly, and the Campbells discovered that they had "moved" to neighboring Hancock County, even though their farm had remained at the same physical location. A map or series of maps which show the boundary shift might be the only way a researcher could tell for sure what had happened 150 years before.

It's also important that you *establish relationships* between jurisdictional conflicts on the large scale (national and international) and your own research. The early power struggle over America reveals the impact of European politics on our ancestors' efforts to hold on to their newly formed colonies and territories. The earliest maps of America show France and Spain with grand discoveries in America, while England claimed only a small cluster of colonies. However, as history points out, the very concentration of settlement becomes a source of close support when struggles with other nations began. While other nations extended themselves over more land than they could manage and ultimately lost their foothold on this continent, the English colonies survived, and the French and Spanish languished or failed altogether.

As some foreign governments relinquished their lands, ownership by individuals was a major factor in the growth and significance of federal power. Therefore, we would expect many records to be kept at a federal level, and we could reasonably expect that they might include the names of our ancestors. Cargo routes from many coastal ports guide us to immigration paths, and maps would show us those. The appearance of forts on those maps could indicate the blocked thrusts of competing nations over such items as furs and skins, and it would suggest the recording of militia or military records which might include your ancestors. Maps, then, represent the changes in political boundaries and, through dating, show us the approximate dates of these movements and events.

Maps Depicting Historical Geography

Maps of historical geography reveal the difference between today's culture of instant gratification and the stretch of time it took for mail to travel from one coast to another when the nation was young. For example, to make distances easier to travel involved the efforts of hundreds of thousands of people, including our ancestors, who provided the labor to build the roads, canals, and railroads. So maps showing the development of these arteries infer the existence of occupational records in certain localities.

Since transportation was more difficult at higher elevations, migration trails developed on rivers, down valleys, passes, and along the coast. Frontier towns became important points of supply for those traveling westward. For a time, steamboats became more important than roads, and then canals became cheaper for moving goods than steamboats. All of these changes are recorded on maps. So maps that depict historical geography show the movements of a restless people going off to new locations, causing conflicts with existing residents, starting brush wars, arriving at solutions—all of this resulting in the cycle of changed boundaries and jurisdictions.

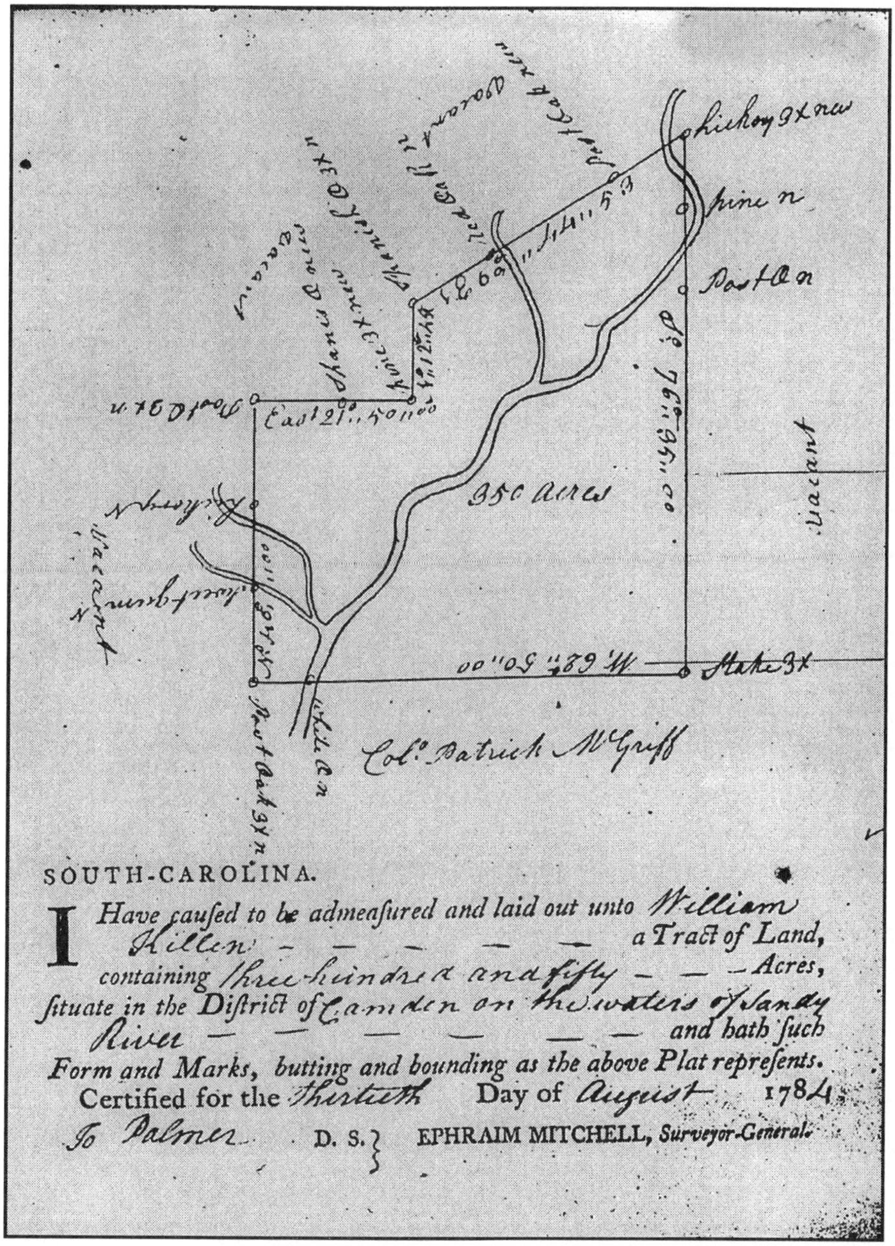

Illustration 7-11 Land Survey Map

Other Resources

As we trace the growth of the nation, especially in the Midwest, **township maps** help to distinguish one area from another. When they are used with county histories, these maps help to plot the proximity of one family to another. In the South, **military district** maps, **cadastral** maps, and **land surveys**, used in conjunction with land and property records, provide important clues for locating otherwise obscure information, such as the maiden names of female ancestors.

Terms to Understand

town·ship map - A descriptive outline sketch of land boundaries with the owners' names written on each section so that neighbors can easily be seen and each owner's distance from other places can be calculated.

Terms to Understand

mil·i·tar·y dis·trict - A division of an area administered by the armed forces sent there to protect the area.

Terms to Understand

ca·das·tral map - A survey map relating to land boundaries.

Terms to Understand

land sur·vey - Determines the boundaries, areas, and elevations of the earth's surface by means of measuring angles, distances, riverways, and neighbors.

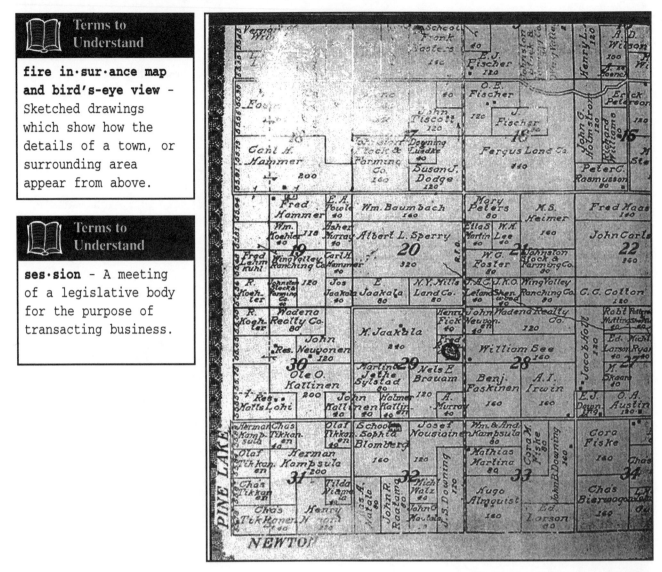

Terms to Understand

fire in·sur·ance map and bird's-eye view – Sketched drawings which show how the details of a town, or surrounding area appear from above.

Terms to Understand

ses·sion – A meeting of a legislative body for the purpose of transacting business.

Illustration 7-12   Township Map

In New England, town maps provide clues for migration movements and the location of records. In Europe, historical maps and gazetteers, used together, provide parish and religious data which can, in turn, help you to locate vital records on your ancestors. These European maps also provide information on political boundary changes and census enumeration districts, which help locate families in unindexed sources. For many of the same reasons, **fire insurance maps** and **bird's-eye view** maps provide a great deal of help to those doing urban research.

Just as it's important to understand the foundation principles in genealogy, it's also important to understand the original sources which form the basis for the marvelous electronic genealogy mapping aids we now have available. Today, more than ever before, you can find thousands of maps, both on the Internet and drawn by computer programs. But, as in all things, the result may not be what you expect or need. For example, the electronic map might be far less detailed than you need, or it might focus on a time period that is not helpful to your particular research. This is when you find yourself asking, "Where did the originals come from?" And then you will be glad that you know how to locate and understand the original sources and how they work. With this background, you will then be able to go back and check the original sources.

Laws created during specific legislative **sessions** are the chief authorities for county creations, changes and boundary descriptions. By carefully reading these session laws from the colonies, territories and states, maps evolved. The laws, previous maps, and other primary and secondary sources added to the creation of new historical maps. This long study resulted in few sources as conclusive as the *Historical Atlas and Chronology of County Boundaries, 1788-1980*, by John H. Long. In five volumes, it condenses the study of laws and county formations to help historians and others understand the jurisdiction of records. Sometimes, maps covering the exact location you are concerned with are in error. By returning to the session laws, you might be able to determine the true location, and thus jurisdiction, for the creation of the record you seek.

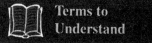

Terms to Understand

Animap™ - A computer mapping program showing the changes in jurisdictional boundaries over time.

By taking that information a bit further and placing the information into electronic format, we have the development of a computer program which depicts, year by year, each boundary change, chronologically. **Animap**™ is the best-known jurisdiction mapping program for the computer, and it is a great aid to the genealogist. Combined with the original maps of the area we are studying, we can then compare the information from both with our research findings. These original maps are located in major university libraries, state and federal archives, Family History Centers, microfilm and microfiche collections available in public libraries, and on the Internet.

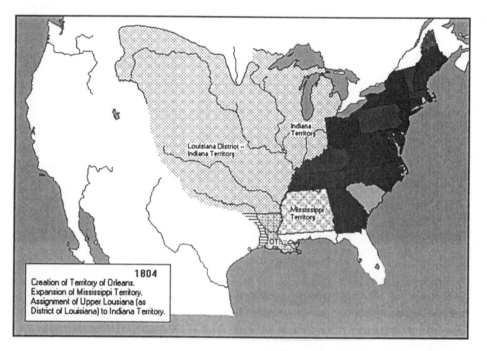

Illustration 7-13   Animap Printout

YOUR TURN

1. During what period of time did your ancestor (the individual you used as the example for the previous exercise) live?

2. Approximately when did your ancestor's parents marry?

3. When was your ancestor born?

4. How old was your ancestor when a major historical event occurred? What was the event?

5. Can you identify when your ancestor moved from one place to another?

A CHRONOLOGICAL PERSPECTIVE

A chronological study of your ancestors' lives can also help you find out what happened to them during those six years between the census in Pennsylvania and the land purchase in Illinois. One way to develop a sense of chronology is to *enter your notes in chronological order*. This way, your information will be most effective in the research process.

Time lines of events also help us understand and remember sequential relationships. They are visual aids that seem to promote the mental arrangement of events in their proper order. Think of these examples: presidential elections, major national wars since the American Revolution, the development of the railroad across the nation, the movement of Native Americans from the East to the

West along the Trail of Tears. Each one of these is a major touchstone in American history, and mentally arranging events in your ancestors' lives in relation to them helps you to see not only their place in that history, but the impact of major events on their movements and choices. There are several sources available to aid in compiling a time line of your family. Some are included in the chapter bibliography.

AMERICA'S INVOLVEMENT IN WAR

Colonial Wars

King Philip's War, 1657-76
King William's War, 1689-97
   European name: War of the Palatinate
Queen Anne's War, 1702-13
   European name: War of Spanish Succession
King George's War, 1744-48
   European name: War of Austrian Succession
French & Indian War, 1754-63
   European name: Seven Years' War

Revolutionary War, 1775-83

Post-Revolutionary Wars

War of 1812 (President Madison), 1812-14
Indian Wars (several presidents), 1817-58
Mexican War (President Polk), 1846-48
Civil War   (President Lincoln), 1861-65
Spanish-American War (President McKinley), 1898

Modern Wars

World War I   (President Wilson), 1917-18
World War II (President Roosevelt), 1941-45
Korean War (Presidents Truman & Eisenhower), 1950-53
Vietnam War (Presidents Kennedy, Johnson, & Nixon), 1961-73
Persian Gulf War (President Bush), 1991

Presidents were involved in wars and so were your ancestors . . . in one way or another.

Illustration 7-14 America's Involvement in War

Cause-Effect Relationships

Once you begin to mentally place your ancestor within these time periods, you are ready to recognize the possible causes for, and the effects of, his or her actions. Let's imagine that you know your earliest ancestor in America was a member of the denomination known as the Quakers. You know he settled in Pennsylvania, but you don't know where he was before that. However, in the course of your research you learn that the Quakers of that period were forced, because of their beliefs, to leave the predominately Catholic area of Maryland and go to Pennsylvania. Aha! Now you know to check for that Quaker ancestor in Maryland during the period prior to his settling in Pennsylvania.

YOUR TURN

1. In the text example, what is a possible cause and what is a possible effect in the life and movements of the Quaker from Maryland?

2. See Illustration 7-14 on "America's Involvement in War." Do you see any dates when one of your male ancestors would have been between 16 and 30 years of age? Identify the ancestor and describe the event.

3. What does this suggest about what your ancestor might have been doing during all or part of this period?

4. How would this have affected his family's well-being?

Conclusion

Since every event takes place both in space and in time, each occurrence has an historical, chronological and a geographical aspect, and these can be better understood with maps of the time and place. Chronological arrangements of events (as outlined in Chapter 4) also provide a sequential relationship for events–"maps" of a different kind. Developing an environmental awareness of your ancestors' history will also result in greater success in locating sources for solving research mysteries as you will discover in the following chapters.

ASSIGNMENT 7: ORGANIZATION OF HISTORICAL EVENTS

Part I: Organization of historical events, as well as vital records, is important. Organization conserves the mind for other tasks. Furthermore, events in history may affect your research goals if you are aware of them. Select one ancestor. Try to answer these questions about his/her life. If you don't know the answer to the question, use the sources indicated below the question to find the answers.

1. When was the town you are researching organized?
   (County histories give this information.)

2. When was the county in which the town lies established?
   (*The Handy Book for Genealogists* and *Ancestry's Redbook* give this information.)

3. When did the state receive statehood?
   (The sources under #2 answer this question.)

4. What counties was your county formed from?
   (The sources under #2 above or the *Map Guide to the U.S. Federal Censuses, 1790-1920* can help.)

5. What groups of people lived in this town, this county?
   (County histories give this information.)

6. What motives attracted settlers to this area?
   (County histories, state histories, and general U.S. histories can help.)

7. What religion or peculiar local customs did the people of this town, or county, have?
   (County histories, state histories, and general U.S. histories can help.)

8. Did any major war take place during the lifetime of the ancestor you are studying?
   (County histories, state histories, and general U.S. histories can help.)

Part 2: Once these questions are answered, the dates which are involved and the event should be placed in the documentation area for the individual upon which you are concentrating your efforts. Have you become aware of other sources for finding information on this ancestor?

YOUR TURN ANSWERS

Analyzing the Environment

1. On a contemporary map, locate the path of the National Road.

    A. What is it called today? Hwy 70.

    B. Through what states does it pass? Illinois, Indiana, Ohio, Pennsylvania, Maryland.

2. Locate the Ohio River.

    A. Through what cities does it pass? Paducah, Illinois; Evansville, Kentucky; Owensboro, Kentucky; Louisville, Kentucky; Warsaw, Kentucky; Maysville, Kentucky; Covington, Kentucky; Cincinnati, Ohio; Portsmouth, Ohio; Gallipolis, Ohio; Marietta, Ohio; Moundsville, West Virginia; Wheeling, West Virginia; Parkersburg, West Virginia; Huntington, West Virginia; Georgetown, Pennsylvania; Beaver, Pennsylvania; Pittsburgh, Pennsylvania.

    B. Where does it end? In Pittsburgh, Pennsylvania when it meets with the Allegheny and the Monongahela Rivers.

3. What does this tell you about its importance as a major route of travel? Since it passes through so many states, it could be a major migration route for all the states mentioned above.

Cause and Effect

1. In the example above, what is a possible cause and what is a possible effect in the life and movements of the Quaker from Maryland? The cause for his movement could have been the persecution caused by his beliefs. The effect on his life was that he moved from Maryland and started a new life in Pennsylvania where he was welcome. The records of that area should be searched.

The other YOUR TURN assignments in this chapter are appropriate for personal preference answers.

COMPUTER CHECKLIST #7

1. Is there a way to enter notes chronologically in your computer program to aid in your development of a sense of chronology? What method will you use to provide chronological notes?

WEB SITES

http://www.usgs.gov
U.S. Geological Survey National Mapping Information.

http://www.lib.utexas.edu/Libs/PCL/Map_collection/Map_collection.html
The Perry-Castaneda Library Map Collection at the University of Texas at Austin.
Includes maps of all areas of the world, not just Texas.

http://scarlett.libs.uga.edu/darchive/hargrett/maps/maps.html
Rare map collection from the Hargrett Library at the University of Georgia
Library covering 500 years, from the sixteenth through the twentieth century.

http://geography.pinetree.org/
World Wide Web Virtual Library: Geography site which contains map information
and Internet links to other areas categorized by subject.

BIBLIOGRAPHY

Cerny, Johni and Wendy Elliott. *The Library: A Guide to the LDS Family History Library.* Salt Lake City: Ancestry, 1988.

Church of Jesus Christ of Latter-day Saints. *Family History SourceGuide.* CD-ROM. Salt Lake City: Church of Jesus Christ of Latter-day Saints, 1998.

Eichholz, Alice. *Ancestry's Red Book.* Rev. ed. Salt Lake City: Ancestry, 1992.

Everton, George B., Sr. *The Handy Book for Genealogists.* 9th ed. Logan, Utah: Everton Publishers, 1999.

Schlesinger, Arthur M., Jr. *Almanac of American History.* New York: Putnam, c1983.

Thompson, Morris M. USGS. *Maps for America, U.S. Geological Survey.* 3rd ed. U.S. Department of the Interior, 1989.

Welsey, Edgar B. *Our United States...Its History in Maps.* Chicago: Denoyer-Geppert Company, 1957.

For various state and county histories, consult:

Meyerink, Kory. *Printed Sources.* Salt Lake City: Ancestry Inc., 1998.

The US Government Printing Office has printed a free 12-page booklet by the US Department of the Interior and the US Genealogical Survey entitled *Maps Can Help You Trace Your Family Tree: How to Use Maps in Genealogy.* Write to: US Geological Survey, National Cartographic Information Center, 507 National Center, Reston, VA 22092.

U.S. Gazetteers

Abate, Frank R., ed. *American Places Dictionary: A Guide to 45,000 Populated Places, Natural Features, and Other Places in the United States.* 4 vols. Detroit: Omnigraphics, 1994.

Abate, Frank R., ed. *Omni Gazetteer of the United States of America: Providing Name, Location, and Identification for Nearly 1,500,000 Populated Places, Structures, Facilities, Locales, Historic Places, and Geographic Features in the Fifty States.* 11 vols. Detroit: Omnigraphics, 1991.

de Colange, Leo. *The National Gazetteer.* London: Hamilton, Adams, and Co., 1884.

A Bibliography of Gazetteers:

Sealock, Richard B., ed., et al. *Bibliography of Place- Name Literature, United States and Canada.* 3rd ed. Chicago: American Library Assoc., 1982.

Postal Directory

Bullinger's Postal and Shippers Guide for the United States and Canada: Containing Post Offices and Railroad Freight Stations with the Nearest Post Offices and Railroads on which Every Place or the Nearest Communicating Point is Located and the List of Railroads and their Terminal Points. Westwood, NJ: Bulllinger's Guides, 1871-. Annual.

CHAPTER 8

Resolving Conflict

"Confusion is a word we have invented for an order which is not understood."

—Henry Miller

Have you ever played the game "Telephone"? You sit in a circle, and the first person reads something written on a piece of paper, and then whispers what he or she has read to the person on right. Player #2 whispers what he or she hears to the next person on the right, and so on. By the time this "information" reaches the last player in the circle, it contains some of the original statement, but much is lacking. There may even be some brand-new information added, based on what players thought they heard. "Telephone" is only a game, but chances are quite high that misinformation—because people passed on what they thought they heard—has happened in the passing-down of your family history. Because so much of our family history is passed on orally, it's understandable that people will mishear, misreport—even embellish that history.

Parlor Games

Family Documents

RESOLVING CONFLICT

Now that you have all your "bits and pieces" of family trivia, documents, and traditions organized, sorted, separated, entered, alphabetized, documented, cited, and filed in notebook form, you have completed the organizational phase, and you can find anything in minutes! Now it's time to resolve conflicts, see what information others have, and decide what to do next.

If your ancestry goes back to the early decades of European settlement in America, chances are high that at least one of your family lines has been researched. Perhaps a book has even been published, or is in the process of being published. Whether this is the case or not, it's time for you to move on to the next phase of your research in order to see if others have been working on your line, compare what you have with other available information, and resolve any conflicts. Others may have clues you need, but until you have followed these steps you may not be able to recognize those clues. The first step is to review the research cycle.

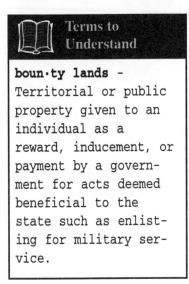

Terms to Understand

boun·ty lands - Territorial or public property given to an individual as a reward, inducement, or payment by a govern- ment for acts deemed beneficial to the state such as enlist- ing for military ser- vice.

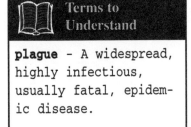

Terms to Understand

plague - A widespread, highly infectious, usually fatal, epidem- ic disease.

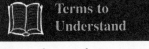

Terms to Understand

ter·ri·tor·ies - An area of land or water under the jurisdiction of an external govern- ment.

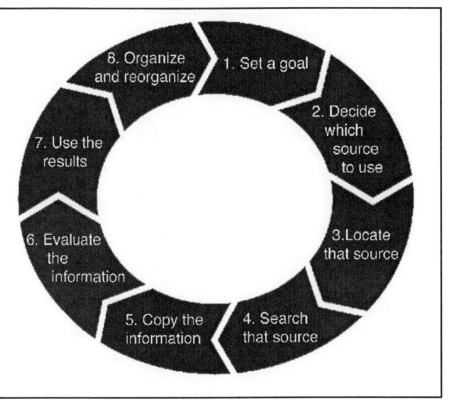

Illustration 8-1   The Research Cycle

Goals

According to Step 1 in the Research Cycle, we must first set a goal. One way to do this is to look at your Pedigree Chart and ask yourself, "What is one specific piece of information I want about one individual on my chart?" Since under the notes for that person you have already listed everything you already know about him/her in chronological order, the new information you want to know now becomes the goal.

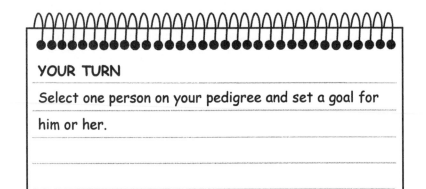

YOUR TURN

Select one person on your pedigree and set a goal for him or her.

Dates

Now look at the dates on both your Pedigree Chart and your chronological notes list. Are any of these dates associated with a significant historical event? Use the resources in the previous chapter to arrive at significant dates, watching for wars, droughts, famines, **plagues**, the acquisition of new **territories**, openings of canals, availability of **bounty lands**, migration, etc.

Do any of these dates raise questions in your mind? Was this person of marriageable age; could he/she have been married before; was the death date of one spouse so early as to cause the other spouse to marry again in order to provide for the needs of young children?

Now ask yourself if any of these facts are possible research topics. For example, since Henry Butler was 12 years older than his wife Katherine, could this be his second marriage? Since their first child was born in Boone County, Kentucky, might they have been married in Boone County as well?

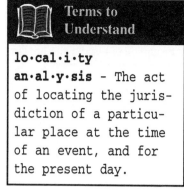

Terms to Understand

lo·cal·i·ty an·al·y·sis – The act of locating the jurisdiction of a particular place at the time of an event, and for the present day.

YOUR TURN

Look at your Pedigree Chart and your Chronological Notes list. Are any dates associated with significant historical events? List them.

Where to Go for Answers to Your Questions

Since you are new to the experience of using genealogical sources for answering your questions, use the Guide to Sources for Extending Your Pedigree (Illustration 8-2) to tell you where to look. This guide provides some of the *sources most commonly used by genealogists* to fill in those missing holes.

INITIAL TECHNIQUES FOR SEARCHING SOURCES

As you begin to search the sources listed in the guide, you should observe the following techniques:

1. Go from the *known* to the *unknown.*

2. Don't skip any *generations or sources.*

3. *Within reason*, get *all* of them. (For example, get those individuals of the same surname in the same locality, neighbors who may have traveled with your ancestors for several generations, and relatives who appear on one record or another. On the other hand, you wouldn't want to get all of the Smiths in New York City; in such cases you have to decide what is within reason.)

4. Find the *present county jurisdiction* for the location where your ancestors lived.

5. Now find the *county of jurisdiction at the time of the event.* They are often different. This is called a **locality analysis.** It is very important that you are looking in the correct place at the time of the event, since records are kept in the county where they were originally created or filed. Use gazetteers of the time period, geographical dictionaries, maps, and books to guide you in the state, county or town information you seek.

GUIDE TO SOURCES FOR EXTENDING YOUR PEDIGREE

INSTRUCTIONS: Line up the goal in the left column with the date of birth or death. Then search the record groups listed under the heading "Key to Record Groups." *(This is only a GUIDE. There can be exceptions.)*

GOAL	PRESENT-1910	1910-1880	1880-1850	1850-1790
Find parent's names	1, 2, 3, 4 & 3 again	7, 11, 8, 9	13, 11, 8, 9, 19	13, 16, 11, 20, 8, 9
Find birth date/place	1, 2, 14	7, 14, 8, 9, 12	7, 6, 8, 9, 11, 19	8, 14, 20, 17, 9
Find marriage	1, 6, 9, 14	1, 8, 9, 11, 14, 19	8, 9, 10, 11, 14, 17, 19	6, 8, 10, 14, 17, 20
Find death date	1, 3, 5, 9	8, 14, 5, 9, 12	5, 12, 8, 15, 14, 9, 19	5, 12, 9, 8, 14, 20
Find spouse's maiden name	1, 3, 6, 4	11, 12, 8, 9, 10, 14	11, 8, 9, 10, 12, 14, 19	11, 8, 9, 10, 12, 14, 20
Find death place	1, 4, 3	5, 8, 9, 10, 14	15, 14, 12, 9, 8, 5, 19	12, 5, 16, 17, 10, 20
Find siblings	4, 18, 9	5, 8, 9, 10, 12, 14, 18	5, 8, 9, 10, 12, 14, 18	5, 8, 9, 10, 12, 14, 16, 18, 20

KEY TO RECORD GROUPS

1. Check family records.
2. Order birth certificate from state of birth.
3. Order death certificate from state of death.
4. Check Social Security Death Index.
5. Check probate index from county of death--both wills [testate] and administrations [intestate].
6. Check marriage record from the state where first child was born.
7. Locate a federal census record: 1) search Soundex; then search 2) county and state.
8. Midwestern states: 1) find ancestors on census records; 2) then search those counties for histories.
9. Locate obituaries in communities where ancestors may have died.
10. Check land and property records in counties where the ancestor lived just before he appeared in census records.
11. Check marriage record indexes in the county in which the first child appears on federal or state census records.
12. Check death and/or cemetery records in the county where the ancestor was last located in federal or state census records, or tax records.
13. Check statewide printed census indexes.
14. Look for church records.
15. Check federal census mortality schedules for deaths occurring the twelve months prior to the federal census.
16. Search the *AIS Accelerated Indexing Systems Census Index on Fiche, 1600's to 1850* for the entire U.S., by surname.
17. Look for county histories, look under the township or post office listed in the federal or state census records, or look at tax records.
18. Search city directories.
19. Search military records - Civil War *State Indexes*, if ancestor was a male, born 1838 to 1852. If you find his name there, order pension/bounty land records.
20. Military records - War of 1812 *State Indexes*, if ancestor was a male, born 1787 to 1795. If you find his name there, order pension/bounty land records.

Illustration 8-2 Guide to Sources for Extending Your Pedigree

6. List *all of the sources that you search*, whether the results are negative or positive.

7. Determine *what other researchers have already discovered*. Avoid duplication of effort by making a **preliminary survey**.

8. Finally, write down *on a planner* the sources you will search next. And do not confuse a log with a **Research Planner**. The Research Log only records what was searched. The planner or calendar records not only what you found, what you did not find, where you searched, and when you made a search, but also what records *should eventually* be searched. Since using a calendar or planner is such an important step in the research process, we will study it in more detail after looking at the ways in which you can find additional information about an ancestor.

TIPS FOR EFFECTIVE USE OF THE RESEARCH PLANNER

One of the greatest aids to you as a genealogist is the Research Planner. It helps to focus your attention on the current research you are doing and reminds you to apply the eight techniques for researching the sources listed in the above chart.

Step 1 of the research cycle, and the first step in the effective use of your Research Planner, is to set specific goals. Those goals are arrived at through an analysis of existing family records. While it is the task of your genealogy computer program to organize the family records so that you can conduct an analysis, *it is the task of the Research Planner to help you, the researcher, go about your research in an orderly fashion.*

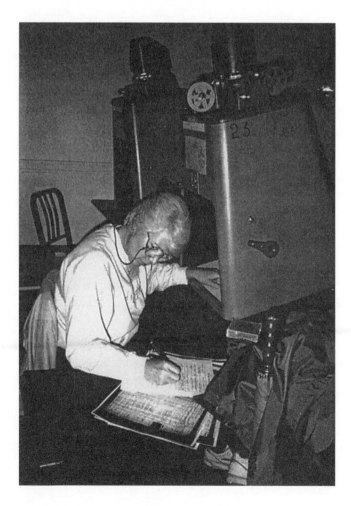

> **Terms to Understand**
>
> **pre·lim·i·nar·y sur·vey** - A comprehensive search of compiled sources and databases to prevent the repetition of previous research performed on a particular family or goal.

> **Terms to Understand**
>
> **re·search plan·ner** - A list of records to be searched for a particular goal, a list of records actually searched for a particular goal, call numbers of sources searched and the results of those searches, including the extract numbers for extractions which pertain to that research.

YOUR TURN

Step 1: Goal Setting

In order to make good use of the ideas you jotted down as you did your initial data entry, here are examples of the kinds of questions a good researcher should ask that could become goals.

1. What do you really know about your grandfather, John Morten, born 1898. You were told he was born in Pennsylvania, but in what town? Turn this question into a goal.

2. Who in my family would have information on this family? Look at the Family Group Records for your aunts and uncles, great-aunts and -uncles, cousins, and grandparents. Keep in mind that youngest daughters often received the family Bible, which would place the Bible in the hands of a different surname line, if the daughter married. Turn this question into a goal.

Previously, you learned that if certain information is missing, that information could become a goal in itself; you also learned that reaching this goal could enable you to go further in your research. You may also have set some goals on your own while you were data entering your information, since the act of organizing that information in the genealogy computer program, and into timelines, often helps to reveal missing or questionable areas. These very questions can be listed on your Research Planner. Just be sure to use a separate planner for each goal, as most goals will need to be broken down into smaller objectives. For example, your goal may be to locate the father of Timothy Hundley, born 1847.

Begin by writing the goal at the top of your research calendar; then, smaller objectives can be written in the space labeled "object of search." This is a sample goal.

Goal: *Locate the father of Timothy Hundley born 1847 in Virginia*

Step 2: As you learn more about the research process, what sources are available, and where they may be obtained, you will be able to set better goals. In the goal to locate the father of Timothy Hundley, born 1847, a will which mentions Timothy as the son of a Mr. Hundley would be proof. Also, a census with a child of the same age as Timothy, listed with his parents, would provide evidence to solve the problem. You're just beginning your search, so you do not as yet have the name of a repository (a library, an archive, or a special collection) where this source might be found. Nor do you know the title of a book, a film number, or a full description of a source. That can be filled in later. Now you can see why these are called "planners"! In essence, you are "planning" work to be done later. Once you learn the whereabouts of a nearby Regional Records Services Facility which has census films, you will be able to proceed. Or you may learn that a local Family History Center has the **probate** records for which you are searching on **microfilm**.

Since you know the approximate time period, you can fill in the "Time Period Column." In the "Note" column, you can write the MRIN for the Family Group Record, in order to use it as a reference, later, as you data enter the information into your program. If you apply these techniques, your Research Planner will look similar to Illustration 8-3.

Terms to Understand

pro·bate - The process of legally establishing the validity of a will; or, all of the legal processes carried out at the death of an individual in order to establish ownership of, or the heir, to the deceased's goods.

Terms to Understand

mi·cro·film - A reproduction of printed or handwritten materials, photographed and stored on film at greatly reduced size in order to save space in libraries and archives.

Goal *Locate the father of Timothy Hundley born 1847 in Virginia*

SURNAME/SUBJECT *Hundley Family*

RESEARCHER *Your Name Goes Here*   AREA *Virginia*

Repository / Call #	Date	Description of Source	Ind / Con	Object of Search	Time Period, Search	Note	Ext #
		Will records		*All Hundley*	*1848-1900*	*Mrin #123*	
		Virginia 1850 Census Index		*Timothy Hundley with father*	*1850*	*Mrin #123*	

Illustration 8-3   Research Planner Showing Step 2

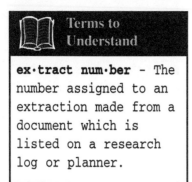

Terms to Understand

ex·tract num·ber - The number assigned to an extraction made from a document which is listed on a research log or planner.

YOUR TURN

Step 2: Guide to Sources

Using the information in Illustration 8-2, select the goal in the left hand column which applies to finding a death date. Now assume that the individual died between 1880 and 1910. Which records should you look at to find this ancestor's death date according to the guide?

Step 3: Next, you learn that the numbers for the microfilms you want are available from the Internet card catalog for a particular repository, so now you can fill in the columns headed "Repository" (name of the library, archive or collection) and "Call #" (call number).

When you plan to visit a repository such as the Family History Center and the National Archives, you will be able to view photo-duplications of original documents on film. When you locate your families, you can also make copies of the filmed documents, which can then become a permanent part of your records. You can also make a "table of contents" for the sources you have searched that day by using the "Ext #" (Extract Document Number) field on your Research Planner.

In the upper right-hand corner of each set of records you have photocopied, write a code number representing the family, such as "H" for Hundley, and an **extract number** starting with the number "1." Therefore the first photocopy or set of photocopies indicating "Hundley family extract item 1," would be "H-1." Also, record that number under the heading "Ext #" on the Research Planner. Later, as you review the many documents and notes you have taken on your research trip, it will be very easy to determine which sources on your Research Planner matches which of the documents you have brought home. See Illustration 8-4

Goal _Locate the father of Timothy Hundley born 1847 in Virginia_

SURNAME/SUBJECT _Hundley Family_

RESEARCHER _Your Name Goes Here_   AREA _Virginia_

Repository Call #	Date	Description of Source	Ind Con	Object of Search	Time Period, Search	Note	Ext #
FHC #1245634		Will records, Henry County, Virginia		All Hundley	1848-1900	Mrin #123	
San Bruno Federal Archives Roll 125		Virginia 1850 Census Index		Timothy Hundley with father	1850	Mrin #123	H-1

Illustration 8-4   Research Planner Showing Step 3

YOUR TURN

Step 3: Keeping track of your documents

Assume you found the census record, a county history, and a probate record for John Smith which you needed in the previous "Your Turn" assignment. Provide an extract number for each one of them.

Step 4: When you searched the will records for Henry County, Virginia, you found nothing that related to the Hundley family. But you did discover that the Hs in the index were filed in error after the letter "I," so you made a note of that under the "Con" ("Condition" heading in the Research Planner), in case you ever need to search that file again. And you found that you ran out of space in a couple of columns, so you simply turned the Planner over and wrote additional notes on the back.

Since you didn't want to waste time reading a roll of census film that had already been indexed, you checked the card catalog for a notation indicating whether it had been indexed or not, and you marked this information on your Research Planner in the "Ind" (Indexed) box. You also noted the indexes you searched on your Research Planner. And when you found the census index for Virginia, you discovered that Timothy Hundley's father lived in Pittsylvania County, Virginia, next door to Henry County. Aha! That's probably why you hadn't found him in the Henry County probate records. But as you packed up to leave at the end of this very successful repository visit, you not only felt pleased that you had tracked down the elusive Mr. Hundley, but you had the satisfaction of seeing that your Research Planner looked like Illustration 8-5, with the name of another county to be searched for the will, at a later date. Now you are ready for the next step in the process.

Goal *Locate the father of Timothy Hundley born 1847 in Virginia*

SURNAME/SUBJECT *Hundley Family*

RESEARCHER *Your Name Goes Here*   AREA *Virginia*

Repository / Call #	Date	Description of Source	Ind / Con	Object of Search	Time Period, Search	Note	Ext #
FHC #1245634		*Will Index, Henry County, Virginia ** (all H's in index after I)*	**	*All Hundley*	*1848-1900*	*Mrin #123*	*Ø*
San Bruno Federal Archives Roll 125		*Virginia 1850 Census Index*		*Timothy Hundley with father*	*1850*	*Mrin #123*	*H-1*
San Bruno Federal Archives Roll 127		*Virginia 1850 Census Pittsylvania County*		"	" pg. 243	"	*H-2*
FHC #1245689		*Will Index, Pittsylvania County, Virginia*		"	"	"	*copied over*

Illustration 8-5   Research Planner Showing Step 4

YOUR TURN

Step 4: Recording Indexes

1. Look at Illustration 8-2 under the goal to find a birth date between 1790 and 1850. Which record groups have indexes? List them.

2. How would you indicate on your Research Planner that there is an index to those records?

Step 5: Now that you're back home, you can't wait to enter the new information into your computer genealogy program. But you remember from class that there's a method for this, as well. You begin by using the ID numbers which you had listed under the "Note" column (the RIN or MRIN numbers). Then you look to the right of the "Note" column to the extract fields, pick up the document, and enter the information you located on that original document or any notes you transcribed on the back of your Research Planner.

Once the information has been entered, you mark lightly in pencil the MRIN number in the upper right-hand corner of the document, circling the number lightly to indicate that you have entered the document fully into your computer. That way, if you are interrupted and must return to the data entry later, you will know it hasn't been completed because the number has not been circled. When all of the data entry is complete, you file the Planners away in the section of your Family History binder titled "Research Planners." Thus, your Planners provide the bibliographic notations that you need for your family history's documentation, and they remind you of all of the sources you have searched, and for whom you were searching.

GENEALOGY RESEARCH ASSOCIATES

Research Planner

Remember to have only *one goal* per Research Planner.

Goal ____

____

Surname/Subject ______________________ Researcher ______________________

Area ______________________ Client ______________________

Source Location		Description of Source	Object	Time	Remarks		
Date source searched	Library or repository & call #	(State, county, type of record, and time period of record)	(Person's name or what is sought)	(Person's age or date of event)	Comment or ID # of family	Index	File

Genealogy Research Associates, Inc. 139 East South Temple, Suite #300 Salt Lake City, UT 84111 Phone (801) 363-3464

Illustration 8-6 Blank Research Planner

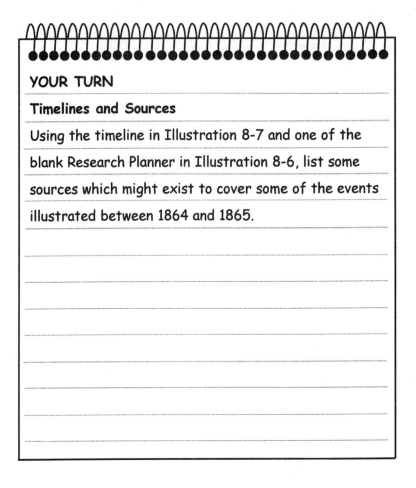

YOUR TURN

Timelines and Sources

Using the timeline in Illustration 8-7 and one of the blank Research Planner in Illustration 8-6, list some sources which might exist to cover some of the events illustrated between 1864 and 1865.

One blank Research Planner will be found as Illustration 8-6. Others will be found in the Appendix. Be sure to put a return address stamp or label in the upper corner, so that they will be returned to you if they are misplaced or left behind after a visit to a library or repository.

THE RESEARCH PROCESS

1. Go from known to unknown.
2. Don't skip sources.
3. Get all of same surname.
4. Check if this is the proper place.
5. Do a locality analysis.
6. List all sources + and -.
7. Do a preliminary survey.
8. Keep a Research Planner.

---

780 NORTH AMERICA

charters, state bank notes were driven out of existence by a tax of 10% (1865).

June 20. West Virginia (the loyal part of Virginia) admitted to the union as the thirty-fifth state.

1864, Nov. 8. Re-election of Lincoln. Andrew Johnson, vice-president.

1865, Feb. 1. Resolution in Congress to submit to the states the **thirteenth amendment** to the constitution, prohibiting slavery within the United States. The amendment was ratified by two-thirds of the states by Dec. 18.

1865-1873. Serious and recurring **epidemics** of smallpox, typhus, typhoid, cholera, scarlet fever, and yellow fever in Philadelphia, New York, Boston, Baltimore, Washington, Memphis, and New Orleans led to the realization of the need for improved sanitation. In 1866 a municipal **board of health** was created in New York and in 1869 a state board of health was established in Massachusetts.

1861-1868. New territories. In the years just before the war the discovery of precious metals in the Pike's Peak country and in the Washoe Mountains led to mining rushes to those regions, with the result that the territories of **Colorado and Nevada** were organized in 1861. Mining rushes elsewhere in the years of the war resulted in the organization of the territories of **Arizona** (1863), **Idaho** (1863), and **Montana** (1864). **Wyoming** was made a territory in 1868.

1862-1886. Taming of the Plains Indians. The constant pressure of white population, combined with broken promises, led to continued outbreaks of the Indians. The **Homestead Act** (1862) played a prominent part in the settlement of the west. The **Morrill Act** (1862), providing for grants of land to states in order to aid the establishment of agricultural colleges, opened up more areas. In 1862 the **Union and Central Pacific Railways** were chartered by Congress and given a large grant of land. They formed the first transcontinental railway (completed May 10, 1869).

In 1862 the **Sioux Indians** of Minnesota were defeated by Gen. Sibley at **Wood Lake.** In 1864 the **Cheyenne** went on the warpath, with the aid of the Arapahoe, Apache, Comanche, and Kiowa tribes. Troops under Col. Chivington staged a massacre of Indians at **Sand Creek**, Colo. (Nov. 1864). Efforts of troops to build an emigrant road from Fort Laramie along the Powder River to the mines of Montana and Idaho led to war with the **Plains Sioux** (1866). A commission authorized by Congress persuaded the Apache, Comanche, and Kiowa tribes to locate in **Indian Territory**, and secured the removal of other tribes from the Plains to more remote regions. In 1869 Congress created the **Board of Indian Commissioners** to supervise all government expenditures for the Indians. Meanwhile the advance of white settlers, slaughter of the buffalo, and the gold rush to the Black Hills caused an outbreak of the Plains Sioux (1876) under **Sitting Bull**, which resulted in the **massacre of Custer** and his men at the **Little Big Horn** (June 25). **Nez Percé Indians** under **Chief Joseph** were defeated (Oct. 1877) and removed to Indian Territory. The last important Indian uprising came in the years 1882–1886, when the **Apaches** in Arizona and New Mexico, under Victorio and **Geronimo**, resisted efforts to confine them to reservations. By 1886 the Indians had all been removed to Indian Territory or to reservations.

c. THE UNITED STATES, 1865-1917

1865, Apr. 14. ASSASSINATION OF LINCOLN; death Apr. 15. Andrew Johnson, vice-president, succeeded.

Cost of the war. National debt in 1860, $64,842,287; in 1866, $2,773,236,173, which great increase was in addition to the debts incurred by the states and municipalities.

May 29. President Johnson issued a **proclamation of amnesty**, granting pardon to all ordinary persons who had participated in the rebellion on taking an oath of allegiance.

Dec. Joint Committee of Fifteen on Reconstruction appointed by Congress.

Dec. 18. Ratification of the **thirteenth amendment**, abolishing slavery.

1866, Feb. Johnson vetoed a measure extending the life of the **Freedmen's Bureau**, thereby increasing tension between himself and Congress.

April. Congress passed over Johnson's veto the **Civil Rights Bill**, declaring all persons born in the United States to be citizens of the United States and entitled to equality of treatment before the law. This was designed to guarantee equal treatment to Negroes in southern states.

June 13. FOURTEENTH AMENDMENT sent to states for ratification. Declared ratified July 28, 1868. It incorporated in the constitution the principle of the Civil Rights Act; gave the southern states the choice of Negro enfranchisement or reduced representation in the lower House of Congress; barred from

Illustration 8-7 From An Encyclopedia of World History, compiled by William L. Langer

CONCLUSION

There are two ways to absorb the research techniques you have learned in this chapter.

1. You read through the rules once, apply the two or three you remember, and ignore the others. (Eventually, you'll learn the other rules, but only after you have had to repeat hours, days, weeks, months or years of research, redoing the steps you missed. In fact, the step you forgot and had to repeat, belatedly, will probably be the one you'll lecture your own students about when you become a genealogy teacher. Personal mistakes are great teachers, but they are soooo time-consuming.)

2. A better method is to learn from the mistakes of others and follow the steps in the research process. Try to memorize and absorb each step, and use the bookplate, on the bottom of page 8-14, to help you memorize these techniques. Cut them out, carry them with you, and learn these eight techiques.

ASSIGNMENT 8: RESOLVING CONFLICT

1. What do you know about all of the people appearing on your Pedigree Chart? In other words, what has been substantiated in your family history? Make up a separate Research Planner for each unsubstantiated, questionable, or unknown event on your Pedigree Chart.

2. Write down a county (or county equivalent for a foreign country) for every locality on your Pedigree Chart.

3. Verify that the county (or county equivalent) actually existed at the time of the event of the person in question.

4. List which relatives might have information on the family you are researching.

YOUR TURN ANSWERS

Step 1: Goal Setting

1. In what town or county was John Morten's birth of 1898 in Pennsylvania?

2. Who would be a direct-line descendant of John Morten, born 1898 in Pennsylvania? Locate all of the spouses and children of the siblings of John Morten as well.

Step 2: Guide to Sources

Numbers 8, 14, 5, 9, which translates to looking for the ancestor on a census, if possible, and then searching for the ancestor in a county history if he or she lived in the Midwest; looking for church records; checking the probate index in the county of death where the person was last found on a census; locating obituaries in communities where the ancestor may have died.

Step 3: Keeping Track of Your Documents

Census record S-1
County history S-2
Probate record S-3

Step 4: Recording Indexes

1. 13, 16, 11, 20

2. Mark this information on your Research Planner in the "Ind" (Indexed) box.

Timelines and Sources

Tax records, territorial records for Colorado and Nevada; occupational or mining records for Arizona, Idaho, Montana, and Wyoming; homestead and other land and property records; Native American records; National Archives records involving Native Americans, military (specifically Civil War records), reconstruction, and Freedman's Bureau; census records, vital records.

COMPUTER CHECKLIST #8

Describe how to accomplish the following tasks in your genealogy computer program:

1. How do you correct a surname?

2. How do you correct a locality?

3. How do you unlink a child from a family without deleting the child and his/her notes?

4. How do you unlink a couple from one another?

5. How do you modify the general notes on an individual?

6. How do you modify the source notes on an individual?

WEB SITES

http://www.four11.com
The White Pages for the Internet to search for phone numbers or e-mail addresses.

http://www.searchint.com/
Search International, Inc. is exclusively in the missing persons business primarily for missing heirs and beneficiaries, but also for their National Adoption Registry.

http://www.familytreemaker.com/ffitop.html
Family Tree Maker's FamilyFinder Index has over 500 million names from census records, marriage records, social security records, and submitted family trees. This is only an index, but a very powerful one, and it continues to grow.

BIBLIOGRAPHY

Cerny, Johni and Wendy Elliott. *The Library: A Guide to the LDS Family History Library.* Salt Lake City: Ancestry, 1988.

Family History SourceGuide. CD-ROM. Salt Lake City: Church of Jesus Christ of Latter-day Saints, 1998.

Everton, George B., Sr. *The Handy Book for Genealogists.* 9th ed. Logan, Utah: Everton Publishers, 1999.

Greenwood, Val D. *The Researcher's Guide to American Genealogy.* 3rd ed. Baltimore: Genealogical Publishing Co., 2000.

Langer, William L. *An Encyclopedia of World History.* Boston: Houghton Mifflin Co., 1940.

Thorndale, William and William Dollarhide. *Map Guide to the U.S. Federal Censuses, 1790-1920.* Baltimore: Genealogical Publishing Co., 1987.

CHAPTER 9

State Vital Record Offices, Public Libraries, Courthouses and Local Repositories

"Let fame, that all hunt after in their lives,
Live register'd upon our brazen tombs."

—William Shakespeare

Now that you have been taught how to organize your materials, how to use a computer program to aid in that organization, how to enter sources properly, how your genealogy computer program may be used to record timelines to aid in research, how to analyze what is known, how to work backward in time with the aid of the "Guide to Sources for Extending Your Pedigree," and how to prepare and use a Research Planner, it is time to locate and obtain more original records.

ARMCHAIR GENEALOGY

Others in your family, or within the communities where your family lived, may have information to help you. Much of that information can be gathered through correspondence. A common term for research conducted through correspondence is *armchair genealogy*.

An **armchair genealogist** is one who does genealogy without having to leave home. That doesn't mean never going out, but it does mean doing as much as possible from home. The computer, with a simple word processing program, can be a great help here. A form letter (such as the one shown in Illustration 9-1) could be made up and used over and over again to write to relatives or friends of the family. In addition to the family, there are others who might be of help to you:

1. The chambers of commerce in an ancestor's home town can be asked for information; use the local telephone book or local area maps.
2. County and city clerks can be of great help. *The Handy Book for Genealogists* or the *County Courthouse Book* are two books you will want to own if you plan to do much research from your home. They include addresses for every county in the United States and a list of the records available from them. The *Handy Book* also includes maps.

Terms to Understand

Arm·chair ge·ne·al·o·gist - One who does genealogy through correspondence or the Internet, without leaving home.

3. Cemeteries can provide names of family members and burial dates, occupations, military service, church affiliation, citizenship, place of birth, etc. *The Source* contains several addresses for cemetery associations. *The Researcher's Guide to American Genealogy* is very informative as well, and public libraries have directories for funeral homes and morticians.

SAMPLE FORM LETTER

Date

Name
Address
City, State, Zip

Dear _____:

My (relationship) lived in your county in (year). This is what I know about (him/her):

Names
Birth date and place
Marriage date and place
Spouse name
Death date and Place
Names of children

Brief sources of information:

I am searching for (his/her) parents. Do you have (state a specific record series to search) which might give me the answer to my question?

I will be happy to pay for photocopies and would be more than happy to share information I have on this family.

Thank you so much for your time and consideration. If you are unable to help me, could you please write at the bottom of this letter the name and address of someone else who could help. Please find enclosed a self-addressed, stamped envelope for your convenience.

Sincerely,

Your name
Complete address
Phone number (optional)
E-mail address

Illustration 9-1   Sample Form Letter

4. Local historians might help you. In small towns the local postmaster might pass the letter on to a person he knows would have information.
5. Newspapers and newspaper offices may help. State libraries can often send copies of their state's old newspapers on interlibrary loan to your local library.

6. Military records are available by correspondence. These include service, pension and bounty land records, which can be ordered from the National Archives, or in some cases on the Internet from the U.S. government, or through a genealogy record look-up service (see *www.GRAonline.com*).

7. Several genealogical periodicals can be of help to you including: *Everton's Genealogical Helper, Ancestry, Heritage Quest,* and similar magazines which are available in many public libraries. They are full of suggestions.

8. Genealogical and historical societies in each state are listed in a book called *The Genealogist's Address Book.* Genealogy societies can also be found on the Web at *www.fgs.org.* They could be contacted regarding information concerning publications.

9. Vital records repositories, where you can order birth, marriage and death records, are also listed in *The Genealogist's Address Book.*

10. Churches may be contacted. The *SourceGuide* produced by the Family History Library on CD for less than $15 and free on the Internet at *www.FamilySearch.org,* provides addresses for major religious repositories in the United States. *The Researcher's Guide to American Genealogy* describes the kind of records available and where these might be located.

11. Naturalization records and ships' passenger lists are available for loan or purchase on films through the National Archives and Records Service. The National Archives also provides forms to request the original naturalization records.

12. Employment and Social Security information is available. Addresses for obtaining the original Social Security application and the death record are available on the Social Security Death Index at most Family History Centers and on the Internet.

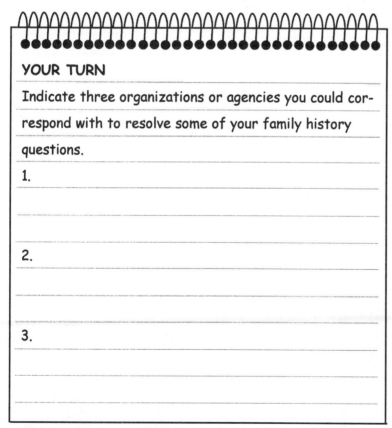

YOUR TURN

Indicate three organizations or agencies you could correspond with to resolve some of your family history questions.

1.

2.

3.

There is No Substitute for Original Records

Original records give an insight into problems that nothing short of speaking with the participants themselves could bring. Not only that, but the genealogist

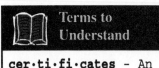

Terms to Understand

cer·ti·fi·cates - An official document stating a fact or event, such as a birth certificate which states the birth date and place.

Terms to Understand

ap·pli·ca·tions - A form filled out in making a request.

Terms to Understand

banns - Official notification of a couple's intention to marry, usually given at a church service several weeks before the wedding.

Terms to Understand

bond - An official document created by a person, his heirs, an administrator, or an executor, promising a certain sum of money to cover expenses, usually in regard to a deceased's property and possessions and the execution or administration of that estate.

will find no substitute for searching original records to obtain the feel of the time and place of a particular problem.

The first primary records that family historians consult are vital records, including birth records, marriage records, and death records. Yet at least 50 percent of the dates and places given to me in research cases have been in error. Either dates, places, people, or events were scrambled over the years. Since vital records are the first pieces of primary evidence sought for by researchers, it is important to understand how to best use them and to realize that they, too, can contain erroneous information, as will be explained.

HOW TO SEARCH FOR VITAL RECORDS

It is a proven fact that searching the last event first will give clues to those which preceded it. Therefore, search death, then marriage, then birth records. By going after the later events first, you will save much time and expense, because you have more information to go on. CAUTION: Many informants on death records make errors regarding birth dates and parents' names of the deceased during their time of grief. Try to verify all information with other sources.

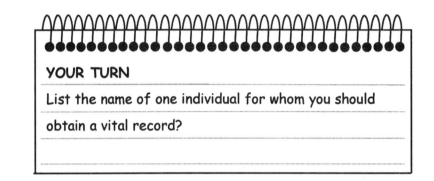

YOUR TURN

List the name of one individual for whom you should obtain a vital record?

Vital Records Have Many Names

In addition to the order in which vital records are searched, the item you are looking for may be listed under a variety of names. Birth records, for example, could be listed under a term which is set by the jurisdiction involved in its creation. For example, state offices call their records "Birth Records." Some religious denominations call their earliest records "Christening" or "Baptismal" records. Hospitals call their records **"Certificates,"** while municipal governments call their records "City Records."

Marriage records, on the other hand, could be listed under the headings **applications, banns,** proclamations, **bonds,** certificates, consent notices,

licenses, returns, register entries, marriage **contracts,** or **intentions.** As with birth records, these headings will vary between jurisdictions.

YOUR TURN

List four terms that refer to the birth of an individual.

1.

2.

3.

4.

YOUR TURN

1. List four terms that refer to the marriage of an individual or couple.

   a.

   b.

   c.

   d.

2. List two people in your family for whom you need a marriage record.

   a.

   b.

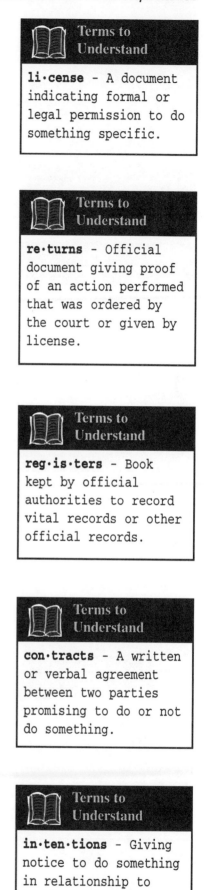

Terms to Understand

li·cense - A document indicating formal or legal permission to do something specific.

Terms to Understand

re·turns - Official document giving proof of an action performed that was ordered by the court or given by license.

Terms to Understand

reg·is·ters - Book kept by official authorities to record vital records or other official records.

Terms to Understand

con·tracts - A written or verbal agreement between two parties promising to do or not do something.

Terms to Understand

in·ten·tions - Giving notice to do something in relationship to marriage agreements.

When someone dies, several things happen. A death record in the hospital or a city certificate may be written up, an obituary may be entered in a newspaper, a mortician or coroner may be contacted, a cemetery may be located,

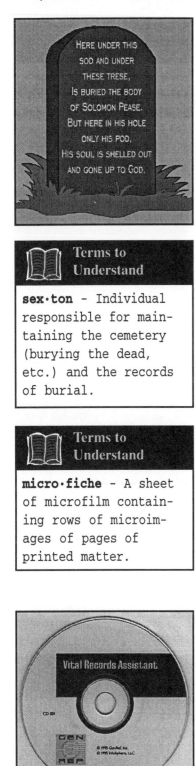

HERE UNDER THIS
SOD AND UNDER
THESE TRESE,
IS BURIED THE BODY
OF SOLOMON PEASE.
BUT HERE IN HIS HOLE
ONLY HIS POD,
HIS SOUL IS SHELLED OUT
AND GONE UP TO GOD.

Terms to Understand

sex·ton - Individual responsible for maintaining the cemetery (burying the dead, etc.) and the records of burial.

Terms to Understand

micro·fiche - A sheet of microfilm containing rows of microimages of pages of printed matter.

Vital Records Assistant

CD ROM

GEN REF

© 1995 GenRef, Inc.
© 1995 Intelphere, LLC

YOUR TURN

List three terms that also refer to the death of an individual.

1.

2.

3.

---

the local **sexton** may be contacted, a special church service may have been held, and relatives may have come to pay their respects.

Therefore, death information can be found through several sources. You can locate the names and addresses of morticians or funeral directors by using the *National Directory of Morticians*. Newspaper obituaries may be located by using the *Union Catalog of Newspapers* (available on **microfiche** through a Family History Center) to search for the paper's title; you can then order the paper on interlibrary loan through your local public library.

Since many vital records are found among church documents, the following sources help you locate them in the United States: Kay Kirkham's *Survey of American Church Records;* Ancestry's *The Source; WPA Inventories of Church Records;* Kory Meyerink's *Printed Sources;* and publications mentioned in *The Researcher's Guide to American Genealogy.* Many vital records are also found among contemporary materials, including Bible records. Don't forget to look for death records on tombstones. Some are very interesting and humorous as well.

A handy guide for ordering vital records is the *International Vital Records Handbook* by Thomas Kemp. Time-saving addresses and costs are provided for ordering vital records for events after about 1905. A good CD that produces your form letter, builds a correspondence catalog, and informs you of the price of vital records in the United States is the *Vital Records* CD by GenRef (available at *genref.com*).

Vital statistics registration in the United States is a relatively modern phenomenon. There has never been a national registration, so it was left up to each state to determine how and what they would do. New Jersey was the first state to bring its vital records together on a statewide basis, beginning in 1848. Registrations are held in different jurisdictions as well. In New England, the practice of registration began very early, on a town basis. In many large metropolitan cities and western states, registrations were not undertaken until the 20th century.

Birth Records

Early birth records are the rarest of the vital records. The heaviest concentration of early birth records is in New England. In most regions during the colonial period, church and Bible records serve as substitutes for missing birth records. By the mid 1800s, Virginia (and, therefore, West Virginia, which was not formed until 1862, out of Virginia counties) started keeping birth records.

Since vital records are relatively modern genealogically speaking, especially the recording of births and deaths, they usually are not microfilmed. However, many indexes are available in electronic (as data) or scanned (an image of a page) media. Some states, such as Kentucky, even have vital records available on the Internet. Illustration 9-2 shows some of the birth and death record microfilm and microfiche collections available in the Family History Library. They can be accessed through the Internet catalog at *www.familysearch.org*. The actual records can be obtained in person at the Family History Library, through loan at a Family History Center, or by requesting a copy through *www.GRAonline.com*.

SAMPLE STATEWIDE VITAL RECORDS IN THE FAMILY HISTORY LIBRARY COLLECTION

STATE	BIRTH INDEX	BIRTH RECS	DEATH INDEX	DEATH RECS
Alabama	1917-1919		1917-1919	
California			1905-1988	
Delaware	1861-1913		1855-88	1855-1910
Florida			1877-1969	
Hawaii	1896-1909	1859-1905	1896-1949	1896-1916
Idaho			1911-1932	1911-1937
Illinois, not Chicago			1916-1938	1871-1942
Chicago, IL		1871-1933	1871-1933	1878-1922
Cook Co, IL	1871-1915	1878-1894 1916-1922		1878-1914
Iowa	1880-1934			
Kentucky	1911-1954		1911-1922	
Maine			1892-1922	
Massachusetts	1893-1900/70	1841-1895	1841-1971	1841-1899
New Jersey		1848-1900		1848-1900
New York City		1881-1965	1900-1965	
North Carolina		1901-1967	1906-1994	
Ohio			1908-1932	
Oregon			1903-1970	
Rhode Island	1853-1900		1853-1943	
South Dakota	1880-1990		1880-1990	
Tennessee	1908-1912	1908-1912	1914-1942	1914-1942
Texas	1900-1945*		1900-1945	
Vermont	1871-1908		1871-1908	
Washington	1907-1954	1907-1936	1907-1979	1907-1952
Wisconsin	1852-1907		1862-1907 1959-1984	1862-1907 1959-1984

Illustration 9-2 Sample Statewide Vital Records in the Family History Library Collection

A RULE

Search the last event first (such as death records) for clues to those events which preceded it (e.g. birth records).

YOUR TURN

Search the list of vital records presented in Illustration 9-2, and indicate if any of these dates or localities cover one of your ancestors. Who is it, and which index is of interest?

Many other birth records after 1910 are available from local courthouses. They are very valuable, but many researchers fail to obtain them because they believe they already know most of the information. This reluctance to obtain these later vital records robs the researcher of vital clues.

Below is the information contained on a standard birth certificate in the 1900s.

Information Often Found on Modern Birth Records		
Regarding the Child	**Regarding the Mother**	**Regarding the Father**
Name	Name, often maiden name	Name
Birthplace	Birthplace	Birthplace
Race	Race	Race
Date of Birth	Age	Age
Hospital or place of birth	Residence	Residence
Time of birth	Occupation	Occupation
Sex	Term of residence in community	
	Marital status	
	Number of other living children	
	Number of other deceased children	
	Number of children born dead	

Illustration 9-3 Information Often Found on Modern Birth Records

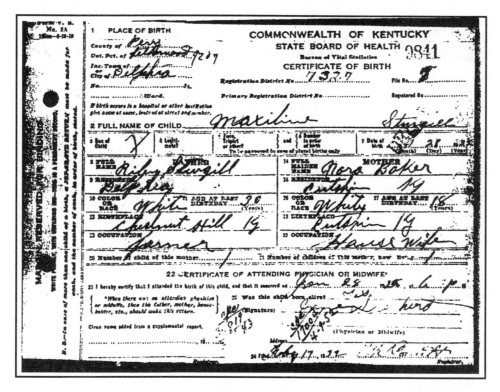

Illustration 9-4 Example of a Certificate of Birth

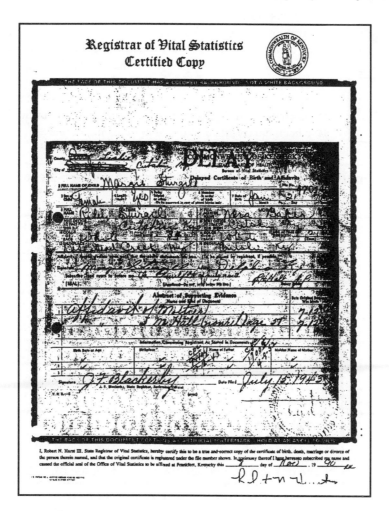

Illustration 9-5 Example of a Delayed Certificate of Birth

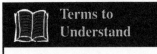

Terms to Understand

af·fi·da·vit - A written declaration made under oath before a notary public or other authorized officer.

YOUR TURN

After studying Illustration 9-3, indicate why you think it might be important to have this certificate for every member of your family including uncles and aunts.

Delayed Birth Certificate

Because birth records are often missing, and because the United States government legislated benefits (such as Social Security and civil service retirement) based on age, delayed birth certificates originated. A delayed birth certificate applicant had to fill out a petition to the county court stating his or her name, address, date and place of birth, parents' names, race, and evidence to support the information presented, such as a baptismal certificate, a school record, a census, or the **affidavit** of living people who witnessed the birth. Many of these records have been microfilmed throughout the United States.

Information Often Found on Modern Marriage Records

Regarding the Event	Regarding the Bride	Regarding the Groom
Name of officiator	Name, including maiden name if widow	Name
Title of officiator	Birthplace	Birthplace
Date of license	Race	Race
Date of marriage	Age	Age
Place of marriage	Residence	Residence
Witnesses to marriage	Occupation	Occupation
Residence of witnesses	Marital status	Marital status
	Name of father	Name of father
	Name of mother, maiden name	Name of mother, maiden name

Illustration 9-6   Information Often Found on Modern Marriage Records

YOUR TURN

After studying Illustration 9-6, indicate why you think it is important to obtain an actual marriage record.

When a birth certificate cannot be located, a Social Security original application form SS-5 can be obtained by writing to the Freedom of Information Officer in Washington, D. C. These applications provide the individual's birth date and place, and by using the application people can apply for a delayed certificate.

Marriage Records

Marriages are not so difficult to locate. They were usually maintained from the time a U.S. county was formed, and that is the way they will need to be obtained—through county jurisdictions, either on microfilm or microfiche, or by correspondence. Marriage records from the late 1800s to the present time contain wonderful information for the family historian, as shown in Illustration 9-6.

Death Records

Early death records were usually recorded in registers, and they provided little more than the name, possibly the age, and the date of death. Sometimes the cause of death was mentioned. Today's death records are much more detailed, as shown in Illustration 9-8.

Modern death records are not standardized, even within the same state. Different state legislative orders required different information be collected. Death certificates are sometimes the most fruitful records for the family historian because they guide the researcher to so many other sources of information. In Illustration 9-8 there is a column on the left covering what was known about the death. Experienced researchers understand that this information is most likely to be accurate, while the other information may be in error. Therefore, following up on the first column, "Regarding the Event," is most likely to bring other rewards.

THE COMMONWEALTH OF KENTUCKY

No._____ __

_____COUNTY COURT

BE IT KNOWN, That we_____
as principal, and_____
as surety, are jointly and severally bound to the Commonwealth of Kentucky, in the sum of ONE HUNDRED DOLLARS.

THIS BOND IS CONDITIONED AS FOLLOWS:

That, whereas Marriage is intended to be solemnized between_____
_____and_____

Now, if there is no lawful cause to obstruct said Marriage, this bond shall be void, otherwise it shall be and remain in full force and effect.

Witness our hands, this_____day of_____192___.

_____Principal.
_____Surety.

Attest:

_____Clerk.
By_____D. C.

REGISTER OF MARRIAGE

No. 11

Full names of parties, Husband_____*Riley Sturgill*_____
Wife_____*Nora Baker*_____
*By Whom Married_____*Isaac M. Day.*_____
*Place of Marriage_____*Isaac M. Day's*_____County of_____*Leslie*_____Kentucky.
*Date of Marriage_____*22nd Day of Dec 1920.*
*Witnesses_____*Martha York*_____and_____*Sarah Day.*
Age of Husband_____*20*_____years; Condition (single, widowed, divorced)_____
Age of Wife_____*18*_____years; Condition (single, widowed, divorced)_____
Race: (white or colored)_____*White*_____
Husband's Place of Birth_____*Letcher Co Ky*_____Residence_____*Perry Co Ky.*
Wife's Place of Birth_____*Leslie*_____Residence_____*Leslie "*
Names of Parents of Husband_____*Jim Sturgill*_____
and_____*Susan Sturgill*_____
Names of Parents of Wife_____*Wm Baker.*_____
and_____*Jane Baker.*_____
Occupation of Husband_____*Miner.*_____
Date of License_____*28"*_____day of_____*December*_____192*0.*

Subscribed and sworn to before me by_____
this_____day of_____192___   *J. M. Howard* _____Clerk.
By_____D. C.

*RECORD OF MARRIAGE CERTIFICATE

*I,_____*Isaac M. Day*_____a_____*Minister*_____
of the_____Church,
or religious order of that name, do certify that on the_____*22*_____day of
_____*Dec*_____192*0*, at_____*Isaac M. Day's*_____Kentucky, under
authority of the above license, I united in Marriage_____*Riley Sturgill + Nora Baker*
_____and_____*Martha York*
the persons named and described therein, in the presence of_____*Sarah Day. Martha York*
_____and_____*Sarah.*
I qualified and gave bond, according to law, authorizing me to celebrate the rites of Marriage in the County of_____*Leslie*_____State of Kentucky.
Given under my hand, this_____*22*_____day of_____*Dec*_____192*0*

A Copy, Attest: _____*Isaac M. Day*
_____*J. M. Howard.*_____Clerk.
By_____D. C.

*Blanks to be filled by Clerk after return of License.

Illustration 9-7 Example of a Marriage Bond

Information Often Found on Modern Death Records

Regarding the Event	Regarding the Deceased	Regarding the Spouse
Date & time of death	Complete name of deceased	Name
Place of death	Birthplace	
Cause of death	Race and sex	
Informant's name	Age at time of death	
Informant's address	Residence at time of death	
Doctor's name	Occupation	
Doctor's address	Marital status	
Funeral Director	Name of father	
Funeral Home address	Name of mother, maiden name	
Informant's relationship	Birthplace of father	
Place of burial	Birthplace of mother	
Address of burial	In armed forces, yes or no	
Hospital or institution	Social Security number	
	Usual place of residence	
	How long in the state	

Illustration 9-8   Information Often Found on Modern Death Records

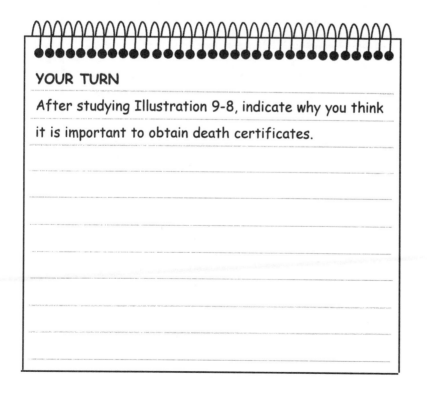

YOUR TURN

After studying Illustration 9-8, indicate why you think

it is important to obtain death certificates.

Registrar of Vital Statistics

Certified Copy

FORM V.S. NO. 1-A
REV. 1-56
FEDERAL SECURITY AGENCY
U. S. PUBLIC HEALTH SERVICE
NATIONAL OFFICE VITAL STATISTICS

COMMONWEALTH OF KENTUCKY
DEPARTMENT OF HEALTH
DIVISION OF VITAL STATISTICS
CERTIFICATE OF DEATH

FILE NO. 116

GA~ 114

REGISTRAR'S NO.

7801

Registration District No. 1170   Primary Registration District No. 7801

1. PLACE OF DEATH	2. USUAL RESIDENCE (Where deceased lived. If institution residence before admission)
a. COUNTY Perry	a. STATE Kentucky b. COUNTY Perry
b. CITY OR TOWN Hazard, Kentucky c. LENGTH OF STAY (in this place) 1 day	c. CITY OR TOWN Delphia IS RESIDENCE ON A FARM? YES ☒ NO ☐
d. FULL NAME OF HOSPITAL OR INSTITUTION Hazard Appalachian Reg.	d. STREET ADDRESS IS RESIDENCE INSIDE CITY LIMITS? YES ☐ NO ☐

3. NAME OF DECEASED (Type or Print)	a. (First) Nora	b. (Middle)	a. (Last) Sturgill	4. DATE OF DEATH (Month) 2 (Day) 10 (Year) 64

5. SEX Female	6. COLOR OR RACE White	7. MARRIED, NEVER MARRIED, WIDOWED, DIVORCED (Specify) Widowed	8. DATE OF BIRTH 3-26 1902	9. AGE (in years last birthday) 61 60	If Under 1 Year	If Under 24 Hrs.

10a. USUAL OCCUPATION Housewife	10b. KIND OF BUSINESS OR INDUSTRY	11. BIRTHPLACE Kentucky	12. CITIZEN OF WHAT COUNTRY? USA

13. FATHER'S NAME William Baker	14. MOTHER'S MAIDEN NAME Jane Baker

15. WAS DECEASED EVER IN U. S. ARMED FORCES?	16. SOCIAL SECURITY NO.	17. INFORMANT

18. CAUSE OF DEATH   MEDICAL CERTIFICATION

PART I. DEATH WAS CAUSED BY:
IMMEDIATE CAUSE (a) Pernicious anemia with degenerative cord disease

2900

Conditions, if any, which gave rise to above cause (a) stating the underlying cause last.   DUE TO (b) Arteriosclerotic heart disease with sinus tachycardia

DUE TO (c)

PART II. OTHER SIGNIFICANT CONDITIONS CONTRIBUTING TO DEATH BUT NOT RELATED TO THE TERMINAL DISEASE CONDITION GIVEN IN PART 1 (a)

19. WAS AUTOPSY PERFORMED? YES ☐ NO ☒

INTERVAL BETWEEN ONSET AND DEATH

20. ACCIDENT ☐	SUICIDE ☐	HOMICIDE ☐	21a. DESCRIBE HOW INJURY OCCURRED (Enter nature of injury in Part I or Part II of item 18.)

21b. TIME OF INJURY   Hour   Month, Day, Year   a. m.   p. m.

21c. INJURY OCCURRED WHILE AT WORK ☐ NOT WHILE AT WORK ☐	21d. PLACE OF INJURY (e. g., in or about home, farm, factory, street, office bldg., etc.)	21e. CITY, TOWN, OR LOCATION	COUNTY	STATE

22. I hereby certify that I attended the deceased from 2-9- 1964 to 2-10-64 , 19 that I last saw the deceased alive on 2-10- 164, and that death occurred at 3:20A, from the causes and on the date stated above.

23a. DATE SIGNED 2-10-64	23b. ADDRESS Hogant, KY	23c. SIGNATURE W. F. O'Donnell, M. D. (Degree or title)

24a. BURIAL, CREMATION, REMOVAL (Specify) Burial	24b. DATE 2-13-64	24c. NAME OF CEMETERY OR CREMATORY Stony Fork Cem.	24d. LOCATION (City, town, or county) Perry Co. (State) KY.

25a. DATE REC'D BY LOCAL REG. 2-16-64	25b. REGISTRAR'S SIGNATURE	26. FUNERAL DIRECTOR Brashear Funeral Home ADDRESS Viper, Ky.

I, Omar L. Greeman, Registrar of Vital Statistics, hereby certify this to be a true and correct copy of the certificate of death of the person therein named, and that the original certificate is registered under the file number shown. In testimony thereof I have hereunto subscribed my name and caused the official seal of the Office of Vital Statistics to be affixed at Frankfort, Kentucky this 3 day of Dec ,1951 .

64189
Fee Control Number

Omar L. Greeman, State Registrar

Illustration 9-9 Example of a Death Certificate

For example, when using the information in this death certificate, the researcher should try to track down the **informant** and see if he or she is still alive. The researcher could also contact the funeral home and ask for its records. They could try to locate the cemetery and obtain the cemetery records. If the deceased was in the armed forces, military records could be obtained. If the deceased had a social security number, the official Form SS-5 Social Security Application could be obtained. And with an exact date of death, provided by the death certificate, you are more likely to locate newspaper obituaries.

So you see, it is very important to obtain death certificates. They are rich in genealogical information and may clarify discrepancies in your family records. Remember: *look for an individual's vital records by obtaining the latest event first: death, then marriage, then the birth record.*

How to Locate Vital Records

In 1967, there were no publications to help you order vital records. Today we have several avenues to take, but there are several unique features to obtaining vital records in the United States which need to be understood first.

The Exceptions

1. Louisiana has "parishes," not counties.
2. There are special "recording districts" in Alaska and Hawaii.
3. There are multiple recording offices in Alabama, Arkansas, Iowa, Kentucky, Maine, Massachusetts, Mississippi, and Tennessee.
4. There are independent cities with their own vital records offices in Virginia.
5. Vital records are at the municipal (town) level in Connecticut, Rhode Island, and Vermont.

In addition, other problems exist due to separate county recording offices, similarly or identically named localities, and other kinds of jurisdictional entities. For example:

ALABAMA: Four counties contain two separate recording offices: Barbour, Coffee, Jefferson, and St. Clair.

ALASKA: Alaskan counties are called "boroughs." There are 23 of them. However, land records are recorded in 34 "recording districts," which have different jurisdictions, so all the boroughs and districts overlap. You would need to know in which recording district any given town or city is located.

ARKANSAS: The counties of Arkansas, Carroll, Clay, Craighead, Franklin, Logan, Mississippi, Prairie, Sebastian, and Yell have two separate recording offices each.

HAWAII: One central office records all districts.

IOWA: Lee County has two recording offices.

LOUISIANA: The parish of St. Martin has two non-contiguous segments.

MAINE: Aroostook and Oxford counties each have two separate recording offices.

MARYLAND: The city of Baltimore has its own separate recording office.

MASSACHUSETTS: Berkshire and Bristol counties each have three recording

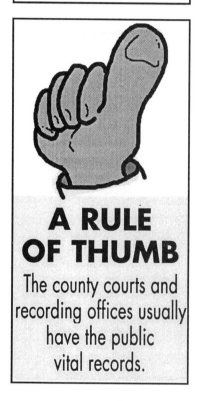

Terms to Understand

in·for·mant - An individual who provides information concerning a life event, such as a death. This individual could be a spouse, a son or daughter, or a next door neighbor.

A RULE OF THUMB
The county courts and recording offices usually have the public vital records.

offices. Essex, Middlesex and Worcester counties each have two recording offices.

MISSISSIPPI: Ten counties have two separate recording offices each: Bolivar, Carroll, Chickasaw, Harrison, Hinds, Jasper, Jones, Panola, Tallahatachie, and Yalobusha.

MISSOURI: The city of St. Louis has its own recording office.

NEVADA: Carson City has its own recording office.

PENNSYLVANIA: Although there is a statewide office, Pittsburgh and Philadelphia have their own recording offices.

TENNESSEE: Sullivan county has two separate recording offices.

VIRGINIA: There are forty-one independent cities in Virginia, but only twenty-seven have separate recording offices. The following fourteen share their recording offices with the surrounding county:

Bedford-Bedford County
Covington-Alleghany County
Emporia-Greenville County
Fairfax-Fairfax County
Falls Church-Arlington or Fairfax County
Franklin-Southhampton County
Galax-Carroll County
Harrisonburg-Rockingham County
Lexington-Rockbridge County
Manassas-Prince William County
Manassas Park-Prince William County
Norton-Wise County
Poquoson-York County
Williamsburg-James City County

States of Confusion

Those states which do not record vital records by county, such as the New England states, have other problems. With all recording being done at a city or town level, people may attempt to find documents in counties which are actually towns (or vice versa). Sometimes they are misfiled, as in the case of the Connecticut towns of Fairfield, Hartford, Litchfield, New Haven, New London, Tolland, and Windham, each having a corresponding Connecticut county by the same name.

In New Hampshire, the counties confused are Carroll, Grafton, Hillsborough, Merrimack, Strafford, and Sullivan.

In Rhode Island, this confusion takes place with Bristol, Newport, and Providence.

In Massachusetts (which does have a statewide vital records office), this also occurs with cities or towns having the names of the following counties: Barnstable, Essex, Franklin, Hampden, Nantucket, Norfolk, Plymouth, and Worcester.

Vermont has similar problems with Addison, Bennington, Chittenden, Essex, Franklin, Grand Isle, Orange, Rutland, Washington, Windham, and Windsor. There are also places in Vermont that have both a city and a town with the names of: Barre, Newport, Rutland, and St. Albans. So, even if you are given the place of birth, is it a town, a city, or a county?

Internet Access to State Offices

Today, most state offices can be reached via the Internet, and most state government offices are accessed on the Internet with a common **URL.** Examples are given below:

www.state.ak.us/	*www.state.al.us/*	*www.state.ar.us/*
www.state.az.us/	*www.state.ca.us/*	*www.state.co.us/*
www.state.ct.us/	*www.state.fl.us/*	*www.state.ia.us/*
www.state.id.us/	*www.state.in.us/*	*www.state.il.us/*
www.state.ks.us/	*www.state.ky.us/*	*www.state.la.us/*
www.state.ma.us/	*www.state.me.us/*	*www.state.va.us/*

A few exceptions:

www.migov.state.mi.us/   Michigan
www.capcityon-line.com   District of Columbia Web site under construction

Also try:

Vital Records Information United States   *http://vitalrec.com*
VitalChek Network   *http://www.vitalcheck.com/*

But for years genealogists have relied on a truly handy book, *The Handy Book for Genealogists,* to provide them with quick information to vital record offices. Genealogists can also consult *The Genealogist's Address Book* and *Ancestry's Red Book,* which provide similar information. And computer genealogists also have a program called *The Vital Records Assistant.* This is a most helpful tool for the genealogist.

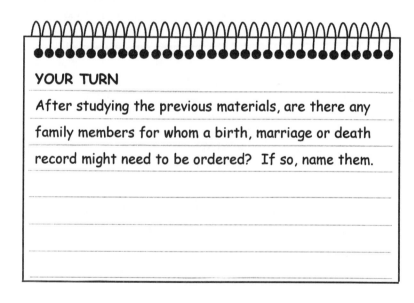

YOUR TURN

After studying the previous materials, are there any family members for whom a birth, marriage or death record might need to be ordered? If so, name them.

Problems with Vital Records

Besides some of the obvious problems such as those shown above, as researchers we must be wary of:

1. Inaccurate information provided by informants.
2. Legibility and misreading of records.
3. The variety of spellings for names, which may cause records to be misfiled, difficult to find in indexes, or ignored (e.g., McPhail, MacPhaill, or McFail).
4. **Transcribed** indexes may contain errors in typing such as the transcriber reading an "L" for an "S" or a "T" for an "F". Try to determine all possibilities.

5. Sometimes records are severely restricted, or at least require a few hoops to be jumped through before going any further. For example, in some states you need to submit a copy of your birth certificate, drivers license, and a pedigree chart showing your relationship to the person on the record you are requesting.

Summary

Vital records offices are very valuable repositories. Duplicate copies of records held in smaller jurisdictions are often found at the county level as well, and they often have a better feel for the spelling of names found. If one set of records is lost or incomplete, try another place. And remember; there are many, many other sources for vital record information. See the bibliography at the end of this chapter for more sources to help you. Now, let's turn our attention to another location for obtaining genealogical sources--the public library.

PUBLIC LIBRARIES

Public libraries are important, and they exist to serve an entire community with a variety of needs. They are usually close to everyone, free of charge, and offer inter-library loan services to aid in obtaining other materials. However, because most of its sources are secondary sources, most *primary* genealogical research cannot be conducted in a public library. It often has a primary focus which caters to the needs of their users and contributors and not all are interested in genealogy.

While it is unlikely for every neighborhood library to have a major genealogy collection, it is not unlikely to find genealogical materials in every public library. Your next step after organizing your family information will be to ascertain what research has already been conducted by others, or who has already compiled a record on your family. This is part of a preliminary survey, the goal being to prevent duplication of effort. Much of this work can be accomplished through a public library. The problem for the beginning researcher lies in locating the materials he or she wants, because libraries use various cataloging systems.

Understanding the various identification systems will aid in locating materials wherever you go. If you look in the front of most new books you will find one or all of the following: the International Standard Book Number, the Dewey Decimal Classification, or the Library of Congress Classification.

A very wise teacher once said to me: IT IS NOT SO IMPORTANT HOW MUCH YOU KNOW AND REMEMBER as to know WHERE TO FIND WHAT YOU NEED TO KNOW.

YOUR TURN

Write the name of a local public library you use.

International Standard Book Number

This is a group of ten numbers identifying a book and its publisher. International Standard Book Numbers, or ISBNs, simplify book ordering and, therefore, aid booksellers, librarians, and publishers. They have been used in the United States since 1969.

An ISBN has four parts separated by hyphens or spaces. The first group is called the "group identifier" and represents the geographical or language group of a book. For example, the English language is represented by the number "0".

The second group of numbers is the publisher prefix and represents the publisher of a book. The third represents the book title and is called the title prefix. The last number is called the "check digit" and is a number under 10 or X. As the ISBN goes through a computer, the check digit indicates errors that may have been made when the number was written.

SAMPLE

ISBN 0-016489-48-5

This is the ISBN number for the book *The Library of Congress: A Guide to Genealogical and Historical Research.*

YOUR TURN

Check the front of a published book in your possession.

What is its ISBN number? What is its title and subject matter?

Dewey Decimal Classification

The Dewey Decimal Classification system was named for Melvil Dewey, who developed it in 1876. This system numbers books by dividing them into ten main groups, each represented by figures as demonstrated below:

000-099	Generalities (encyclopedias, bibliographies, periodicals, journalism)
100-199	Philosophy and Related Disciplines (philosophy, psychology, logic)
200-299	Religion
300-399	Social Science (economics, sociology, civics, law, education, vocations, customs)
400-499	Language (language, dictionaries, grammar)
500-599	Pure Sciences (mathematics, astronomy, physics, chemistry, geology, paleontology, biology, zoology, botany)
600-699	Technology (medicine, engineering, agriculture, home economics, business, radio, television, aviation)
700-799	The Arts (architecture, sculpture, painting, music, photography, recreation)

800-899   Literature (novels, poetry, plays, criticism)
900-999   General Geography and History

Each of these ten main classes are divided further into specialized fields. When the classification becomes very exact, the decimal is used. Specialists add or modify about 6,000 classification numbers yearly to account for current events and new knowledge.

The Family History Library in Salt Lake City, Utah, uses a modified version of the Dewey system in order to aid in browsing. However, browsing is not the best way to approach a library, since it might prevent a search of the true primary sources (those in *microform*). The library catalog should always be consulted.

Library of Congress Classification

This method of organizing and filing materials is found in many large research and university libraries because it provides greater precision in most fields and more room for expansion than the Dewey Decimal Classification system. While in 1900 only one library in the United States, the Library of Congress, had over a million items, by the 1980s, over 150 libraries in the United States had collections of over a million items.

The classification is broken down by a series of letters and numbers. The first letter in the set indicates one of twenty-one major areas of knowledge:

A=General Works	H=Social Science	Q=Science
B=Philosophy, Religion	J=Political Science	R=Medicine, Psychology
C=History	K=Law	S=Agriculture
D=History	L=Education	T=Technology
E=History	M=Music	U=Military Science
F=History	N=Fine Arts	V=Naval Science
G=Geography, Anthropology	P=Language, Recreation, Literature	Z=Bibliography, Library Science

The second letter stands for a subclassification. The numbers represent a specific topic. Many genealogy books start with "C" and "F" because of their historical background. F443 R5 W4 is the *History of Roane County, Tennessee* at the Sutro Library.

Approaching the Unfamiliar Library

Most genealogists are interested in similar areas: local histories, newspapers, maps, gazetteers, local biographies, old pictures, censuses, inventories of collections, and directories, to name a few. These materials are easy to find in a Family History Center because a FHC caters to genealogists. But what do you do when you enter a public library, a law library or other specialty library?

First: Have a Goal in Mind

You need to come prepared with specific questions you want answered.

Second: Always Use the Library Catalog

A library catalog is the easiest and fastest way to locate information in a library no matter what form of filing classification they use, because once you have found an item, the librarians can help you by using their knowledge of their own filing system.

First, look at the outside of the catalog, if it is in card form. Is it set up by locality, by subject, or by author-title? If it is on computer, look at the instructions in order to see if it is set up by locality, subject or author-title.

What is it you are trying to find? A county history under a "subject" catalog might be listed under the "history" category, or under the name of the county in the "locality" or "title" category. In summary, you need to understand the cataloging system used in the particular library you are using.

Second: Talk to the Reference Librarian

The local reference librarian could answer questions such as: Do you have newspapers on microfilm? Where are your maps and gazetteers? Do you have any "loose files" or "clip and save" drawers where biographical sketches of local people might be kept? Is there an old picture collection in this library? Do you have an inventory list of your collection?

The reference librarian also has information on interlibrary loan materials and other libraries or societies in the area that could help you. Often the local genealogical or historical society shares facilities with the local library, and it is possible that the librarian could put you in touch with others interested in genealogy.

Third: When All Else Fails, Browse

Although not the best way to locate information quickly, browsing the shelves and hideaways of libraries has been very fruitful over the years for this researcher when time was not of importance. And as you consider the history surrounding an individual's life, other sources may come to you. Perhaps those sources will lead you to a county courthouse.

COURTHOUSES

Courthouses often contain vital records, wills, and tax and land records. If the records have not been microfilmed, you might be required to visit a courthouse, or arrange for an agent to visit the courthouse, to obtain copies of records for you. Or you could write to the courthouse.

Courthouse

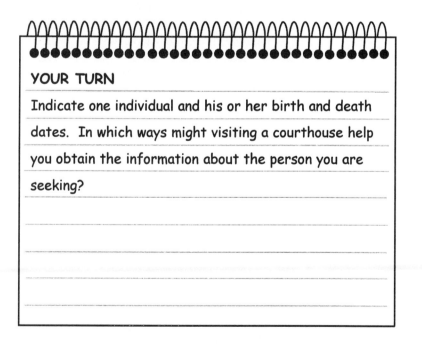

YOUR TURN

Indicate one individual and his or her birth and death dates. In which ways might visiting a courthouse help you obtain the information about the person you are seeking?

The *County Courthouse Book* (Genealogical Publishing Company) is an excellent source for information on courthouses you are interested in. It describes not only the locations, phone numbers, and e-mails, but also the cost of individual copies of records.

A word of caution. The public officials may be very overworked and underpaid in those departments dealing with the records you are searching. If at all possible, try to locate your court records on microfilm or fiche, if you are not close enough for a quick visit. This way, you have all the time you need to look carefully over the records, and the copies are much less expensive. I have found American courthouses very busy, and often the records are no longer in their care. The *County Courthouse Book* helps remedy much of the problem.

Courthouses are most important to search when people have lived in the 20th century. Many of their records are too recent to have been microfilmed and cataloged. There are excellent chapters on court records in both *The Source* and *The Researcher's Guide to American Genealogy.* Records from the past are often sent off to state archives or libraries. Except for records of the past hundred years, try the Family History Library first for the records you need.

HISTORICAL SOCIETIES

Historical Society

Throughout America, historical societies are involved in areas which touch the subjects dealt with by genealogists. They are cataloging memorabilia including diaries and vital records which could be of value to you. Often historical and genealogical societies are combined into one organization in a county. Sources in the bibliography for this chapter give suggestions for locating societies in the areas in which you may have an interest. Because of time limitations, they may not be able to do searches for you, but most can recommend someone who will.

I have always found some type of success visiting these wonderful places. Remember to search Mary Wheeler's *Directory of Historical Organizations in the United States and Canada.*

CONCLUSION

While we have only covered four basic repositories in this chapter, vital record offices, public libraries, local repositories such as genealogical societies and historical societies, and courthouses, more will be described in subsequent chapters. While you are learning which repository to use to solve which problem in your research, a "Repository Guide for Local Genealogists" has been prepared to help you (Illustration 9-10) determine where you might obtain a particular record in person, through correspondence, or on a loan basis.

REPOSITORY GUIDE FOR LOCAL GENEALOGISTS

FHC=Family History Center

RECORD	IN PERSON	BY CORRESPONDENCE	ON A LOAN BASIS
FEDERAL CENSUS	National Archives or its branch facility Libraries with census on film FHCs Purchase copies on CD	Hire record look-up assistance	Public library Heritage Quest loan program On loan at FHC Archival loan
STATE CENSUS	State Library	Hire record look-up assistance	"
VITAL RECORDS AFTER 1902	Courthouse in county of event	Write to state vital records repository	N/A
VITAL RECORDS BEFORE 1902	Courthouse in county of event State Library	Write to county of event; *Handy Book*; hire record look-up assistance	On loan at FHC Some on interlibrary loan
LAND & PROPERTY RECORDS	"	Write to county in question Hire record look-up assistance	On loan at FHC; indexes for others at FHC; some published in libraries
PROBATE RECORDS	"	Write to county in question Hire record look-up assistance	"
COMPILED FAMILY HISTORIES	Major libraries	Write societies; Hire record look-up assistance	On loan at FHC Heritage Quest loan program Major library interlibrary loan NEHGS loan; NGS loan
REVOLUTIONARY WAR & INDEXES	National Archives and field branches FHL	Order from National Archives Hire record look-up assistance	On loan at FHC Heritage Quest loan program Major library interlibrary loan
CIVIL WAR & 1812 SERVICE BOUNTY LAND* & PROBATE*	National Archives & some field branches; State Libraries have Confederate copies	State Adjutant General Hire record look-up assistance	On loan at FHC Some Heritage Quest Some interlibrary loan
COMPILED CENSUS INDEXES/1790-1920	National Archives & field branches & FHL	FHL photoduplication order, hire searcher	Some at local FHC such as AIS 1790-1850
FAMILY VITAL RECORDS	Family, periodicals, historical societies	Historical & lineage societies	On loan at FHC Some Heritage Quest
COURT RECORDS	Local courthouse	Hire record look-up assistance	On loan at FHC
CHURCH RECORDS	Local church or regional center	Hire record look-up assistance Local church or records center	On loan at FHC Some interlibrary
IMMIGRATION	Courthouse of jurisdiction	Hire searcher to visit courthouse	On loan at FHC
CEMETERY/BURIAL	Visit cemetery	Write to sexton	On loan at FHC

Illustration 9-10   Repository Guide for Local Genealogists

REPOSITORY GUIDE FOR GENERAL BACKGROUND

RECORD	IN PERSON	BY CORRESPONDENCE	ON A LOAN BASIS
FOREIGN & HISTORICAL	Public Libraries FHC	Hire record look-up assistance Historical & ethnic Societies Periodicals	Public library Heritage Quest On loan at FHC Archival loan
MAPS	State Library Public Libraries	Hire record look-up assistance Write to county Map sellers Historical societies	On loan at FHC Public Library
JURISDICTIONS AND COUNTY FORMATION	*Handy Book, Map Guide* County histories from public libraries	Write to county in question	Histories from FHL On loan at FHC Heritage Quest loan services

Illustration 9-11 Repository Guide for General Background

ASSIGNMENT 9: DETERMINING THE BEST REPOSITORY

1. Look over your pedigree. What records do you need to solve your current family history mystery?

2. Using the Repository Guide for Local Genealogists, determine the most economical and most easily available repositories for solving your research problems.

3. Read a chapter in one of the books suggested in this chapter on repositories. List the chapter's title.

4. Write a sample form letter (on a separate piece of paper) which could be used for most correspondence to a genealogical or historical society. Keep in mind the following suggestions from your assigned reading: Limit your request to one or two items; make your request easy to answer; make copies of your letter; express appreciation; offer a fair exchange; and provide for return postage on a self-addressed, stamped envelope (SASE).

5. Visit your public library. Locate four of the following:
   a. A gazetteer (preferably the oldest one possible).
   b. An atlas of the area in which you are doing research.
   c. A history of your county.
   d. Newspapers or an index to them.
   e. The history of the state or country you are interested in researching.

6. Does your public library have a major genealogy collection? Could the reference librarian tell you where to go for more genealogical information in the area?

7. Select someone from your own research. Notice where he/she was born, married and died. Use some of the sources mentioned thus far in this book; *The Almanac of American History* by Arthur M. Schlesinger, Jr.; an area research guide for the states in which these events took place; an encyclopedia from a public library; or a history book of the place in question. Indicate an event which took place in the state in question during the years your ancestor lived there. Fill in the form below to help you get started thinking chronologically. Now try to locate some resources in your public library to understand these events.

Ancestor's Name: _____

Year of Birth: _____ Place of Birth: _____

What Happened That Year in This State: _____
_____
_____
_____
_____
_____
_____
_____
_____

Marriage Year: _____ Marriage Place: _____

What Happened That Year in This State: _____
_____
_____
_____
_____
_____
_____
_____
_____
_____

Year of Death: _____ Place of Death: _____

What Happened That Year in This State: _____
_____
_____
_____
_____
_____
_____
_____

List Other Sources Which Might Now Be Searched:
_____
_____
_____
_____
_____
_____
_____
_____
_____
_____
_____

YOUR TURN ANSWERS

Organizations or Agencies

A chamber of commerce in an ancestor's home town, county and city clerks, local cemeteries, local historians, local postmasters, newspaper offices, state libraries, the National Archives, a genealogy record look-up service, genealogical and historical societies in each state, vital record repositories, churches, employment and Social Security offices are all possibilities.

Birth Terms

Christenings, baptisms, hospital certificates, city records of births.

Marriage Terms

Applications, banns, proclamations, bonds, certificates, licenses, returns, register entries, consent notices, marriage contracts, or intentions.

Death Terms

Hospital death records, city death certificates, obituaries, mortician or coroner records, cemetery records, sexton records, church records of death.

General Value of Certificate of Vital Events

These could verify maiden name of mother, birthplaces of both parents, places of residence at various times, parents' occupations, if other children were born the descendants were unaware of, and the ages and location of birth, marriage and death for each person.

COMPUTER CHECKLIST #9

1. How does your program record repository addresses?

2. How do you link sources to their repository addresses in your program?

WEB SITES

Vital Records Information United States *http://vitalrec.com*

At the *www.state.ak.us/* sites, once you get to the page, look under the Department of Health, Vital Statistics, or FAQ to locate how to order birth and death certificates.

BIBLIOGRAPHY

Bentley, Elizabeth Petty. *County Courthouse Book.* 2nd ed. Baltimore: Genealogical Publishing Co., 1996

Bentley, Elizabeth Petty. *The Genealogist's Address Book.* 4th ed. Baltimore: Genealogical Publishing Co., 1998

Carter, Fran. *W.P.A., Works Progress Administration: Surveys, Guides, Inventories, City Town-County-States-National, Depositories-Unpublished-Published, Private Collections, Printed Church Surveys.* Galveston, TX: Frontier Press, c1990.

Eichholz, Alice, ed. *Ancestry's Red Book.* Rev. ed. Salt Lake City: Ancestry, 1992.

Ernst, Carl R. and Michael L. Sankey, eds. *Public Records Online: The National Guide to Private & Government Online Sources of Public Records.* 2nd ed. Facts on Demand Press, 1999.

Everton, George B., Sr. *The Handy Book for Genealogists.* 9th ed. Logan, Utah: Everton Publishers, 1999.

Greenwood, Val D. *The Researcher's Guide to American Genealogy.* 3rd ed. Baltimore: Genealogical Publishing Co., 2000.

Kemp, Thomas Jay. *International Vital Records Handbook.* 4th ed. Baltimore: Genealogical Publishing Co., 2000.

Kemp, Thomas Jay. *Virtual Roots: A Guide to Genealogy and Local History on the World Wide Web.* Wilmington, DE: Scholarly Resources, 1997.

Kirkham, E. Kay. *Survey of American Church Records.* 3rd ed. Logan, Utah: Everton, 1971.

Kot, James Douglas and Elizabeth Gorrell Kot. *United States Cemetery Address Book.* Vallejo, CA: Indices Publishing, c1994.

The National Directory of Morticians. Youngstown, Ohio: National Directory of Morticians, 1950—Irregular.

Neagles, James C. and Mark C. Neagles. *The Library of Congress: A Guide to Genealogical and Historical Research.* Salt Lake City: Ancestry, 1990.

The Sourcebook of Public Record Providers: The National Guide to Companies that Furnish Automated Public Record Information, Search Services, and Investigative Services. 2nd ed. Tempe, AZ: BRB Publications, c1994.

Schlesinger, Arthur M., Jr. ed. *Almanac of American History.* New York: Putnam, 1983.

Sperry, Kip. *New England Genealogical Research: A Guide to Sources.* Bowie, MD: Heritage Books, c1988.

Szucs, Loretto Dennis and Sandra Hargreaves Luebking. *The Source: A Guidebook of American Genealogy.* Rev. ed. Salt Lake City: Ancestry, Inc., 1997.

Wheeler, Mary Bray, ed. *Directory of Historical Organizations in the United States and Canada.* Nashville, TN: American Association for State and Local History Press, c1990.

U.S. Newspaper Program National Union List. 4th ed. Dublin, OH: Online Computer Library Center, 1993.

CD-ROM

Church of Jesus Christ of Latter-day Saints. *Family History SourceGuide.* CD-ROM. Salt Lake City: Church of Jesus Christ of Latter-day Saints, 1998.

Vital Record's Assistant. CD-ROM. GenRef, 1995. (Order through www.GRAonline.com.)

Magazines:

Everton's Genealogical Helper. 1947-. Published by The Everton Publishers, P.O. Box 368, Logan, UT 84323.

Ancestry. 1994-. Published by Ancestry Incorporated, P.O. Box 476, Salt Lake City, UT 84110.

Heritage Quest Magazine. 1985-. Published by Heritage Quest, 593 West 100 North, Bountiful, Utah 84011.

CHAPTER 10

Resources of the Family History Library

"A library is thought in cold storage."
—*Lord Samuel*

The next major repository you should become familiar with is the Family History Library (FHL) in Salt Lake City, Utah, the largest genealogical library in the world. In addition, there are thousands of local Family History Centers around the world, which are "branch" libraries of this huge repository. Information on how to access and use a Family History Center will be given in Chapter 12.

In 1894, the Genealogical Society of Utah was organized for the purpose of collecting and making available all the genealogical information possible to interested persons who wanted to search out their ancestral lines. Over the years, the society tried to keep pace with the upsurge in genealogical needs, all the way from negotiating with nations for permission to microfilm their records to actually microfilming the vital records of the world.

By the late 1950s, computer technology was added, and in 1958 a shattering blast detonated a canyon wall southeast of Salt Lake City beginning what would take eight more years to complete—the Granite Mountain Records Vault. This vault was made to protect the library's precious resources, with 700 feet of solid granite overhead and three electronically operated, solid steel doors, each weighing over nine tons and all beveled inward so that any pressure or force, even from an atomic blast, would only seal them more tightly. Here, thousands of rolls of film are processed weekly and shared with anyone in the world who wishes to find his or her ancestors.

Then in June of 1999, the largest Internet site in the world for genealogists was introduced, making it possible for The Church of Jesus Christ of Latter-day Saints to share their computer databases of vital information freely with the world. The LDS site began to receive a half-million hits per day. I can but stand in awe!

But in order to benefit from these riches, you must become familiar with the *Family History Library Catalog (FHLC)*, so that you can access the non-electronic holdings. And to access the electronic databases of this repository, you will need to use the Internet.

Family History Library

Granite Mountain Records Vault

www.familysearch.org

Terms to Understand

e·lec·tron·ic re·sources - Refers to materials published or maintained in a computer or Internet format.

Terms to Understand

ser·ver - A computer with enough memory and ability to provide support to several other computers.

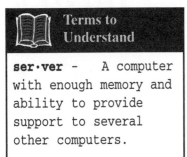

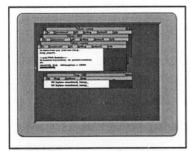

This chapter will cover the Internet, book, microfiche, and microfilm collections of the library, while the next chapter will cover the **electronic resources**. The basic purpose of this new Internet resource as explained by their representative, Randy Bryson, is to "Provide access to genealogical data in the home, to assist individuals with the research process, and to facilitate collaboration between individuals and families." While each of the catalog mediums (whether they are in electronic or non-electronic formats) has its own strengths and weaknesses, the strength of the new search technology introduced by the Internet is its ability to identify individuals based upon a relationship to parents or spouse, the ability to currently isolate a search by a "year" and eventually by a "place," as well, and its ability to be used any time of the night and day at home. Its weakness is its current inability to be downloaded to a diskette or computer file, for more efficient processing. But that is something we gladly live with in light of its availability. How to use this new resource will be explained after an understanding of the other media is introduced.

With the many resources available for the genealogist through the Family History Library, a medium was sought that could be a guide to all the major sources of the facility, yet be inexpensive, able to contain thousands of pages of printed instructions, maps, and word lists, and light enough to be carried easily from place to place. What evolved was *SourceGuide*. Using this guide on a compact disc together with the *Family History Library Catalog* is but one step below the ultimate facilitator to this genealogical repository. Having a knowledgeable, personal assistant holding your hand could be better, but for less than $15 this is just amazing.

Since a sizeable portion of your research sources will come from this repository, let's begin by learning how to use the *FHLC* in its many formats, and then how to use *SourceGuide* to determine which source to search first.

USING THE FAMILY HISTORY LIBRARY CATALOG

The *FHLC* can be found in several formats:
- on the Internet (*www.familysearch.org*),
- on microfiche, at local centers or the main library,
- on CD-ROM at local centers or by individual purchase (see www.familysearch.org),
- on computers linked through **servers** in larger centers,
- or in a more robust version known as "Webview" in the main library.

The Internet version is very friendly and easy to use, but the catalog at a center allows much more information to be gathered even more quickly.

On the microfiche version, information is divided into four major indexes with four different colored headings and many sub-headings in each. These four major headings, Author/Title, Subject, Locality, and Surname, along with how they differ, will be covered below.

1. AUTHOR/TITLE: If you know the actual name of a book, or are looking for books by a particular author, you would find that information fastest by looking in the Author/Title section. Perhaps you heard of the Andrea Collection on South Carolina research. Look up "Andrea" and see what this collection contains.

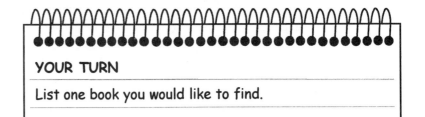

YOUR TURN

List one book you would like to find.

2. SUBJECT: This section contains entries about particular subjects of a general nature that might cover more than one locality, such as LDS Church Records, Native Americans, Heraldry, or Quaker Records. This index will lead you to books, micro-

YOUR TURN

List one subject you would like to know more about.

_____

| Jews - Genealogy |
| Jews in Virginia - History |
| Italians in Brazil |
| Geography - England - Kent |

Illustration 10-1 Microfiche FHLC Subject Headings

films, microfiche, and other resources available on those subjects.

3. LOCALITY: This section is probably used the most, as people want to know what is available in a particular area where their ancestors lived. You can look up any locality to see what films, fiche, books, or maps are available for that area. Basically you will want to obtain information from the most specific to the least specific locality first, starting with a city, then a county, state, region, and country. Within each level (city, county, state, or country), records are broken down further by categories. In this manner, you will not overlook a potential source of information on your family.

By looking at the locality fiche, you will also see major subdivisions of material in each country much like you see within states in the U.S. Information within each geographical area is listed alphabetically on the *FHLC* locality fiche, *starting with the largest area first*. For example, to find Bremerhaven, you would first look in Germany.

HELPFUL CLUE: On the first fiche for each major locality there is a gazetteer-like section to help you know where to look, and it tells you if there are records available for that particular area. For example, if you want to know what the Family History Library had available for Hastings, Nebraska, you would take the Nebraska microfiche and look at the beginning and see if Hastings is listed. If it is, it will read: "Hastings - Nebraska, Adams, Hastings." Now you know that there are at least some records specifically for the town of Hastings, that it is located in Adams County, and that you can also see what is listed county-wide. This gazetteer is particularly helpful if you are looking for information on a foreign country and do not know how it is filed in the library, or if there is even anything listed for that area. On the computer and Internet versions of the *FHLC* there is a browse feature available to aid in locating an area. The computer version is labeled "Locality **Browse**," while the Internet version of the *FHLC* automatically becomes a "browse" feature if two localities have the same same name (e.g., Portland, Maine and Portland, Oregon).

Once again, on microfiche, information is listed *according to the largest area first*, alphabetically by category, then by category within counties, and categories within towns. Let's take Nebraska as an example once again. The first things listed will be references to information that pertains to the *whole state*. These are *categories* which are listed alphabetically, such as Autobiographies, Biographies, Cemetery Records, Church Records, **Ethnology,** Histories, Land Records, Probate Records, Vital Records, etc.

After you have gone through all the statewide categories on the fiche (and some states have more than others), you will find the counties listed. Again, *countywide information will be listed first*, alphabetically, for each county. After the countywide information, each town for which they have specific references will be listed (alphabetically) with their categories (alphabetically).

Therefore, if we are looking up information on Hastings, Nebraska, we would

📖 **Terms to Understand**

`browse` - While using the *Family History Library Catalog*, the ability to casually inspect various localities when, for example, an exact spelling in a locality is unknown.

📖 **Terms to Understand**

`Eth·nol·o·gy` - A study of human cultures including nationalities, races and their origins, viz., Huguenots, Cherokees, etc.

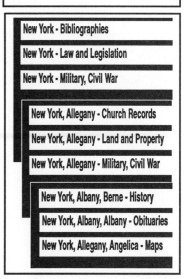

| New York - Bibliographies |
| New York - Law and Legislation |
| New York - Military, Civil War |
| New York, Allegany - Church Records |
| New York, Allegany - Land and Property |
| New York, Allegany - Military, Civil War |
| New York, Albany, Berne - History |
| New York, Albany, Albany - Obituaries |
| New York, Allegany, Angelica - Maps |

Illustration 10-2 Microfiche FHLC Locality Headings

look first to see what is specifically listed for Hastings. There may or may not be a lot of references for your particular town. After checking that, check to see what countywide references are available that fit your research needs. Then, if necessary, go to the state listings to see if you might pick up additional references there. If you use the *FHLC* on the *FamilySearch* computer program, you may start at any locality level. Most of the categories are self-explanatory (see categories listed in Illustration 10-3). Those few terms which might cause confusion are pointed out on the chart, or in the instructions which follow.

However, you will need to do a little thinking to find some topics. If you cannot find a category for the kind of record for which you are looking, stop and think what broader category it may fall under. For example, birth records will be listed under Vital Records, as will a whole variety of other records that could provide a birth, marriage, or death date, such as ministers' returns, cemetery and sextons' records, and death records. If you are looking for a ship's list, check Emigration or Immigration; while wills and orphan's court records will be listed under Probate Records. It would be to your advantage to study the makeup of some of the entries

YOUR TURN

List one locality you would like more information about.

to understand what records will show up under which categories.

4. SURNAME: This section contains references for family histories, biographies, autobiographies, personal journals, and other related information. Individual surnames are searched using key word searches to focus on those records most likely to contain the correct information. These entries will be arranged alphabetically in surname order, *regardless of the country of origin or residence of the individual.* By using this section of the *FHLC,* you can determine if there is already a published history for your family from which you can gain additional information and save much duplication of effort.

Each entry is also cross-referenced according to the other major names listed in the history. Every name mentioned will not have an entry, but the major ones will. Because of time and space limitations, only the surnames mentioned on the title page of a work are normally listed in the microfiche version. The computer version, however, searches by all names in the catalog file and seems to locate many more references. If the name of the history is *The Clark Anderson Family, Including the Names of Jones, Adams, Clark and Jackson*, there will be entries for that history listed under Jones, Adams, Clark and Jackson as well as under Anderson. There will also be a short description of what is contained, such as, where they lived, when they came to the U.S.A., and so on. It will give you an idea of whether this family matches information you already know about your family. If it says they were long-time residents of Maine, and your family came

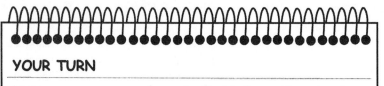

YOUR TURN

List one surname you hope to find information about.

FHLC Category Headings

Almanacs
Archives and Libraries
Bible Records
Bibliography
Buddhist Directories
Business Records and
　Commerce
Cemeteries
Census
Centennial Celebrations, etc.
Chronology
Church Directories
Church History
Church Records
Civil Registration
Colonization
Correctional Institutions
Court Records
Description and Travel
Directories
Dwellings
Emigration and Immigration
Encyclopedias and Dictionaries
Ethnology *3
Folklore
Gazetteers
Genealogy *1, 2
Guardian and Ward
Handwriting
Heraldry
Historical Geography
History
Islamic Directories
Islamic Records
Jewish History
Jewish Records
Land and Property
Language and Languages
Law and Legislation
Manors
Maps

Medical Records
Merchant Marine
Migration, Internal
Military History
Military Records
Minorities
Names, Geographical
Names, Personal
Native Races
Naturalization and Citizenship
Newspapers
Nobility
Notarial Records
Obituaries
Occupations
Officials and Employees
Orphans and Orphanages
Pensions
Periodicals
Politics and Government
Poor Houses, Poor Law, etc.
Population
Postal and Shipping Guides
Probate Records*
Public Records
Religion and Religious Life
Schools
Shinto Directories
Shinto Records
Slavery and Bondage
Social Life and Customs
Societies
Sources
Statistics
Taxation
Town Records
Visitations, Heraldic
Vital Records
Voting Registers
Yearbooks

* Includes Wills
*1 Family Histories - Genealogy
*2 Research Aids - Genealogy, How To
*3 Studies of groups, nationalities, races and their origins, viz.,
　Huguenots, Cherokees, etc.

Illustration 10-3　FHLC Category Headings

from North Carolina, it probably isn't yours.

Samples of FHLC Entries

- First, go to the state you are interested in.
- Second, go to the county you are interested in.
- Third, go to the subject you are interested in.

NOTE: "Probate" covers wills, administrations, estate settlements, etc.

```
****************************************************************************
TENNESSEE, POLK - PROBATE RECORDS

Polk County (Tennessee).  County Clerk.                      _____
    Wills, 1873-1970. -- Nashville : Tennessee State Library & |U.S. & CAN|
        Archives, 1970. -- 1 microfilm reel ; 35 mm           |FILM AREA |
                                                              |0840024   |
        Includes index.                                       |_____|


****************************************************************************
TENNESSEE, POLK - PROBATE RECORDS

Tennessee.  County Court (Polk County).                      |U.S. & CAN|
    Probate records, 1890-1965.- [S.l.] : Tennessee State Lib |FILM AREA |
        and Archives, 1970. -- 3 microfilm reels; 35 mm.     |_____|

    Microfilm made from originals.
    Includes index in each volume.

        Administrators' bonds & letters, v. 1-3 1890-1965......... 1012136
        Executors' bonds & letters, v. 1      1903-1964........ 1012137
            Guardians' bonds & letters, v. 1-2  1894-1963
            Insolvent estate accounts, v. 1     1895-1932
        Settlements, v. F-H                     1894-1936...... 1012140
****************************************************************************
VIRGINIA - MILITARY RECORDS - COLONIAL PERIOD, CA. 1600-1775
                                                             _____
    Crozier, William Armstrong, 1864-1913                    |U.S. & CAN|
        Virginia Colonial Militia, 1651-1776/ edited by William |BOOK AREA |
            Armstrong Crozier. -- Baltimore, Md.: Genealogical  |975.5     |
            Publishing Company, 1982. -- 144 p.              |M2c       |
                                                              |1982      |
    Reprint of original published: New York: Genealogical    |_____|
        Association 1905. (Virginia county records; v. 2)   Includes index.
        ISBN 0-8063-0566-5


****************************************************************************
NORTH CAROLINA, ALBEMARLE - LAND AND PROPERTY

North Carolina.  County Court of Pleas and Quarter Sessions  _____
        (Pasquotank County).                                 |U.S. & CAN|
    Deed records, 1700-1910; general index, 1700-1915. Raleigh |FILM AREA |
        N.C.: Filmed by North Carolina Department of Archives & |_____|
        History; Salt Lake City: Filmed by the Genealogical Society
        of Utah, 1969. --75 microfilm reels; 35 mm.
    Microfilm of original records in Elizabeth City, North Carolina and in
    the North Carolina Department of Archives and History in Raleigh,
      North Carolina.   Dates are mixed.
    Albemarle County was discontinued in 1739.
    Includes general index with most volumes individual indexed.

        Grantor index, A-E         1700-1915......................0019527
        Grantor index, F-L         1700-1915......................0019528
        Grantor index, M-R         1700-1915......................0019529
        Grantor index, S-Z         1700-1915......................0019530
        Grantee index, A-E         1700-1915......................0019531
        Grantee index, F-L         1700-1915......................0019532
        Grantee index, M-R         1700-1915......................0019533
        Grantee index, S-Z         1700-1915......................0019534
            Deed records           1700-1747......................0019503
            Deed records, v. B     1745-1750......................0019507
****************************************************************************
TENNESSEE, POLK - LAND AND PROPERTY

Polk County (Tennessee).  Register of Deeds.                 _____
    Deed records, 1894-1927. -- [S.l.]: Tennessee State Lib. |U.S. & CAN|
        and Archives, 1970. -- 9 microfilm reels; 35 mm.     |FILM AREA |
    Microfilm made from originals  Includes index in each volume.
```

```
        General Index              1897-1938.................  1012147
        Deeds,       v. 1-2        1897-1927 (re-recorded)...  1012141
*****************************************************************************
VIRGINIA - MILITARY RECORDS - REVOLUTION, 1775-1783 - PENSIONS
                                                         _____
Revolutionary War bounty warrants and index (Virginia)-Salt |U.S. & CAN|
  Lake City: Filmed by the Genealogical Society of Utah,1954 |FILM AREA |
  31 microfilm reels; 16 mm and 35 mm.                       |_____|
      Microfilm of original and typescript at the state library in
        Richmond, Virginia.
  Index, Aaron, William to Payner, Wm. ......................  0029850
  Index, Pea, Thomas to Zimmerman, Wm. ....................    0029851
  Warrants, Aaron, William to Ayres, John.................     0029821
      Warrants, Baber, Edw'd to Bates, Thos.
  Warrants, Box 10, Batson, Thos to Beazley,...............    0029822
      Ephraim.
      Warrants, Box 11, Beck, John to Belvin, William
      Warrants, Box 12, Benjamin, Joseph to Biggs, Tom
*****************************************************************************
```

How do you limit common surname histories that are linked to yours? One possibility is using the KEY WORD SEARCH feature of the *FHLC* on computer. By striking the F6 function key, you are given the option of entering two words that could also link to that surname. The two most successful methods are to enter the state or county and the surname of the spouse. Perhaps your Aunt Maude is mentioned in a history about her famous husband, or she might be mentioned in a history of a group of people from a particular county.

The list of records produced by the catalog may include family histories, genealogies, Bible records, and biographies containing the surname. You can use this list to help you decide which Family History Library materials you would like to order through your local Family History Center, or you can request detailed searches of library materials through professional record look-up services (see *http://www.GRAonline.com*).

Instructions at a Local FHC:

1. Go to a *FamilySearch* computer with a printer. Select the *Family History Library Catalog* from the menu, press ENTER.

2. Choose the "Surname" search.

3. Type in the surname and view results list.

    A. If there aren't very many records listed for the exact spelling, print (F2) to make a copy of the possible variations of the name, and print all the exact spellings, plus the most probable variations.

    B. If there are many entries and no keywords given, go to the list and print out at least those with the surname in the title (DO NOT GET THE SMITH FAMILY HISTORY IF THEIR LAST NAME IS JONES).

    C. Always print (F2) sources where the subject's surname is the primary surname in the book (included in the title of the book, instead of just the notes) and when it is also in the same locality.

    D. Also check for the records that are written by the individual with the same surname.

The information from your search may be printed to a **text file** or an **ASCII** file so that it can be brought into a word processing program for reporting.

The next chapters will teach you how to obtain the records you have printed. However, other things can be learned from studying the catalog entries which we wish to cover first. Various indexing codes, for example, guide you to other resources.

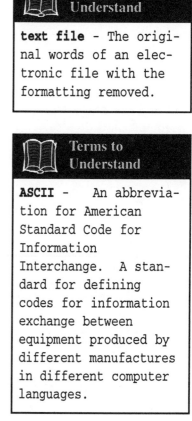

Terms to Understand

text file - The original words of an electronic file with the formatting removed.

Terms to Understand

ASCII - An abbreviation for American Standard Code for Information Interchange. A standard for defining codes for information exchange between equipment produced by different manufactures in different computer languages.

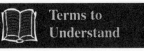

Terms to Understand

Par·ish and Vi·tal Re·cords List - A microfiche listing of sources by locality which have previously been extracted. This list guides the researcher to another way of obtaining information in unindexed sources.

Family History Library Index Codes

Below is a sample of a microfiche entry on the *FHLC*. The codes beside the film numbers indicate whether a microfilm is being extracted for insertion into the *International Genealogical Index (IGI)* which we will cover in the next chapter. This means that, eventually, the information in an unindexed resource will soon be indexed and in one of the electronic databases available in the Family History Library. Similar information can be obtained by using the **Parish and Vital Records List** on microfiche to see if an area you wish to do research in has had records extracted already. To locate areas previously extracted listed by locality, use this listing.

I = In Process of Being Extracted
X = Extracted
P = Partially Extracted

```
***************************************************************************
ENGLAND, YORK, RASTRICK - CHURCH RECORDS

Church of England.  Parish Church of Elland.               -----------------
  Bishop's transcripts, 1600-1841. -- Salt Lake City      | BRITISH        |
  Filmed by the Genealogical Society of Utah, 1977.       | FILM AREA      |
  on 3 microfilm reels; 35 mm.                             -----------------

  Microfilm of manuscripts in the Borthwick Institute, York.
  Elland is a chapelry in the parish of Halifax.
  Includes chapelries of Norland, Rastrick, and Ripponden.

  Christenings 1600-1787 -------------------------------- 0990607
  Marriages    1600-1786
  Burials      1600-1788
  Christenings 1788-1824 -------------------------------- 0990608  I
  Marriages    1787-1824
  Burials      1789-1825
***************************************************************************
ENGLAND, YORK, RATHMELL - CHURCH RECORDS

Church of England.   Chapelry of Rathmell.                -----------------
  Bishop's transcripts, 1843-1846. -- Salt Lake City      | BRITISH       |X
  Filmed by the Genealogical Society of Utah, 1976.       | FILM AREA     |
  on 1 microfilm reel; 35 mm.                             | 0919138       |
                                                          |   item 2      |
                                                          -----------------
  Microfilm of original records in the Borthwick Institute, York.
  Rathmell is a chapelry in the parish of Giggleswick.
  Christenings, marriages and burials.  No burials, 1845.
***************************************************************************
ENGLAND, YORK, ROSEDALE - CHURCH RECORDS

Church of England.  Parish Church of Rosedale.            -----------------
  Parish registers 1616-1875 -- Salt Lake City:           | BRITISH       |P
  Filmed by the Genealogical Society of Utah, 1968.       | FILM AREA     |
  1 microfilm reel; 35 mm.                                | 0551573       |
                                                          |   item 2      |
                                                          -----------------
  Microfilm of originals in the County Record Office, Northallerton.
***************************************************************************
```

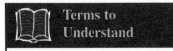

Terms to Understand

nav·i·ga·tion bar - On an Internet screen, a menu of options which take you somewhere else within the program.

The Internet FHLC

As you come to the opening screen of the Internet *FamilySearch* screen, you will be able to go immediately into an ancestor search, a keyword search, or a custom search by selecting one of the tabs in the center of the screen. You will also notice a **navigation bar** along the left hand margin of your screen. There are various functions along the bar including search, browse categories, collaborate with others, preserve your genealogy, add a site, order family history resources, provide feedback, and get help.

By clicking on the *Keyword Search* button you can go to various Web sites or to the *SourceGuide* which we will discuss later. By clicking on the *Custom Search* button, you are given the option of selecting the *Ancestral File, International Genealogical Index* (as far as it is completed), the *Family History Library Catalog*, the Family History Center addresses, *SourceGuide*, Web sites, and collaboration lists. By selecting the *Family History Library Catalog*, you may search over two million microfilm and over eight hundred thousand books and microfiche.

At the *Family History Library Catalog* **front page** you may elect to do a place search, surname search, or all searches. If you select a place, you will be given the choices of an author search, film or fiche search (lists the contents of a particular roll of film or slide of fiche), place search, surname search, or call number search.

If you select a place search, you may enter a town such as Portland and then another locality option, such as Oregon. By clicking on the Search button, the program will provide you with matching places. Once you have the area you desire and you click on it, the various categories which were mentioned previously under the microfiche *FHLC* will come up, as well as some notes on the date of the creation of that city or county.

To go deeper into the sources available on a particular locality, merely click on the category topic you are interested in. By clicking on "Oregon, Portland, Cemeteries," I would be given a list of those references in the Family History Library collection. To view the film notes, I would click on the *View Film Notes* button, and read what information is available on that film. If I were quite impressed with those records, I could print a copy of the screen and take my printout to my local Family History Center and order the microfilm.

To make it easier on everyone, there is a button to click to find the addresses of local Family History Centers. It is very simple to go to the *Custom Search* tab and select Family History Centers, type in the town you live in, and see which one is closest to you. The hours, location, and phone numbers are provided. More on Family History Centers will be given in chapter 12.

Using the *Family History Library Catalog* with the *SourceGuide* will increase your research skills by leaps and bounds.

THE SOURCEGUIDE

The *SourceGuide* CD contains four major items necessary for a family historian:

- Instructions on what sources are the most important to search in each state or country
- How and in what order to approach the sources in each area
- Word lists to help you interpret records of various nations, and
- Maps of diverse time periods.

For example, you might be interested in doing research in Germany. Just put in the CD, scroll down to Germany and you will see options for German word lists, maps, and genealogy how-to sections. Bring up the genealogy how-to information and scroll through the instructions. If you see something you like, print it or copy it to a computer file. By using a disk file you can add notes to yourself about who you would like to search in those particular records.

Once you have determined a record source from the *SourceGuide*, go to the *Family History Library Catalog* and locate that source. Many sources are given a computer number in the *SourceGuide* to make this task even faster. While using the CD, print out a copy of the map which most represents the time period under study. You may also want to print a modern map in order to compare where the sites are today. The *SourceGuide* will give you foreign references to gazetteers which could point out specific places as well which are not on the CD

📖 **Terms to Understand**

front page - In an Internet program, it is the main page of a particular subsection of a Web site.

but available through loan at a local Family History Center.

You can order a copy of the *SourceGuide* online from the *FamilySearch* Online Distribution Center at *http://www.familysearch.org* or by calling the Salt Lake City Distribution Center at (800) 537-5971. You can use the *SourceGuide* online at the above site, but it works so well in CD format that I like owning my own copy.

CONCLUSION

The *SourceGuide* and the *Family History Library Catalog* are powerful guidance tools to the collection of the Family History Library. Each *FHLC* format has its own advantages as well. Using the *FHLC* on microfiche allows you to take photocopies of several records at a time, to do searches you cannot do currently on the CD version such as author/title and subject searches, and they are quick to use when all the computers are tied up at the library or center you are using. Using the *FHLC* on CD or on a server at a local center allows you to download the information you want to a diskette, take it home, study it further, pull it into your own word processor or GEDCOM-compatible genealogy computer program, and continue your research. Using the *FHLC* on the Internet is the ultimate in availability and ease for those already accustomed to the Internet.

With four versions of the *Family History Library Catalog* available, I would rank them as follows:

1. Webview terminals available in the Family History Library contain the most current information because they are updated weekly with new library acquisitions. They have more functionality than #2 below, such as having author/title and subject searching capabilites.

2. The Internet version at *www.familysearch.org* is more current than #3 below and is available wherever you might have an Internet connection.

3. The newest Window's version CD-ROM *FHLC* is available for $5. It can be ordered at *www.familysearch.org*, but needs particular computer viewers, so check those specifications at the purchasing site. You can do author/title searches.

4. The DOS CD-ROM *FHLC* available at most of the Family History Library terminals and local Family History Centers is still easier and faster for certain searches, such as family histories, but you cannot do author/title searches. If you want to know which FHCs hold a particular roll of microfilm on indefinite loan, this is also the format to use.

Mastering the use of these tools will bring you years of enjoyment and cut your frustration levels in half. The next chapter will cover the electronic resources of the Family History Library.

ASSIGNMENT 10: USING THE FHLC AND SOURCEGUIDE

1. Using *SourceGuide,* become familiar with one state where your ancestors lived by locating that state and printing out the guide to its records. What is the result of this search?

2. Use the *Family History Library Catalog* (*FHLC*) to search for a published history on one of your family surnames which you selected in the "Your Turn" assignments in Chapter 9. What did you find?

3. Use the *Family History Library Catalog* (*FHLC*) to search for the locality you selected on in the "Your Turn" assignments in Chapter 9. What did you find?

YOUR TURN ANSWERS

See Assignment 10 for application of answers.

COMPUTER CHECKLIST #10

Explain how you could use the *Family History Library Catalog* to obtain the complete citation for a film or book in the library, copy it to a disk file, bring it up into a word processor which can read ASCII or .TXT files (or WordPad on your Accessories List), and then cut and paste it to your notes fields and source fields of your computer program.

WEB SITE

http://www.familysearch.org
The largest genealogy site in the world. It was introduced May 24, 1999. It averages roughly 8.5 million hits a day. New information is always included. By the end of 2000, 240 million new names will be added to the FamilySearch™ Internet genealogy database, primarily from Western Europe, Scandinavia, and Mexico.

BIBLIOGRAPHY

Church of Jesus Christ of Latter-day Saints. *Family History SourceGuide.* CD-ROM. Salt Lake City: Church of Jesus Christ of Latter-day Saints, 1998.

Church of Jesus Christ of Latter-day Saints. *Family History Library Catalog.* CD-ROM. Salt Lake City: Church of Jesus Christ of Latter-day Saints, 2000.

CHAPTER 11

Major Databases of the Family History Library

"It is a capital mistake to theorize before one has data."
—*Sir Arthur Conan Doyle*

Learning to use specific resources in specific repositories is part of the success of a family history researcher. Databases have been developed for use in the Family History Library by taking computer-entered information from vital records or other sources and sorting the information by surname, dates or events. These databases prove very helpful to the genealogist who is just beginning research, for they often lead to primary sources, which are critically important for accurate research.

FAMILY HISTORY LIBRARY DATABASES

There are several sets of databases available through the Family History Library, and each has its own function. For example, there are those which:

- Provide access to original records internationally, as they also provide clues to relationships *(IGI)*.
- Link continuous generations, based on the submissions of many individuals *(Ancestral File)*.
- Provide death and residence information for those deceased in the U.S. since the 1940s *(Social Security Death Index)*.
- Provide the death date for those who have died in some of America's wars *(Military Index)*.
- Index the christening and marriage records of the established church of Scotland up to 1855 *(Scottish Parochial Index)*.
- Act as a finding aid to the millions of individuals who were enumerated in England, Wales, Scotland, and Ireland in 1881 *(1881 British Census Index and Abstracts)*.
- Act as a finding aid to the vital records of Australia, North America, and other regions (Vital Records CDs).

 **Terms to Understand**

International Genealogical Index (IGI) - Started in 1969, this index now contains over 300 million names on the computer *FamilySearch* program. It is arranged by surname and locality. Millions of names have been "extracted" by volunteers who copy information from original documents (birth, christening, marriage records, etc.) onto computer cards. Using this index can help you locate an elusive ancestor, find others searching your lines, locate primary sources, and pinpoint localities for unusual surnames.

 Terms to Understand

ex·trac·ting - The process of copying essential information from an original record.

 **Terms to Understand**

sub·mit·ter - One who provides information to a database or other collection.

The above databases are found at the Family History Library and at its branch Family History Centers. Some databases are available for searching on the Internet, and others are available for purchase on CD-ROM, to be used in your home. See Illustration 11-1.

Database	Family History Library	Family History Center	Internet	Available to purchase
IGI	***	***	***	
Ancestral File	***	***	*** (modified usage...not able to perform GEDCOM downloads)	
Social Security Death Index	***	***		Available through other companies
Military Index	***	***		
Vital Record CDs	***	***		***
1881 British Census	***	***		***
1851 British Census	***	***		***
Scottish Parochial Index	***	***		

Illustration 11-1 Databases of the Family History Library
(*** Available at this locality)

We will begin with the largest of all databases for genealogists, the *International Genealogical Index.*

WHAT IS THE IGI?

The ***International Genealogical Index (IGI)*** is an index to names found in the computerized files of the Family History Department (FHD) of the LDS Church with the Family History Library as the FHD's repository. As of 1999, it contained more than 300 million names, and it continues to grow by millions of names each year, through the efforts of volunteers involved in a worldwide vital records **extraction** program of the LDS Church and other **submitters.**

The *IGI* contains names of *deceased persons only*, so don't use it for locating **living** relatives. Most of the names are of persons living from the early 1500s to about 1875, although some are from more recent times. In recent years, the information linking the *IGI* to records submitted by LDS Church members *since 1969* was separated from the *IGI* and placed into the LDS Ordinance Index, to make it easier to work with the two files.

The *IGI* is literally the largest database in the world, containing church records of almost every denomination, extracted for their vital information. It is, therefore, a tremendous tool for genealogists internationally, since in many areas of the world church records provide the birth, marriage and death information genealogists seek to establish their relationships.

The IGI Lists Individuals, Not Families

While the *IGI* does link one individual to another, such as a child to a parent, or a husband to a wife, it does not continue to link an entire family in order to show family relationships.

Neither does it link any records (birth or marriage, for example) listed for the same individual. For each record, the *IGI* includes the following:

1. Name of an individual
2. Name of the parents for an individual or the name of a spouse
3. Sex of the individual
4. Type of event (birth, christening or marriage)
5. Date of event
6. Place of event
7. LDS ordinance dates (part of a subset of records, the *LDS Ordinance Index*)
8. Source references

The *IGI is only an index.* It does not necessarily include all genealogical information known about a person. Most of the entries in the *IGI are extracted or indexed from vital records created by governments or churches,* and are, therefore, not limited to names of LDS Church members or their ancestors. *It is the largest general index of information of its kind, anywhere.*

The *IGI* is published on microfiche and on CD, and it is also available on the Internet. Each *IGI* microfiche contains 357 pages, or frames, with up to 62 names per page. Each page has both a page number and a grid number (a letter-number combination, such as M-03) in the upper left-hand corner. Since the *IGI* is updated and reprinted periodically, you should look at the top of each microfiche for the date of that edition (see Illustration 11-2).

At the top of each page, or frame, you will also find the name of the region (e.g., North America), and the state or province. The first line of data will give you the following information: the first name on that page, an explanation of the different columns and the source of the information with a batch number and serial sheet (source references).

At the bottom of each page, or frame, is an explanation for the letter codes used. Each microfiche also contains an index page which lists the first name that appears at the top of each page of that microfiche. You will find this index as the last page or frame on each microfiche.

The names on the microfiche edition of the *IGI* are arranged by geographical regions (such as North America or England), by localities within those regions (such as Utah or Yorkshire), then alphabetically by surname, and then by given names.

In Norway, Finland, Sweden, Iceland, Wales, Scotland and Monmouthshire, England entries are arranged alphabetically by GIVEN name, as well as by SURNAME. This is because in those countries, historically, the surname changes in accordance with a **patronymic naming system.**

Terms to Understand

liv·ing - In many genealogical databases, including *Ancestral File*, this term is used in place of an individual's name, if he or she was born in the last 95 years and no death date was listed. In the *IGI*, this term refers to individuals who do not have a known death date, or whose birth date is less than 110 years prior to publication.

Terms to Understand

pat·ro·nym·ics - Of, relating to, or derived from the name of one's father or a paternal ancestor.

```
International Genealogical Index (R) - Version 4.01

11 AUG 1999                          HOLDING FILE ENTRIES                          Page 1
=====================================================================================================
                                                                        Batch and Source
Names (Sex)                    Event  Date/Place                        Information
-----------------------------------------------------------------------------------------------------
John Hindman PAUL (M)............... B: 25 Dec 1840                      Ba: 8676001 19
   Father: Moses PAUL                   Lisbreen, Antrim, Ireland        So: 1396239
   Mother: Elizabeth HYNDMAN

John Reuben PAUL (M)............... C: 15 Nov 1840                       Ba: C053911
   Father: John PAUL                    All Souls, St. Marylebone, London,  So: 580892
   Mother: Elizabeth Caroline           England                          Pr: 0883632
```

Illustration 11-2 Sample Holding File from the International Genealogical Index

Names in the CD version can be grouped and searched on a larger scale. For example, all of the United States can be searched at once, rather than state by state. All of England, Wales, Scotland and Ireland can be searched at once if you are unsure of a specific locality, or you may limit your search to one or two states. The possibilities become quite numerous.

Spellings of names have been standardized for filing purposes, and both the actual and standardized spellings appear in the microfiche version of the *IGI*. A cross-reference (=) is found between the *actual spelling* and the *standard spelling*. The standard spelling is marked with an asterisk (*). Given names are filed alphabetically and not assigned standard spellings, *so look under all possible spelling variations and abbreviations for given names.* In the computer version, all name variations are listed together, if you request this to be done, and then they are grouped chronologically.

In the CD version of the *IGI*, the information may be printed on paper or to a computer disk so that it can be entered into a home computer through the use of the GEDCOM data transfer system.

IGI Sources of Information

The names in the *IGI* come from two major sources:

1. Records processed through the Extraction Program of The Church of Jesus Christ of Latter-day Saints. Through this program, volunteer church members extract the names from original or compiled records of births, christenings and marriages. The *Parish and Vital Records List* shows which records have been extracted for each area and time period. It is arranged alphabetically by state or country.

2. Forms that LDS Church members submitted years ago with information about their ancestors. Previously, these forms contained information about individuals or couples only. Presently, LDS Church members are also submitting information via Family Group Records where complete documentation is not possible to prove vital statistics, but where combined sources can be used to prove the individual. Many records are also being submitted via the *FamilySearch TempleReady* program which is available at local Family History Centers. *TempleReady* converts data from the PAF genealogy program to the program used for the LDS Church temple submissions. The results are found on the *LDS Ordinance Index of Family Search.*

This latter source should not be confused with Family Group Records submitted by LDS Church members as part of the Four Generation Program prior to 1980. *These were not put into the IGI.* Those records submitted after 1980 are part of the *Ancestral File.* Many LDS members are unaware that they may need to resubmit some information to bring their records up to date. Non-LDS Church members may also submit their genealogical data. This is one way that their personal research can appear on the *IGI* to help others.

HOW THE IGI HELPS IN RESEARCH

The *IGI* can help with your research in many ways. It can help you locate original genealogical sources. It can lead you to the individuals who submitted the research. It prevents duplication of research. It can lead you to LDS Ordinance dates. The *IGI* localities may be able to guide you to an area where a preponderance of ancestors with your name lived.

The IGI is not, however, considered an original source for documentation. You should usually check the input sources of *IGI* entries in which you are interested. *Names coming from the extraction program are generally taken from original sources,* such as church records, but the information is only as accurate as the extraction. *If it was submitted by an individual, the information is only as accurate as his or her research.*

You can tell if an item has been extracted or submitted by looking at the batch number. If it was **patron submitted**, the batch number will be all digits, such as 7020219 (meaning batch 20219 of the year 1970), and it will begin with the number 69-99. If it appears through extraction, the number will be prefixed with M, P, or C (such as M004161). (These are very simplified rules to several pages of instructions.)

There is an *IGI* manual, and information is available in the *SourceGuide* to aid the researcher. However, the easiest thing to do is to look up a name on the CD version or the Internet version of the *IGI,* both of which identify all the source numbers for you.

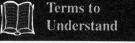

Terms to Understand

pa·tron sub·mit·ted – Unverified information, from an individual's genealogy files or personal research.

To Avoid Duplication in Research

If a name appears in the *IGI,* you can save yourself time and effort by determining where the information came from. If it was extracted, you can go directly to the film source used for extraction (some have a printout) and augment your research. If submitted by an individual, you can obtain his/her name and address and compare data.

There may also be more information in the Family History Library Archives, especially if the baptism or endowment date is very early. Many of the extracted films are very old and difficult for an untrained person to read. Through the Extraction Program, this information is available without your having to find a way to read the film.

A patron can order either a microfilm or a photocopy of the source entry he or she is interested in by using the film number provided in the computer printout and labeled "Source" or "So" (see Illustration 11-2, and look at the right-hand column, headed "Batch and Source Information").

To Determine LDS Ordinance Dates

Members of The Church of Jesus Christ of Latter-day Saints use the Ordinance Index to obtain baptismal and temple marriage dates for their deceased family members. The Ordinance Index is not the only source of LDS Temple Ordinance information. If you do not find the information you are seeking in the *IGI,* you should check the original Temple files on film.

To Extend Pedigree Information

By using the *IGI,* you can often put many members of a family together, or extend your pedigree, especially if the information comes from extraction. By looking through the entries for your surname and watching for all those with the same parents, for example, you can add missing family members to your research. Of course, you will still need to consult the primary sources to verify the possible connections.

With the computer or CD version of the *IGI,* but not the Internet version, you can request that all children of the same-named parents be listed together by doing a parent search. You can also find marriages by doing a marriage search.

To Determine Localities Where Your Surnames Appear

You can see what surnames appear in the record(s) of a certain place. For example, you could find the counties and towns in Pennsylvania where persons with the surname of Eastwood are found. This could help you narrow your search area and give you material to check for possible relatives.

LIMITATIONS OF THE IGI

It is an Index Only for Those Records Entered Into It

The *IGI* is NOT an index to ALL records for any place or time period. Nor is it an index to all records available at the Family History Library. For LDS Church members, it is NOT an index to all Temple information.

It May Leave out Names in the Original Record

As with any index, names found in the original records may be omitted, or a name may have been misinterpreted and indexed incorrectly. Even though the vital records of a place have been extracted, some names were illegible and so were not copied or entered into the *IGI*. Although every effort is made to assure correctness, some names are interpreted incorrectly. For example, Herfoot may be listed as Kerfoot, or Hubbins may be listed as Stubbins. Sometimes, due to rights of privacy, certain years are not included.

It Does Not List All the Information on An Individual

Because the *IGI* is an index, only the information sufficient to identify a person is given. But it does identify each person listed and provides a reference number for the source of the information. There may be additional information in the source document.

It Does Not Cross-Reference All Events

There are millions of listings of events (births, christenings, marriages and some miscellaneous events) in the *IGI*, but there are no cross-references or links between those events. There are search capabilities to pull up individuals by the same name in the same time period which might indicate a relationship, but research in the original records should be done to verify that assumption. A name referring to the same individual may be entered more than once, by birth and by marriage. This also applies to families. The brothers and sisters and parents may all be listed in the *IGI,* but there was no capability to cross-reference between them until the computerized version made it possible. The new *Custom Search* feature of the Internet *IGI* allows the specification of an event year. Soon that feature will also allow a search by place as well. Special filters on the Internet *IGI* can identify individuals based upon a relationship to parents or spouse during the search. No list is pulled together for you on the current version of the Internet *IGI*. However, by looking down the section of your surname on the microfiche, CD, or computer versions, you can watch for people who have the same parents; and you can look for those who have a modification of the spelling of the surname. In this way, you can put together hypothetical families through the *IGI*. Of course, you would have to use other sources to prove these connections.

Remember: *THE IGI IS ARRANGED BY THE LOCALITY OF THE EVENT.* If you are looking in the wrong county in many countries, or the wrong state in the U.S. on the CD or computer versions, for example, you will not find the entry, although it may be elsewhere in the *IGI*. The Internet version does a broader search for you automatically. You may want to try looking in additional localities with various spellings as well. The locality is determined *by where the event took place*. If your ancestor was born in Vermont, married in Maine and had children in Maine, New Hampshire and New York, you had better check all of those locations for possible entries in the *IGI*.

Many IGI Entries Represent Persons Who Died as Infants

In earlier times, many children did not survive childhood. Deaths and burials are not generally extracted in the *IGI*, so an individual's birth record may have been extracted, but not his death as a child. As a general rule, the Family History Department does not index burial records, and those burial records that have been indexed have not always been matched against birth and christening records.

Many names in the IGI represent persons who died as infants, even though they may not be identified as such. If you find an entry in the *IGI* that appears to be for one of your ancestors, you should check the input source. If the individual died within a few years of birth (even though he or she had the same name and christening time period as your ancestor), this could not be your ancestor. You should also check the burial records for that area and time period to be sure that the individual lived to maturity.

The IGI is a Secondary Source

The data in the *IGI* is only as accurate as the person who submitted it. It is always wise to verify information by checking original records. The Family History Department does *not* check the accuracy of submitted information. Duplicate information may also have been entered due to typing errors or different spellings of localities.

The Family History Department has many, many rolls of microfilm, and much of it has not been extracted or indexed. IF YOU DON'T FIND AN ENTRY IN THE *IGI,* SEARCH OTHER RECORDS AVAILABLE FOR THAT AREA.

It is always important to locate the sources others have used. As mentioned previously, the computerized version of the *IGI* gives the source film with the entry. There are several things to be gained by ordering a copy of the microfilmed entry forms, if the source is an individual entry. For example:

1. You will see a copy of the actual entry form, as submitted by the patron. (Now you know why you should be sure that *your* entry forms are neat and legible!)

2. You will know the name and address of another person who is also working on the same line. You could write to the address given and share information. If the address is very old, the submitter may not still be alive or living there, but it is something to check out.

3. You will be able to see a reference to the *source* from which the submitter obtained the information. It may give you valuable information by listing a family history or the name of a book that you have never heard of. It may tell you that the submitter has the family Bible or other documents that you would not have had access to any other way.

More Hints About the IGI

In searching the *IGI,* you may find many entries for your family members with the same batch number but different serial/sheet numbers. This often indicates that the same individual submitted all the entries. If there are many entries, it would be to your advantage to order the film so that you could then look

through it and gain much insight into the sources being used by others. The submitter was supposed to list a primary source on each individual entry or marriage record. You could learn a lot by looking at that film. (You will also see why "Family Records" doesn't quite cut it as a research source!)

However, you may find that there is only one, lone entry for your ancestor. It is still invaluable to go after the source of that information. You could find that the submission is totally false and that by adhering to its information it may be stopping you from progressing further.

YOUR TURN

Use the Internet version of the *IGI* by going to *http://familysearch.org* to search for your grandparents or great-grandparents. At the home page, click on "Custom Search" along the tabs below the "Search for Ancestors" title. Select the option for *IGI*. Enter as much information in the fields that are then provided including your ancestors' first and last names, birth dates and localities. Now select the birth, christening, marriage, death, or burial dates option. What were the results?

WHAT IS THE ANCESTRAL FILE?

Simply put, *Ancestral File* is a lineage-linked, surname-indexed database of pedigrees and Family Group Records submitted since 1980 by researchers all over the world. This file is constantly growing. Submitters' names and addresses are provided for the purpose of sharing source materials. Data may be downloaded to a floppy disk and added to a computer genealogy program.

Many family lines may be found on *Ancestral File*, and if we find something our first impulse is to download everything and immediately bring the information into our own files. CAUTION: We may also find numerous submissions for the same individual, incorrect linkages, conflicting dates and places, and missing children or siblings. While we should definitely use *Ancestral File* to build the foundation of our personal family history, we should use it only after removing the pests that plague it.

YOUR TURN

1. Use the Internet version of the *Ancestral File* by going to *http://familysearch.org* to search for your grandparents or great-grandparents. At the home page, click on "Custom Search" along the tabs below the "Search for Ancestors" title. Select the option for *Ancestral File*. Enter as much information in the fields that are then provided including your ancestors' first and last names, birth dates and localities, and then ask for the birth, christening, marriage, death, or burial dates. What were the results?

2. Did you find any erroneous information in the *Ancestral File*? What is wrong with the information?

HOW TO CORRECT ERRORS IN THE ANCESTRAL FILE

Here are some ways to fix the *Ancestral File* before you load it into your own files:

First, set your goals for using the Ancestral File

Consider these examples of goals others have set:

1. Each of the maternal lines branching off the _____ line needs to be examined for correctness and completion.

2. If LDS, determine whether Temple ordinances have been performed on any of those individuals who did not currently have Temple ordinances listed in the Family Submissions to *Ancestral File*.
3. If the family was located in the LDS data files (see next step), prepare an electronic copy of the materials to pull into your family file to save time, effort, and spelling or data entry errors.
4. Correct any erroneous data, and provide documentation for information that was corrected.
5. Provide documentation to prove or verify relationships between family members added to the family tree, and add to information in your genealogy computer program notes fields.
6. Obtain lists of submitters for new individuals added to the family tree in order that correspondence between your family and interested parties might be undertaken.
7. If LDS, and if information was not available in the LDS databases on Temple or individual ordinance data, then seek that information in the original files of the church, update the records for the family, and notify the family if Temple work has not been completed, or if individuals have been missed, so everyone can help.
8. Prepare charts and diagrams to help your family determine which lines need to be worked on in the future.
9. Provide the family with reports in electronic format (e.g., *PAF,* GEDCOMs and WordPerfect), so that the information might be pulled into family histories or other family publications in the future.

Second, determine exactly which lines to focus on

Below are goals others have set.

1. An overall analysis of the ancestral lines of _____
2. Going back to the 5th generation from _____, there are eight major lines. . .
3. Each of these eight lines will be covered separately. The maternal line branching from each line is a direct-line and will be covered. Looking at each of these surname lines closely, there are, of course, several other lines attached to each of them which can be seen in ancestral fan charts.
4. The earliest ancestor, or as far back as the family has gone on the _____ line, was. . . In *Ancestral File*, Samuel had two sons christened in the same year a few months apart (one in February and one in March). One was our direct line, _____, and the other was George. This always raises a red flag that the direct line connection might be in error. This should be searched using original records.
5. Another problem. Samuel's direct line descendant had two daughters both named Mary, which is okay if one of them died, but the second was born three months after our direct line ancestor. Therefore, we believe there is an error in the family record at that point.
6. Also, Samuel had only two children listed, and his first wife had no children listed. We would assume, therefore, that there are missing individuals in the family record, or that in years gone by, only the direct-line ancestor was copied.

Third, use other large databases to speed up the process of correcting errors in the file

1. *Ancestral File*: To see if others have also submitted on the same families.
2. *IGI:* To see if the work has been done via the Extraction Program of the LDS Church.

3. *LDS Ordinance File:* See if all the Temple work (especially sealing work) has been done.
4. *FHLC Surname Search:* See if any books have been published on your family.
5. Library of Congress: Same as #4.

Fourth, determine how to correct errors in what you find

Many people believe they can change information that is already in the *Ancestral File* simply by submitting a record with the correct information. When several relatives submit similar family information to the *Ancestral File* without first downloading the existing information, checking it, verifying information, and then correcting what is already in the file, a big problem occurs. Many "almost" duplicate entries result in "new" entries in this master file, so that a man who married twice may be listed with four or five wives. If you submit a proper birthplace for an individual who has an improper birthplace currently in the file, and you do not use the correction method, the new correct information will be ignored and the old, incorrect information will remain in place.

Corrections may be made to the Ancestral File three different ways

- In writing.
- While using the *Ancestral File* program (Edit F3 key).
- Through submissions using *PAF* 3.0 and higher (while you can contribute new information to *Ancestral File* using earlier versions, you cannot use earlier versions to submit corrections).

Corrections can be made to the records for

- Individuals and marriages.
- Families.
- Submitter, interested researcher, and history of changes lists.

Before you make corrections you should know

- What corrections you need to make (compare what is currently in the *AF* with your own family records).
- What documentation (or reasoning) would verify the correction (a complete citation so others can also find that documentation in the future).
- How to coordinate your correction with other family members or *AF* submitters in case they can add to your documentation.
- If the privacy rights of living persons are protected. If you do not have a death date for an individual born in the past 95 years, he or she will be listed as "LIVING" in the file. If you find in the *AF* the complete information for a person who is still alive, please write to the Family History Department, ATTN: *Ancestral File* Corrections, 50 East North Temple Street, Salt Lake City, UT 84150-3400.

Corrections which are only made in writing

If you need to submit corrections to the *AF,* there are four things which can be done in writing but which *cannot be done* with the Edit feature of *AF.*

- Change the sex codes of parents or spouses in the *Ancestral File.*
- Add or correct a marriage and sealing information for a couple in which the word LIVING appears on one or both of the spouses' records. (LIVING indicates that the person was born within the last 95 years, and that the record does not contain death, burial, and LDS baptism information. Also, if the

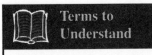

Terms to Understand

merge - To blend the information on an individual, family or event, so as to provide a concise, complete and accurate record.

name of the individual whose correction you want to make is spelled differently, by submitting it in writing the person processing the correction can verify that the names are the same and can manually **merge** the names, even if the spellings are slightly different.)

- Remove an individual from one family and link him or her to another family.
- Correct information about a person who was born before the year A.D. 1500.

Corrections made via PAF 3.0 or higher

- If you want to submit more than one generation of a person's family, because the Edit feature will not allow more than one generation to be added.
- When you want to add new people who have never been in the file.
- If you want to add death and burial information for a person who is currently listed as "LIVING" in the file.
- To include missing baptismal dates and Temple ordinance dates.
- To add or correct names, dates and places of all vital events, as well as the dates and locations of LDS baptisms, endowments and sealings.

Corrections made using the Edit feature of Ancestral File

- To add the death date for someone whose death date is missing from the file.
- To include missing baptismal dates or Temple ordinance dates (LDS submitters).
- To add or correct names, dates and places of all vital events, as well as the dates and locations of LDS baptisms, endowments and sealings.
- To merge people who are listed as LIVING (because of insufficient information at the time of submission) with the same person whose name is actually listed in the file.
- To merge duplicate individuals in the file.
- To add or correct a deceased couple's marriage and sealing information.
- To add new individuals and families to deceased individuals.
- To remove individuals from families.
- To correct your name and address in the "submitter" or "interested researcher" list in the file.
- To register a research interest in someone you found in the *Ancestral File.*
- To indicate that a person shown on the "submitter" or "interested researcher" list is deceased.

How to submit corrections on paper

- Print the appropriate record from the *Ancestral File* (it must have the *Ancestral File* number showing). To correct information for one individual, print only the individual record. It is not necessary to print the Pedigree and Family Group Record as well. If you are correcting information on several children in a family, print the Family Group Record.
- Write the corrections clearly, in black or blue ink, on the printout, or include a separate Family Group Record that contains the corrected information.
- Write your name and full mailing address on EACH page.
- Write a source or reason for each change, or the change will not be made.
- Mail the printouts to: Family History Department, ATTN: *Ancestral File* Corrections, 50 East North Temple Street, Salt Lake City, UT 84150-3400.

How to submit corrections on disk from PAF 3.0 or higher

- Convert *AF* information to a format *PAF* can use by making a GEDCOM. In *AF,* press F2 (print/copy) and select C. Create a GEDCOM. Follow instructions on screen.
- In *PAF* 3.0, use Import to upload the GEDCOM file.

Guide for Making Corrections to *Ancestral File*™, Part I

To	Do this to identify an individual	Do this to edit
Correct an individual's: name or title, birth or christening, death or burial, baptism, endowment or sealing-to-parents.	Highlight the individual on one of these screens: F5 Index, F6 Family record, F7 Pedigree, Or display Individual Record, Or the individual's Submitter List	Press F3 and select **A. Edit individual info**, Delete incorrect info, Type new info, Press F12 to save, Type source or reason, Press F12 to save, Read editing completed, Press ENTER when done
Correct sex for a child	Same	Same
Correct person listed as LIVING who has died	Same	Same (must provide death or burial info)
Correct person listed as LIVING (with no name given who is LDS)	Same	Same (must provide baptismal date)
Coordinate research about a deceased person	Same or start from submitter list F9	Select **E. Register research interest** and follow directions.
Correct a person with more than one record	Highlight the person on one of these screens: F5 Index, F6 Family record. NOTE: If duplicates are not listed as children in the same family start with Index F5.	Press F3 and select **B. Merge two individuals**. Move highlight bar to duplicate person. Press SPACE BAR. (If duplicate record is not shown on Index screen, press F4 to find duplicate individual.) Press F12 and read warning. Press ESC. Correct info on Merged Record window. Press F12. Type source or reason. Press F12 to save. Read editing completed. Press ENTER when done
Correct submitter's name or address or interested researcher's name, address, or telephone number	Highlight an individual the submitter contributed. Read notice and press ENTER. Highlight submitter or researcher you want, Press F3. Select **B. Edit submitter or researcher information**	Make the needed corrections. Press F12 to save. Read editing completed. Press ENTER when done
Register that a submitter/interested party has died	Same except last line select **C. Mark submitter or researcher as deceased**	Read editing completed. Press ENTER when done

Illustration 11-3 Guide to Making Corrections to Ancestral File, Part 1

Guide for Making Corrections to *Ancestral File*™, Part II

To	To identify and correct	To start the edit	To finish the edit
Correct a deceased couple's marriage and sealing information	Highlight the individual on either: F6 Family record F7 Pedigree Press F3 and select **C. Edit marriage and family data**	Highlight "Edit marriage data (& LDS sealing to spouse)" Press ENTER Delete incorrect info Type new info	Press F12 to save Type source or reason Press F12 to save Read editing completed Press ENTER when done
Correct individual's information in a family	Same as above	Highlight the individual's name Press ENTER Delete incorrect info Type new info	Same as above
Merge records of the same child listed more than once	Same as above	Highlight the names of one of the children Press SPACE BAR. (If duplicate record is not shown on Index screen, press F4 to find duplicate individual) Press F12 and read warning Press ESC Type correct info on Merged Record window	Same as above
Remove an individual from a family.	Same as above	Highlight the individual's name Press DELETE (the individual is removed from this family only)	Same as above
Add a parent	Same as above	Highlight the place where the parent should appear Press ENTER Type new info on parent if not in AF If parent is in Aft, press F4 to find the parent	Same as above
Add a child	Same as above	Highlight the words "Add a Child" which appear beneath the last child in the family Press ENTER Type new info on child if not in AF If child is in AF, press F4 to find the child	Same as above
Add an entire family	Highlight the person either: F6 Family record F7 Pedigree Press F3 and select **D. Create a new family**	Select whether you want to add a new family, with the individual as a child or as a parent Highlight area where you want to add information Press ENTER. Type information and press F12	Repeat until family is in Type source or reason Press F12 to save Read editing completed Press ENTER when done

Illustration 11-3 Guide to Making Corrections to Ancestral File, Part 1

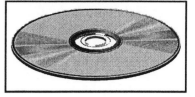

- Make the corrections.
- Use Export in *PAF* 3.0 to create a file to send to *Ancestral File*. Select *Ancestral File* Submission. Use the Corrected option in the *Ancestral File* submission process. If you want to add new individuals, use the New option in the *PAF* 3.0 program, but submit that information on a different diskette.
- When you have finished, write on the label of the diskette, "*Ancestral File* Corrections," your name, address, and phone number, and your computer's operating system. If you are also submitting new information, use a different diskette for the new information. It would be labeled "Ancestral File Submission" rather than "correction" and it would need to be labeled with the version of *PAF* you used, plus your name, address, phone number, and computer operating system.
- Mail the disk(s) to: Family History Department, ATTN: *Ancestral File* Corrections, 50 East North Temple Street, Salt Lake City, UT 84150-3400.

How to submit corrections on disk from Ancestral File

- Decide what you wish to correct. Select the option you desire from the *Correcting Information in Ancestral File* handout available from the Family History Department (address located above), or use Illustration 11-3, *Guide for Making Corrections to Ancestral File.*
- Locate the individual you are seeking in *Ancestral File,* and highlight that person.
- Press F3 to edit.
- Insert a blank, formatted, floppy disk, and indicate which drive you want to use.
- Enter your name, mailing address, and telephone number.
- Press F12 to save this information onto the floppy disk.
- Make the corrections and provide the reason or source for each change. If possible, use a source that is publicly available, so that another can find that source.
- Review or print your corrections by pressing F3 and selecting F, which allows you to Review/print edits made. Select the drive into which you have placed your diskette and highlight the file name (they all begin with AFEDIT). Press F12 and review the corrections by using the Pg Up and Pg Dn keys. If you find an error or something you don't want to submit, highlight that correction and press "delete" to remove it. The item won't disappear, but it has been marked for deletion. When you press the ESC key, the correction will be deleted, and you can review it again to be sure. To print your corrections, press F2 and select A (Summary of Edits), then press F12 to print to paper. Press R when you are ready to quit reviewing and printing edits.
- When finished, write on the label of the diskette, "*Ancestral File* Corrections," your name, address, and phone number, and the name of your computer's operating system.
- Mail the disk(s) to: Family History Department, ATTN: *Ancestral File* Corrections, 50 East North Temple Street, Salt Lake City, UT 84150-3400.

To review all these steps, see Illustrations 11-2 and 11-3.

What if my family is not located in the Ancestral File?

If the individual's parents, siblings, and children have not been located in these major files, then original research must be done in the records of the country by beginning with the last known place of residence. When the research is completed, data enter the information into a genealogy computer program. The free version of *PAF* 4.0 does an excellent job of this. Then submit a copy of the information via the Internet site, or mail a copy to Ancestral File, 50 East North Temple Street, Salt Lake City, UT 84150-3400. Remember to include your name, address, phone number, and the name of your computer's operating system (DOS, Windows 95, Windows 98, Macintosh, etc.).

WHAT IS THE FAMILY HISTORY LIBRARY CATALOG?

The *Family History Library Catalog* is a database of the Family History Library collection in Salt Lake City. Besides helping you to locate records from all areas of the world, it will permit you to search the database by surname. If the surname is a common one yielding several hundred or several thousand books, key-word searches, such as a location or collateral surname, may be added to the search to concentrate it and yield better results. This catalog was covered in Chapter 10.

WHAT IS THE SOCIAL SECURITY DEATH INDEX?

This database covers individuals who died between 1937 and the current year who had a social security number, and whose death was reported to the Social Security Administration. Although middle names are not given and many people are not listed, when your individual is located, information is available as to where to obtain a death certificate, if there are other living heirs, the date of birth, the state of birth, and the date and place of death.

With the social security number listing from this index you can obtain a copy of the individual's original Social Security Application Form SS-5, and/or Form OA-C790. Both forms basically contain the same information, including the name of the applicant, the town and country of birth (even the parish or small town in a foreign country), the date of birth, the names of the parents (usually the mother's maiden name), the home address, the occupation, and the personal signature of the individual you are researching.

This is a very helpful index for the post-1937 period, but it mostly covers those who died after 1960. The first Social Security card was issued in 1936. The Social Security Administration began keeping records in electronic form in 1962, and the majority of birth dates in the Social Security Death Master File

Illustration 11-4 Social Security Application Form SS-5

YOUR TURN

1. Use the Internet version of the *Family History Library Catalog* by going to *http://familysearch.org* to search for a published history on one of your ancestors. At the home page, click on "Custom Search" along the tabs below the "Search for Ancestors" title. Select the option for *Family History Library Catalog*. Select the "Surname" button. Enter the surname of your ancestor in the field provided. What were the results? How many entries were located?

2. Click on the title of the book. Any item that has a "View film" button indicates that more information is available in a film or fiche version. The film or fiche number is provided so that you can go to your local Family History Center and order that item on loan; and then you can study the contents at your convenience. If the item is only in a book format, you may print out a copy of the page and take it to your local public library to see if it might be ordered on interlibrary loan. If you cannot get the material on loan, you can go to *www.GRAonline.com* and select the option to have a searcher obtain the material and request certain items be copied from the book. What did you find?

range from just after 1870 through 1960. Those individuals who died before 1962 may be in the file, but a death certificate, obituary, and a social security number, if available, will be needed to prove to the SSA that it would be worthwhile for them to make a search.

The *Social Security Death Index* is available at the Family History Library and its Family History Centers, but not yet on their Internet site. However, you can access the *Social Security Death Index* in another format at *www.ancestry.com*.

WHAT IS THE MILITARY RECORDS INDEX?

These are master indexes of those who died in the Vietnam and Korean Wars. They will soon be augmented by those who served in the Civil War.

WHAT ARE THE VITAL RECORDS INDEX CDs?

There are several Vital Records Index CDs for various parts of the world, including North America, the British Isles, Australia, and soon for Germany. Each index includes several million births, christenings, and marriages taken from a partial collection of records in various places and time periods (usually prior to 1900). Each contain from four to five million names. They are fully searchable, sourced, easy to use, and extremely inexpensive (usually about $1 per CD). They can be purchased for use in your home. They may be ordered at

YOUR TURN

Go to *www.ancestry.com* and click on the *Social Security Death Index*. Enter a name of someone in your family who died between 1960 and 1997. What did you find?

www.familysearch.org, and this Web site also indicates from which localities of the world most of the records were derived (for example if the majority of the sources were from Texas, Georgia, and Iowa, and your families came from that area, this would be an excellent source to use). If your states were not covered, it would not be of value to you.

WHAT IS THE 1881 BRITISH CENSUS CD?

The 1881 British Census CD is a fully searchable index to the millions of individuals who were enumerated in England, Wales, Scotland, and Ireland in 1881. But in addition to being an index alone, the index links you immediately to an actual transcription of the information from the census, including full names, ages, sex, color, birthplace, and relationships. You may also ask for a neighbor search and see the neighbors on each side for possible collateral families. This comes on over thirty CDs, and again it is very reasonably priced and marvelous to use on your home computer.

WHAT IS THE 1851 BRITISH CENSUS CD?

The 1851 British Census CD also is more than an index. It includes transcriptions of the census records of Devon, Norfolk, and Warwick counties in England taken on 31 March 1851, and it gives names, ages, relationships, occupations, and birthplaces.

WHAT IS THE SCOTTISH OLD PAROCHIAL INDEX?

Prior to the establishment of Civil Registration in Scotland, the established Church of Scotland, the Presbyterian Church, maintained vital information on the citizens. Until this index was put together, if you didn't know which parish your ancestor was from, you would have to search every parish in Scotland, one-by-one. Since many Scottish ancestors came to the United States before the 1860s when parish names were not often recorded on ships' passenger lists or death records, this was nearly an impossible task. With this index, however, a name can be searched throughout Scotland and the birth and marriage dates located from the late 1600s to 1855. Of course, the more you know about your ancestor, such as other brothers and sisters, possible localities in Scotland, occupation, parents' names, etc., the more likely you are to find exactly who you are looking for in this index. Again, you should search the original records as well.

WHAT IS THE PEDIGREE RESOURCE FILE?

Like the *Ancestral File,* the *Pedigree Resource File* is a lineage-linked, surname-indexed database of pedigrees and Family Group Records. However, this newest addition to the LDS databases (introduced in May 2000) includes the source notes if patron submitters entered their documentation. Also unlike the *Ancestral File*, no attempt has been made to merge family files. Each submission stands alone as it was submitted. Submitters may submit as often as they would like to upgrade their information. For this reason, it is wise to look at the later submissions where upgrades to the family and their documentation are more likely given.

The index to each of the *Pedigree Resouce Files* will be available on the Internet at *www.familysearch.org* as each CD-ROM is completed. Individuals may locate the family or individual they are seeking on the index, and the index will point to the correct CD. These CDs may then be purchased for $5.00 each on the Web site.

CONCLUSION

As we have demonstrated, powerful databases have been developed for use in the Family History Library and at home by taking computer-entered information from vital records or other sources and sorting the information by surname, dates or events. However, these databases are most helpful to the genealogist who is prepared to use them. Each database is a terrific finding aid, but you should never forget to look for the original sources to prove or disprove your hypotheses. More exciting databases are provided in this chapter's "Web sites" listing.

ASSIGNMENT 11: *SEARCHING DATABASES*

1. Locate one individual in your family history on the *Social Security Death Index*. He or she would have to have died after 1937 and not been self-employed. Print out the page of information on where to write for more information from both the Vital Records Office and the Social Security Administration. You may do this search by going to *www.ancestry.com* or *www.ssa.gov* on the Internet, or visiting your local Family History Center.

2. Do a search on the *Ancestral File* for a grandparent in your family to determine if someone else is tracing your line. Print out the page of sources and correspond with the person who submitted the information. You may do this search by using the Internet at *www.familysearch.org*, or by visiting your local Family History Center.

3. Select an ancestor from your Pedigree Chart who was born around the 1850s and try to locate him/her in the *International Genealogical Index*. If you did not find the individual, explain what you learned by the experience. You may do this search by using the Internet at *www.familysearch.org*, or by visiting your local Family History Center.

YOUR TURN ANSWERS

Personal preferences are expected on all Chapter 11 responses.

COMPUTER CHECKLIST #11

1. Explain how you could export a GEDCOM file from your computer to share with the *Ancestral File.*

WEB SITES - Searchable Databases

http://xcat.stauffer.queensu.ca/census/
1871 Ontario Census

http://www.islandnet.com/bccfa/
The British Columbia Cemetery Finding Aid

http://www.islandnet.com/ocfa/homepage.html
Ontario Cemetery Finding Aid for over 2 million interments from over 3,800 different cemeteries in Ontario, Canada

http://feefhs.org/index/indexsur.html
Surname databases from the Federation of East European Family History Societies

http://thor.ddp.state.me.us/archives/plsql/archdev.Marriage_Archive. search_form/
Index to Maine Marriages 1892-1966

http://143.207.5.3:82/search/
Seventh-day Adventist Periodical Index

http://www.usgenweb.com/census/
For transcribed federal and state census records on the Web

gopher://gopher.uic.edu/11/library/libdb/landsale
State of Illinois Public Domain Land Tract Sales, 1815-1880

BIBLIOGRAPHY

Contributing Information to Ancestral File™. Salt Lake City: Family History Department, 1998.

Correcting Information in Ancestral File™. Salt Lake City: Family History Department, 1998.

Howells, Cyndi. *Netting Your Ancestors: Genealogical Research on the Internet*. Baltimore: Genealogical Publishing Company, 1997.

Kemp, Thomas Jay. *Virtual Roots: A Guide to Genealogy and Local History on the World Wide Web*. Wilmington, Delaware: Scholarly Resources Inc., 1997.

Using Ancestral File™. 5th ed. Salt Lake City: Family History Department, 1998.

Using the International Genealogical Index® 6th ed. Salt Lake City: Family History Department, 1998.

Using the Ordinance Index™. Salt Lake City: Family History Department, 1998.

CHAPTER 12

Using Local Family History Centers

"Madam, a circulating library in a town is as an evergreen tree of diabolical knowledge! It blossoms through the year! And depend on it, Mrs. Malaprop, that they who are so fond of handling the leaves, will long at last for the fruit."

—Richard Brinsley Sheridan

Because the Family History Library in Salt Lake City, Utah has as its major aim family history, you are very correct in assuming that they focus on primary sources. However, not everyone can travel to Utah to do research. Luckily, your local Family History Center (FHC) can provide you with a great many primary records, especially vital data and land, property, probate, church and military records.

YOUR LOCAL FAMILY HISTORY CENTER

Some Family History Centers have been in existence for over thirty years, while others are only a few months old. Most centers have the *Family History Library Catalog* in both microfiche and CD-ROM versions, but since the computers at local Family History Centers are usually being used by others, it is a good idea to have an alternative method of locating sources. One strategy is to search the catalog on the Internet before you go to the center so that you have in mind what you wish to order when you arrive.

How to Locate a Center

There are several ways to locate a local Family History Center:

1. Look in your telephone book under The Church of Jesus Christ of Latter-day Saints (Mormons).
2. Go to the Web site at *http://www.familysearch.org*.
3. Order a copy of addresses to local Family History Centers from the Family History Library, 35 North West Temple, Salt Lake City, UT 84150.

When Are They Open?

Most FHCs are open only certain days and hours of the week because they are manned by volunteers. Be sure to call or write ahead of time to find out the hours of the FHC nearest you. You can also go to *http://www.familysearch.org* and obtain the hours and phone number of specific FHCs.

Orientation to a Family History Center

Family History Centers were started over 33 years ago as branches of the Genealogical Society of Utah in Salt Lake City. They are operated by Mormon and non-Mormon volunteers who have various levels of expertise in family history research.

Volunteers are usually trained in the use of equipment, holdings, and basic techniques of research, but they are not expected to do research for patrons. They are, rather, like guides to lead patrons to the various source materials, rather than research assistants. However, often you will find very qualified research specialists volunteering at a local FHC, and you may have a difficult time keeping them from helping you if they know you are in need of help.

Most centers have microfiche and microfilm reader-printers, as well as standard copy machines, so you will be able to make copies of the materials you find. You will be charged for the price of the copies and enough to cover maintenance on the center's machines.

STEP-BY-STEP GUIDE TO THE FHC

Often, basic supplies are available, at cost, to help you organize your family. These may include Pedigree Charts, Family Group Records, census forms, correspondence forms, *IGI* forms, etc.

NOTE: The most common reason for not finding a record is looking in the wrong place.

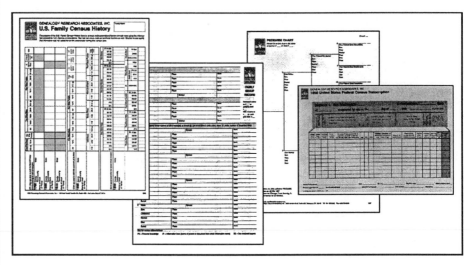

Illustration 12-1 Basic Supplies You May Find at Your Family History Center

Also available are resources *on microfiche* of the most commonly-used reference materials such as historical atlases, maps, or gazetteers for various areas of the world. (Since centers are often short on space, they try to obtain as much information as possible on microfiche.)

RESEARCH STRATEGIES IN A FAMILY HISTORY CENTER

While Chapter 11 explained the various files of the Family History Library, the purpose of this chapter is to explain when and why to search these files. The main reason for searching the databases of the Family History Library is to avoid duplication of research by conducting a preliminary survey. Its purpose is to find sources which indicate that others have already researched and perhaps published information on your family.

Use the "Guide to the Family History Center" to begin your research (see Illustration 12-3). It is a great do-it-yourself aid for the beginning genealogist. Copy it for your personal use, and fill one out *on each line* you are researching. The end result will be a record of the major sources you have searched on an individual. Chances are you will have solved your problem by the time you have completed all the steps. Notice that you are asked to indicate the surname or locality you are searching. Sometimes you may want to do a locality or environmental study before you start on a surname. The guide can be used for either project.

Be sure to date the guide and indicate the smaller localities where your ancestor lived if you elect to do a surname search. The *Family History Library Catalog* (*FHLC*) on the Internet, on computer at local Family History Centers, and on microfiche also acts as a locating guide. Remember, by looking at the first fiche for a state or country on the fiche version of the *FHLC*, a small gazetteer-type index is available to locate the county in which a town will be located in the Family History Library collection. Regular gazetteers, maps, and atlases may also be used.

The guide encourages you to check off items you have accomplished. For example, it asks you to organize your family into Pedigree Charts and Family Group Records. Since you have already accomplished this task, remember to bring them with you to the center.

Start with the *Ancestral File* even if you already experimented with it on the Internet. It has other features in the computer format, such as downloading families, which are very helpful. Plus the *Ancestral File* is extremely valuable for pre-1800 families, for those having royal lines, and as a general reference for all families in the United States. It is one of the first sources searched in a preliminary survey.

Next, search the *FHLC* Surname File. You will find the computer's ability to filter common names such as Smith, Brown, and Green by a second surname (such as a wife's maiden name), or a location where the family lived, impressive as you determine if a published resource is available on your family. Detailed instructions were provided on page 10-7 for accomplishing this task.

If the computers are busy, see if your center has its own indexes, such as a surname index to their periodicals, or a collection of printed family histories that have been donated by their patrons. Next move on to the *International Genealogical Index* which is particularly valuable if your ancestors are from New England, Great Britain, or Mexico. The files are particularly strong in those areas, but no areas of the world are completely neglected.

Perhaps the center you are visiting has a local library source list of specific references, finding aids, or loan films and fiche. Perhaps your center has purchased other CDs or databases which are available for you to use. Many centers have their own Family History Center Catalog (FHCC) or a cataloging system on computer for keeping track of resources in their own center. Some also have a Patron Locality Surname File, which is an index to local patron genealogies or files for patrons to place copies of their research materials. In this way patrons can share their information with others.

Many centers have copies of the published multi-volume set of indexes covering surname histories in the Library of Congress. If your center has such a set,

Terms to Understand

Pa·tron Locality Sur·name File - A file containing the names of Family History Center patrons, along with the surnames they are searching, their addresses, and phone numbers. This permits local patrons to contact each other regarding lines or names they have in common. You are invited to fill out a form as well. (This service is not available at every FHC.)

that is also an item to check on your preliminary survey for the family you have selected. However, remember that it is far from complete.

Catalogs from Nearby or State Libraries

Often long-established centers will have catalog collections for nearby libraries. For example, at the Monterey, California, Family History Center, the card catalog for the California State Library, Sutro Branch, is available on microfiche. California's largest collection of family history materials *not related to California* is located at the Sutro Library just south of San Francisco. This repository is a two-hour drive from the center.

YOUR TURN

Check each of the following resources at your local Family History Center and report on your findings:

1. Does your center have a Patron Locality Surname File? Did you find anything in it?

2. Does you center have a Family History Center Catalog of their own local sources? What did you find in that?

3. Did the center you visited have a collection of printed family histories? Do they accept copies from others who wish to donate?

4. Does your center have a copy of the Library of Congress indexes for surname histories? Did you find anything?

Original Research

Once the preliminary survey phase of the Family History Center has been conducted on the family you are interested in, you can avail yourself of a variety of resources for pursuing original research, some of which are available at your FHC.

Accelerated Indexing System (AIS)

The *AIS* is an alphabetically arranged surname index of town, tax, or census records in the United States. It is nearly complete between 1690 and 1850, but it is incomplete beyond that date. Its value lies in its ease in use. If you don't know the location of your ancestor in a particular decade and you know only his or her name, this can help locate the county where he or she lived. County vital records can then be searched for further clues. Just be aware that there is a 20 percent error rate with this database, due to the difficult handwriting transcribers were faced with in these records.

> **YOUR TURN**
>
> Check your Pedigree Chart. Do you have a male who would be over the age of 21 in 1850? Try to find him on the *AIS* index.
>
> 1. Did it tell you which state and county he lived in? If so, where was he living?
>
> 2. Before locating him on the *AIS*, where did you think he was living?

Terms to Understand

FHLC Sur·name File - The Family History Library in Salt Lake City has a catalog of its holdings available on microfiche or CD through the FamilySearch program. The Surname portion of the catalog will lead you to published histories and collateral-line histories available through the Family History Center's loan system. Thousands of new items are accessed by the library each month, so as part of a preliminary survey, in order to avoid duplication, you should search the surname section in order to see if others have produced a book on your family lines.

Census Records

Many Family History Centers have printed census indexes to the various states. Don't forget to also use the *AIS* mentioned above for states prior to 1850 because no Internet or CD-ROM index covers the entire U.S. at the same time for all these years as yet, though indexes in both formats are imminent. When you don't know the state of residence for an individual, the *AIS* can be your best source. Also many centers today have CD-ROM census indexes produced by Brøderbund (now Genealogy.com) or Heritage Quest. The Family History Department has produced an 1851 and 1881 every name index to the British census, and several other valuable resources as well. Use those which apply to the localities in which you are searching. Also search the card catalog of the local center to see if they have a census you are interested in on indefinite loan at their center already. You will learn more about census records in Chapter 14. Just be aware of their existence in your center.

Terms to Understand

in·de·fi·nite loan
- Films and microfiche are often kept at a local Family History Center for an indefinite period. They are usually not sent back unless the local center does not have the storage space to retain them.

Family History Library Catalog

The goals you have set for yourself should be aligned to the locations in which your ancestors resided during the time period of your goal. Now is the time to expand your knowledge of sources through the *FHLC*. At your center the *Family History Library Catalog* (*FHLC*) will be available on microfiche and on the computer. Having determined the location of your ancestors, the *FHLC* should be searched for original records to assist in the research. If you use the computer version of the *FHLC* in the center, and you have a film number or fiche number on the screen in front of you, highlight the film number you are interested in and strike the enter key. The *FHLC* will provide you with a list of centers where that film has been sent on indefinite loan. Happily, you may just find that it is already at your local center.

YOUR TURN

Look at your "Guide to the Family History Center,"
Illustration 12-3. What goal did you set for yourself?

1. What topic or individual could you search to find additional information on the *Family History Library Catalog?*

2. What locality (e.g., state, township, country, city, county) should you search in order to find reference materials on that topic or individual?

3. Did you check a reference book to see what year the county where your ancestor lived was organized?

4. Did you notice the county formation date as you searched the *FHLC* for its name?

5. What other information did it give you?

Ordering Films and Fiche

Once an item of interest is located you may request a microfilm for a six-week or six-month loan to the center nearest you, but they may *not* be taken home. In addition, those already on loan at a local center may be used by anyone who uses the facility. Fees are very reasonable, costing less than $4 per roll. Microfiche are always put on **indefinite loan**, and their cost is less than $.50 each. Ask a librarian for a loan form. Films may take from 2 to 3 weeks to arrive, and you may be notified by phone or mail.

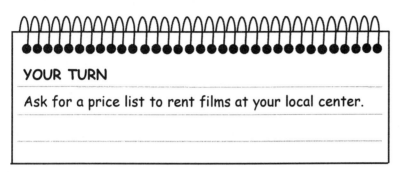

YOUR TURN

Ask for a price list to rent films at your local center.

Additional Research Guidance

We discussed the *SourceGuide* in Chapter 11. But there are also Area Research Guides, individual "how-to guides" on research, in particular parts of the world, for sale at FHCs. You may purchase the entire packet of Area Research Guides for the world, including maps, word lists, and other information, for under $20 on the *SourceGuide* itself (a CD available through the Distribution Center.) Prepared by the Family History Library staff, these Area Research Guides are excellent references to the essential items to search in each geographical locality. They are available through the Salt Lake Distribution Center, 1999 West 1700 South, Salt Lake City, UT 84104-4233, or on the Internet at *www.familysearch.org*. Centers may have individual guides, for about $1.00 each.

Another set of reference materials that will help you if you find yourself doing research about a foreign country in which you know very little is the *World Conferences on Records* reports. Two world conferences have been held in Salt Lake City under the auspices of the Family History Library: the first was in 1969, and the second was in 1980. International experts on genealogy and the preservation of historical or vital documents gathered to share their expertise in research, documentation, preservation, collection, and retention of the records of the world. The lectures were all translated into English and printed. This information covered topics and localities of varied interest, and it is available in book form or fiche at most Family History Centers. You can make photocopies of articles of interest.

Both world conference reports provide research aids for various areas of the world, as well as information on how to use special kinds of records. There is also information regarding the physical properties of records, their makeup and preservation, as well as much technical data that you would be hard put to find any other way. Remember, this was a *World Conference*, the *very best experts in all fields were there, so the reports contain a wealth of information* on a variety of subjects and material pertaining to genealogy.

Social Security Death Index

The *Social Security Death Index* is on CD discs through the *FamilySearch* program. It helps to locate the death place and date of individuals who may have had a social security number and died between 1937 and the present year. The original application for a social security number contains the date of birth, the original town in the foreign country if foreign born, and the parents of an individual. See also page 11-16.

Periodicals

Current genealogical periodicals are often available at FHCs. Ask for a list of their titles, or if an index is available. Also ask about any special indexes or catalogs for that particular library. The Monterey, California FHC has an extensive Library Periodical Surname Notebook and card catalog system which indexes their thirty-five year collection of genealogical periodicals by major surnames and localities. Most centers have a copy of *PERSI* in microfiche or CD-ROM, or the printed version. *PERSI* stands for Periodical Source Index. It is a surname and locality index to nearly every genealogy periodical ever published since the 1830s. Once you locate an individual in that index, you can request a copy of the article from the Allen County Public Library in Fort Wayne, Indiana. Fees are very nominal.

Basic Genealogy Reference Books

Basic books for genealogy research may be available at your local Family History Center in printed format in addition to the "Most-Used Reference Books" collection on microfiche. Check this microfiche collection for over 500 histories, indexes, and finding aids which form the foundation of most FHC collections.

Local Interests

Many centers receive donations from local groups who have enjoyed using the center's services. I have seen large collections of Native American records, county sources, Portuguese research, Midwestern states resources, Pennsylvania German records, Germans from Russia information, and other items, such as CDs, all of which have been donated. (Some centers also index their local obituary notices.) These centers have grown with the needs and uses of their patrons, while at the same time keeping within their budgets.

YOUR TURN

1. List some unique resources or sources of your local Family History Center.

2. What do you wish they had?

HELP FOR THE RESEARCHER

The *Parish and Vital Records List* was introduced in Chapter 10. It is a computer-generated list of parishes, towns and other places whose records have been included in the Family History Department's Extraction Program. This list is arranged by geographical area, then alphabetically by parish or town. The list includes the film numbers for the computer-generated records, is revised quarterly, and is presently available on microfiche, labeled *Parish and Vital Records List*.

In the Extraction Program, names are extracted from parish and town records. In many cases, alphabetized computer printouts are produced which show the names and genealogical information contained in these records, which is a great help, because many times the records are old and very difficult to read without special training. Being able to view a printout will be more helpful than trying to decipher old script.

Before proceeding with genealogical research in a country where you do not read the language or the handwriting very well, you should determine whether the parish or county records of the area you are interested in have been included in an Extraction Program. To do this, you should examine the *Parish and Vital Records List* to save you a lot of unnecessary effort. These are also valuable if you do not read handwriting of the seventeenth and eighteenth century in this country. By obtaining a copy of the computer printout of the extractions, you can do your work faster, and then go back and obtain the original copies for the additional information such records often provide. (See Illustration 12-2.)

SELF-HELP RESOURCES

There are finding aids available in bound volumes, on microfiche and on film for use at a local FHC. Some are listed below but may not be available in all centers.

Film Registers

Film registers are indexes to films available on a particular subject such as census, military, passenger and immigration, etc. They have been prepared to make the ordering faster and easier from the Family History Library in Salt Lake City and from other major film repositories.

A sampling of those at the Monterey, California, Family History Center is given below, but you may find similar ones at your own Family History Center.

F REG 1	AGLL Catalog: American Genealogical Lending Library
F REG 2	Four-Generation Family Group Records 1967-1976 (separate filmings)
F REG 3	Index to Civil Registrations of Births, Marriages, Deaths of England and Wales from 1837 forward.
F REG 4	Boyd's Marriage Index of England, 1st & 2nd Series, 1500-1837
F REG 5	U.S. Census 1790-1880
F REG 6	U.S. Census 1900
F REG 7	U.S. Census 1910
F REG 8	Register of L.D.S. Church Records
F REG 9	Passenger Lists of Vessels Arriving in the U.S.
F REG 10	Federal Population Census, 1790-1880 (National Archives numbers)
F REG 11	Register for the Revolutionary War Pensions & Bounty Land Warrant Application Files (FHL numbers)
F REG 12	Federal Population Census, 1900 (National Archives numbers)
F REG 13	Federal Population Census, 1910 (National Archives numbers)

F REG 14   AGLL Canadian Census Listings, 1666-1891 (AGLL film numbers)

F REG 15   Canadian Marriage Index, Loiselle & Rivest Marriage Index

F REG 16   FHL Film Register of LDS Church Record Call Numbers, Vols. 1 & 2

```
*** E 08 ***                                                                           *** E 08 ***
ENGLAND                         PARISH AND VITAL RECORDS LIST        JAN 1988
                                                                                 PAGE    370

 1.          2.                              3.      4. |------5------|   6.        7.
COUNTY   TOWN AND/OR PARISH                PERIOD  RECD|PRINTOUT  NUM|  PROJECT   SOURCE
                                           FROM - TO TYPE|CALL NO.  FCH|            CALL NO.

DURHAM   HEWORTH                           1826-1875  CHR |* 0933997    |  C  98-2    894912
         HEWORTH                           1696-1753  MAR | NONE        |  M  98-1    091095
         HEWORTH                           1754-1808  MAR |* 1037076    |  M  98-2    894912
                                           1808-1854  MAR |             |             894913
                                           1865-1880  MAR |             |             894914
         HOUGHTON LE SPRING                1581-1812  CHR | 0471854     |  P  47-1    021023
                                                      CHR |             |             091023
         HOUGHTON LE SPRING                 -1545     MAR | NONE        |  M  47-1    091023
                                           1563-1812  580 |             |             091023
         HOUGHTON LE SPRING, ST. MICHAELS ROMAN CATHOLIC 1831-1840 CHR |* 0883949 | C 6469-1 593802 (RG4 2283)
         HOUGHTON LE SPRING, WESLEYAN METHODIST 1837-1840 CHR |* 883934 | C 6470-1 593802 (RG4 477)
         HUNSTANWORTH                      1659-1777  CHR | NONE        |  C 227-3 ** 1068651
         HUNSTANWORTH                      1777-1875  CHR | 0455511     |  P 227-1    252544
                                                      CHR |             |
         HUNSTANWORTH                      1672-1777  MAR | NONE        |  M 227-3 ** 1068651
         HUNSTANWORTH                      1776-1812  MAR | NONE        |  M 227-2 ** 252544
         HUNSTANWORTH                      1813-1876  MAR |* 1037040    |  M 227-1    252544
         HURWORTH ON TEES                  1561-1799  CHR | 0411399     |  P  86-1    090785
                                                      CHR |             |
                                                      CHR |             |
         HURWORTH ON TEES                  1559-1812  MAR |* 1037040    |  M  86-1    090785
         JARROW                            1572-1696  CHR | 0472536     |  P  48-1    021096
                                                      CHR |             |
                                                      CHR |             |
```

Illustration 12-2 Parish and Vital Records List

Indexes to Local Collections

Each FHC may have guidebooks, instructions for using a particular collection, clip and save files, etc. Ask your local volunteer to show you around the center.

BRITISH CENSUS RECORDS

Since so many American's have British roots, a brief introduction to their fundamental records will be given here.

Great Britain, England and Wales

The British census began in 1841 and continued *every ten years* thereafter. It is advantageous to learn the exact dates of these censuses so as to know if the ages listed were given BEFORE or AFTER the person's birthday. These are: 7 June 1841, 31 Mar 1851, 8 Apr 1861, 3 Apr 1871, 4 Apr 1881, and 5 Apr 1891.

As soon as 100 years have passed since the census was taken, it becomes available for genealogical research. The 1891 census was made available in 1991. The Family History Library has the censuses between 1841 and 1891 on loan films. These census films were not indexed by surname until the 1851 indexing project which was mentioned in Chapter 11 (only three counties were included), and the 1881 index and transcripts which were released in 1999. A place index to the census records is on microfiche and is available at many Family History Centers. The 1841 street index is on microfiche number 6026393, items 1 through 9; the 1851 index is on microfiche numbers 6054458 through 6054476; the 1861 index is on microfiche number 6026702, items 1 through 19; the 1871 index is on microfiche numbers 6054442 through 6054457; and the 1881 index is on microfiche number 6026715, items 1 to 44.

To locate the place of an ancestor for searching these census records, first locate a birth, marriage or death record of an ancestor whose birth, marriage or

death occurred near one of the census years indicated above. This is done by:
1. Locating the individual's vital dates from home sources,
2. Locating the individual's birth year from federal census records in the United States,
3. Requesting a death certificate from a state in the U.S.,
4. Searching church records, or
5. Searching naturalization records.

Fam·i·ly His·to·ry So·ci·e·ties – In England, Genealogical societies.

Once the place has been located (England, Scotland, Ireland, or Wales), find the year of birth for the individual in these same records. Now search for your ancestor in the Civil Registration records. The indexes for these registrations are also available on interlibrary loan at your local FHC. The Civil Birth Registration, for example, will indicate the place of the event, including the street address of the individual, the individual's parents, and where they were living at the time of the event. Now go to the street indexes listed above, if no printed surname index exists, and locate the family on the census. There you will find the brothers, sisters, and perhaps aunts, uncles and grandparents *with their parishes of birth provided.* Now you can search the parish records. Some parish registers are on microfilm and they are much less expensive than ordering copies of the original Civil Registrations. Sometimes, however, the Civil Registration is a bargain at any price when it gives the researcher solid information to begin a project.

The British censuses are, as a general rule, very well done. The 1841 census differs slightly from the other years in that the ages of a person over 15 years are estimated to the nearest 5 years below true age. All members of a family at home are shown, but no relationships are stated. The birthplace is not recorded but it will state if they were born in the county or not.

The 1851 and later censuses show EXACT declared age, relationships of all members of one household, the name of the *parish of birth* (or country if not in England) and occupation. A series of pamphlets known as "The McLaughlin Guides" provide easy-to-understand information on English records. These guides are available at many Family History Centers.

Many **Family History Societies** have indexed their own particular census records and may search them for you for a fee. For example, the Nottinghamshire Family History Society has published surname indexes for the whole county for both 1851 and 1881. Other counties with indexing projects include: Derbyshire, Devon, Essex, Hampshire, Lancashire, Lincolnshire, Norfolk, Oxfordshire, Staffordshire, Warwickshire, Surrey and Yorkshire.

The great advantage of using the censuses is that it leads one to further research at the *parish level*. On the other hand, the great advantage of ordering a birth certificate is it will give you the address to find the correct census. It may be necessary to pay for the birth certificate of a sibling in order to locate a census address at the correct time for your own ancestor, but ultimately greater success on the entire family is achieved.

When the 1861 census was taken in England, people on board ships at sea and docked in English ports were also included. The FHL has microfilm copies of the census returns for these ships. A surname index on microfiche to the census records for ships at sea and in port is available on microfiche 6025598 and entitled *Surname Index to the 1861 Ships at Sea and in Port*. The ships which were enumerated are on microfiche 6025599, and the listing is called *Ships Enumerated During the 1861 British Census: A Companion List*. The microfilms themselves are located under:

ENGLAND - CENSUS
ENGLAND - MERCHANT MARINE

Scotland

Scotland censuses up to 1891 are open to the public and contain nearly the same information as Great Britain.

Ireland

Irish censuses of the nineteenth century are nearly non-existent. At least the parts you want are never available. The National Archives of Ireland, Bishop Street, Dublin 8, has a few. The 1901 and 1911 censuses are open to inspection, but they normally give only the county for birthplace. They do give religious affiliation which may be of help to those searching these records.

CONCLUSION

Family History Centers are conveniently located around the United States, provide access to major genealogical materials and instruction on computer usage, and are open to the public. They are one repository we all should take advantage of in our family history pursuits.

The only way you will learn of the great value of a Family History Center is to use it frequently. Remember to thank the volunteer staff whenever you visit the center. Perhaps they need more volunteer helpers, and you perhaps could give an hour or two. They do a marvelous job and receive no monetary compensation for their efforts.

GUIDE TO THE FAMILY HISTORY CENTER

Surname or locality you are searching _____

Today's Date _____ GOAL_____

The family you are searching is thought to have lived in these counties or states: *(Records are recorded by county name...locate the county if you know the city or town by using a gazetteer)* _____

_____   _____   _____

CHECK OFF WHEN ACCOMPLISHED

  1. I have organized family information onto a pedigree chart   _____

  2. I have organized family information onto family group records _____

PRELIMINARY SURVEY BY...

  3. Searching the *Ancestral File*   ( )

  4. Searching the *FHLC Surname File* on computer *(FamilySearch Program)*   ( )

  5. Searching a Surname Index to Periodicals such as PERSI   ( )

  6. Searching printed Family Histories at the center   ( )

  7. Searching the IGI by county, state, surname *(FamilySearch Program)*   ( )

  8. Searching any other local library source lists if any   ( )

  9. Searching the Library of Congress Published Surname Histories   ( )

10. Searching the Pedigree Resource File   ( )

ORIGINAL RESEARCH...

11. The federal census records of the county already available at the FHC   ( )

12. The AIS: census indexes 1600-1850/60 by surname on microfiche   ( )

13. Census films from FHL, Heritage Quest or Genealogy.com CDs

14. FHLC Locality File for Vital Records and Vital Records Indexes CDs   ( )

15. The Locality file of any other major repository catalog available there   ( )

16. The Locality file FHC Card Catalog containing their holdings   ( )

17. Area Research Guides for specific help on localities/subjects   ( )

18. THE HANDY BOOK FOR GENEALOGISTS for localities, or other basic books   ( )

19. MAP GUIDE TO THE U.S. FEDERAL CENSUSES 1790-1920   ( )

20. Research Papers by the experts in genealogy worldwide   ( )

21. WORLD CONFERENCE ON RECORDS   ( )

22. Category/Surname/Title References in the FHC Card Catalog   ( )

23. Loose Files for maps, miscellaneous information, pedigree charts   ( )

24. Jacobus, PERSI, and other periodical indexes   ( )

  OTHER WAYS THEY HELP YOU...

25. Information on computerizing your genealogy through the PAF program   ( )

26. Seminars and workshops on your personal area of interest   ( )

27. Family History SourceGuide   ( )

28. Forms, charts, photocopies of books,   ( )

29. Social Security Death Index (abt. 1937-1989 by surname *FamilySearch*)   ( )

30. Local CDs applying to your area of research   ( )

31. Film Register Books   ( )

32. Information on creating a GEDCOM to submit family data to FHL   ( )

Illustration 12-3 Guide to the Family History Center

ASSIGNMENT 12: VISIT A LOCAL FAMILY HISTORY CENTER

1. Plan a visit to a local Family History Center or major genealogical library. Using the "Guide to the Family History Center" (Illustration 12-3), become familiar with as many of the sources discussed as possible. What did you find?

2. If the guide is not usable at your nearest facility, make up a guide of your own to match your available resources.

3. Call up in advance to schedule the use of a computer at the local Family History Center, and experiment with the features available on the center computers that are not available on the Internet in *FamilySearch*.

4. Order a film or fiche on a surname you are researching.

ALTERNATIVE ASSIGNMENT:

1. If a Family History Center is not available to you, locate an historical or genealogical repository nearby. What were you able to find?

2. Try to get other relatives involved, if they live near a center. Perhaps they can help you to look through films.

YOUR TURN ANSWERS

Personal preferences are expected on all Chapter 12 responses.

COMPUTER CHECKLIST #12

1. Enter the repository name and address for your local center into the repository locality portion of your notes fields.

2. Cite one source in your notes that you searched at your local center or located from the Web site.

3. Explain how you would import a GEDCOM "download" from the *Ancestral File* into your own files.

WEB SITES

http://www.cyndislist.com
A directory to genealogical sites on the Web by Cyndi Howells. Go down her list to the topic you are interested in where you will find links established to a great many sites.

http://www.usgenweb.com/
To visit a *USGenWeb* county page, go to the main project home page above, or visit the U.S. state pages on Cyndi's List given above. Be sure to keep a Research Planner of your queries because Web sites are very easy to update. They change, grow, and evolve on a daily basis. Keep track of what you found, where you were, and what date you checked that Web page. The next time you visit that site, check the revision date and you'll know if anything has changed. Now visit the *USGenWeb* archives page of each state and/or county you are interested in. Keep a separate Research Planner on each locality. To determine what counties are next door to the counties you are searching, check a county outline map such as *http://www.census.gov/datamap/www/*.

BIBLIOGRAPHY

Adkins, Wilma. "Periodical Source Index (PERSI)." *Genealogical Journal* 22, no. 1 (1994): 12 17.

Butler, Steven R. ""Finding Your Mexican War Veteran Ancestor." *Genealogical Journal* 22, no. 3 (1994): 73-77.

Cerny, Johni and Wendy Elliott. *The Library: A Guide to the LDS Family History Library.* Salt Lake City: Ancestry, 1988.

Chapman, Colin R. *Pre-1841 Censuses & Population Listings in the British Isles.* 3rd ed. England: Lochin Publishing, 1992.

Clifford, Karen. "California's Gem - The Sutro Library." *Genealogical Journal* 23, no. 1 (1995): 28-35.

Davenport, David Paul. "The State Censuses of New York, 1825-1875." *Genealogical Journal* 14, no. 4 (1985/1986): 172-197.

Davies, Ian and Chris Webb. Using Documents. *English Heritage,* 1996.

Deputy, Marilyn and Pat Barben, *Register of Federal United States Military Records: A Guide to Manuscript Sources Available at the Genealogy Library in Salt Lake City and the National Archives in Washington, D.C.* Bowie, Md.: Heritage Books, 1986.

Dilts, G. David. "Hamburg Passenger Lists 1850-1934: A Hometown Finder for Central and East European Emigrants." *Genealogical Journal* 22, no. 4 (1994): 100-108.

Foot, William. *Maps for Family History.* London: PRO Publications, 1994.

Galles, Duane L.C.M. "Using Life Insurance Policies in Genealogical Research." *Genealogical Journal* 20, no. 3 & 4 (1992): 156-171.

Gardner, David E. and Frank Smith. *Genealogical Research in England and Wales.* Vol 2, 12th printing. Salt Lake City: Bookcraft Publishers, 1976.

Gardner, David E. and Frank Smith. *Genealogical Research in England and Wales.* Vol. 1, 11th printing. Salt Lake City: Bookcraft Publishers, 1976.

Gay, Beth. "Dreams Do Come True-Odom Library." *Genealogical Journal* 23, no. 4 (1995): 186 188.

Green, Arnold H. "Baptismal Registers of the Coptic Orthodox Church." *Genealogical Journal* 19, no. 3 & 4 (1991): 123-137.

Hey, David. *Family History and Local History in England.* New York: Longman Inc., 1987.

Horan, Dorothy. "The Family History Library Nebraska Collection." *Genealogical Journal* 22, no. 1 (1994): 28-40.

Humphrey-Smith, Cecil. *The Phillimore Atlas and Index of Parish Registers.* 2nd ed. West Sussex: Phillimore & Co. Ltd., 1995.

Hunter, Dean J. "British Archives: England's Public Record Office." *Genealogical Journal* 26, no. 4 (1998): 172-181.

____. "Scottish Census Substitutes." *Genealogical Journal* 17, no. 3 & 4 (1990): 145-161.

Kartous, Peter. "Genealogical Research in Slovakia." *Genealogical Journal* 22, no.3 (1994): 59 64.

Kenyon, Sherrilyn. *The Writer's Guide to Everyday Life in the Middle Ages.* Cincinnati: Writer's Digest Books, 1995.

Kitzmiller II, John M. "British Military Ancestry: Part I." *Genealogical Journal* 20, no. 3 & 4 (1992): 134-155.

____. "British Military Ancestry: Part II." *Genealogical Journal* 21, no. 2 (1993): 26-55.

____. "British Military Ancestry: Part III" *Genealogical Journal* 21, no. 3 & 4 (1993): 109-125.

La Count, Louise. "Loyalists." *Genealogical Journal* 26, no. 1 (1998): 3-23.

McCleary, Linda C. "The Arizona State Genealogy Library." *Genealogical Journal* 21 no. 3 & 4 (1993): 95-97.

Mehr, Kahlile. "German-Russian Genealogical Records." *Genealogical Journal* 22, no. 1 (1994): 1-8.

____. "The International Genealogical Index (IGI), 1993." *Genealogical Journal* 22, no. 3 (1994): 45-58.

____. "The International Genealogical Index, 1992 Microfilm Edition. *Genealogical Journal* 20, no. 1 & 2 (1992): 5-15.

Parker, J. Carlyle. *Going to Salt Lake City to Do Family History Research.* 2nd ed. Turlock, California: Marietta Publishing Co., 1993.

Owens, Preston J. "The Use of Twentieth-Century Military Records: A Case Study." *Genealogical Journal* 26, no. 3 (1998): 65-70.

Rawlins, Bert J. "Records of the Established Church in Wales." *Genealogical Journal*, 17, no. 3 & 4 (1988-1989): 166-176.

Rencher, David E. "Tracing Your Irish Protestant Ancestor." *Genealogical Journal* 20, no. 2 (1993): 71-81.

Roberts, Jayare. "Ellis Island: Bibliography." *Genealogical Journal* 23, no. 4 (1995): 147-175.

____. "Ellis Island and The Making of America." *Genealogical Journal* 23, no. 2 & 3 (1995): 51 142.

____. "Ellis Island: Up Date." *Genealogical Journal* 23, no. 4 (1995): 176-185.

____. "Treasures of the Genealogical Library: Unites States Sources." *Genealogical Journal* 14, no. 4 (1985/1986): 135-171.

____. "Using U.S. Newspapers." *Genealogical Journal* 23, no. 1 (1995): 3-11.

Ryskamp, George R. "Basic Concepts of Archival Research: Lessons Learned in Southern European Archives." *Genealogical Journal* 26, no. 3 (1998): 71-86.

Slater-Putt, Dawne. "Where Did They Come From and Where Did They Go?" *Genealogical Journal* 26, no. 4 (1998): 163-171.

Smith, Clifford Neal. "Some Eighteenth-Century Emigrants to America from Durlach, Wuerttemberg-Baden, Germany." *Genealogical Journal* 14, no. 3 (1985): 99-104.

Starks, Wade C. "Norwegian Ecclesiastical Sources: Finding Your Ancestors in Norwegian Church Records." *Genealogical Journal* 21, no. 3 & 4 (1993): 56-64.

Suess, Jared H. "Some Notes on the Sound Changes of German and English." *Genealogical Journal* 13, no. 3 (1984): 96-99.

Triptow, Adelphia. "A Brief History of the Utah Genealogical Association." *Genealogical Journal* 18, no. 3 & 4 (1990): 101-107.

CD-ROM

Church of Jesus Christ of Latter-day Saints. *Family History SourceGuide.* CD-ROM. Salt Lake City: Church of Jesus Christ of Latter-day Saints, 1998.

Church of Jesus Christ of Latter-day Saints. *Family History Library Catalog.* CD-ROM. Salt Lake City: Church of Jesus Christ of Latter-day Saints, 1998.

CHAPTER 13

National Archives and Regional Records Services Facilities

"Knowledge is of two kinds. We know a subject ourselves, or we know where we can find information upon it."

—Samuel Johnson

The last major repository that we will cover in this volume is the National Archives and Records Administration (NARA), also referred to as the Federal Archives, which is most commonly known for three great sources of records: census, military, and passenger or **immigration** lists. However, there are many other records available through the National Archives or their Regional Records Services Facilities. In fact, there are so many records that it takes three volumes just to list the record groups and what they contain. Some of these include piracy, Native American, mobster, **mutiny**, bankruptcy, and **draft** records. However, since most beginners use National Archives field branches, or Regional Records Services Facilities, for census records, and since they form part of the basic structure of your primary research, the next chapter will discuss censuses more thoroughly.

THE REGIONAL RECORDS SERVICES FACILITIES

Before we discuss military records and ships' passenger lists, may I point out that you may have a service facility of the National Archives very close to you. They are located in the following cities:

- Atlanta, Georgia
- Pittsfield, Massachusetts
- Chicago, Illinois
- Denver, Colorado
- Kansas City, Missouri
- Fort Worth, Texas
- Dayton, Ohio

- Laguna Niguel, California
- New York, New York
- Philadelphia, Pennsylvania
- San Francisco, California
- Seattle, Washington
- Anchorage, Alaska

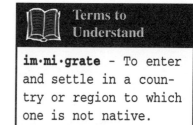

Terms to Understand

im·mi·grate - To enter and settle in a country or region to which one is not native.

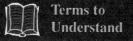

Terms to Understand

mu·ti·ny - Open rebellion against constituted authority, especially rebellion of sailors against superior officers.

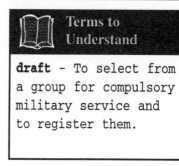

Terms to Understand

draft - To select from a group for compulsory military service and to register them.

The address, telephone number, hours and holdings of your local Regional Records Services Facility may be located by reading Loretto Szucs and Sandra Luebking's *The Archives: A Guide to the National Archives Field Branches,* or by going on the *Internet to http://www.nara.gov.* More information is available at *http://www.nara.gov/genealogy.*

Regional archives branches have text, microfilm, and indexed materials that are common to all, or most, branches. The best way to know what is available at your favorite branch is to find out by visiting, as things are constantly changing. In addition, there are text, microfilm, and indexed materials unique to each branch because of its specific location and the interest of its patrons. For example, the records of San Francisco ships' passengers to Angel Island are at the San Francisco branch and not in New York. The admiralty records for Key West are in Atlanta. The Atlanta Branch even has Admiralty Court records from the South Carolina colonies, 1716 to 1756, even though we were not yet a country.

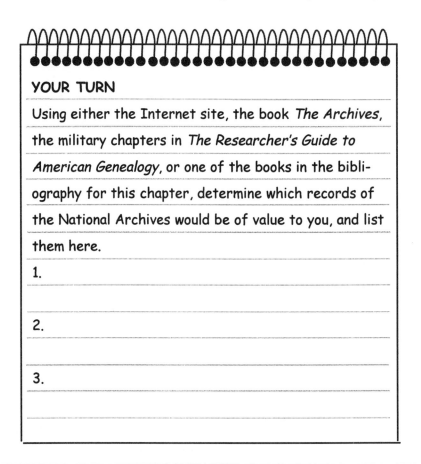

YOUR TURN

Using either the Internet site, the book *The Archives,* the military chapters in *The Researcher's Guide to American Genealogy,* or one of the books in the bibliography for this chapter, determine which records of the National Archives would be of value to you, and list them here.

1.

2.

3.

Summary

Since this is a beginner's book, I will not go into depth on the many records in the National Archives, but I will, hopefully, help you to gain a desire to search the records of these marvelous collections. Let's discuss the records which cover our immigrants during just one time period.

IMMIGRATION RECORDS

You learned in previous chapters about the Extraction Program of the FHL. Similarly, volunteer extractors are also working with records pertaining to the National Archives. Climbing the family tree today takes a lot less clawing with the help of these volunteers and the many organizations who are trying to make information available to the public.

One nonprofit foundation is nearing the completion of a $15 million project to post **Ellis Island** immigration records on the Internet. When it is finished, this project will revolutionize genealogical research for many of the more than 113 million Americans who already actively pursue their family histories—many of which include immigrant ancestors.

Officials at the Statue of Liberty-Ellis Island Foundation in New York, the same organization that gave Lady Liberty a face lift in 1986 without any public funding, estimate that more than 40 percent of Americans can trace their European ancestry back to Ellis Island. Working with others, this organization's goal is to allow people to be able to enter any information they know about a progenitor, and a program will search more than twenty million records for a match. The software will even be able to tolerate misspellings. If a match is found, the researcher can choose to print out a photo of the ship and a copy of the original **passenger manifest** that marked the immigrant's arrival.

The database, which organizers say could be ready by the end of 2000, will catalog the records of the almost twenty million immigrants who flooded the tiny New York harbor island. Until now, those documents have been stored at the National Archives, and at the Immigration and **Naturalization** Service, in microfilm format. Information on the project may be found at *www.ellisisland.org* on the Internet.

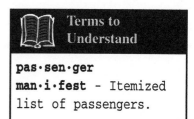

Terms to Understand

Ellis Island - An island southwest of Manhattan, the chief immigration station of the United States from 1892 to 1943.

Terms to Understand

pas·sen·ger man·i·fest - Itemized list of passengers.

Terms to Understand

nat·u·ral·ize - To grant full citizenship to one of foreign birth, or to acquire citizenship in an adopted country.

YOUR TURN

Do you have ancestors who came to this country during the period from the late 1800s to the mid 1900s? If so, go to the Web site at *www.ellisisland.org* and see if any of the records listed there could be of interest to you. List below the records or the names of the individuals whose records you hope to find:

1.

2.

3.

MILITARY RECORDS

Military records have solved many family mysteries. Not only can they provide you with wonderful background material on your ancestors, they may also provide you with vital records that no longer exist in any other way. Since a soldier or his heirs had to prove their identity, their relationships, and their service in order to receive benefits, many vital documents may be found among these papers that are not strictly military.

Terms to Understand

boun·ty land - Public land given as a reward, inducement, or payment, especially one given by a government for acts deemed beneficial to the state, such as enlisting for military service.

Terms to Understand

pay vouch·er - An official written document which promises to give money in return for goods or services rendered.

Terms to Understand

war·rant - A voucher authorizing payment or receipt of money or land.

Military records kept prior to the Revolutionary War period contain mostly the names of individuals, their places of service, the conflicts their units served in, and, very occasionally, information on the soldier's origin. Records kept since the Revolution, however, contain facts relating to birth, marriage, death, relationships, migration movements, and other genealogical clues.

Categories of Military Records

There are three major categories of military records helpful to the family historian:

- Service Records
- Pension Records
- **Bounty Land Warrants**

Service Records

These contain very little in the way of vital data, but they provide excellent supplementary information. They include descriptions of events which happened to the soldier during his tour of duty, **pay vouchers**, records of enlistment, captivity, issuance of clothing allowance, and notices of separation or discharge.

There are eight series of service records in the National Archives:

- Revolutionary War, 1775-1783
- Post-Revolutionary War, 1784-1811
- War of 1812, 1812-1815
- Indian Wars, 1816-1860
- Mexican War, 1846-1848
- Civil War, 1861-1865 (Union/Confederate)
- Spanish-American War, 1898
- Philippine Insurrection, 1898-1901

Pension Records

Beginning with the Revolutionary War, regular payments, or pensions, were paid for injury or service rendered. The records which resulted may contain a treasure trove of information, such as marriage licenses, children's birth certificates, letters establishing relationships, family movements, names of family members, the health and occupation of the soldier, etc. Four types of pension records are usually available. A pension given for a soldier's disability is called an *invalid pension*. That given to a surviving widow at the death of her husband is called a *widow's pension*. That given to the minor children of a deceased father is called a *child's pension*. And that given to a mother who was solely supported by a son who died in the service is called a *mother's pension*.

Bounty Land Records

Land warrants were provided for wartime service rendered between 1775 and 1855. The information found in these records is similar to that in pension records, and they can contain many important clues and sources for the genealogist since the soldier (or his heirs) had to prove his identity in order to gain rights to bounty land. Generally, this required that the soldier mail his discharge papers to the Secretary of War. If everything was approved, he would receive a warrant (a certificate granting him land in the public domain). Once the soldier located the land he wanted, he mailed in his warrant, and received a **patent**. Most men sold their warrants. A man did not have to serve for years to receive a pension or bounty land. Often, service of only a few weeks was required.

How to Find Military Records

Most of the federal service and pension records have survived and are available at the National Archives in Washington, D.C. A major exception is the collection of early Revolutionary War records which are thought to have been destroyed during the War of 1812. The indexes to the other service and pension records are available through the National Archives, the Family History Library, and the Sutro Library, among others. While the indexes to the Confederate veterans' records are in the National Archives, the actual records are located in their respective states. They have also been micro-filmed in many cases and most are now available from the Family History Library (FHL).

A majority of the existing records involving World Wars I and II were cen-tralized at the Federal Records Center in St. Louis, Missouri. The FHL has the World War I Draft Records and an index to them on microfilm.

For each set of records, consult the indexes before trying to locate the actual records. Because of spelling inaccuracies, check all name variations for your ancestor. Various pension acts, beginning in 1776, gradually liberalized pension requirements and allowed **enlisted men's**, widows' and orphans' ben-efits. Congressional Acts, beginning in 1776 and continuing until 1885, grant-ed bounty lands to veterans of the U.S. military and of state militia.

Indexes to the Revolutionary War, Indian Wars, the War of 1812, the Mexican War, and the Civil War (Union forces) are available on microfilm through the loan services of the National Archives, the Family History Library and its centers, Heritage Quest microfilm rental program, and through state and local libraries. The Confederate Army indexes and most of the Confederate records have been microfilmed by the states and are available through the Family History Library and its centers, as well as the state archives and libraries. The pension and bounty land records for the Revolutionary War are available at most National Archives branches, as well as the above cited repositories.

The pension and bounty land packets for the Old Wars (Indian Wars between the Revolutionary War and the War of 1812), the War of 1812, Indian Wars, the Mexican War and the Civil War are available by correspondence with the National Archives, a personal visit, or hired researcher. These records have not, as yet, been filmed. Be sure to request a complete packet if you desire every paper belonging to the soldier's case. Some packets contain hundreds of papers, but the staff will generally select ten of the most pertinent pages, so you could miss clues you need. Recently, some of these military records have been abstracted and indexed in printed form and are available at major genealogical and research libraries (see the chapter bibliography).

After the Treaty of 1783, both the United States and Great Britain provid-ed a way for *Loyalists,* those who were loyal to Great Britain during the Revolutionary War, to be compensated for their property losses. These claims were preserved and are available on microfilm through the Family History Library loan service, the National Archives, and other repositories.

A Regular Army was permanently established in 1789 (as opposed to a **vol-unteer** Army), and the records relating to the personnel involved have also been preserved. Indexes are available through the sources previously cited. In the National Archives, Regular Army records are filed in two major groups: the peri-od between 1789 and 1821, and those for the period between 1821 and 1912.

Terms to Understand

pat·ent - A land grant made by a government.

Terms to Understand

en·list·ed man - Male member of the armed forces who ranks below a commissioned officer or warrant officer.

Terms to Understand

vol·un·teer - Somebody who has offered to serve in one of the armed services without being required to join by law.

Ordering Military Records

Army, Navy and Marine Corps service records were not compiled by the federal government. Therefore, check the archives of the state in which your ancestor served for regular military service records. Once you have identified the unit and a time period, check federal pension records.

To request a copy of the service, pension or bounty land packets prior to World War I, ask for a form entitled *ORDER FOR COPIES OF VETERANS RECORDS, NATF Form 80.* You may request: (1) the Pension Application; (2) the Bounty-Land Warrant Application; or (3) the Military (service) Record on this form. You must submit a separate form for each file you request, even when requesting this information for the same person, and you should allow a minimum of eight to ten weeks for processing. Requests for blank forms should specify how many forms are needed and should be addressed to:

General Reference Branch (NNRG)
National Archives and Records Administration
7th and Pennsylvania Avenue, NW
Washington, D.C. 20408

The forms are free, but there is a minimum fee of $10 for copying ten pages of the documents you request. Normally, the staff at the National Archives will copy those pages they feel are most representative of the information, but not the entire packet. If you wish the complete packet, write on the form that you wish to be informed of the cost of copying the entire packet, or you can charge it to your credit card. You will need the following information to request a copy of the military packet:

Name of soldier
State from which he served
Infantry, Cavalry, Artillery
Officer or Enlisted
Volunteer or Regular
Pension or Bounty Land File Number

All of this information will come from the indexes and the instructions which pertain to them. If you also know the date and place of birth and death, it will be helpful. To request information on World War I and World War II soldiers, write to:

National Personnel Records Center
Military Personnel Records, NARA
9700 Page Boulevard
St. Louis, MO 63132-5100

YOUR TURN

Check your own family records. Do any of the individuals listed qualify to have served in one of the wars mentioned above? If so, write their names here:

1.

2.

3.

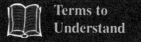

Terms to Understand

reg·i·men·tal his·to·ry- The chronological record of events of a military unit of ground troops consisting of at least two battalions, usually commanded by a colonel.

CONCLUSION

There are many other kinds of helpful military records in addition to these major categories, including **regimental histories** and Adjutant General Records. You can search the Internet at *http://www.nara.gov* for information you are seeking. In fact, there are so many sources available through the federal government that we must stay focused in order to obtain our desired results. Before we search immigration and military records, we need the very important information contained in the U.S. census records, so that will be the basis of our next chapter.

ASSIGNMENT 13: USING RECORDS OF THE NATIONAL ARCHIVES

1. Become familiar with the records of the federal government by reading the introduction to *The Archives* or to the *Guide to Genealogical Research in the National Archives*. Describe the differences between the Regional Records Services Facilities and the National Archives.

2. Make a note on your Research Planner to search at least one set of records pertaining to the National Archives for one of your ancestors. Indicate what record you selected and where you hope to search that record.

YOUR TURN ANSWERS

Personal preferences are expected for all Chapter 13 responses.

COMPUTER CHECKLIST #13

Determine how you would enter military sources into the Notes field of your computer program.

WEB SITES

http://members.aol.com/veterans/warlib6.htm
Veteran and Military Web sites with links to others.

http://www.itd.nps.gov/cwss/
Civil War Soldiers and Sailors System Web site contains more than 230,000 soldiers' names.

http://image.vtls.com/collections/CW.html
Confederate Pension Rolls, Veterans and Widows.

http://www.nara.gov
Federal records of Adjutant General.

http://www.nara.gov/regional/cpr.html
National Personnel Records Center.

http://web.syr.edu/~laroux/lists/alpha.html
French and Indian War site.

http://jefferson.village.Virginia.EDU/vshadow2/contents.html
Valley of the Shadow: The Civil War as Seen by Franklin County, Pennsylvania (Union), and Augusta County, Virginia (Confederate).

BIBLIOGRAPHY

Deputy, Marilyn and Pat Barben, *Register of Federal United States Military Records: A Guide to Manuscript Sources Available at the Genealogy Library in Salt Lake City and the National Archives in Washington, D.C.* Bowie, MD: Heritage Books, 1986.

Greenwood, Val D. *The Researcher's Guide to American Genealogy.* 3rd ed. Baltimore: Genealogical Publishing Co., 2000.

Guide to Genealogical Research in the National Archives. Rev. ed. Washington, D.C.: National Archives Trust Fund Board, 1985.

Heitman, Francis B. *Historical Register and Dictionary of the United States Army, from its Organization, September 29, 1789 to March 2, 1903.* Washington, D.C.: Government Printing Office, 1903.

Horowitz, Lois, A. *Bibliography of Military Name Lists from Pre-1675 to 1900: A Guide to Genealogical Research.* Metuchen, NJ: Scarecrow Press, 1990.

Military Service Records: A Select Catalog of National Archives Microfilm Publications. Washington, D.C.: National Archives and Records Service, 1985.

Neagles, James C. *U. S. Military Records: A Guide to Federal and State Sources, Colonial America to the Present.* Salt Lake City: Ancestry, 1994.

Neagles, James C. and Mark C. Neagles. *The Library of Congress: A Guide to Genealogical and Historical Research.* Salt Lake City: Ancestry, 1990.

Szucs, Loretto Dennis and Sandra Hargreaves Luebking. *The Archives: A Guide to the National Archives Field Branches.* Salt Lake City: Ancestry, 1988.

White, Virgil D. *Genealogical Abstracts of Revolutionary War Pension Files.* 4 vols. Waynesboro, TN: National Historical Publishing Co., 1990-92.

White, Virgil D. *Index to Indian War Pension Files, 1892-1926.* Waynesboro, TN: National Historical Publishing Co., 1987.

White, Virgil D. *Index to Mexican War Pension Files.* Waynesboro, TN: National Historical Publishing Co., 1989.

White, Virgil D. *Index to the Old Wars Pension Files, 1815-1926.* 2 vols. Waynesboro, TN: National Historical Publishing Co., 1987.

White, Virgil D. *Index to Volunteer Soldiers in Indian Wars and Disturbances 1815-1858.* 2 vols. Waynesboro, TN : National Historical Publishing Co., 1994.

White, Virgil D. *Index to War of 1812 Pension Files.* Rev. ed. 2 vols. Waynesboro, TN: National Historical Publishing Co., 1990-92.

CHAPTER 14

Census Records Between 1850-1920

"Anything processed by memory is a fiction."

—*Michael Ratcliffe*

Oral histories and traditions can be in error. There are several records which can clear up some of these earlier discrepancies, but none as useful as federal census records. Census records are public records, and therefore they may be used free of charge at a federal public facility. If you use a loaned census film from another repository, however, you may have to pay a small fee. Because they are free, because they provide so much information on the family, and because they are generally quite accurate for the majority of the population, census records are among a genealogist's favorite sources.

Besides providing you with the obvious clues, such as the names of siblings, dates of birth, years of marriage, relationships, and nativity, census records provide other subtle clues. For example, a village name or post office is usually listed on a census page. This could lead you to an unindexed county history where information in the table of contents about the post office might bring you within pages of information on your direct family. Also, lists of neighbors could be followed, if your own family line disappears, in the hopes that they kept in contact and moved together to another area. At any rate, a good understanding of census records is very helpful.

GENERAL GUIDELINES

Every item on the census can give you a clue. If it says that your ancestor could not read and write and you have found a handwritten document bearing his signature, you should think twice about its having been written by your ancestor. The document could have been written by someone with the same name. The occupation of your ancestor, the value of his real estate, his place of birth, the names of his children and his wife's name all help to identify this particular individual from others of the same name.

Terms to Understand

o·ral his·to·ries - A transcribed or a tape-recorded history made from the memories and recollections of an individual who experienced the history or heard the history. Usually done through an interview.

Terms to Understand

pho·ne·tic spel·ling -
Spelling based on the
sounds of speech
rather than an accept-
ed orthography.

Terms to Understand

var·i·ant - Tending to
differ; deviating from
a standard, usually by
only a slight differ-
ence. For example,
variant name spellings
indicate different
ways to spell a name.
The name Gahan can
also be spelled
Gahann, Gahagn, Gahen,
Gaghan, Gaghann, or
Gehan.

Copy Information Correctly

Copy *all* information given, *exactly* as it appears. Be sure to copy the information from the top of the page, as to the county, township, ED (Enumeration District), page or sheet number, etc. You need this for proper documentation of your information and research! Otherwise, you will ask yourself some day, "How do I know that?" "Where did I find that?" It is always easier to write it down the first time than to have to go back and do it all again.

While there are errors in the information in the census, it is amazing how often the information is correct and family tradition is incorrect. If you know that your ancestor was a school teacher, and the family in the census are all listed as unable to read and write, they may not be your family. You should look further. Remember: There were many people with the same names living in the same places.

Caution: Phonetic Spellings Abound

Because **phonetic spellings** were commonly used in the early decades of the census, *be sure to look at all **variant** name spellings*. Sometimes the information was given by a child or a neighbor, and sometimes your ancestors just gave wrong information. People who could not read and write could not always remember exactly when they were born, either. There is much of value to the census, but you should be prepared for some interesting surprises.

YOUR TURN

1. Write down a way an ancestor's surname could be spelled differently, i.e., Smith vs. Smyth, Thompson vs. Thomson:

2. Write down a way an ancestor's given name could be written differently, i.e., Mary vs. Polly, Jack vs. John, William vs. Bill:

Learn How Various Census Years Differ

Not all U.S. censuses were exactly alike, so it's important that you learn what particular information is available from each census year. Before 1850 only the head of the household was listed by name, while all other members were enumerated by age group: males and females. These censuses can still be valuable, as you can "track" a family by whether or not they have children of the same age and gender as the family you are seeking. Below are the key points about each of the census records we will study.

GENEALOGY RESEARCH ASSOCIATES, INC.
1850 United States Federal Census Transcription

Street/ route name	Street/ route number	Dwelling in order of visit	Family in order of visit	The name of every person whose usual place of abode on the first day of June, 1850, was in this family	Age	Sex	Color	Profession, occupation, or trade of each male person over 15 years of age	Value of real estate owned	Place of birth, naming the state, territory or country	Married within the year	Attended school within yr.	Person over 20 who can't read/write	Deaf, dumb, blind, insane, idiotic, pauper, convict	Estimated birth year

Head of Household _____ State _____ County_____ City/Township _____ Written page number ____

Printed page number _____ Enumeration District _____ Microfilm roll number _____ Call number _____ Repository _____

© 1997 Genealogy Research Associates, Inc.   4/97

Illustration 14-1 United States 1850 Federal Census Transcription Form
(Larger versions of each of these Census Transcription Forms are located in the Appendix)

1850 Census. 1850 was the first year that all members of a household were listed by name, and that little fact makes 1850 a very important year to search. For the first time, you can see family members' names, ages, and where they were born. Since birth years are provided, you can determine the exact ages of family members; so if the wife is 24 and the oldest child is 18, you have a good idea that she is a second wife, and you know to look for other marriage records. In addition, you may find "lost" children and, generally, better identify the family that is yours. After 1850, each census has a little bit of information that is characteristic of that particular year, as will be shown. Looking at Illustration 14-1, which is a transcription form for the 1850 census, you will see the way the information is recorded.

Illustration 14-2 1850 Census Handwriting Example

GENEALOGY RESEARCH ASSOCIATES, INC.
1860 United States Federal Census Transcription

SCHEDULE 1.—Free Inhabitants in *Mt Hope* in the County of *McLean* State of *M* enumerated by me, on the *2* day of *June* 1860. *A.P. Allen* Ass't Marshal

Post Office *McLean*

Street/ route name	Street/ route number	Dwelling in order of visit	Family in order visit	Name of every person whose usual place of abode on 1 Jun 1860, was in this family	Age	Sex	Color	Occupation or trade of each male person over 15 years of age	Value of real estate owned	Value of personal estate	Place of birth, naming the state, territory or country	Married within the year	Attended school	Person over 20 who can't read/write	Deaf, dumb, blind, insane, idiotic, pauper, convict	Estimated birth

Head of Household .... State .... County .... City/Township .... Written page number ....

Printed page number .... Enumeration District .... Microfilm roll number .... Call number .... Repository ....

Illustration 14-3 United States 1860 Federal Census Transcription Form
(Larger versions of each of these Census Transcription Forms are located in the Appendix)

1860 Census. In the 1860 census, property value was listed for the first time. This information can lead you to further researches in tax, land, and probate records. The census information is shown in Illustration 14-3.

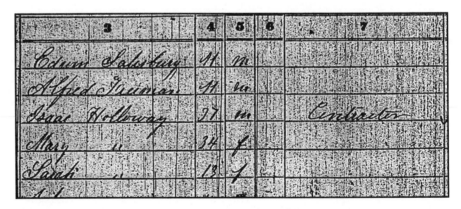

Illustration 14-4 1860 Census Handwriting Example

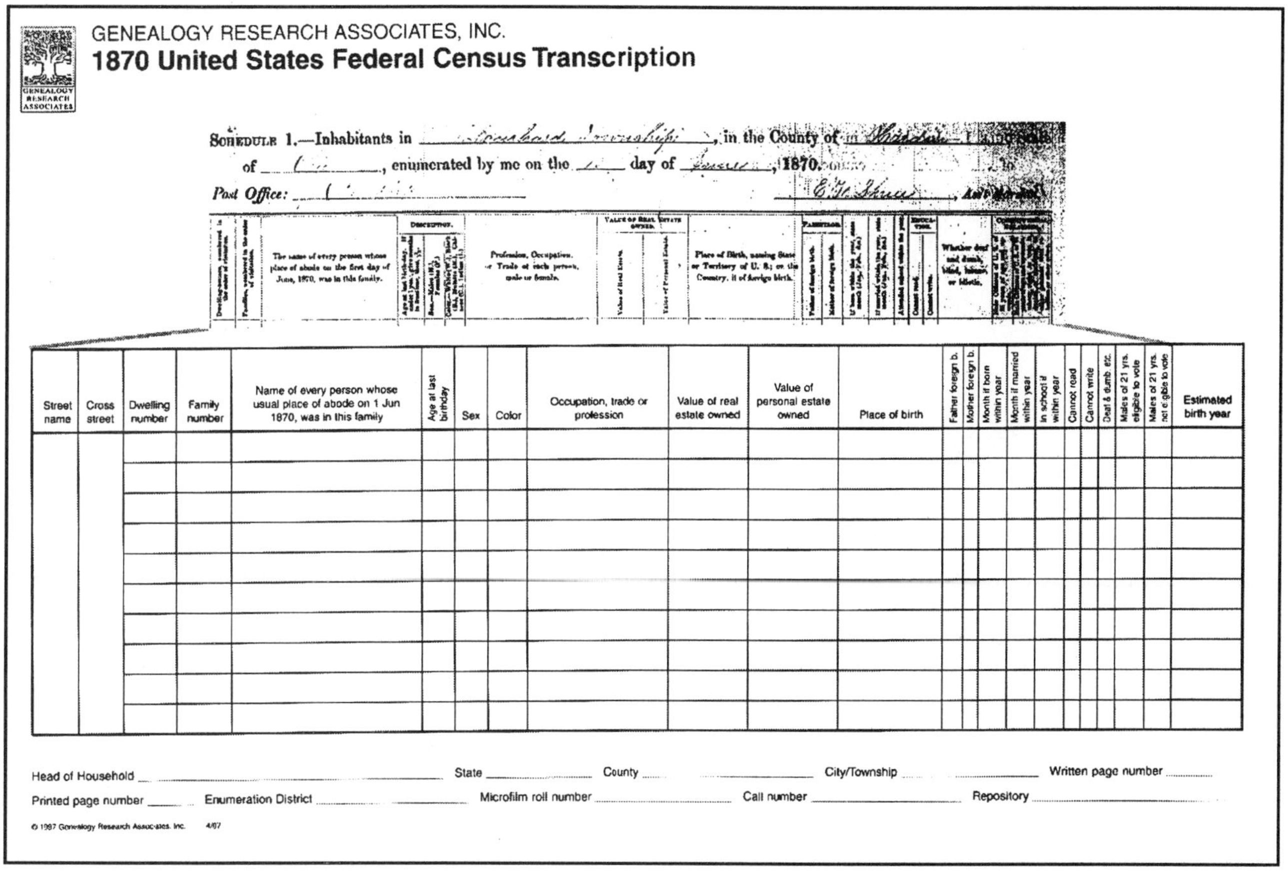

Illustration 14-5 United States 1870 Federal Census Transcription Form
(Larger versions of each of these Census Transcription Forms are located in the Appendix)

1870 Census. In the 1870 census, parents of foreign birth were indicated. This can be the information you need to discover the immigrant generation. Black Americans were recorded with their own surname for the first time in the Southern States. The census information is shown in Illustration 14-5.

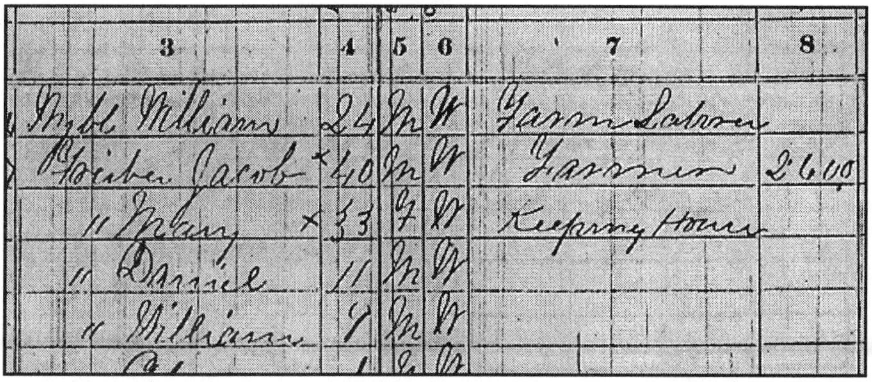

Illustration 14-6 1870 Census Handwriting Example

GENEALOGY RESEARCH ASSOCIATES, INC.
1880 United States Federal Census Transcription

Street name	House number	Dwelling number	Family number	Name of every person whose usual place of abode on 1 June, 1880 was with this family	Estimated year of birth	Color- White, Black, Mulatto, Indian or Chinese	Sex	Age	Month born if within census year	Relation to head of this household	Single	Married	Widowed/Div.	Married this yr.	Occupation, trade or profession	Months unemployed	Illness	Blind	Deaf & dumb	Idiotic	Insane	Disabled	School-yr.	Can't read	Can't write	State, territory, or country of Birth	Birthplace of father	Birthplace of mother

Head of Household .... State .... Conty .... City/Township .... Written page number ....

Printed page number .... Enumeration District .... Microfilm roll number .... Call number .... Repository ....

© 1997 Genealogy Research Associates, Inc.

Illustration 14-7 United States 1880 Federal Census Transcription Form
(Larger versions of each of these Census Transcription Forms are located in the Appendix)

Terms to Understand

Sound·ex - A coded surname indexing system in which the vowels, as well as the silent letters, w, h, and y, are removed, and a progression of consonants rather than the alphabetical spelling of the surname is used; the name is phonetically "sounded" rather than spelled in the usual way. The Soundex system was adopted by the federal government for several indexing projects because of widespread misspelling on records that caused difficulties in locating individuals.

1880 Census. The 1880 census is the first year of the **Soundex**! More will be covered on this subject in the next few pages. The head of household's surname, however, is only indexed if there was a child 10 years of age or under living in the home. If your family is not in the Soundex, you will have to read the actual census film to find them. However, early in 2000 a transcription of the entire 1880 census will be out in a CD-ROM format. (If you are doing research in Utah for this period, be aware that there was some juggling of households due to polygamous families.) The census information is shown in Illustration 14-7.

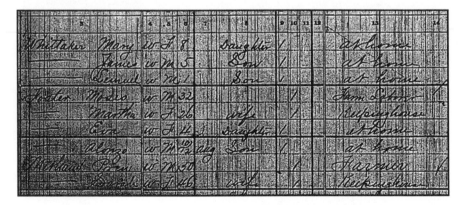

Illustration 14-8 1880 Census Handwriting Example

FAMILY SCHEDULE—1 TO 10 PERSONS.   476

[7-556 a.]   Eleventh Census of the United States.

Supervisor's District No._____
Enumeration District No._____
SCHEDULE No. 1.
POPULATION AND SOCIAL STATISTICS.

Name of city, town, township, precinct, district, beat, or other minor civil division }_____ : County:_____ : State:_____

Street and No.: *1612 — 14* ; Ward:_____ ; Name of Institution:_____

Enumerated by me on the *10* day of June, 1890.   *Enumerator.*

INQUIRIES.	1	2	3	4	5
A.—Number of Dwelling-house in the order of visitation.					E.—No. of Persons in this family. *7*
1 Christian name in full, and initial of middle name.	George	Robert L	Clara V	Gladys M	Jeanne C
Surname.	Coombs	Swart	—	—	—
2 Whether a soldier, sailor, or marine during the civil war (U.S. or Conf.), or widow of such person.					
3 Relationship to head of family.	Lodger	Head	Wife	Daughter	Daughter
4 Whether white, black, mulatto, quadroon, octoroon, Chinese, Japanese, or Indian.	white	White	White	White	White
5 Sex.	Male	Male	Female	Female	Female
6 Age at nearest birthday. If under one year, give age in months.	40	26	25	2	2/12
7 Whether single, married, widowed, or divorced.	Single	Married	Married	Single	Sin
8 Whether married during the census year (June 1, 1889, to May 31, 1890).		no	no		
9 Mother of how many children, and number of those children living.			2 – 2		
10 Place of birth.	Maryland	D. C.	D. C	D. C	D. C
11 Place of birth of Father.	do	Va ‡	Md		
12 Place of birth of Mother.	do	D. C	D. C		
13 Number of years in the United States.	40				
14 Whether naturalized.					
15 Whether naturalization papers have been taken out.					
16 Profession, trade, or occupation.	merchant	Clerk		at Home	
17 Months unemployed during the census year (June 1, 1889, to May 31, 1890).	.	½			
18 Attendance at school (in months) during the census year (June 1, 1889, to May 31, 1890).					
19 Able to Read.	Yes				
20 Able to Write.	do				
21 Able to speak English. If not, the language or dialect spoken.	Yes				
22 Whether suffering from acute or chronic disease, with name of disease and length of time afflicted.					
23 Whether defective in mind, sight, hearing, or speech, or whether crippled, maimed, or deformed, with name of defect.					
24 Whether a prisoner, convict, homeless child, or pauper.					
25 Supplemental schedule—and page.					

TO ENUMERATORS.—See inquiries numbered 26 to 30, inclusive, on the second page of this schedule. These inquiries must be made concerning each family and each farm visited.

(12878—15,000,000.) 1ᵈ   43

Illustration 14-9 United States 1890 Federal Census Example

1890 Census. The 1890 census is extremely fragmentary, as most of it was destroyed by fire. However, you should still check the census guides in case your family may be listed. It was indexed by Soundex, but with so few families left in the census, the printed indexes are faster to use. Illustration 14-5 shows what would be available on this census.

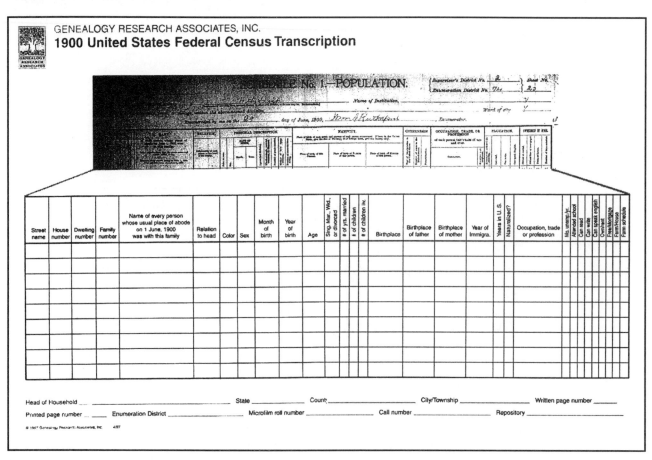

Illustration 14-10 United States 1900 Federal Census Transcription Form
(Larger versions of each of these Census Transcription Forms are located in the Appendix)

1900 Census. The 1900 census *is the best of all for including everyone in the Soundex.* Every state is indexed and it gives the month as well as the year of birth, the year of immigration, the year the couple was married, and if a first or second marriage, the number of children born and the number living, whether naturalized or not, and information on the ownership or rental of land, in addition to the information given in the other censuses. Thus, you have some excellent clues as to the total number of children and who you still have to look for. Because you have the children's birthplaces, you also have a possible place of marriage. The information found on this census is shown in Illustration 14-10.

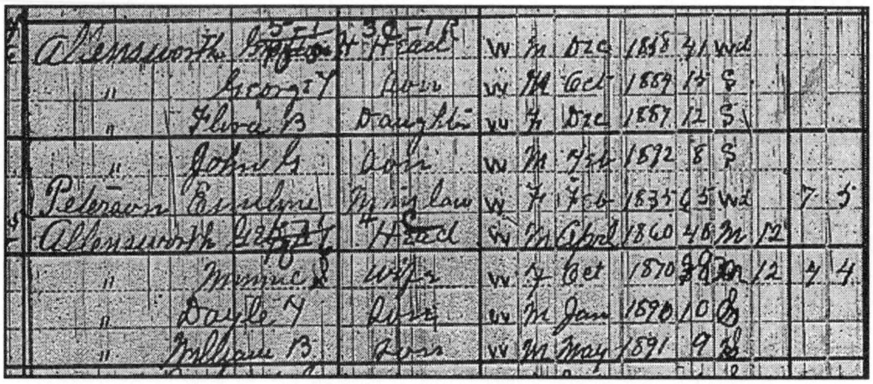

Illustration 14-11 1900 Census Handwriting Example

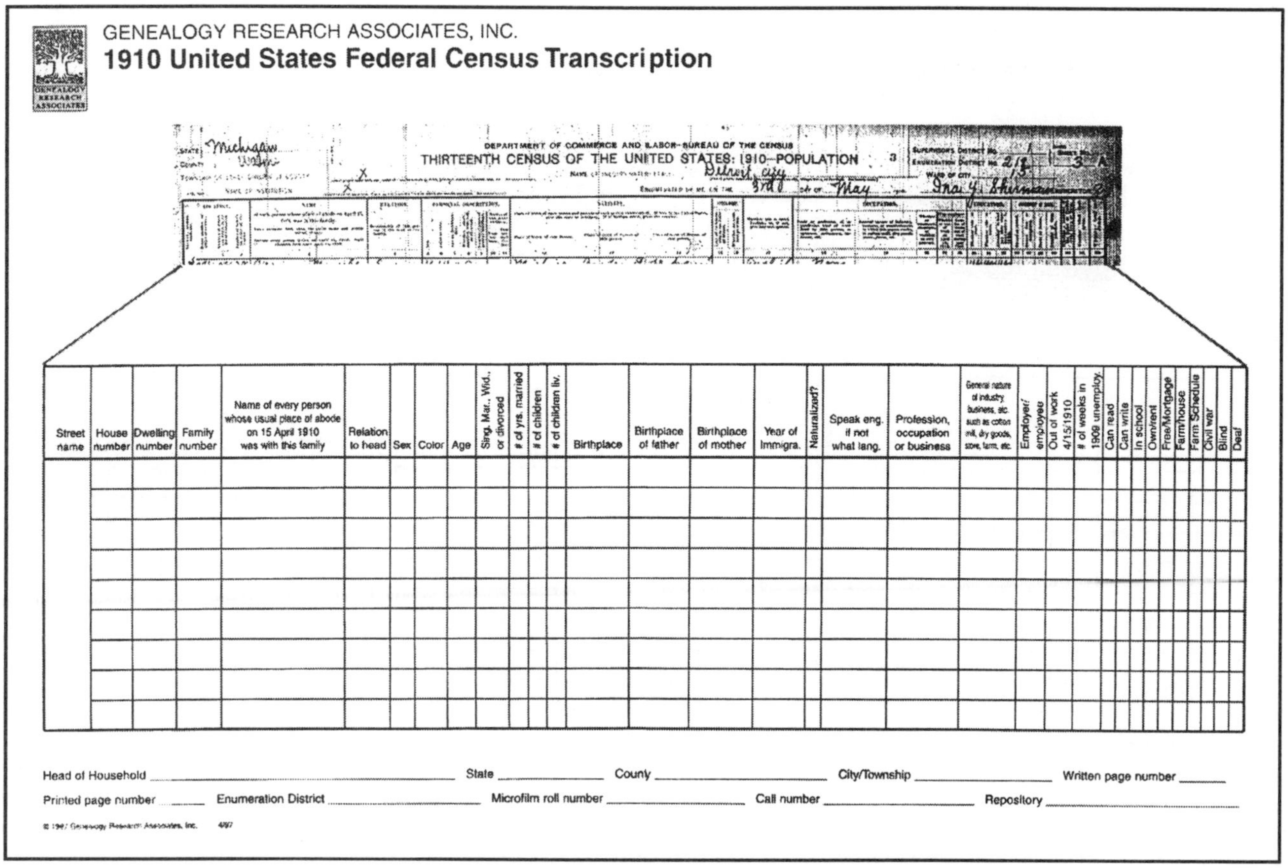

GENEALOGY RESEARCH ASSOCIATES, INC.

1910 United States Federal Census Transcription

Street name	House number	Dwelling number	Family number	Name of every person whose usual place of abode on 15 April 1910 was with this family	Relation to head	Sex	Color	Age	Sing., Mar., Wid., or divorced	# of yrs. married	# of children	# of children liv.	Birthplace	Birthplace of father	Birthplace of mother	Year of Immigra.	Naturalized?	Speak eng. if not what lang.	Profession, occupation or business	General nature of industry, business, etc. such as cotton mill, dry goods, store, farm, etc.	Employer/employee	Out of work 4/15/1910	# of weeks in 1909 unemploy.	Can read	Can write	In school	Own/rent	Free/Mortgage	Farm/house	Farm Schedule	Civil war	Blind	Deaf

Head of Household ______ State ______ County ______ City/Township ______ Written page number ______

Printed page number ______ Enumeration District ______ Microfilm roll number ______ Call number ______ Repository ______

Illustration 14-12 United States 1910 Federal Census Transcription Form
(Larger versions of each of these Census Transcription Forms are located in the Appendix)

1910 Census. In 1910, the federal government produced indexes for only twenty-one states. Other indexes were produced by private companies for Nevada and Wyoming. It is also important to realize that many large cities have separate indexes from their state counterparts. There are also street indexes to certain large cities available through the Family History Library (see FHL fiche # 6331480-1). 1910 is an important census for immigrants from the Germanic countries because a more complete description of the place of birth is often given. The information found on this census is shown in Illustration 14-12.

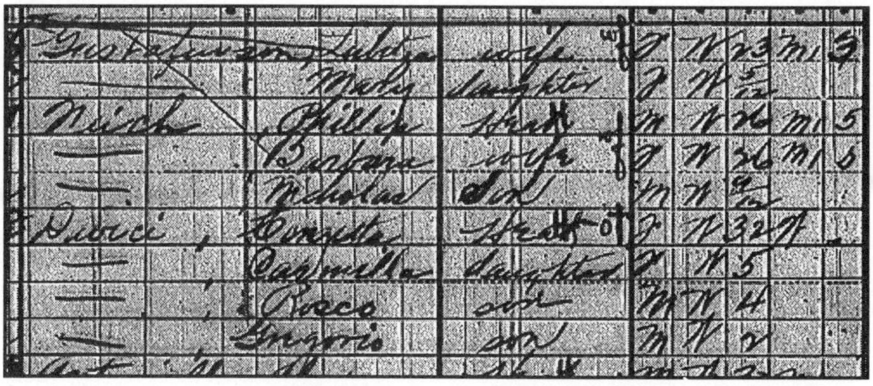

Illustration 14-13 1910 Census Handwriting Example

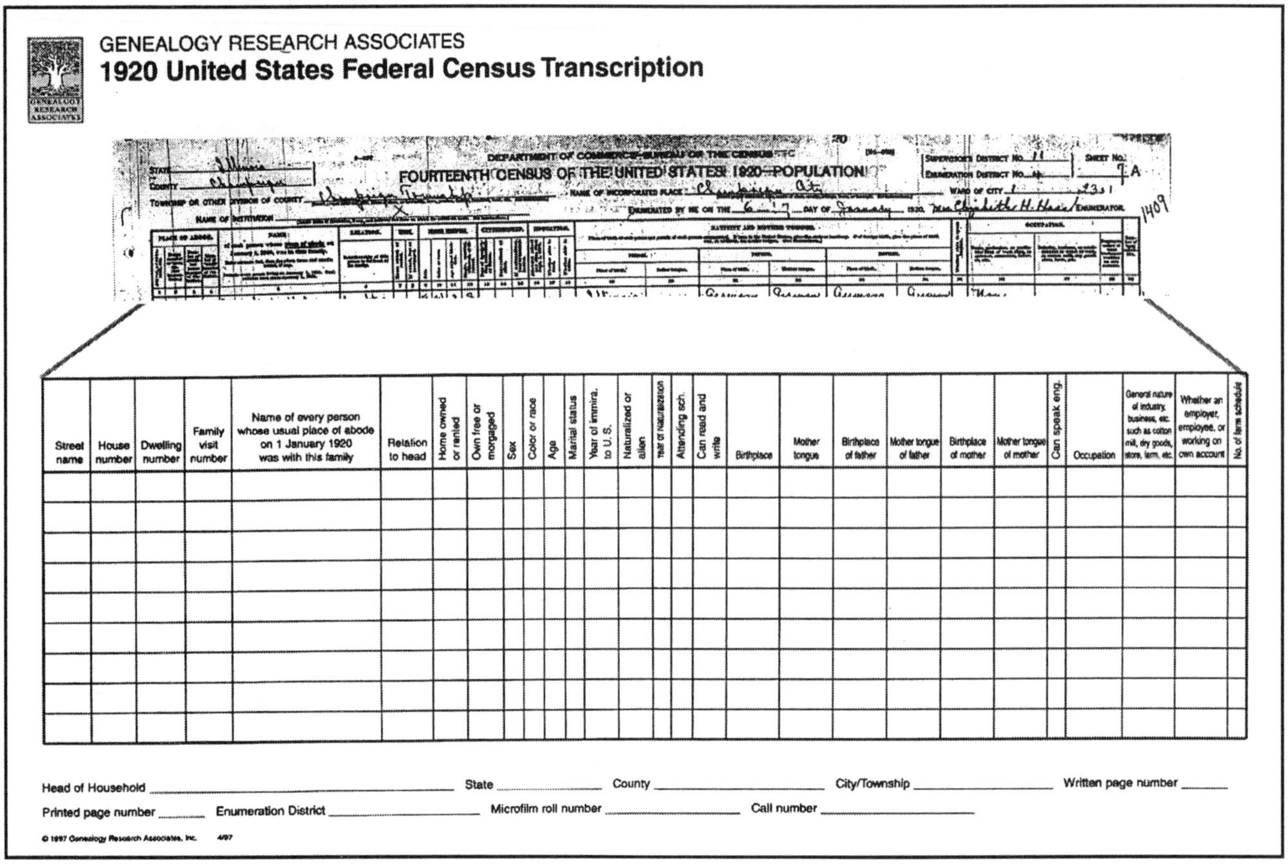

GENEALOGY RESEARCH ASSOCIATES

1920 United States Federal Census Transcription

Street name	House number	Dwelling number	Family visit number	Name of every person whose usual place of abode on 1 January 1920 was with this family	Relation to head	Home owned or rented	Own free or morgaged	Sex	Color or race	Age	Marital status	Year of immira. to U.S.	Naturalized or alien	Year of Naturalization	Attending sch.	Can read and write	Birthplace	Mother tongue	Birthplace of father	Mother tongue of father	Birthplace of mother	Mother tongue of mother	Can speak eng.	Occupation	General nature of industry, business, etc. such as cotton mill, dry goods, store, farm, etc.	Whether an employer, employee, or working on own account	No. of farm schedule

Head of Household ______ State ______ County ______ City/Township ______ Written page number ______

Printed page number ______ Enumeration District ______ Microfilm roll number ______ Call number ______

Illustration 14-14 United States 1920 Federal Census Transcription Form (Larger versions of each of these Census Transcription Forms are located in the Appendix)

1920 Census. The 1920 census has been indexed nationwide and is the latest index open to the public. This census should not be ignored. Often a date for immigration and naturalization is provided for your ancestors in this census if they were from the old country, or if one of their parents was living with them and listed this information. The information found on this census is shown in Illustration 14-14.

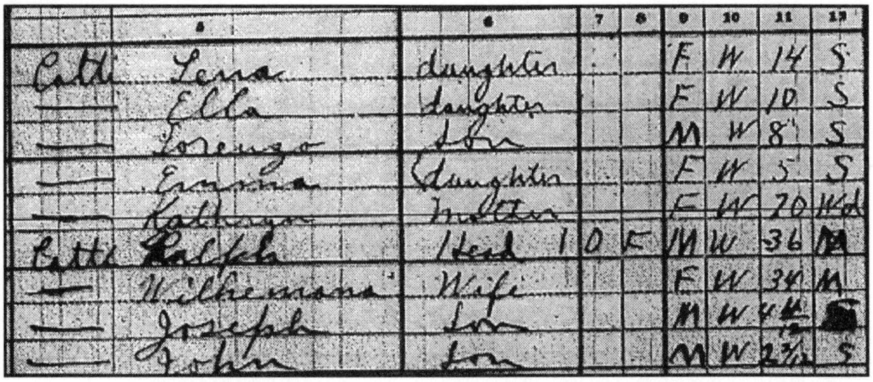

Illustration 14-15 1920 Census Handwriting Example

YOUR TURN

1. Which census records would be most valuable for finding information on one ancestor? List them below:

Ancestor   Census Year

2. In what states did this ancestor live during the years listed in #1?

3. Was the ancestor male or female?

4. If the ancestor was a female, was she married? Yes   No   What would her last name have been during this census?

6. If the ancestor was a male, was he 21 years old or older? Yes   No What was his age in each census year?

These are the kinds of questions you must ask yourself with each census you search.

Terms to Understand

Mir·a·code - The Miracode indexing system is very similar to the Soundex system, using the same rules to code a surname. However, the Miracode card is a typewritten census card instead of a handwritten census card. The Miracode also indexes by family visitation number instead of sheet number. Miracode was used to index several states for the 1910 federal census.

RESEARCH AIDS

There are several census aids that can help you in locating an individual on a federal census:

1. Soundex or **Miracode** indexes on microfilm (1880-1920)
2. Statewide head-of-household indexes (1790-1870) or CD-ROM indexes
3. Statewide every-name indexes
4. Countywide every-name, or head-of-household indexes
5. Accelerated Indexing System™ (AIS) nationwide computer indexes on fiche
6. Map guides.

Soundex or Miracode Indexes on Microfilm (1880-1920)

Both the Soundex and Miracode indexing systems allow for *most* names that "sound the same" to be grouped together, regardless of the actual spelling. (There are problems such as Carr and Karr, Thompson and Thomson not being grouped together.) Your ancestor was not given the opportunity to write down his or her name, but was asked to give it orally. The person writing would then write it the way he heard it, "accent and all." It was also a fact that phonetic spelling was the norm until recent times. Therefore, you may find some rather interesting spellings of your own surnames.

Soundex and Miracode forms have been designed for your use in extracting information from the index rolls, and their use should help you keep all of the information in proper order so that you can locate the original census record on microfilm. Below is a sample of one of the forms.

1910 CENSUS SOUNDEX FORM				

CODE	HEAD OF FAMILY OR INDIVIDUAL NAME		ED	SHEET
COLOR	AGE	BIRTHPLACE	VOL.	
COUNTY	CITY		STATE	

ENUMERATED WITH:

NAME	RELATIONSHIP	AGE	BIRTHPLACE

Illustration 14-16 1910 Census Soundex Extraction Form

Miracode is essentially the same as Soundex in coding a name, but the typescript produced differs from the handwritten Soundex cards. Care should be used in transcribing the information from the card so as not to confuse the

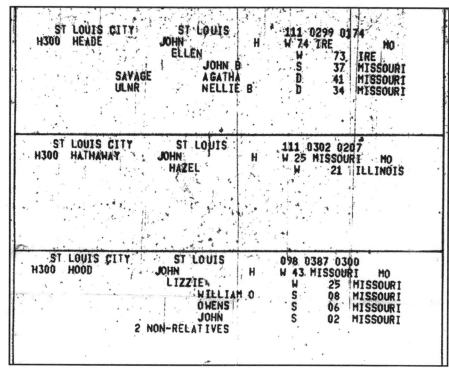

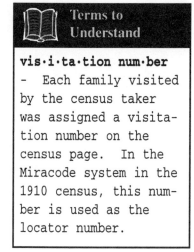

Terms to Understand

vis·i·ta·tion num·ber - Each family visited by the census taker was assigned a visitation number on the census page. In the Miracode system in the 1910 census, this number is used as the locator number.

Illustration 14-17 1910 Census Miracode Example

1910 MIRACODE					
COUNTY	CITY	VOLUME	ED #	VISITATION	
CODE SURNAME	GIVEN NAME	RELATIONSHIP	RACE /AGE	BIRTH PLACE	RESIDENCE

SURNAME	GIVEN NAME	RELATIONSHIP	RACE/AGE	BIRTH PLACE

Illustration 14-18 1910 Federal Census Miracode Extraction Form

Enumeration District on Soundex cards with the **Visitation Number** on Miracode cards. An Enumeration District is usually recorded on the actual census in the upper-right or left-hand corner, while the Visitation Number is the number found in the far left column of the actual census, beside the individual's name. See an illustration of the 1910 Miracode card in Illustration 14-17 and a sample of the Miracode Extraction Form in Illustration 14-18 so you can compare it with the Soundex Form shown in Illustration 14-16.

```
┌─────────────────────────────────────────────────────────────┐
│                   1920 CENSUS SOUNDEX FORM                    │
│                                                               │
│ ┌──────────┬──────────────────────────┬──────────┬─────────┐ │
│ │ CODE     │ HEAD OF FAMILY OR INDIVIDUAL │ ED     │ SHEET   │ │
│ │          │ NAME                         │        │         │ │
│ ├──────────┼──────────┬───────────────┼──────────┴─────────┤ │
│ │ COLOR    │ AGE      │ BIRTHPLACE    │ VOL.               │ │
│ ├──────────┼──────────┴───────────────┼────────────────────┤ │
│ │ COUNTY   │ CITY                     │ STATE              │ │
│ ├──────────┴──────────────────────────┼────────────────────┤ │
│ │ STREET                              │ HOUSE              │ │
│ │                                     │ NO.                │ │
│ ├─────────────────────────────────────┴────────────────────┤ │
│ │ ENUMERATED WITH:                                          │ │
│ ├──────────────┬────────────┬──────┬────────────┬─────────┤ │
│ │ NAME         │ RELATIONSHIP│ AGE  │ BIRTHPLACE │ CITIZEN.│ │
│ ├──────────────┼────────────┼──────┼────────────┼─────────┤ │
│ │              │            │      │            │         │ │
│ └──────────────┴────────────┴──────┴────────────┴─────────┘ │
└─────────────────────────────────────────────────────────────┘
```

Illustration 14-19 1920 Federal Census Soundex Extraction Form

Miracode was used to index part of the twenty-one states in 1910, and Soundex was used in 1880, 1900, part of 1910, and 1920. The 1890 census was nearly all destroyed by fire, so it has only a printed index.

Since we previously broke down the census years individually, let us now look at 1880, 1900, 1910, and 1920 as a unit and see which one to start with. It is always preferable to search records from the known to the unknown, without skipping any ground in the middle. So we should normally begin with the latest one open to the public, which is both indexed and easy to use.

Most of us are too young to remember what happened in the 1910 census, so we should look at that record, *even if our family information already takes us a generation or more beyond that.* You never know what clues may be found in these records. However, there's trouble in 1910! As mentioned previously, only twenty-one states were indexed for the federal census, and the percentage of individuals left off the census appears to be higher than in other years. Those states which were indexed include:

Alabama	Kentucky	Oklahoma
Arkansas	Louisiana	Pennsylvania
California	Michigan	South Carolina
Florida	Mississippi	Tennessee
Georgia	Missouri	Texas
Illinois	North Carolina	Virginia
Kansas	Ohio	West Virginia

If your family was in one of those states, then you should begin with that search. If not, start with the 1920 or the 1900 census, because every state was indexed and every head of household was indexed.

In the Soundex of 1880, only heads of families who had children 10 years of age or under living with them were put in the index. People without children 10 or under are on the actual census, but not in the index.

Only heads of household with children under 10 were indexed in 1880

YOUR TURN

1. Do you have the name of an ancestor who would have been the head of a household in 1910?

2. In which state would this ancestor have lived in 1910?

3. Does that state have a 1910 index? Yes   No

Using the Soundex System

The Soundex is helpful if the county of residence is unknown but you know the state, because all names from a given state are listed together in the Soundex. But remember, when you read this index *you will not be reading the actual census*. The actual census indicates so much more than the Soundex card.

If, for example, you do not find your direct-line ancestor on the 1880 Soundex, can you think of any aunts and uncles who may have had younger children and lived nearby? This might get you within pages of your own family, and then you can conduct a page-by-page search. If you know the county and township of your family, it is also possible to go directly to the census, but an index usually saves much time. Soon the entire 1880 census, will be searchable on numerous CDs, and this will make the job much easier.

Look at it this way. . . When you finish with census records, probate records will be a breeze.

Are census records primary sources or *pry-Mary* sources? It depends on who gave the information.

1880 CENSUS SOUNDEX FORM

SOUNDEX NO:	YEAR:	STATE:		
HEAD OF FAMILY:			VOL:	ED:
			SHEET:	LINE:

COLOR:	MONTH:	AGE:	BIRTHPLACE:	CITIZENSHIP:
COUNTY:			MCD	
CITY:		STREET:		HOUSE #

NAME	RELATION-SHIP	AGE	BIRTHPLACE	CITIZENSHIP

Illustration 14-20 1880 Census Soundex Extraction Form

1900 CENSUS SOUNDEX FORM

SOUNDEX NO:	YEAR:	STATE:		
HEAD OF FAMILY:			VOL: SHEET:	ED: LINE:

COLOR:	MONTH:	AGE:	BIRTHPLACE:	CITIZENSHIP:
COUNTY:			MCD	
CITY:		STREET:		HOUSE #

NAME	RELA-TION-SHIP	BIRTH MONTH	BIRTH YEAR	AGE	BIRTHPLACE	CITIZENSHIP

Illustration 14-21 1900 Census Soundex Extraction Form

On the Soundex, you will see filmed rows of index cards that are either handwritten (Soundexed) or typed (Miracoded). The Soundex code will be in the upper left-hand corner of these cards. The surname will be given first, then the given name. When you get to your correct Soundex code, *look for the given name* next, and ignore the surname until you find the given names you are looking for.

The cards are alphabetized according to given name. Other information on the card includes the county, the city or township, the age and birthplace of head of household and then everyone who is listed in that household, with age, place of birth, etc. *But not even half of the information from the actual census is given.* So don't stop yet. You will want to look at the actual census.

If you are looking for someone who was a child in the 1880 census and you do not know the father's or mother's name, the Soundex can still be very helpful. Locate the proper section of the Soundex according to the surname you are searching, then go through that section and watch for all possible spellings of your surname. When you find a family, see if they have a child with the same name and age as the person for whom you are looking. This takes longer, but it can often work to your advantage. Watch also for siblings of your person, as well.

The Soundex card will provide the actual location in the census where you can find the family that interests you. This information is listed by an *Enumeration District* (ED) number, but it is very important that you copy down the name of the county as well as the Enumeration District and *sheet number.* Extract forms for the various census records have been provided to aid you in recording the necessary information from these indexes. (See Illustrations 14-16, 14-19, 14-20, and 14-21.)

Since several surnames will have the same code, the cards are arranged alphabetically by given name. In addition, there are usually divider cards to let you know that you have gone from one Soundex code into another. However, sometimes there are **mixed codes** in a given range. Instead of being in numerical order, they are inter-filed alphabetically by given names.

Since Soundex cards are filed by given name, not surname, when you get to your Soundex code, don't waste time looking for your surname. If you are looking for William Jason Brown, go directly to the Ws. If he is not there, he may have been listed as Jason, Jason W., W., W. J., J. W., J., Will, Bill, Wm., or another nickname, so check the first part of the W's first, and then go to the Williams and look for your ancestor.

![Terms to Understand icon]	**Terms to Understand**

mixed codes - Instead of being in numerical order, these Soundex codes are inter-filed alphabetically by given names.

Summary

You will save yourself much time if you remember these details:

1. Look for the given name first (including possible variations).
2. Record the county, state, Enumeration District (or Visitation Number), and sheet or page number.

OTHER INDEXES

Statewide Head of Household Indexes (1790-1870)

Many statewide head of household indexes are available in book form on the shelves of Family History Centers, National Archives branches, and major

---

OHIO 1880 CENSUS INDEX

NAME	CODE	PAGE	NAME	CODE	PAGE	NAME	CODE	PAGE
REYMAN, HENRI	ERW5	334B	REYNOLDS, ANN	HKPE	121A	REYNOLDS, EDWD	CYW3	173D
REYMER, FRED	MTBU	004D	REYNOLDS, ANNA	MTW2	093A	REYNOLDS, EDWD.	LUW5	297B
REYMER, HENRY	LGPE	180D	REYNOLDS, ANNA	VNSW	159D	REYNOLDS, EDWIN	LREY	481B
REYMER, JOHN	LGPE	180D	REYNOLDS, ANNIE	JFW3	499D	REYNOLDS, ELI	VNMC	051D
REYMER, WALTER	EROX	141C	REYNOLDS, ARTHUR	SUW5	100D	REYNOLDS, ELISEBATH	HULY	099D
REYMILLER, HANNAH	MMSP	314D	REYNOLDS, ASHER	WYCR	516D	REYNOLDS, ELISHA	BUW3	410C
REYMOND, AUGUSTUS	HKLA	088B	REYNOLDS, BARNEY	GUJK	086A	REYNOLDS, ELIZ.	CHRU	337A
REYMOND, CHARLES	VWUN	275C	REYNOLDS, BARNEY	HMW4	428B	REYNOLDS, ELIZA	HMW5	041B
REYMONK, NETTE	CYSO	351A	REYNOLDS, BARNEY	MHSM	207C	REYNOLDS, ELIZA	LKPA	399B
REYNALD, SAMUEL	HLRL	379B	REYNOLDS, BASCOM H.	LGZA	286C	REYNOLDS, ELIZABETH	FUAM	049A
REYNALDS, JNO.	CKGE	053D	REYNOLDS, BELLE	HMW1	610B	REYNOLDS, ELIZABETH	HNJA	489B
REYNALDS, MARY	CMMM	159B	REYNOLDS, BELLE	MTW5	191A	REYNOLDS, ELIZABETH	JFW2	470D

Illustration 14-22 1880 Census Index from a Printed Register

libraries, and nearly all printed census indexes are available at the Family History Library in Salt Lake City. If you are unable to find the one you need in a local facility, you may request, through a photo duplication order form at a local Family History Center, that certain names be copied from an index available in Salt Lake City. Some statewide head of household indexes are also available on the Internet through Ancestry.com, HeritageQuest.com, and Genealogy.com. Ancestry.com and HeritageQuest.com will soon have scanned images of all the actual census pages available online through a subscription service. Genealogy.com links their new census CD-ROM indexes directly to the image on the CD. All provide some form of printing capability. The technology each company has developed for users provides different possibilities for viewing and saving the images in your research

Statewide Every-Name Indexes

Although not as common, there are some census indexes to every name in a state. Often, individuals who are indexing a set of records do not just index the head of the household: they may type out the entire census, placing an index to all names in the back. Thus, they make an every-name index. Some of the newer indexes are every-name indexes, so be sure to read the *FHLC* entry carefully to see if it is an every-name index.

OCCUPANT	ACCT#	TWP	PGE#	HH	A	S	OCCUP	B/P	DTE
Lee, Mary	00582	Hamilt	103		19	F		In	8/15
Lee, May	00325	Hamilt	100		31	F		Tn	8/9
Lee, Robert	00328	Hamilt	100		01	M		In	8/9
Lee, Samuel	00324	Hamilt	100	HH	32	M	Farmer	In	8/9
Lee, Symantha	01135	Hamilt	110		14	F		Ky	8/23
Lee, William	00581	Hamilt	103	HH	25	M	Cooper	Ky	8/15
Leeson, Benjamin	10808	Grassy Fork	232		08	M		In	9/19
Leeson, James	10807	Grassy Fork	232		10	M		In	9/19
Leeson, John	10804	Grassy Fork	232	HH	55	M	Laborer	Va	9/19
Leeson, John	10806	Grassy Fork	232		13	M		Va	9/19
Leeson, Nancy	10805	Grassy Fork	232		49	F		Va	9/19
Leeson, Nancy J	10809	Grassy Fork	232		04	F		In	9/19
Leeson, William	10814	Grassy Fork	233		20	M	Laborer	Oh	9/19
Lennor, Mary	06910	Driftwood	183		30	F		England	8/16
Lennox, Catharine	06912	Driftwood	183		16	F		Ky	8/16
Lennox, Isabella	06911	Driftwood	183		21	F		Pa	8/16
Leonard, Celestis	06810	Driftwood	181		06	F		In	8/15
Leonard, Ludice	06809	Driftwood	181		28	F		In	8/15
Leonard, Paschal	06808	Driftwood	181	HH	32	M	Farmer	Ky	8/15
Leonard, Sarah	08492	Owen	202		16	F		In	8/27

Illustration 14-23 1850 Jackson County, Indiana Census Index (compiled by Carol Stultz, FHL US/CAN 977.223 28s)

Countywide Every-Name, or Head of Household Indexes

Using the catalog of the Family History Library on microfiche or computer might lead you to other county or state every-name census indexes. To use this source, look up the STATE, then the topic CENSUS, then INDEX. If you know the county you are looking for, try looking up the STATE, COUNTY, CENSUS, INDEX in that order. Hundreds of these have been written.

Accelerated Indexing System™ (AIS)

The *AIS* or *Accelerated Indexing System*™, provides an index of heads of households in the federal census for the period 1790-1850. This means that only the father, husband, mother, widower, or single person would be listed. There are some years in some states that have been indexed for the years after 1850. The reason the *AIS* is so important is that it is the equivalent of a "nationwide" search.

The microfiche sections of the *AIS* are called "searches." A search, in this case, is a microfiche printout for a particular time period. For example, Search 1 covers Early Colonial Records and the US, 1600-1819. Searches 5 to 7A cover the 1850 census, with each sub-search in Search 5 covering a particular section of the country, and Search 7 covering the entire United States. Search 8 is the **Mortality Schedule**, which contains information on people who died within the year prior to the census.

The information recorded on the *AIS* (whether on microfiche or in a printed index) will be:

1. The name of the head of household.
2. The county of residence.
3. The page on the census upon which he or she appears.
4. The town or area in which he or she lived. Sometimes it will give a district number, sometimes it will list a city, sometimes "No Township Listed" will be indicated.

The *AIS* can, therefore, aid you in locating the county and state in which your ancestor lived, if you do not know this information. This is very important because vital records, land and property records, probate records, etc., are usually maintained at a county or town level. Other important records, such as military records or original land patents, might be at a statewide level. The more you find out about the locality of your individual, the easier it will be to pinpoint research sources.

> **Terms to Understand**
>
> **Mor·tal·i·ty Sched·ule**
> - Contains information on people who died within the exact year prior to the census.

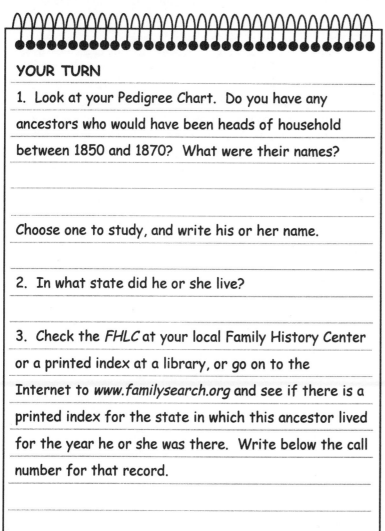

YOUR TURN

1. Look at your Pedigree Chart. Do you have any ancestors who would have been heads of household between 1850 and 1870? What were their names?

Choose one to study, and write his or her name.

2. In what state did he or she live?

3. Check the *FHLC* at your local Family History Center or a printed index at a library, or go on to the Internet to *www.familysearch.org* and see if there is a printed index for the state in which this ancestor lived for the year he or she was there. Write below the call number for that record.

Terms to Understand

pre·pon·der·ance - Superiority in weight, force, importance, or influence.

Terms to Understand

mi·gra·tion path - A route traveled by a group of people while moving from one region and settling in another.

Even if you do not locate a known relative in the *AIS,* you can see what areas of the country had a **preponderance** of the name you are looking for. Or, if your family was on the move, you might see a **migration path** developing as you trace them from one place to another. If your ancestor's name suddenly disappears in New York and appears in Michigan, you have an idea of when he was traveling and can better track him that way.

Once you have located your family in the AIS, go to the original record by ordering the roll of film for that family and verifying the information. It is also a good idea to check the information in other statewide indexes now that you know the state to look in. Since many indexes have been made by various individuals and organizations, it could be that your ancestor was left off of one index but has been included in another.

Map Guides

One of the problems of locating early ancestral records is that county boundaries changed as the states became more settled. What had been a particular county in 1850 may not even exist today, or it may have been part of another county. The *Map Guide to the U.S. Federal Censuses, 1790-1920,* by William Thorndale and William Dollarhide, is extremely helpful for locating county boundary changes.

If your family says they lived in Buchanan County and you can't find them there, it doesn't mean that they have been telling you stories. Perhaps the boundaries changed for that county. The *Map Guide* contains maps for each state for *each census year,* beginning either with 1790 (the first census) or the first census year that the state existed.

It is important, before searching for records, to look at the census maps for the proper year and see if the county was the same then as it is now. Perhaps they were exactly where they said they were, but the names have since changed. Or, perhaps that particular county doesn't even exist anymore. It's even possible that you have been looking in the wrong county (as we now know it). Each map in the *Map Guide* has the current counties in black and the counties as they were in that census year in white. You can see where perhaps one little corner belonged to another county during the time period you are searching, and that may give you just the clue you need to find the appropriate records.

Animap™ is a computer program that was introduced to you in Chapter 7. It provides the county boundary changes for every year since the colonial period and therefore goes beyond the printed map book in yearly ranges. When you find the maps you want, they can be printed to a file and brought into your own records.

YOUR TURN

1. Look at your family. Do you have an ancestor who stayed in the same state from 1850 to 1920, or for several decades in a particular state? What was his or her name?

2. Try to obtain one of the maps mentioned above and see if the boundaries for the county where your ancestor lived ever changed. What did you discover?

OBTAINING CENSUS FILMS

The actual census records may be obtained in many ways. You can see some originals in archives, courthouses, and state libraries; surviving census records up to 1920 are available on film; many are available in scanned electronic format on the Internet through a subscription service through either HeritageQuest.com or Ancestry.com, and others are available in CD-ROM format by purchasing through HeritageQuest.com or Genealogy.com. All provide some form of printing (either line by line or an entire page).

The film version is available through:

1. FHC film orders through the Family History Library.
2. Film rental through Heritage Quest, which also produces them on CD.
3. Interlibrary loan at your local public library.
4. A personal visit to a National Archives branch.
5. The purchase of the film from the National Archives or Heritage Quest.
6. Record Look-up Services at *www.GRAonline.com* provides a copy of the census page in photocopy or scanned image formats.

YOUR TURN

Determine which repository is the best place for you to obtain copies of federal census records. Write the name here.

Since the process for using census records varies at the different repositories, instructions will be given on how to use them at a National Archives branch. The techniques will need to be modified for other localities using other film numbers.

USING CENSUS RECORDS AT REGIONAL RECORDS SERVICES FACILITIES

For Ancestors Living 1880-1920

Compute the Soundex code for any census films from 1880, 1900, 1910 or 1920 by following the instructions below, or by using a feature of your genealogy computer program which automatically computes the information.

SOUNDEX CODING GUIDE

Code   Key Letters and Equivalents

Code	Key Letters and Equivalents
1	b,p,f,v
2	c,s,k,g,j,q,x,z
3	d,t
4	l
5	m,n
6	r

Illustration 14-24 Soundex Coding Guide

The letters *a, e, i, o, u, w, h,* and *y* are NOT coded. (Just remember "WHY vowels," and you'll have an easy way to remember those letters which are *not* coded.)

The *first letter* of a surname is *not coded, but it is written* as the beginning of your Soundex Code. Therefore, Cook would be: C 200.

Every Soundex Code must have a three-digit number. If a name yields no code numbers, then zeroes would follow. Lee would be L 000, for example. Kuhne would be K 500, Ebell would be E 140 and Ebelson is E 142 not E 1425.

When two key letters (see chart above) appear together, such as ll in Kelly, or when two or three letters combine to make a single sound, such as ck in Buerck, sch in Schaefer, or sck in Buscker, they are coded as one letter. Kelly would be K 400, Buerck would be B 620 and Buscker would be B 260. Schaefer would be S 160.

EXAMPLES: Eckhardt = E263; Jones = J520; Clifford = C416; Fritzenheimer = F632; Bauer = B600.

Prefixes such as "van", "Von", "Di", "du", etc., are sometimes disregarded, so be careful. Nuns were sometimes recorded as though Sister were their surname, and Indians may have shortened names.

YOUR TURN

1. Write the surname code of the individual you are

seeking, here _____.

2. Write the name of the state in which the person

your are seeking lived, here _____ _____.

Now, follow the steps in the "Step-by-Step Procedures" chart in Illustration 14-25.

Ancestors living prior to 1880 may be found in printed indexes. Most censuses have been indexed between 1790 and 1860, and several are being worked on for 1870 at this time. The next section will cover searching for your ancestor prior to 1880. Follow the steps in the procedures chart in Illustration 14-26.

Step-by-Step Procedures for Locating Your Ancestor on the 1880 to 1920 Census Rolls at the National Archives or Branch Archives

1. Go to the appropriate U.S. government-produced census booklet (either 1920, 1910, 1900, or 1790-1890) which contains the film numbers for the state Soundex you seek.
2. In the Soundex portion of the booklet, locate the state where your ancestor lived in the census year you are researching.
3. Now, look down the columns until you locate the Soundex code number within the range of numbers allowed.
4. Write down the "T" number (located beside the state name), which helps locate the drawer in which the films are located, and then write down the number of the film itself (located to the far left of the Soundex range). The "T" number is: _____. The film number is: _____.
5. Take the Soundex film from the drawer and place it onto the microfilm reader.
6. Roll the film forward until you locate the Soundex code number in the upper-right or left-hand corner. There are often several numbers on each roll, and they are usually in numerical order. Sometimes, however, the codes are mixed.
7. Now, search for the given name, not the surname, of the individual you seek. If it is William Thomas, look for: William, William Thomas, William T., W. T., Wm., Wm. T., Thomas, Tom, or Bill. Once you have found the given name under the particular Soundex code, look for the correct last name (or as close to correct as possible). The spelling is often incorrect.
8. Once you have found the right family, write down all of the information on the appropriate Soundex transcription card. Particularly important are the name of the county in which the family was living, the state, the ED (Enumeration District), the sheet number, and the line number. [To assist you, Appendix A contains forms to help you in this step as you are learning to correctly copy raw material.]
9. Having now obtained the correct county and ED number, go to the appropriate booklet again. Look under the section which covers the actual census films. Go to the state you are interested in and find the particular county given on the Soundex card. Sometimes there are so many Enumeration Districts in a particular county that you will need to check two rolls of film to cover your district. Write down the film number(s) to the far left of the county. The film number(s) is/are: _____.
10. Now, go to the film cabinet, find the film you want, and put it onto the machine. Often, you will see a list of the counties on that roll, so you can see how many counties you will need to roll through to get to your county.
11. Roll ahead until you find your county (the name is usually written in the far left corner).
12. Now, look at the far right-hand corner for the Enumeration District you are seeking.
13. Once you have found the Enumeration District, go to the sheet number (page).
14. Finally, go down the page to the line where the Soundex card indicated you would find your family.
15. Copy all of the information in every column (including that in the top part of the form, which will give the township, the post office, and the date the census was actually taken); better yet, have a photocopy made. Be sure to look back five or six pages before and after your ancestor to see if in-laws, cousins, brothers, sisters, aunts, uncles, parents, etc., are living close by, and photocopy those pages as well.

Illustration 14-25 1880-1920 Procedures

Step-by-Step Procedures for Locating Your Ancestor on the 1790 to 1870 Census Rolls at the National Archives or Branch Archives

1. Decide in what state the individual you are researching was living at the time of a census.
2. Go to the printed census indexes, which are filed in alphabetical order, or check the *AIS*™, or CD-ROM indexes.
3. Locate the individual you seek in the index, and copy the county abbreviation and page number for the census.
4. Go to the appropriate booklet (1790-1880), and look under the year you are researching.
5. Find the state in which you are interested.
6. Go to the county indicated in the above printed index, locate the film number for that county and write it here:_____.
7. Locate the film in the drawer. NOTE: If you find a notation like this in the printed index book, 0120423-12304 (the actual numbers will be different but there will be a long line of them), it indicates that the actual information on that census has already been transcribed. You might think it is not necessary to look at the original census, but when you do, you may find that the numbers were not transcribed correctly, you might find another locator clue such as a township name, military district number, or a riverway, and you might locate possible neighbors. Those numbers (0120423-12304) refer to the family numbers (0 means no male 0 to 5 years, 1 means a male under 10, 2 indicates 2 males between 10-15, etc.). Having a copy of a Census History Form available (see Appendix A for ordering information or contact your local genealogy supply store) is very helpful. If you record these numbers in order on such an extract form, it will make the ages readily apparent.
8. Place the film onto the viewer. Roll it to the correct county, then to the particular page number indicated in the index. This is often tricky, because some indexers used the printed numbers on the pages, which changed with every county, while other indexers used the hand-written numbers that ran through the entire film. Other films have stamped page numbers throughout. If you can first locate the correct county and township, the page will be easier to locate.
9. Copy down all of the information on your census abstract forms. Be sure to look around at the neighbors on the surrounding pages. Very likely there are in-laws, cousins, brothers, sisters, aunts, parents, etc., living nearby.
10. Not all indexes are complete for 1870, but the census films are available. Try looking up the individual you just found in the same county and township ten years earlier, and go page by page through the area. You may very well locate him. You could also check county histories to see when the townships developed, and then go back to the census films to locate those new townships. Keep checking for new indexes, which are being published each year.

Illustration 14-26   1790-1870 Procedures

CONCLUSION

Federal census records are important primary sources of information for your family. Family research should include census records early in the research phase, and it should exhaust the information in them. Remember these tips when using the Soundex:

1. The first letter of the surname becomes the first part of the code.
2. Every Soundex number must be a three-digit number.
3. Double or triple letters which sound alike are only counted once.
4. If a letter is repeated but separated by another letter (except the silent sounded letters w, h, and y), you would use the number twice.
5. All vowels, plus w, h, y, are not coded.

ASSIGNMENT 14: CENSUS RECORDS

1. Obtain copies of the appropriate maps for the states in which an ancestor lived between 1850 and 1920. Highlight the area in which he or she lived, and notice the boundary changes.

2. Using the previous guidelines, locate an ancestor in each of the following years (or at least a sample of each of the following census records):

   a. 1920 census _____ (ancestor's name)

   b. 1910 census _____ (ancestor's name)

   c. 1900 census _____ (ancestor's name)

   d. 1880 census _____ (ancestor's name)

   e. 1870 census _____ (ancestor's name)

   f. 1860 census _____ (ancestor's name)

   g. 1850 census _____ (ancestor's name)

3. Compare the variety of information given on each of these census records. Compare the legibility and availability of these records.

YOUR TURN ANSWERS

Personal preferences are expected on all Chapter 14 responses.

COMPUTER CHECKLIST #14

1. Describe how you would enter census records for the following years into your genealogy computer program:

   a. 1880-1920

   b. 1850-1870

2. Data enter census records into your genealogy computer program.

3. Print out the results of what you entered.

WEB SITE

Soundex Conversion Program
http://www.genealogy.org then select "soundex".

BIBLIOGRAPHY AND REFERENCE LIST

Adams, Enid Eleanor. "Who is 'XZLLY MZFGIN'?" *The American Genealogist* 59 (1983).

Brewer, Mary M. *Index to Census Schedules in Printed Form.* Huntsville, Alabama: Century Enterprises, 1969. Supplement, 1970-71.

Buckway, G. Eileen, et al. *U.S. 1910 Federal Census: Unindexed States: A Guide to Finding Census Enumeration Districts for Unindexed Cities, Towns, and Villages.* Salt Lake City: Family History Library, 1992.

_____ and Fred Adams, *U.S. State and Special Census Register: A Listing of Family History Library Microfilm Number.* Rev. ed. 2 vols. Salt Lake City: Family History Library, 1992.

Eakle, Arlene Haslam. "Census Records," in *The Source: A Guidebook of American Genealogy.* Edited by Loretto Dennis Szucs and Sandra Hargreaves Luebking. Rev. ed. Salt Lake City: Ancestry, 1997.

Lainhart, Ann S. *State Census Records.* Baltimore: Genealogical Publishing Co., 1992.

McMillon, Lynn C. "An Index Can Be A Roadblock." *Virginia Genealogist* 21 (1977): 205-06.

Records Indexed by AIS. Genealogical Library Reference Aids Series B, no. 11. Salt Lake City: Genealogical Society of Utah, 1984.

Saldana, Richard H. *A Practical Guide to the "Misteaks" Made in Census Indexes.* Salt Lake City, Utah: R.H. Saldana & Co., 1987.

Steuart, Bradley W. *The Soundex Reference Guide: Soundex Coded to Over 125,000 Surnames.* Bountiful, Utah: Precision Indexing, 1990.

Szucs, Loretto Dennis. "Research in Census Records," in *The Source: A Guidebook of American Genealogy.* Edited by Loretto Dennis Szucs and Sandra Hargreaves Luebking. Rev. ed. Salt Lake City: Ancestry, 1997.

Thorndale, William and William Dollarhide. *Map Guide to the U.S. Federal Censuses, 1790-1920.* Baltimore: Genealogical Publishing Co., 1987.

Vallentine, John F. "Census records and Indexes." *Genealogical Journal* 2 (1973): 133-39.

CHAPTER 15

Analysis and Goal Setting

"Once more on my adventure brave and new."

—Robert Browning

The need for goal setting was mentioned much earlier in this book, but as we return to this topic once more, you will notice a remarkable difference. You now have the background and understanding to set realistic, meaningful goals. Without a plan, it's unlikely that the purposes you set out to accomplish could be achieved. But now that this book has guided you through the Research Cycle and the principles of good research, it is time to revisit that topic so that you can think about what you specifically hope to find.

In genealogy research, the majority of goals focus upon:

Finding the parents' names
  Finding an individual's birth date or place
    Finding a marriage date or place
      Finding a death date or place
        Finding a spouse's name, or maiden name
          Finding the names of siblings
            Finding background information on the family.

ORGANIZATION

As we proceed in our research, we must make a logical move from one level of questioning to another. The first question should always be, "What do I already know?" and you can now answer that question because you have organized your materials. Remember what a hard time you had finding what you wanted because it was just *too much*! Now, the *principle of organization* has prepared you for greatest success further down the line, but this principle must be practiced over and over again. Just like a beginner who comes into a library with a suitcase full of old documents, notes, and letters and then must spend most of the time in the library finding this or that piece of information, long-time family

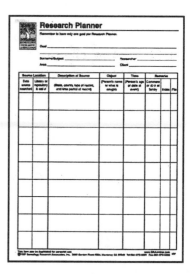

Terms to Understand

rel·e·vant - Having a bearing on or connection with the matter at hand.

Terms to Understand

re·cord type
Information about a group or class of records; i.e., military records, land records, or vital records.

Terms to Understand

pri·or·i·ty -
Precedence by order of importance or urgency.

historians find so many clues and are working on so many family lines that they may forget what they were supposed to be doing and tend to feel out of control.

Success in genealogical research requires *careful planning and successful recording of information*. All facts relating to this person should be recorded in chronological order, if possible. Previously completed research should be itemized in a brief, descriptive form, and as much information as possible should be obtained about the **relevant** events in question. Then you should seek out available record sources, for the correct and wise use of genealogical records is the ultimate goal. Each major **record type** should be studied for its general value to your research problem.

Sorting information by chronology and sorting goals by **priority** can be a tremendous help. We can get our thoughts about every individual lined up. We can then take stock of the priorities we have left, make out a plan of attack with the use of a good Research Planner, and begin a new phase of our project. When we do this, we feel better about ourselves, and our best efforts are given to those things that are most important.

DETERMINE WHAT IS MISSING

Now we must determine what is missing and try to fill in the gaps. Part of the questioning includes: "Who would have this information? Where can this information be found if someone knowledgeable is not available?" Then we ask: "How do I get this information? How do I search that source?" And the research cycle begins anew. So let's take another look.

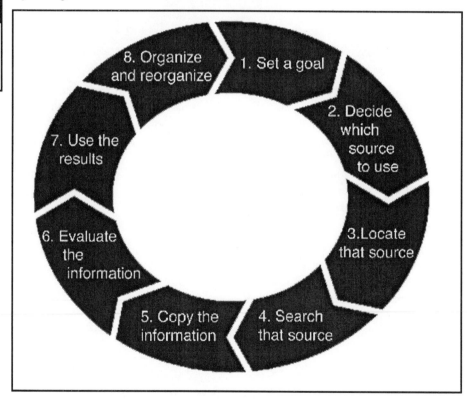

Illustration 15-1 The Research Cycle

You will want to repeat this process over and over again, and one of the easiest ways to determine which goals to pursue is to look at the existing family Pedigree or Ancestral Chart, Family Group Records, or individual data fields on your computer genealogy program. Is anything missing or questionable? Could those missing items fall under one of the goals mentioned above?

Basically, goal setting involves asking questions, recording questions, and listing sources. And while it's true that greater success involves applying good research techniques, the foundation of our success depends upon focusing on appropriate goals from the very beginning. Also, as you selected a goal, did you put into practice those research techniques introduced previously to prevent researching the wrong family line? Let's review them for a minute.

Go from Known Information to Unknown Information

You cannot set a goal if you have not separated fact from tradition, hypothesis from actuality. If someone on the Internet or in a published genealogy has extended your family line three generations, don't just accept it as fact and start going backward from the end of the purported "new" third generation. First, verify the relationships between your known ancestors and the new-found ancestors. Then you can move into the "unknown" once again.

"What do you really know about this person?"

"I was told he was born in Virginia."

"But how did I come to know that information?"

"Oh, I remember, I found that on the 1880 census record."

"Since records are kept on a county level in Virginia, what county was the person living in?"

"I don't know! Wait! Yes, it was written on that 1880 census. It was Franklin County. But this only tells me where he was living in 1880 and that he was born in Virginia. I will need to go back in time starting with 1880 and see if he remains in this same county."

"Correct! So what will your goal be?"

"My goal is to find the birthplace of this person."

"You've got the idea."

"But I really want to find out who this person's parents are, too."

"That is another goal. There are now two goals for this person."

Don't Skip Generations or Sources

In the above example, it would be very tempting to skip the present generation, since you already know a person's name, the year of birth and the location, then just jump back to the parents' names. Resist that temptation. Don't skip generations or sources. By finding the birthplace of the individual, you may also find the parents' names. And you might find even more.

Let's say that in the above example, you also have the individual's marriage date and place, so you're tempted to skip looking it up because you think you already "know" it. You do not, however, have a *primary source* for the information. You only have hearsay evidence from a published family history, so you must select as another goal to find the marriage record or marriage application.

When you find the original marriage location, you may also find in the marriage application the names of the parents. Had you not sought these primary sources, the information would have been lost to you. Therefore, your third goal would be to find documentation for the marriage date for the individual you're searching because it might contain information on the person's parents.

WITHIN REASON, Get Them All

You need to record all of the individuals of the same surname in the same locality (even the common surnames, such as Smith, if you are searching in a small town or township), the neighbors who may have traveled with them for several generations, and the relatives who appear on one record or another. You obviously wouldn't want to get all the Smiths in New York City, but would want to get all of the Smith individuals in the same block or building. You are doing this because, even though your third great-grandfather did not state on his marriage record the names of his parents, his sister, who lived in the same county, might have stated the names of her parents— just what you were looking for.

Find the Current County Jurisdiction

Look at a current atlas or map and determine where the location would be today. Then make a copy of that area, in case you want to contact genealogy societies, historical societies, or local libraries there to see if they have records or information on the individual for whom you are searching.

Locality Analysis

Next, you must determine the name of the location at the time of the event, since records are cataloged and retained in their original jurisdiction. Use gazetteers of the time period, geographical dictionaries, maps, and books to guide you to the name of the county, and possibly the town which might have existed during the years your relatives lived there. County boundaries during the early years of settlement in the United States were constantly changing, and towns were sprouting like dandelions, only to find themselves absorbed into larger municipalities as the nation grew, or in some cases, dying and blowing away like tumbleweeds in sparsely populated areas.

List All Sources Searched, Both Negative and Positive

Because we must list our negative searches (so we don't repeat them), as well as our positive searches, it is a good idea to put all of this information onto a Research Planner, which we discussed in Chapter 8. That way, we can just note whether we found something or not.

Determine What Others Have Already Discovered

Avoid the duplication of effort with a preliminary survey. This involves searching major biographical databases, the *Ancestral File,* the *International Genealogical Index,* the Library of Congress database, Internet sources, etc. Often this information is secondary, but it can help you find locations for primary sources. *The Great Ancestral Hunt,* a beginning computer course available on CD and the Internet at www.GRAonline.com, guides you through the Preliminary Survey.

Plan Your Research Process with the Help of a Research Planner

Do not confuse a *Research Planner* with a *Research Log*. The latter records only what was found. The former records *not* only what was found, but also what was not found when an item was searched, and what records *should* eventually be searched. Using a Research Planner is a very important step in setting goals, as it helps to focus your attention on what you are doing, and it reminds you to apply the other seven basic rules of research.

YOUR TURN:

List below three new goals you can now set for your family.

1.

2.

3.

Goal planning could also include learning more about topics surrounding family history, talking more to relatives, and finding out more about sources.

COMMUNICATION

How can you learn more from your relatives? This involves the principle of communication, and there is a game that demonstrates this principle: Pair off two people, and make one the "describer" and the other the "listener." Have them sit back-to-back, with the describer facing the screen for an overhead projector. Show a simple design on the screen, and give the listener a blank piece of paper and a pencil. Have the describer tell the listener exactly what to draw, in order to reproduce the design on the screen. Only verbal instructions can be given, and the players have three minutes to complete the task. The resulting "design" can be quite a surprise, and nothing whatsoever like the original.

If visual communication had been used in addition to verbal, the results

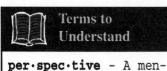

Terms to Understand

per·spec·tive - A mental view or outlook; the relationship of aspects of a subject to each other and to a whole.

Terms to Understand

cus·tom - A practice followed by people of a particular group or region.

Terms to Understand

ven·er·ate - To regard with respect, reverence, or heartfelt deference.

Terms to Understand

tomb·stone in·scrip·tion - A memorial engraving on a grave marker, which is customarily made of stone. The engraving usually includes the deceased's name and birth and death dates; it may also include information about the deceased's family, or a few words which are meant to characterize the deceased's life.

would have been much different. This is equally true in family history research. Have you ever had someone try to explain a genealogy problem to you, orally? Do you find yourself wishing it could be on paper in Pedigree Chart fashion, or at least in a list, with one generation succeeding another? This is because we think better when we can use as many of our senses as possible.

Often, we may receive very astute answers to our genealogy problems, either in conversations or in written form, and these may inspire us, encourage us and help us to set other goals. But visually, the Pedigree Chart and Family Group Records keep the problem in focus. In difficult moments, the correct **perspective** can be most valuable. Try to use the forms and charts you have learned about as you communicate with others so that they can better help you, and vice versa.

It's important for all of us as genealogists to ponder our commonality as a human family. Such a collective overview will provide you with wider insights about records. This is why we spent several pages in this book on history, since it is the combined story of the lives of individuals. Think of what we do today that our ancestors also did in the past.

We too are born.

We too are surrounded by the traditions of the day.

We too are involved with the economic, social, political and religious backgrounds of those around us.

We too may marry.

We too may have to fight against others to preserve our way of life.

We too may have children to raise, to be anxious about, to teach, to set out on a path of their own.

And, finally, we too will die.

Each of these events is common to all of mankind, yet each event may seem very different when it is set against the background or environment in which we and they have lived. Because of this, it is vitally important for a good genealogist to know the historical background of his or her ancestors. Did they take part in any of the great struggles of their countries? Out of necessity, were they pilgrims to a new land? How many were forced out as refugees? Can these great struggles provide clues to the types of records available at those terrifying times?

Humans must work for their survival. What did your ancestors do? If someone spent his or her entire life in a particular occupation, it might provide clues to finding and unveiling an individual. A tin miner in Cornwall, England can be found digging coal thousands of miles away in Pennsylvania. A cloth maker in Ireland can be found among the mills of Massachusetts.

Were your ancestor's circumstances such that he or she was left to struggle throughout life? Were his or her children able to move up the social ladder? What correspondence passed between separated family members? This will never be discovered until we communicate with all family members, for each member carries a personal piece of the family puzzle. Therefore, correspondence with others is another principle of research.

CUSTOMS

Since all of us must die some day, cemetery searching or probate browsing are other tasks to be undertaken. In different cultures, various **customs** surround death. In China, for example, a deceased individual is **venerated** and given a new name at death. Without this knowledge you could find yourself looking for the wrong name. **Tombstone inscriptions** of a lengthy and descriptive nature became increasingly important in some areas of New

England, and this could be very helpful in your cemetery searching. Therefore, knowing the customs can help you to find the correct records.

The same principles apply when searching birth information. If I had been born in Finland, I would have been given a patronymic name, Karen Brunostytar. I would also have received the name of the farm where I was born as my surname. If my brother had been born on a different farm, he would have been given a different surname. This makes it easy to trace localities, but difficult to find people, unless you also know that the Lutheran Church in Finland took a survey of each family each year and grouped them all together, and that these records have been **microfilmed** for the years between 1680 and 1860.

But if I had been born of a certain tribe of Native Americans, my name could have been given to me because of a dream my mother had the night I was born. When I came of age, I would have received another name, and if a favorite relative died, I would have been given his or her name as a remembrance. Without a knowledge of these customs, you might make serious errors in your research; but with a knowledge of this background, your search is more rewarding.

In conclusion, the history of the family as a unit should be considered. What periods of time are involved? What places may be of consequence? Are names of villages or farms important? Are the occupations known? Can a good map or local history be located?

DIALECT

Dialect is the form in which a language develops in a particular locality, and it is usually conspicuous in its peculiarities of vocabulary, pronunciation and usage. When you do not have firsthand knowledge of a locality, dialect can provide some interesting situations, and if you combine dialect with phonetic spelling, more challenges await you.

Since a uniform method of spelling words is relatively modern, names and places were written down as they sounded to the transcriber—or as he or she thought they should be spelled. For example, the name *Hare* is listed in an English register. Sometimes, the "H" is dropped from the beginning of the word when it should have remained. Sometimes, it is added when it does not belong there. The result is that this same name was later spelled Aire, and when the family immigrated to America, it became *Eyre*. Careful attention should be placed on the spelling variations of any surname beginning with a vowel or the aspirate "H."

The same can be true of place names. I have seen the word Albemarle, which is a county in North Carolina, spelled *Arber Marble*. I can almost hear it with a southern accent. I have seen the English town Bicester spelled *Bister,* and Barugh Green, Yorkshire, England spelled *Bark Green*, because these spellings reflect local pronunciations.

NAMING CUSTOMS

Naming patterns, **nicknames** or interchangeable names, such as Mary-Polly, Sally-Sarah, Ann-Agness, Ann-Hannah, Peggy-Margaret, Jenny-Jane, and Nancy for Ann, are all part of family history. Children with more than one given name may use the middle name on one census and the first name on another census. Were the names Biblical (such as David, Solomon, Hezekiah), historical (George Washington, Thomas Jefferson, Henry Harrison), royal (Elizabeth, Charles, Henry), or were they in honor of a patron saint (Bernadet, Christopher, etc.)? Was the mother's maiden name used as a given name in subsequent generations?

Even though we think of surnames as fixed from generation to generation, it is folly to think that all people with the same surname are related. Surnames are

---

Terms to Understand

di·a·lect - A regional variety of a language distinguished by pronunciation, grammar, or vocabulary, especially a variety of speech differing from the standard literary language or speech pattern of the culture in which it exists.

Terms to Understand

nick·name - A descriptive name added to or replacing the actual name of a person, place, or thing; a familiar or shortened form of a proper name.

Terms to Understand

mi·cro·form - An arrangement of images reduced in size, as on microfilm or microfiche.

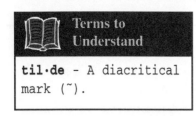

Terms to Understand

til·de - A diacritical mark (˜).

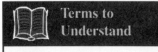

Terms to Understand

thorn - The runic letter Þ originally representing either sound of the Modern English *th*, as in *the* and *thin*, used in Old English and Middle English manuscripts.

Terms to Understand

con·trac·tion - A word, as *won't* from *will not*, or phrase, as *o'clock* from *of the clock*, formed by omitting or combining some of the sounds.

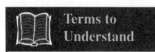

Terms to Understand

sus·pen·sion - The omission of one or more letters from a word, and replacing them with a period or color as a form of abbreviation.

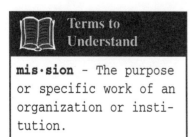

Terms to Understand

mis·sion - The purpose or specific work of an organization or institution.

a recent invention in the history of mankind and they came from localities, occupations, hero worship, given names, things in nature, animals, and much more.

Then there are writing customs. This includes **contractions,** in which letters are left out in the middle of the word, and this process is tagged with a certain stroke or other sign. A "P" with a **tilde** on the top may stand for *per, par, pre,* or *pro,* or sometimes an apostrophe stands in for missing letters, as in *P'fect* or *Edm'nd's.*

Then there are "superior letters," consisting of omitting a letter or letters from a word and raising some of the letters above the line, resulting in , *wth* for *with* and *wch* for *which,* and *yt* and *ye* representing *that* and *the,* the *y* being a survival of the "**thorn,**" a letter found in ancient alphabets and pronounced like *th* yet written somewhat like the letter y. Examples also include abbreviated words, such as the name *Jno Richrd* for *John Richard,* or *chamrs* for *chambers,* as well as *His Matie* for *His Majesty. Mr.* and *Mrs.* are a survival of this practice.

Suspensions leave off the final letters of a word and replace them with a period, colon, or various strokes. The oldest form of suspension was the use of the initial letter of a word. ℞, for example, was the abbreviation for recipe, a sign still displayed by druggists at prescriptions centers, as well as *wid.* for *widow,* and *ite.* for *item.* Then there are special alphabets, legal languages (like Latin), calendar changes, and saints' days to become acquainted with.

In the months to come, you may want to set a goal to learn to read the language of the ancestor you are researching (both the handwriting and non-English words). In addition, you can learn what kind of records are available and where they are available for public use in the area where the ancestor lived.

LEARNING MORE ABOUT REPOSITORIES

There are differences, commonalities, and unique **missions** for archives, public libraries, and family history centers. Some we have covered in depth, but we

	Archives	Family History Centers	Libraries
Differences	Primary materials, often in their original medium, limited to the time period and localities of the mission statement of the facility.	Primary materials in **microform** and secondary printed materials in book, microform, or electronic format from all over the world but limited by the open records of the various countries and the budget of the Family History Library.	Secondary materials in book, microform, or electronic format, limited to the particular mission of the library.
Commonalities	Each repository provides a part of the puzzle you need to solve your research problem and each may have materials unavailable in other repositories. Because of their unique missions and space limitations, each is limited to obtaining materials regarding specific time periods, localities and events.		
Unique mission	To preserve original materials.	To help people trace their families.	To provide reference materials for the public.

Illustration 15-2 Repository Decision Table

can only cover others in a very general manner. Illustration 15-2 can help you decide which repository is best for the type of record you want to find.

At present, the best repository for you may be the one closest to your home. That's fine! Use what you have, and go from there. The most important principle is perseverance. Imagine that I have given you a piece of salt water taffy, and like the taffy, our research also starts out sweetly. Answers come quickly. But the further back in time we go, fewer and fewer records are available. This might mean a thorough, painstaking review of all existing probate or property records, or a page-by-page search of an unindexed census. We have to chew harder now. While we started out with good intentions, the obstacles find their way to us. The words are hard to read, and the film machine may make us dizzy as we roll it on and on. We may become fatigued or rushed, and the pressures cause our resolve to dissolve like the taffy we just ate; it was sweet when we started but it was soon gone.

Now imagine I've given you a stick of gum. We can prove we are made of tougher ingredients if we will persevere, even though the times are rough and the pressures mount. No matter how many times we apply pressure and chew, the gum still remains. Ultimately, that perseverance will pay off, because even the lack of success in one set of records is one area checked off, never to be repeated. One of the biggest reasons most people hire professional researchers is that they want them to do the jobs they do not like to do themselves. But if you possess the necessary perseverance, you will find great reward in doing the work on your own.

Understandably, fatigue, weariness and exasperation over a particular problem may occur. We may also find ourselves rushed or pressed, and as a result we may think and write things we would not have done if we were fresh and had time to ponder and remember. This brings me to another principle. The principle of cooperation. By exploring options and combined examples with friends and associates, we can help to identify the necessary principles involved and discover our own research **deficiencies**. Perceptive questions and logical reasoning with one another produces profound results. This is critical thinking at its best.

Imagine you have only ten pieces of a one-hundred-piece puzzle in front of you, so you can see only parts of the picture. This can make it difficult to come up with a solution. But if everyone works on the puzzle together and contributes the pieces which they have, you all see a more complete picture, you have accomplished the job more easily, and it is more fun.

CONCLUSION

Goal setting, therefore, draws on the sum total of your knowledge, research skills, and organizational abilities. As goals are reached, they must be recorded with sufficient detail to give a clear and accurate picture of what took place. And when you have completed this documentation, you can begin the Research Cycle anew. A review of all of the elements that contribute toward successful research may sound intimidating, but once you've applied these techniques you will find them empowering and rewarding. While you might achieve results by chance, a systematic, organized, goal-centered research approach is the best way to achieve consistent results.

Another point to consider is attitude. Individuals with positive attitudes have a greater chance of achieving success. This may be because those with a positive attitude persevere, are more "attuned" to the people involved, or are more focused on the details in the records. I see this in my own work. If I hire two researchers for the same project, and one thinks that a resource will never be found and the other thinks it will, it is amazing that both are right. The optimist locates the information and the pessimist does not. If you will keep your goals clearly defined, write down your strategy, enlist **allies**, and gather applicable resources, you will be able to visualize your plan, recognize when you're making progress, and note your accomplishments. After all, if you don't know where you're going, how will you know when you've arrived?

	Terms to Understand
	de·fi·cien·cy - The quality or condition of being incomplete or insufficient.

	Terms to Understand
	al·lies - Persons in helpful association with others, often working toward a common goal.

ASSIGNMENT 15: MAKE PLANS FOR THE FUTURE

1. Select one line to focus on in the intermediate level of study, preferably including those who lived in the U.S. and were born before 1830. Write down which line you have selected.

2. Where did this selected family live? List states and counties.

3. Include all of the information you have on this line as a baseline of information. You may do this in the form of a GEDCOM or print-outs from your genealogy computer program, but be sure to include all notes as well.

4. What do you want to know about this family?

YOUR TURN ANSWERS

Personal preferences are expected on all Chapter 15 responses.

COMPUTER CHECKLIST #15

1. Assume that you know you have entered a note on someone but you don't remember where that note is. How would your program find a note in your general notes field?

2. How do you find and make a list of all of the individuals for whom you made TO DO notes?

WEB SITES

Allen County Public Library
Allen County, Indiana
http://www.acpl.lib.in.us/genealogy/genealogy.html

Boston Public Library
Boston, Massachusetts
http://www.bpl.org/WWW/socsci/genealogy.html

DAR Library
Washington, D.C.
http://dar.library.net/

Indiana Archival and Historical Repository
Indiana
http://cawley.archives.nd.edu/sia/guide/reposito.htm

Library of Congress
Washington, D.C.
http://lcweb.loc.gov/library/

National Archives
Washington, D.C.
http://www.nara.gov/genealogy/

National Archives Regional Records Services Facilities
http://www.nara.gov/regional/nrmenu.html

New England Historic Genealogical Society Library
Boston, Massachusetts
http://www.nehgs.org/

Newberry Library
Chicago, Illinois
http://www.newberry.org/nl/genealogy/genealogyhome.html

Sutro Library
San Francisco, California
http://206.14.7.53/GENCOLL/gencolsu.htm

Utah Valley Regional Family History Center
at Brigham Young University, Provo, Utah
http://www.lib.byu.edu/dept/uvrfhc/

BIBLIOGRAPHY

Bowker, R. R. *American Library Directory 1999-2000.* 52nd ed. New Providence, New Jersey: 1999.

Carson, Dina, ed. *Directory of Genealogical and Historical Society Libraries, Archives and Collections in the U.S. & Canada.* Niwot, Colorado: Iron Gate Publishing, 1998.

Clifford, Karen. *The Great Ancestral Hunt* [CD]. Salt lake City, Utah: Genealogy Research Associates, Inc., 1998.

National Historical Publications and Records Commission. *Directory of Archives and Manuscript Repositories in the United States.* Phoenix: ORYX Press, 1988.

The Genealogical Index of the Newberry Library. 4 vols. Boston: G.K. Hall, 1960.

Genealogies in the Library of Congress: A Bibliography. Baltimore: Magna Charta Book Co., 1972.

Greenlaw, William Prescott, comp. *The Greenlaw Index of the New England Historic Genealogical Society.* 2 vols. Boston: G.K. Hall, 1979.

Guide to Genealogical Research in the National Archives. Rev. ed. Washington, D.C.: National Archives Trust Fund Board, 1985.

Guide to the National Archives of the United States. Washington, D.C.: National Archives and Records Administration, 1987.

Grundset, Eric G. and Steven B. Rhodes. *American Genealogical Research at the DAR.* Washington, D.C: DAR, 1997.

Kvasnicka, Robert M., comp. *The Trans-Mississippi West 1804-1912, Part I: A Guide to Records of the Department of State for the Territorial Period.* Washington, D.C.: NARA, 1993.

Schaefer, Christina K. *The Center: A Guide to Genealogical Research in the National Capital Area.* Baltimore: Genealogical Publishing Co., 1996.

Szucs, Loretto Dennis and Sandra Hargreaves Luebking. *The Archives: Guide to the National Archives Field Branches.* Salt Lake City: Ancestry, 1988.

Library Catalog. 3 vols. Washington, D.C.: DAR, 1982.

CHAPTER 16

Sharing Your Family History Research

Sure, I said, heav'n did not mean,
Where I reap thou shouldst but glean,
Lay thy sheaf down and come,
Share my harvest and my home.

—Thomas Hood

The true joy of genealogy lies in sharing your successes and failures with family and friends. Every research experience will add to your knowledge, experience, and understanding. Sharing not just the results of your inquiries, but the insights you've gained along the way will make your learning more meaningful and will help others at the same time. As exciting as family history research is, you cannot expect to become an expert in the discipline overnight.

Terms to Understand
NON NOBIS SOLUM - We are not alone.

SHARING

Family history research is intrinsically rewarding. Always share the results of your efforts!! By sharing, you add to the great pool of information from which each of us can benefit. You will also benefit personally as others respond to the data you provided, and you will meet "living, breathing" relatives you did not know existed. At the same time, you will gain a greater understanding of the world in which you live, and you will make lasting friendships.

As the motto of the National Genealogy Society states: **NON NOBIS SOLUM**. We are certainly NOT alone. Genealogy research is most enjoyable and productive when it is a shared activity, and there are many ways to share your family history findings. Perhaps you have already experimented with some of these methods.

1. Shared through GEDCOM files certain surnames you've researched with those of similar surnames.

2. Shared your entire file with millions of people by submitting to the:
   a. *Ancestral File™*. No charge for others to search for your submission or to search for theirs on the Internet at *http://www.familysearch.org*.
   b. *World Family Tree™*. No charge for others to find you or for you to

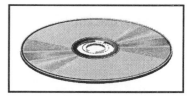

search for others on the *http://www.familytreemaker.com* Internet index, but the person who finds your information will have to purchase or borrow (often at a library) the actual CDs to find you.

c. *Kindred Konnections*™. No charge for others to search for your submission or to search for theirs on the Internet *http://www.kindredkonnections.com*, but there is a charge for obtaining a copy of the actual information, unless you make a submission yourself.

d. Built and posted your own Web page. Web sites are easily built with commercial products. You can do this free of charge at the *FamilySearch* Internet site, mentioned above (a.).

e. Shared copies of electronic files, printed files, and published books by placing copies in local libraries or submitting articles to genealogical periodicals.

f. MyFamily.com. No charge for others to find you, but some restrictions apply.

g. Pedigree Resource File™. A lineage-linked database on CD-ROM containing family history records submitted through the FamilySearch

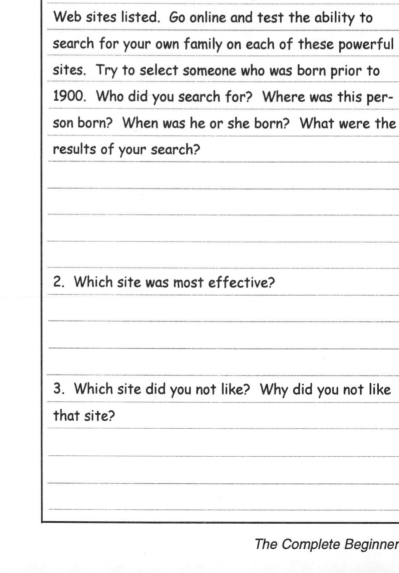

YOUR TURN

1. Turn to the back of this chapter and notice the Web sites listed. Go online and test the ability to search for your own family on each of these powerful sites. Try to select someone who was born prior to 1900. Who did you search for? Where was this person born? When was he or she born? What were the results of your search?

2. Which site was most effective?

3. Which site did you not like? Why did you not like that site?

Internet Genealogy Services. The family information is organized in family groups and pedigrees and may include notes and sources. The Indexes to all Pedigree Resource Files are free to search at *www.family search.org*. Submission is via GEDCOM files. No one is allowed to correct or add to your files, but they may submit their own "versions" of the family history

What is the Process for Sharing Online

I will use the *FamilySearch™* Internet site as my example just to illustrate how easy it is to share your information. Once you log on to the site using *http://www.familysearch.org*, click on the navigation bar option entitled "*Preserve Your Genealogy.*" Information on the screen asks you how you want your genealogy to be preserved? That information submitted through the Internet site will be preserved at the Granite Mountain Records Vault located in Salt Lake City, Utah. Your genealogy would also be preserved on the databases that will be publically available on compact disc or at the Internet site itself. Although the information may later be added to *Ancestral File™*, they ask that you follow the normal process for contributing information to that file as explained in Chapter 11 of this book.

In order to contribute information to either file, you will need to save your genealogy as a GEDCOM file. We have covered this information in earlier chapters and information is also available at the *www.GRAonline.com* Web site on how to do this. A GEDCOM file can be accepted by the *World Family Tree,*

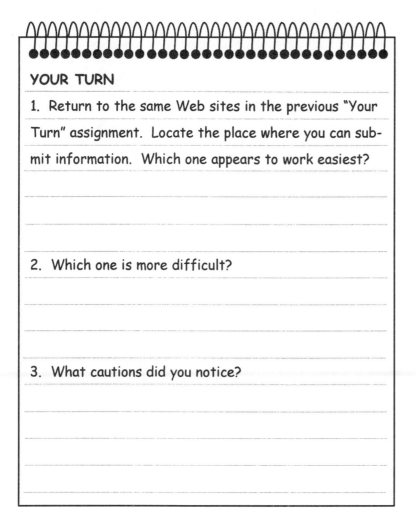

YOUR TURN

1. Return to the same Web sites in the previous "Your Turn" assignment. Locate the place where you can submit information. Which one appears to work easiest?

2. Which one is more difficult?

3. What cautions did you notice?

Kindred Konnections, Ancestry, and many others. To send a GEDCOM file from your computer to the Internet, you must use Netscape Navigator 2.0 or higher or Microsoft Internet Explorer 4.0 or higher. Instructions are provided on the screen on how this is done. In addition, an agreement is posted which you should read giving permission for *FamilySearch™* to share the information with the world.

You are then given three steps. Click on the button shown to help the program find your GEDCOM on a diskette or computer file. Next you are asked to type in a description of the file including the main surname. Finally you are asked if you wish to link that file to your own Web page or to a Web page this site can build for you.

Continue Your Research

It is very easy to share with others. It doesn't matter how you share, but it is hoped that you will share. Without the sharing that has been done in the past, none of us would reap the benefits of what is available today. And then continue your research. Use the Research Cycle over and over with each new name or goal you determine to pursue. Maintain the organization you started with your Family History Notebook archives. You have acquired some solid foundation skills and you are ready to move on to the next level of genealogy. This second phase of your education will include the in-depth study of research sources needed to solve family mysteries prior to the year 1850. New sources will also help you "cross the waters" to your immigrant ancestor's homeland, and this activity will permit you to become involved in another culture. You will also learn how the computer can help *solve* research problems, not merely record the results of your work.

If you are like most researchers, once you have completed this next level, you'll want to publish the results of your adventures! The process of transferring information from a computer database program to a publishing program with narratives, photographs, and even multi-media sound and video is speedily and easily accomplished using today's computer programs. Other specialized reports that meet national standards, such as those set by the National Genealogical Society or the New England Historic Genealogical Society, can also be printed.

THE FUTURE

This book and its successors are dedicated to helping you learn more research techniques, insightful suggestions on sources, fascinating details about your own origins, and ultimately how to publish your own family history in electronic format or by traditional means.

Watch the Web site *http://www.GRAonline.com* for updated information on research, more online lessons (a free 26-lesson "Tracing Your Immigrant Origins" lesson is on the site already), and new techniques for working with computer programs.

ASSIGNMENT 16: SHARING YOUR FAMILY HISTORY RESEARCH

Of course you are not finished with your family history at this time. That does not mean you should not share what you have in order to obtain more. Study your Pedigree Chart. Which family could you share information on now? Do not include living people in your study. They will not be included on what you share because of privacy rights. Which family did you select?

YOUR TURN ANSWERS

Personal preferences apply to these answers.

COMPUTER CHECK LIST

1. Prepare a submission of your family materials for the *Ancestral File*™, a Web site online, or the *World Family Tree*™ and indicate which one you did.

2. Which of all the Web sites did you like the most for sharing your information?

WEB SITES

All these sites accept submissions. This is not a complete list but it is sufficient for the beginning student:

http://www.familysearch.org
You may create a Web site of your own on their site or you may send in your genealogy to be preserved in several ways.

http://www.familytreemaker.com
If you own their program, you may create your own Web site. You may also submit your family for sharing and preservation even if you do not own their program.

http://www.ancestry.com
Accepts submissions from anyone.

http://www.kindredkonnections.com
Accepts submissions from anyone which then allows you to search and use their database.

BIBLIOGRAPHY

Polk, Timothy W. *How to Outlive Your Lifetime! A Complete Guide to Preserving a Place in Your Family's Heart and History.* Sunnyvale, California: Family Life International, 1994.

Sources Used in this Book for "Terms to Understand"

Bremer, Ronald A. *Compendium of Historical Sources.* Bountiful, Utah: AGLL, Inc., 1997.

Encarta World English Dictionary. New York: St. Martin's Press, 1999.

The American Heritage Dictionary for DOS. Sausalito, California: Writing Tools Group, Inc., 1991.

Webster's New World Dictionary of the American Language. New York: Warner Books, Inc. 1985.

The Internet and Genealogy

One of the most popular uses of the Internet is for Genealogy. As demonstrated throughout this book, there are several types of sites on the Internet that are useful for those who are tracing their relatives—either living or dead.

Users of the Internet should be familiar with the different search engines available to them. Search engines allow the Internet user to enter a string of characters which brings up a "hit list" containing that string of characters in its title or description of contents. Some of the most popular search engines are Yahoo, Alta Vista, and Excite. Others are DogPile, Mamma, Google, Go.com., and Ask.com. All search engines use a little different logic, so the search results may be different and certainly will be displayed on the monitor differently.

The Internet has allowed one aspect of genealogy to fully evolve—finding living relatives. Several of the search engines mentioned above provide the means of finding living individuals with whom the Internet user may have lost touch. One of the most popular locators of living individuals is Yahoo's "People Search." Just enter the name and choose a state or other locality and a list of individuals with addresses and telephone numbers is delivered to your screen.

Finding genealogy sources is another aspect of family history research which has benefitted from the Internet. There are many sites on the Web that will help a genealogist to locate records. This book covers, for example, *familysearch.org*, which allows a genealogist to determine what records are available at the Family History Library in Salt Lake City—hence, what is available to Family History Centers, the local branches of the Family History Library. Several other libraries also have catalogs of their holdings online.

The Library of Congress (*www.lcweb.loc.gov*) has many of their collections either cataloged or imaged and online. The Library of Virginia (*www.lva.lib.va.us*) is also digitally imaging many of their documents and placing them online. Some of the larger genealogy libraries around the country also have Web sites, such as the New York Public Library (*www.nypl.org*), the Allen County Public Library (*www.acpl.lib.in.us*), and the New England Historic Genealogical Society (*www.nehgs.org*).

There are many Web sites that provide indexes and abstracts of genealogical records. USGenWeb is a nationwide project that places information about every county and every state on the Internet. Information being placed on these sites includes compilations of cemetery inscriptions, Bible records, biographies, etc.

Remember that information abstracted from original records is secondary, at best, and can have transcription errors in it. The same can be said for information compiled by individuals and submitted to such programs as Ancestral File and Pedigree Resource File, maintained by The Church of Jesus Christ of Latter-day Saints in Salt Lake City. Information in such files is only as correct and complete as the submitter makes it. Too many beginning genealogists simply download such information without checking its accuracy and completeness. These beginners then add a few new personal pieces of information and resubmit it—errors and all. Hopefully this will not be the method employed by the users of this book.

Other programs available on the Internet which may be helpful to genealogists are the genealogical queries sites, such as GenForum and RootsWeb. There are also chat rooms, where Internet users can have a real-time discussion on a subject of their choosing.

The Internet of today offers many benefits to the genealogist. But remember, it also has much inaccurate information on it. Everything that is found and downloaded from the Internet should be verified for accuracy and documented for future users of that information.

Genealogical Forms

The following section contains:

- U.S. Census Transcription Forms
- Soundex/Miracode Transcription Forms.
- Research Planners
- Guide to the Family History Center

Schedule I.—Free Inhabitants in

of ———— enumerated by me, on the ———— day of ———— 1850. ———— Ass't Marshal.

In the County of ———— State

Dwelling-houses numbered in the order of visitation.

Families numbered in the order of visitation.

The Name of every Person whose usual place of abode on the first day of June, 1850, was in this family.

DESCRIPTION.

Age.

Sex.

Color, White, black, or mulatto.

Profession, Occupation, or Trade of each Male Person over 15 years of age.

Value of Real Estate owned.

Place or Birth. Naming the State, Territory, or Country.

Married within the year.

Attended School within the year.

Persons over 20 y'rs of age who cannot read & write.

Whether deaf and dumb, blind, insane, idiotic, pauper, or convict.

Street/ route name	Street/ route number	Dwelling in order of visit	Family in order of visit	The name of every person whose usual place of abode on the first day of June, 1850, was in this family	Age	Sex	Color	Profession, occupation, or trade of each male person over 15 years of age	Value of real estate owned	Place of birth, naming the state, territory or country	Married within the year	Attended school within yr.	Person over 20 who can't read/write	Deaf, dumb, blind, insane, idiotic, pauper convict	Estimated birth year

Head of Household ———— State ———— County ———— City/Township ———— Written page number ————

Printed page number ———— Enumeration District ———— Microfilm roll number ———— Call number ———— Repository ————

GENEALOGY RESEARCH ASSOCIATES, INC.
1860 United States Federal Census Transcription

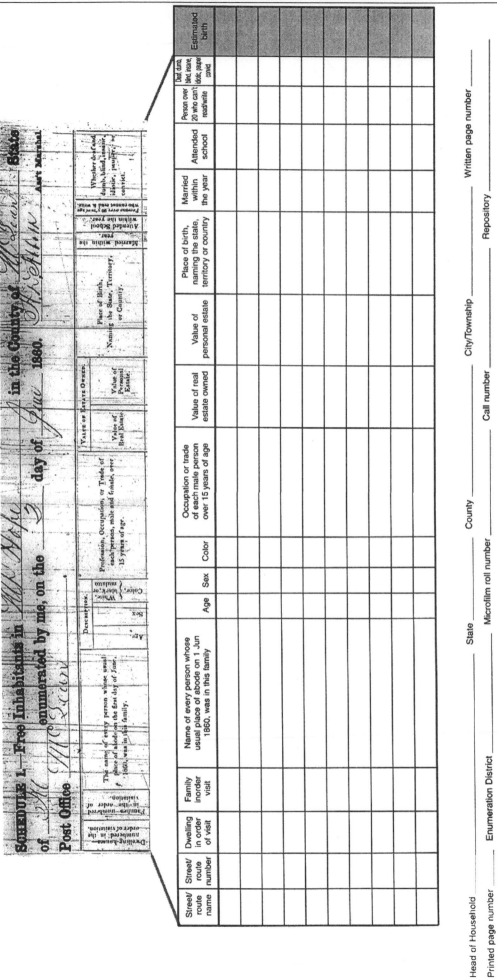

Street/ route name	Street/ route number	Dwelling in order of visit	Family in order of visit	Name of every person whose usual place of abode on 1 Jun 1860, was in this family	Age	Sex	Color	Occupation or trade of each male person over 15 years of age	Value of real estate owned	Value of personal estate	Place of birth, naming the state, territory or country	Married within the year	Attended school	Person over 20 who can't read/write	Deaf, dumb, blind, insane, idiotic, pauper, convict	Estimated birth

Head of Household _____ State _____ County _____ City/Township _____ Written page number _____

Printed page number _____ Enumeration District _____ Microfilm roll number _____ Call number _____ Repository _____

GENEALOGY RESEARCH ASSOCIATES, INC.
1870 United States Federal Census Transcription

SCHEDULE 1.—Inhabitants in _____, in the County of _____, enumerated by me on the ___ day of _____, 1870.

Post Office: _____

Street name	Cross street	Dwelling number	Family number	Name of every person whose usual place of abode on 1 Jun 1870, was in this family	Age at last birthday	Sex	Color	Occupation, trade or profession	Value of real estate owned	Value of personal estate owned	Place of birth	Father foreign b.	Mother foreign b.	Month if born within year	Month if married within year	In school if within year	Cannot read	Cannot write	Deaf & dumb, etc.	Males of 21 yrs. eligible to vote	Males of 21 yrs. not eligible to vote	Estimated birth year

Head of Household _____

Printed page number _____

State _____   County _____   City/Township _____

Enumeration District _____   Microfilm roll number _____   Call number _____   Repository _____   Written page number _____

GENEALOGY RESEARCH ASSOCIATES, INC.

1880 United States Federal Census Transcription

Street name	House number	Dwelling number	Family number	Name of every person whose usual place of abode on 1 June, 1880 was with this family	Estimated year of birth	Color - White, Black, Mulatto, Indian, or Chinese	Sex	Age	Month born if within census year	Relation to head of this household	Single	Married	Widowed/Div.	Married this yr.	Occupation, trade or profession	Months unemployed	Illness	Blind	Deaf & dumb	Idiotic	Insane	Disabled	School yr.	Can't read	Can't write	State, territory, or country of Birth	Birthplace of father	Birthplace of mother

Head of Household _____

State _____   Conty _____   City/Township _____   Written page number _____

Printed page number _____   Enumeration District _____   Microfilm roll number _____   Call number _____   Repository _____

© 1997 Genealogy Research Associates, Inc.   497

GENEALOGY RESEARCH ASSOCIATES, INC.
1900 United States Federal Census Transcription

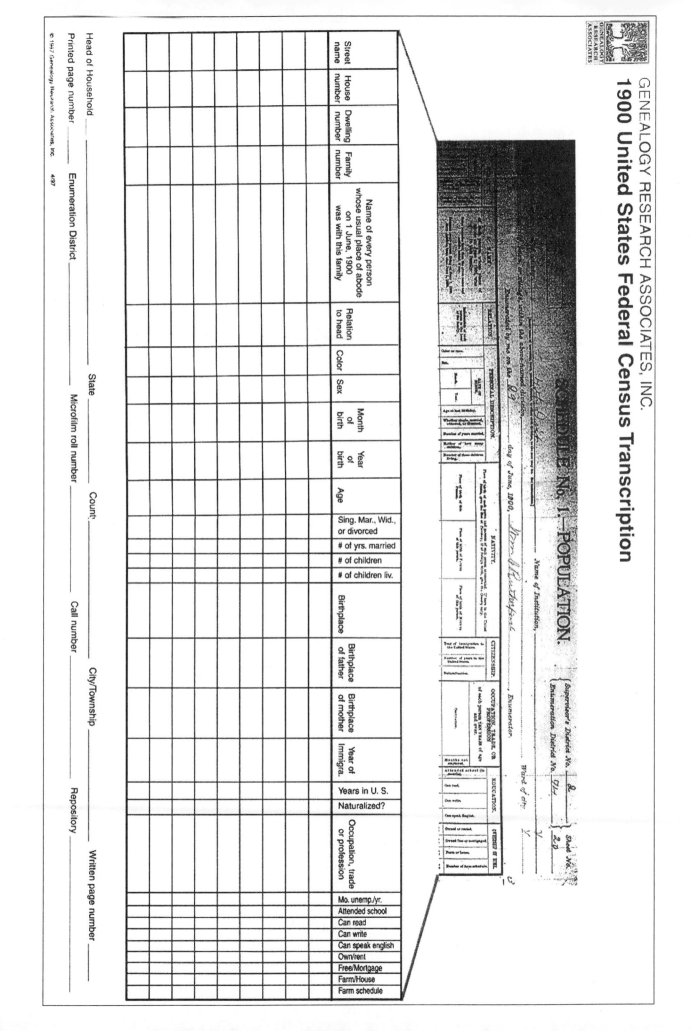

Street name	House number	Dwelling number	Family number	Name of every person whose usual place of abode on 1 June, 1900 was with this family	Relation to head	Color	Sex	Month of birth	Year of birth	Age	Sing. Mar., Wid., or divorced	# of yrs. married	# of children	# of children liv.	Birthplace	Birthplace of father	Birthplace of mother	Year of Immigra.	Years in U. S.	Naturalized?	Occupation, trade or profession	Mo. unemp./yr.	Attended school	Can read	Can write	Can speak english	Own/rent	Free/Mortgage	Farm/House	Farm schedule

Head of Household _____

Printed page number _____

State _____

Enumeration District _____

Microfilm roll number _____

County _____

City/Township _____

Call number _____

Repository _____

Written page number _____

GENEALOGY RESEARCH ASSOCIATES, INC.
1910 United States Federal Census Transcription

Street name	House number	Dwelling number	Family number	Name of every person whose usual place of abode on 15 April 1910 was with this family	Relation to head	Sex	Color	Age	Sing, Mar., Wid., or divorced	# of yrs. married	# of children	# of children liv.	Birthplace	Birthplace of father	Birthplace of mother	Year of Immigra.	Naturalized?	Speak eng. if not what lang.	Profession, occupation or business	General nature of industry, business, etc. such as cotton mill, dry goods, store, farm, etc.	Employer/ employee	Out of work 4/15/1910	# of weeks in 1909 unemploy.	Can read	Can write	In school	Own/rent	Free/Mortgage	FarmHouse	Farm Schedule	Civil war	Blind	Deaf

Head of Household _____ State _____ County _____ City/Township _____

Printed page number _____ Microfilm roll number _____ Call number _____ Repository _____

Enumeration District _____ Written page number _____

GENEALOGY RESEARCH ASSOCIATES
1920 United States Federal Census Transcription

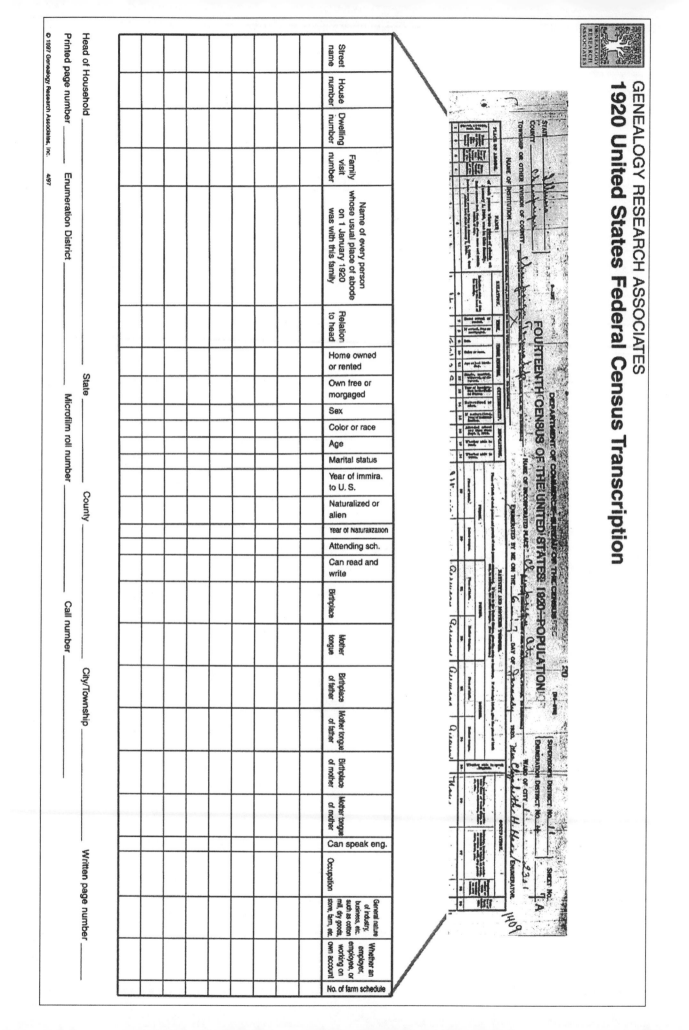

Street name	House number	Dwelling number	Family visit number	Name of every person whose usual place of abode on 1 January 1920 was with this family	Relation to head	Home owned or rented	Own free or morgaged	Sex	Color or race	Age	Marital status	Year of immira. to U.S.	Naturalized or alien	Year of Naturalization	Attending sch.	Can read and write	Birthplace	Mother tongue	Birthplace of father	Mother tongue of father	Birthplace of mother	Mother tongue of mother	Can speak eng.	Occupation	General nature of industry, business, etc. such as cotton mill, dry goods, store, farm, etc.	Whether an employer, employee, or working on own account	No. of farm schedule

Head of Household _____

Printed page number _____   Enumeration District _____   State _____   County _____   City/Township _____   Written page number _____

Microfilm roll number _____   Call number _____

1880 CENSUS SOUNDEX FORM

SOUNDEX NO:	YEAR:	STATE:		

HEAD OF FAMILY:		VOL:	ED:
		SHEET:	LINE:

COLOR:	MONTH:	AGE:	BIRTHPLACE:	CITIZENSHIP:

COUNTY:	MCD

CITY:	STREET:	HOUSE #

NAME	RELATION-SHIP	AGE	BIRTHPLACE	CITIZENSHIP

1880 CENSUS SOUNDEX FORM

SOUNDEX NO:	YEAR:	STATE:		

HEAD OF FAMILY:		VOL:	ED:
		SHEET:	LINE:

COLOR:	MONTH:	AGE:	BIRTHPLACE:	CITIZENSHIP:

COUNTY:	MCD

CITY:	STREET:	HOUSE #

NAME	RELATION-SHIP	AGE	BIRTHPLACE	CITIZENSHIP

1900 CENSUS SOUNDEX FORM

SOUNDEX NO:	YEAR:	STATE:		
HEAD OF FAMILY:			VOL: SHEET:	ED: LINE:
COLOR: MONTH: AGE: BIRTHPLACE: CITIZENSHIP:				
COUNTY:		MCD		
CITY:	STREET:		HOUSE #	

NAME	RELA-TION-SHIP	BIRTH MONTH	BIRTH YEAR	AGE	BIRTHPLACE	CITIZENSHIP

1900 CENSUS SOUNDEX FORM

SOUNDEX NO:	YEAR:	STATE:		
HEAD OF FAMILY:			VOL: SHEET:	ED: LINE:
COLOR: MONTH: AGE: BIRTHPLACE: CITIZENSHIP:				
COUNTY:		MCD		
CITY:	STREET:		HOUSE #	

NAME	RELA-TION-SHIP	BIRTH MONTH	BIRTH YEAR	AGE	BIRTHPLACE	CITIZENSHIP

1910 CENSUS SOUNDEX FORM

CODE	HEAD OF FAMILY OR INDIVIDUAL NAME		ED	SHEET
COLOR	AGE	BIRTHPLACE	VOL.	
COUNTY	CITY		STATE	

ENUMERATED WITH:

NAME	RELATIONSHIP	AGE	BIRTHPLACE

1910 CENSUS SOUNDEX FORM

CODE	HEAD OF FAMILY OR INDIVIDUAL NAME		ED	SHEET
COLOR	AGE	BIRTHPLACE	VOL.	
COUNTY	CITY		STATE	

ENUMERATED WITH:

NAME	RELATIONSHIP	AGE	BIRTHPLACE

1910 MIRACODE

COUNTY	CITY	VOLUME	ED #	VISITATION
CODE SURNAME	GIVEN NAME	RELATIONSHIP	RACE /AGE	BIRTH PLACE	RESIDENCE

SURNAME	GIVEN NAME	RELATIONSHIP	RACE/AGE	BIRTH PLACE

1910 MIRACODE

COUNTY	CITY	VOLUME	ED #	VISITATION
CODE SURNAME	GIVEN NAME	RELATIONSHIP	RACE /AGE	BIRTH PLACE	RESIDENCE

SURNAME	GIVEN NAME	RELATIONSHIP	RACE/AGE	BIRTH PLACE

1920 CENSUS SOUNDEX FORM

CODE	HEAD OF FAMILY OR INDIVIDUAL NAME		ED	SHEET
COLOR	AGE	BIRTHPLACE	VOL.	
COUNTY	CITY		STATE	
STREET			HOUSE NO.	
ENUMERATED WITH:				

NAME	RELATIONSHIP	AGE	BIRTHPLACE	CITIZEN.

1920 CENSUS SOUNDEX FORM

CODE	HEAD OF FAMILY OR INDIVIDUAL NAME		ED	SHEET
COLOR	AGE	BIRTHPLACE	VOL.	
COUNTY	CITY		STATE	
STREET			HOUSE NO.	
ENUMERATED WITH:				

NAME	RELATIONSHIP	AGE	BIRTHPLACE	CITIZEN.

Research Planner

Remember to have only one goal per Research Planner.

Goal _____

_____

Surname/Subject _____   Researcher _____

Area _____   Client _____

Source Location		Description of Source	Object	Time	Remarks		
Date source searched	Library or repository & call #	(State, county, type of record, and time period of record)	(Person's name or what is sought)	(Person's age or date of event)	Comment or ID # of family	Index	File

GENEALOGY RESEARCH ASSOCIATES

Research Planner

Remember to have only one goal per Research Planner.

Goal _____

_____

Surname/Subject _____   Researcher _____

Area _____   Client _____

Source Location		Description of Source	Object	Time	Remarks		
Date source searched	Library or repository & call #	(State, county, type of record, and time period of record)	(Person's name or what is sought)	(Person's age or date of event)	Comment or ID # of family	Index	File

Research Planner

Remember to have only one goal per Research Planner.

Goal _____

_____

Surname/Subject _____   Researcher _____

Area _____   Client _____

Source Location		Description of Source	Object	Time	Remarks		
Date source searched	Library or repository & call #	(State, county, type of record, and time period of record)	(Person's name or what is sought)	(Person's age or date of event)	Comment or ID # of family	Index	File

Research Planner

Remember to have only one goal per Research Planner.

Goal _____

_____

Surname/Subject _____   Researcher _____

Area _____   Client _____

Source Location		Description of Source	Object	Time	Remarks		
Date source searched	Library or repository & call #	(State, county, type of record, and time period of record)	(Person's name or what is sought)	(Person's age or date of event)	Comment or ID # of family	Index	File

www.GRAonline.com 5/97

GUIDE TO THE FAMILY HISTORY CENTER

Surname or locality you are searching _____

Today's Date _____ GOAL_____

The family you are searching is thought to have lived in these counties or states: *(Records are recorded by county name...locate the county if you know the city or town by using a gazetteer)* _____

_____ _____ _____

CHECK OFF WHEN ACCOMPLISHED

1. I have organized family information onto a pedigree chart _____
2. I have organized family information onto family group records _____

PRELIMINARY SURVEY BY...

3. Searching the *Ancestral File* ( )
4. Searching the *FHLC Surname File* on computer *(FamilySearch Program)* ( )
5. Searching a Surname Index to Periodicals if any ( )
6. Searching printed Family Histories at the center ( )
7. Searching the IGI by county, state, surname *(FamilySearch Program)* ( )
8. Searching any other local library source lists if any ( )
9. Searching the Library of Congress Published Surname Histories ( )
10. Searching the Patron Locality Surname File ( )

ORIGINAL RESEARCH...

11. The federal census records of the county already available at the FHC ( )
12. The AIS: census indexes 1600-1850/60 by surname on microfiche ( )
13. Census films from FHL, AGLL or record numbers for local archives visit ( )
14. The Locality file of the FHLC for Vital Records ( )
15. The Locality file of any other major repository catalog available there ( )
16. The Locality file FHC Card Catalog containing their holdings ( )
17. Area Research Guides for specific help on localities/subjects ( )
18. THE HANDY BOOK FOR GENEALOGISTS for localities, or other basic books ( )
19. MAP GUIDE TO THE U.S. FEDERAL CENSUSES 1790-1920 ( )
20. Research Papers by the experts in genealogy worldwide ( )
21. WORLD CONFERENCE ON RECORDS ( )
22. Category/Surname/Title References in the FHC Card Catalog ( )
23. Loose Files for maps, miscellaneous information, pedigree charts ( )
24. Jacobus, PERSI, and other periodical indexes ( )

OTHER WAYS THEY HELP YOU...

25. Information on computerizing your genealogy through the PAF program ( )
26. Seminars and workshops on your personal area of interest ( )
27. Loan Books of a general genealogical nature ( )
28. Forms, charts, photocopies of books, ( )
29. Social Security Death Index (abt. 1937-1989 by surname *FamilySearch*) ( )
30. Local CDs applying to your area of research ( )
31. Film Register Books ( )
32. Information on creating a GEDCOM to submit family data to FHL ( )

GUIDE TO THE FAMILY HISTORY CENTER

Surname or locality you are searching _____

Today's Date _____ GOAL_____

The family you are searching is thought to have lived in these counties or states: *(Records are recorded by county name...locate the county if you know the city or town by using a gazetteer)* _____

_____ _____ _____

CHECK OFF WHEN ACCOMPLISHED

1. I have organized family information onto a pedigree chart _____
2. I have organized family information onto family group records _____

PRELIMINARY SURVEY BY...

3. Searching the *Ancestral File*   ( )
4. Searching the *FHLC Surname File* on computer *(FamilySearch Program)*   ( )
5. Searching a Surname Index to Periodicals if any   ( )
6. Searching printed Family Histories at the center   ( )
7. Searching the IGI by county, state, surname *(FamilySearch Program)*   ( )
8. Searching any other local library source lists if any   ( )
9. Searching the Library of Congress Published Surname Histories   ( )
10. Searching the Patron Locality Surname File   ( )

ORIGINAL RESEARCH...

11. The federal census records of the county already available at the FHC   ( )
12. The AIS: census indexes 1600-1850/60 by surname on microfiche   ( )
13. Census films from FHL, AGLL or record numbers for local archives visit ( )
14. The Locality file of the FHLC for Vital Records   ( )
15. The Locality file of any other major repository catalog available there ( )
16. The Locality file FHC Card Catalog containing their holdings   ( )
17. Area Research Guides for specific help on localities/subjects   ( )
18. THE HANDY BOOK FOR GENEALOGISTS for localities, or other basic books   ( )
19. MAP GUIDE TO THE U.S. FEDERAL CENSUSES 1790-1920   ( )
20. Research Papers by the experts in genealogy worldwide   ( )
21. WORLD CONFERENCE ON RECORDS   ( )
22. Category/Surname/Title References in the FHC Card Catalog   ( )
23. Loose Files for maps, miscellaneous information, pedigree charts   ( )
24. Jacobus, PERSI, and other periodical indexes   ( )

OTHER WAYS THEY HELP YOU...

25. Information on computerizing your genealogy through the PAF program   ( )
26. Seminars and workshops on your personal area of interest   ( )
27. Loan Books of a general genealogical nature   ( )
28. Forms, charts, photocopies of books,   ( )
29. Social Security Death Index (abt. 1937-1989 by surname *FamilySearch*) ( )
30. Local CDs applying to your area of research   ( )
31. Film Register Books   ( )
32. Information on creating a GEDCOM to submit family data to FHL   ( )

GUIDE TO THE FAMILY HISTORY CENTER

Surname or locality you are searching _____

Today's Date _____ GOAL_____

The family you are searching is thought to have lived in these counties or states: *(Records are recorded by county name...locate the county if you know the city or town by using a gazetteer)* _____

_____ _____ _____

CHECK OFF WHEN ACCOMPLISHED

1. I have organized family information onto a pedigree chart _____
2. I have organized family information onto family group records _____

PRELIMINARY SURVEY BY...

3. Searching the *Ancestral File* ( )
4. Searching the *FHLC Surname File* on computer *(FamilySearch Program)* ( )
5. Searching a Surname Index to Periodicals if any ( )
6. Searching printed Family Histories at the center ( )
7. Searching the IGI by county, state, surname *(FamilySearch Program)* ( )
8. Searching any other local library source lists if any ( )
9. Searching the Library of Congress Published Surname Histories ( )
10. Searching the Patron Locality Surname File ( )

ORIGINAL RESEARCH...

11. The federal census records of the county already available at the FHC ( )
12. The AIS: census indexes 1600-1850/60 by surname on microfiche ( )
13. Census films from FHL, AGLL or record numbers for local archives visit ( )
14. The Locality file of the FHLC for Vital Records ( )
15. The Locality file of any other major repository catalog available there ( )
16. The Locality file FHC Card Catalog containing their holdings ( )
17. Area Research Guides for specific help on localities/subjects ( )
18. THE HANDY BOOK FOR GENEALOGISTS for localities, or other basic books ( )
19. MAP GUIDE TO THE U.S. FEDERAL CENSUSES 1790-1920 ( )
20. Research Papers by the experts in genealogy worldwide ( )
21. WORLD CONFERENCE ON RECORDS ( )
22. Category/Surname/Title References in the FHC Card Catalog ( )
23. Loose Files for maps, miscellaneous information, pedigree charts ( )
24. Jacobus, PERSI, and other periodical indexes ( )

OTHER WAYS THEY HELP YOU...

25. Information on computerizing your genealogy through the PAF program ( )
26. Seminars and workshops on your personal area of interest ( )
27. Loan Books of a general genealogical nature ( )
28. Forms, charts, photocopies of books, ( )
29. Social Security Death Index (abt. 1937-1989 by surname *FamilySearch*) ( )
30. Local CDs applying to your area of research ( )
31. Film Register Books ( )
32. Information on creating a GEDCOM to submit family data to FHL ( )

GUIDE TO THE FAMILY HISTORY CENTER

Surname or locality you are searching _____

Today's Date _____ GOAL_____

The family you are searching is thought to have lived in these counties
or states: *(Records are recorded by county name...locate the county if
you know the city or town by using a gazetteer)* _____

_____ _____ _____

CHECK OFF WHEN ACCOMPLISHED

  1. I have organized family information onto a pedigree chart   _____
  2. I have organized family information onto family group records _____

PRELIMINARY SURVEY BY...

  3. Searching the *Ancestral File* ( )
  4. Searching the *FHLC Surname File* on computer *(FamilySearch* ( )
     Program)
  5. Searching a Surname Index to Periodicals if any ( )
  6. Searching printed Family Histories at the center ( )
  7. Searching the IGI by county, state, surname *(FamilySearch* ( )
     Program)
  8. Searching any other local library source lists if any ( )
  9. Searching the Library of Congress Published Surname Histories ( )
10. Searching the Patron Locality Surname File ( )

ORIGINAL RESEARCH...

11. The federal census records of the county already available ( )
     at the FHC
12. The AIS: census indexes 1600-1850/60 by surname on microfiche ( )
13. Census films from FHL, AGLL or record numbers for local ( )
     archives visit
14. The Locality file of the FHLC for Vital Records ( )
15. The Locality file of any other major repository catalog ( )
     available there
16. The Locality file FHC Card Catalog containing their holdings ( )
17. Area Research Guides for specific help on localities/subjects ( )
18. THE HANDY BOOK FOR GENEALOGISTS for localities, or other ( )
     basic books
19. MAP GUIDE TO THE U.S. FEDERAL CENSUSES 1790-1920 ( )
20. Research Papers by the experts in genealogy worldwide ( )
21. WORLD CONFERENCE ON RECORDS ( )
22. Category/Surname/Title References in the FHC Card Catalog ( )
23. Loose Files for maps, miscellaneous information, pedigree ( )
     charts
24. Jacobus, PERSI, and other periodical indexes ( )

   OTHER WAYS THEY HELP YOU...

25. Information on computerizing your genealogy through the PAF ( )
     program
26. Seminars and workshops on your personal area of interest ( )
27. Loan Books of a general genealogical nature ( )
28. Forms, charts, photocopies of books, ( )
29. Social Security Death Index (abt. 1937-1989 by surname ( )
     FamilySearch)
30. Local CDs applying to your area of research ( )
31. Film Register Books ( )
32. Information on creating a GEDCOM to submit family data to ( )
     FHL

Index